LEEDS/BRADFORD ATLAS

INCLUDING HALIFAX, BRIGHOUSE, BAILDON, BINGLEY, HORSFORTH, MORLEY, PUDSEY, SHIPLEY, SOWERBY BRIDGE

Geographia, part of John Bartholomew & Son Ltd, was founded over 70 years ago. This Geographia street atlas is one of a new and up to the minute series of street atlases, each one of which has clear easy to read mapping and a full street index.

The greatest care and attention is taken when we produce these atlases but, if you find any errors, we would be grateful to hear from you.

If you wish to send us information relating to this product, please contact:-

The Chief Cartographer,
Geographia Limited,
105/107 Bath Road,
Cheltenham,
Glos. GL53 7LE

Revised edition 1988

Published by Geographia, an imprint of John Bartholomew & Son Ltd, Duncan Street, Edinburgh EH9 1TA.

Printed in Scotland by John Bartholomew & Son Ltd

CONTENTS

LOCAL INFORMATION GUIDE

Each entry in this guide has a reference to enable the user to locate it in the map section. If, through lack of space, an entry does not appear on the map then the reference will direct the user to the street on which the entry is located.

Abbreviations used in this guide:

Cath.—Cathedral	Hosp.—Hospital	Sec.—Secondary
Coll.—College	Infirm.—Infirmary	Swim.—Swimming
Comp.—Comprehensive		

PUBLIC SERVICES

LOCAL GOVERNMENT

City of Bradford Metropolitan Council	**Calderdale Metropolitan Borough Council**	**Leeds Metropolitan City Council**
City Hall	Town Hall	Civic Hall
Bradford	Halifax	Leeds
Tel: 0274 752111	Tel: 0422 57257	Tel: 0532 463000
p49 N12	*p94 F19*	*p55 AA10*

LIBRARIES

Bradford Central Library	**Halifax Central Library**	**Leeds Central Library**
Prince's Way	Northgate	Municipal Buildings
Bradford	Halifax	Calverley Street
Tel: 0274 753657	Tel: 0422 57257	Leeds
p49 N12	*p94 F19*	Tel: 0532 462062
		p55 AA11

POST OFFICES

Bradford Head Post Office	**Halifax Head Post Office**	**Leeds Head Post Office**
Forster Court	Commercial Street	Wellington Street
Bradford	Halifax	Leeds
Tel: 0274 394466	Tel: 0422 54611	Tel: 0532 434191
p49 N11	*p94 F19*	*p55 AA11*

POLICE STATIONS

Bradford Police Station	**Halifax Police Station**	**Leeds Central Police Station**
Prince's Way	Richmond Close	Millgarth Street
Bradford	Halifax	Leeds
Tel: 0274 723422	Tel: 0422 60333	Tel: 0532 435353
p49 N12	*p94 E19*	*p56 BB11*

HOSPITALS

BRADFORD HEALTH AUTHORITY

Bierley Hall Hospital
Bierley Lane
Bradford
Tel: 0274 682837
p67 O15

Bradford Children's Hospital
St. Mary's Road
Bradford
Tel: 0274 499721
p48 M10

Bradford Royal Infirmary
Duckworth Lane
Bradford
Tel: 0274 42200
p47 K10

Calverley Hospital
Woodhall Road
Thornbury
Tel: 0274 664746
p50 Q10

Green Lane Hall
Green Lane
Shelf
Tel: 0274 678788
p82 J16

Heaton Royds Hospital
Bingley Road
Shipley
Tel: 0274 42016
p29 J8

Leeds Road Hospital
Leeds Road
Bradford
Tel: 0274 729661
p49 O11

Lynfield Mount Hospital
Heights Lane
Bradford
Tel: 0274 498121
p47 J10

Northern View Hospital
Rooley Lane
Bradford
Tel: 0274 729130
p67 N15

St. Luke's Hospital
Little Horton Lane
Bradford
Tel: 0274 734744
p66 M13

Shipley Hospital
Kirkgate
Shipley
Tel: 0274 599011
p30 L7

Stoney Ridge Hospital
Stoney Ridge Road
Cottingley
Tel: 0274 42156
p29 J8

Waddiloves Hospital
Queens Road
Bradford
Tel: 0274 497121
p48 M10

Westwood Hospital
Cooper Lane
Bradford
Tel: 0274 882001
p65 J14

Woodlands Hospital
Woodlands Drive
Rawdon
Tel: 0532 503181
p15 S6

LEEDS EASTERN HEALTH AUTHORITY

Crooked Acres Hospital
Spen Lane
Leeds
Tel: 0532 786245
p35 W8

Killingbeck Hospital
York Road
Leeds
Tel: 0532 648164
p58 FF10

Meanwood Park Hospital
Tongue Lane
Leeds
Tel: 0532 758721
p19 Z6

St. George's Hospital
Wood Lane
Rothwell
Tel: 0532 822211
p75 EE15

St. James University Hospital
Beckett Street
Leeds
Tel: 0532 433144
p56 CC10

Seacroft Hospital
York Road
Leeds
Tel: 0532 648164
p58 GG10

LEEDS WESTERN HEALTH AUTHORITY

Chapel Allerton Hospital
Harehills Lane
Leeds
Tel: 0532 623404
p38 CC8

Cookridge Hospital
Hospital Lane
Leeds
Tel: 0532 673411
p17 W5

Dental Hospital
Leeds University Campus
Leeds
Tel: 0532 440111
p55 AA10

vi

General Infirmary
Great George Street
Leeds
Tel: 0532 432799
p55 AA10

Ida and Robert
Arthington Hospital
Hospital Lane
Leeds
Tel: 0532 677292
p17 W6

St. Mary's Hospital
Green Hill Road
Leeds
Tel: 0532 790121
p53 W11

CALDERDALE HEALTH AUTHORITY

Halifax General Hospital
Huddersfield Road
Salterhebble
Tel: 0422 57171
p94 F21

Northowram Hospital
Hall Lane
Northowram
Tel: 0422 201101
p81 H17

Royal Halifax Infirmary
Free School Lane
Halifax
Tel: 0422 57222
p94 F20

DEWSBURY HEALTH AUTHORITY

Oakwell Geriatric
Hospital
Owler Lane
Birstall
Tel: 0924 478113
p87 U17

SECONDARY EDUCATION

METROPOLITAN BOROUGH OF BRADFORD

SECONDARY COMPREHENSIVE

Beckfoot Grammar
School
Wagon Lane
Bingley
Tel: 0274 563803
p10 H6

Belle Vue Boys School
Thorn Lane
Bradford
Tel: 0274 493533
p29 J9

Belle Vue Girls School
Thorn Lane
Bradford
Tel: 0274 492341
p29 J9

Bingley Grammar
School
Keighley Road
Bingley
Tel: 0274 562557
p10 G5

Buttershaw Upper
School
Reevey Road West
Bradford
Tel: 0274 676285
p65 K15

Carlton-Bolling School
Undercliffe Lane
Bradford
Tel: 0274 633111
p49 O10

Eccleshill Upper School
Harrogate Road
Bradford
Tel: 0274 614928
p32 Q8

Fairfax School
Lister Avenue
Bradford
Tel: 0274 392311
p67 O13

The Grange School
Haycliffe Lane
Bradford
Tel: 0274 573953
p66 L14

Hanson School
Sutton Avenue
Bradford
Tel: 0274 636278
p31 N9

Nab Wood Grammar School
Cottingley New Road
Shipley
Tel: 0274 567281
p29 J7

Oakbank Grammar School
Oakworth Road
Keighley
Tel: 0535 662787
p7 A5

Queensbury School
Deanstones Lane
Queensbury
Tel: 0274 882214
p64 G15

Rhodesway School
Oaks Lane
Allerton
Tel: 0274 498015
p47 J11

St. Bede's Grammar School
Highgate
Heaton
Tel: 0274 41221
p30 L9

St. Joseph's College
Cunliffe Road
Bradford
Tel: 0274 41177
p30 M9

Salt Grammar School
Higher Coach Road
Baildon
Tel: 0274 584681
p11 K6

Thornton School
Leaventhorpe Lane
Thornton
Tel: 0274 881082
p46 H12

Tong School
Westgate Hill Street
Tong
Tel: 0274 681455
p69 R15

Wyke Manor School
Wilson Road
Wyke
Tel: 0274 674186
p83 M17

Yorkshire Martyrs Collegiate School
Westgate Hill Street
Tong
Tel: 0274 681262
p69 R15

MIDDLE SCHOOLS

Allerton Middle School
Garforth Street
Allerton
Tel: 0274 41515
p46 H10

Belmont Middle School
West Lane
Baildon
Tel: 0274 598115
p12 L5

Bierley Middle School
Bierley House Avenue
Bradford
Tel: 0274 682176
p67 O15

Bronte Middle School
Keighley Road
Oakworth
Tel: 0535 605991
p7 A5

Buttershaw Middle School
Farfield Avenue
Buttershaw
Tel: 0274 678544
p65 K15

Clayton Middle School
John Street
Clayton
Tel: 0274 882263
p65 J13

Cottingley Manor R.C. Middle School
Cottingley New Road
Shipley
Tel: 0274 562876
p28 H7

Daisy Hill Middle School
Hazelhurst Brow
Bradford
Tel: 0274 46059
p47 K10

Delf Hill Middle School
Common Road
Low Moor
Tel: 0274 670686
p83 M16

Drummond Middle School
Drummond Road
Bradford
Tel: 0274 43260
p48 M10

Eccleshill North Middle School
Rillington Mead
Greengates
Tel: 0274 611327
p32 P8

Edmund Campion R.C. Middle School
Rhodesway
Bradford
Tel: 0274 42992
p47 J11

Fairweather Green Middle School
Thornton Road
Bradford
Tel: 0274 43061
p47 J11

Fenby Middle School
Lorne Street
Bradford
Tel: 0274 22441
p67 O13

Frizinghall Middle School
Salisbury Road
Shipley
Tel: 0274 43091
p30 M8

Gilstead Middle School
Warren Lane
Bingley
Tel: 0274 568361
p11 J5

Great Horton Middle School
Cross Lane
Bradford
Tel: 0274 573288
p66 L13

Gregory Middle School
Rooley Lane
Bradford
Tel: 0274 390165
p67 O14

Hainsworth Moor Middle School
Hainsworth Moor Grove
Queensbury
Tel: 0274 882883
p63 F15

Hartington Middle School
Rawdon Road
Haworth
Tel: 0535 42359
p24 ZZ7

Heaton Middle School
Haworth Road
Bradford
Tel: 0274 492096
p29 J9

Highfield Middle School
Tong Street
Bradford
Tel: 0274 604101
p68 P14

Holme Middle School
Knowles Lane
Bradford
Tel: 0274 681502
p68 P13

Hutton Middle School
Victoria Road
Bradford
Tel: 0274 639382
p32 P8

Ladderbanks Middle School
Coverdale Way
Baildon
Tel: 0274 594686
p13 N5

Lapage Middle School
Lapage Street
Bradford
Tel: 0274 664483
p50 P11

Leaventhorpe Middle School
Chelwood Drive
Allerton
Tel: 0274 881955
p46 H11

Lidget Green Middle School
Cemetery Road
Bradford
Tel: 0274 573293
p47 K12

Mandale Middle School
Cooper Lane
Bradford
Tel: 0274 672184
p65 J15

Manningham Middle School
Manningham Lane
Bradford
Tel: 0274 723648
p48 M10

Nab Wood Middle School
New Close Road
Shipley
Tel: 0274 592815
p29 J7

Parkland Middle School
Old Park Road
Bradford
Tel: 0274 611458
p32 P7

Parkside Middle School
Parkside Terrace
Cullingworth
Tel: 0535 272752
p26 D8

Pollard Park Middle School
Barkerend Road
Bradford
Tel: 0274 726158
p49 O11

Priestman Middle School
Hutton Road
Bradford
Tel: 0274 572088
p66 M14

Ryan Middle School
Ryan Street
Bradford
Tel: 0274 723617
p66 M13

St. Blaise R.C. Middle School
Newhall Road
Bierley
Tel: 0274 685313
p67 O14

St. Georges R.C. Middle School
Cliffe Road
Bradford
Tel: 0274 638754
p49 N10

Stoney Lee Middle School
Cottingley Moor Road
Cottingley
Tel: 0274 567545
p28 H8

Swain House Middle School
Swain House Road
Bradford
Tel: 0274 638027
p31 O8

Swire Smith Middle School
Cherry Tree Rise
Keighley
Tel: 0535 604182
p8 D4

Thornbury Middle School
Leeds Old Road
Bradford
Tel: 0274 665812
p50 Q11

Thorpe Middle School
Albion Road
Idle
Tel: 0274 611428
p31 O7

Tyersal Middle School
Fearnville Drive
Bradford
Tel: 0274 664438
p50 P12

Undercliffe Middle School
Undercliffe Old Road
Bradford
Tel: 0274 639380
p49 O10

Waverley Middle School
Stratford Road
Bradford
Tel: 0274 573297
p48 L12

Wellington Middle School
Leeds Road
Bradford
Tel: 0274 639938
p31 O9

Whetley Middle School
Whetley Lane
Bradford
Tel: 0274 43755
p48 L11

Wibsey Middle School
North Road
Bradford
Tel: 0274 678016
p66 L14

Woodend Middle School
Wrose Brow Road
Shipley
Tel: 0274 583555
p30 M7

Woodroyd Middle School
Woodroyd Road
West Bowling
Tel: 0274 727524
p67 N13

Woodside Middle School
Fenwick Drive
Bradford
Tel: 0274 676898
p83 L16

Wrose Brow Middle School
Wrose Brow Road
Shipley
Tel: 0274 599330
p30 M7

Wycliffe Middle School
Saltaire Road
Shipley
Tel: 0274 584779
p30 L7

Wyke Middle School
Huddersfield Road
Wyke
Tel: 0274 678383
p83 M17

CALDERDALE METROPOLITAN BOROUGH COUNCIL

SECONDARY GRAMMAR SCHOOLS

Crossley Heath Grammar School
Savile Park
Halifax
Tel: 0422 60272
p94 E21

North Halifax Grammar School
Parkinson Lane
Halifax
Tel: 0422 52107
p94 E20

SECONDARY COMPREHENSIVE SCHOOLS

Brighouse High School
Halifax Road
Brighouse
Tel: 0484 715932
p97 L21

Brooksbank School
Victoria Road
Elland
Tel: 0422 74791
p99 G24

Halifax Catholic High School
Holdsworth Road
Holmfield
Tel: 0422 245411
p80 E16

Hipperholme and Lightcliffe High School
Stoney Lane
Lightcliffe
Tel: 0422 201029
p97 L19

Holy Trinity Senior School
Holdsworth Road
Holmfield
Tel: 0422 244890
p80 E16

Ryburn Valley High School
St. Peters Avenue
Sowerby Bridge
Tel: 0422 832070
p92 A21

Sowerby Bridge High School
Albert Road
Sowerby Bridge
Tel: 0422 831011
p93 C20

SECONDARY MODERN SCHOOLS

Clare Hall School
Oxford Road
Halifax
Tel: 0422 52106
p94 F20

Exley Secondary School
Park Lane
Exley
Tel: 0422 62215
p99 G22

Haugh Shaw Secondary School
Moorfield Street
Halifax
Tel: 0422 52182
p94 E20

Holmfield High School
Holdsworth Road
Holmfield
Tel: 0422 244323
p80 E16

Ostler Secondary School
Battinson Road
Halifax
Tel: 0422 53719
p93 D19

Ovenden Secondary School
Nursery Lane
Ovenden
Tel: 0422 52836
p79 D17

LEEDS METROPOLITAN CITY COUNCIL

SECONDARY HIGH SCHOOLS

Abbey Grange High School
Butcher Hill
Horsforth
Tel: 0532 757877
p35 W7

Agnes Stewart High School
Cromwell Street
Leeds
Tel: 0532 482834
p56 CC11

Allerton Grange School
Talbot Avenue
Lidgett Park
Tel: 0532 661052
p20 CC6

Allerton High School
King Lane
Leeds
Tel: 0532 684216
p19 AA5

Benjamin Gott High School
Lenhurst Avenue
Leeds
Tel: 0532 752890
p54 X10

Benton Park Grammar School
Harrogate Road
Rawdon
Tel: 0532 502330
p15 R4

Bruntcliffe High School
Bruntcliffe Lane
Morley
Tel: 0532 533803
p88 W17

Cardinal Heenan R.C. High School
Tongue Lane
Leeds
Tel: 0532 741166
p19 AA6

City of Leeds School
Woodhouse Lane
Leeds
Tel: 0532 454825
p55 AA10

xi

Cockburn High School
Burton Road
Hunslet
Tel: 0532 707451
p74 BB13

Corpus Christi R.C. High School
Neville Road
Leeds
Tel: 0532 482666
p57 EE11

Cross Green School
Cross Green Lane
Leeds
Tel: 0532 491501
p56 CC12

Foxwood School
Brooklands View
Leeds
Tel: 0532 602141
p40 FF9

Harrington High School
Chapel Lane
Farnley
Tel: 0532 630741
p53 W12

Horsforth School
Lee Lane East
Horsforth
Tel: 0532 581265
p16 U6

Hough Side High School
Hough Top
Pudsey
Tel: 0532 576337
p52 U11

Intake High School
Calverley Lane
Leeds
Tel: 0532 564881
p34 U9

John Smeaton High School
Smeaton Approach
Seacroft
Tel: 0532 644251
p41 JJ9

Lawnswood School
Westpark Ring Road
Westpark
Tel: 0532 782321
p36 X7

Matthew Murray High School
Brown Lane
Leeds
Tel: 0532 713031
p73 Z13

Morley High School
Fountain Street
Morley
Tel: 0532 532952
p88 W17

Mount St. Mary's R.C. High School
Richmond Hill
Leeds
Tel: 0532 455248
p56 CC11

Notre Dame R.C. High School
St. Marks Avenue
Leeds
Tel: 0532 430753
p55 AA10

Parklands High School
South Parkway
Seacroft
Tel: 0532 731964
p40 GG9

Priesthorpe School
Priesthorpe Lane
Pudsey
Tel: 0532 572618
p51 R10

Primrose Hill High School
Hill Street
Leeds
Tel: 0532 454818
p56 CC10

Pudsey Grangefield School
Richardshaw Lane
Pudsey
Tel: 0532 570278
p52 T11

Ralph Thoresby High School
Farrar Lane
Leeds
Tel: 0532 679911
p17 W5

Roundhay School
Gledhow Lane
Roundhay
Tel: 0532 650051
p39 DD7

St. Michael's College
St. John's Road
Leeds
Tel: 0532 452336
p55 Z10

Silver Royd High School
Swallow Crescent
Armley
Tel: 0532 630745
p54 X12

Stainbeck High School
Carr Manor Road
Leeds
Tel: 0532 688352
p37 AA7

Temple Moor High School
Selby Road
Halton
Tel: 0532 645278
p58 GG11

West Leeds Boys' High School
Whingate
Armley
Tel: 0532 639047
p54 X11

West Leeds Girls' High School
Congress Mount
Armley
Tel: 0532 633426
p53 W11

West Park High School
Spen Lane
Leeds
Tel: 0532 756065
p36 X7

MIDDLE SCHOOLS

All Saints' Middle School
Pontefract Lane
Leeds
Tel: 0532 482014
p56 CC11

Allerton Grange Middle School
Talbot Avenue
Leeds
Tel: 0532 666250
p20 CC6

Archbishop Cranmer Middle School
Lingfield Approach
Leeds
Tel: 0532 695191
p19 AA5

Armley Middle School
Strawberry Lane
Armley
Tel: 0532 638019
p54 Y11

Arthur Greenwood Middle School
Hunslet Hall Road
Leeds
Tel: 0532 709439
p73 AA13

Beckett Park Middle School
Foxcroft Close
Leeds
Tel: 0532 757252
p36 X8

Bedford Field Middle School
Cliff Mount
Leeds
Tel: 0532 783611
p37 AA9

Belle Isle Middle School
Middleton Road
Belle Isle
Tel: 0532 702322
p74 CC15

Blenheim Middle School
Crowther Place
Leeds
Tel: 0532 471580
p37 AA9

Braim Wood Middle School
Elmete Lane
Roundhay
Tel: 0532 655418
p39 EE7

Bramhope Middle School
Breary Rise
Bramhope
Tel: 0532 843166
p2 W2

Bramley Middle School
Hough Lane
Bramley
Tel: 0532 573794
p53 V10

Broad Lane Middle School
Broad Lane
Bramley
Tel: 0532 576275
p35 W9

Clapgate Middle School
Cranmore Drive
Middleton Park
Tel: 0532 716700
p91 CC16

Cross Flatts Park Middle School
Harlech Road
Leeds
Tel: 0532 716754
p73 AA14

Cross Gates Middle School
Poole Crescent
Cross Gates
Tel: 0532 646769
p58 GG10

Earl Cowper Middle School
Cowper Street
Leeds
Tel: 0532 621725
p38 CC9

Fir Tree Middle School
Lingfield Drive
Moortown
Tel: 0532 685233
p20 BB5

Greenhill Middle School
Gamble Hill Drive
Leeds
Tel: 0532 635271
p53 V11

Halton Middle School
Templegate Walk
Halton
Tel: 0532 606203
p58 GG11

Harehills Middle School
Harehills Road
Leeds
Tel: 0532 492181
p38 CC9

Hillside Middle School
Beeston Road
Leeds
Tel: 0532 717259
p73 AA13

Holt Park Middle School
Farrar Lane
Leeds
Tel: 0532 678608
p17 W5

Holy Name Middle School
Iveson Approach
Leeds
Tel: 0532 678315
p17 W6

Holy Trinity Middle School
Green Lane
Cookridge
Tel: 0532 678845
p17 V4

Hugh Gaitskell Middle School
St. Anthony's Drive
Beeston
Tel: 0532 716963
p73 Z14

Hunslet Middle School
Church Street
Hunslet
Tel: 0532 717204
p74 CC13

Intake Middle School
Coal Hill Drive
Rodley
Tel: 0532 563463
p34 T9

John Blenkinsop Middle School
Sissons Terrace
Middleton Park
Tel: 0532 700873
p90 AA17

John Smeaton Middle School
Smeaton Approach
Seacroft
Tel: 0532 602116
p41 JJ9

Kirkstall Middle School
Argie Road
Kirkstall
Tel: 0532 756186
p54 Y10

Lawrence Oates Middle School
Stainbeck Lane
Leeds
Tel: 0532 682493
p37 AA7

Manston Middle School
Sandbed Lane
Seacroft
Tel: 0532 645883
p41 HH9

Middlethorne Middle School
Shadwell Lane
Leeds
Tel: 0532 666179
p21 DD4

Morris Silman Middle School
Primley Park Road
Moortown
Tel: 0532 693595
p20 BB5

North Farm Middle School
Thorn Walk
Leeds
Tel: 0532 657441
p39 EE9

Oak Tree Middle School
Thorn Walk
Leeds
Tel: 0532 657440
p39 EE9

Osmondthorpe Middle School
Wykebeck Mount
Osmondthorpe
Tel: 0532 483008
p57 EE11

Royal Park Middle School
Queen's Road
Leeds
Tel: 0532 756123
p55 Z10

Ryecroft Middle School
Stonebridge Grove
Leeds
Tel: 0532 632433
p53 W12

St. Andrew's Middle School
Harrogate Road
Leeds
Tel: 0532 681952
p20 BB6

St. Benedict's R.C. Middle School
Leeds and Bradford Road
Leeds
Tel: 0532 576408
p35 V8

St. Brigid's R.C. Middle School
Torre Road
Leeds
Tel: 0532 480380
p57 DD11

St. Dominic's Middle School
Leopold Street
Leeds
Tel: 0532 621287
p38 CC9

St. Gregory's Middle School
Stanks Gardens
Seacroft
Tel: 0532 643708
p41 HH8

St. Kevin's R.C. Middle School
Barwick Road
Leeds
Tel: 0532 608714
p41 HH9

St. Matthew's Middle School
Wood Lane
Chapel Allerton
Tel: 0532 681489
p38 BB7

St. Michael's Middle School
Wood Lane
Headingley
Tel: 0532 755890
p37 Z8

St. Peter's Middle School
Cromwell Street
Leeds
Tel: 0532 451490
p56 CC11

SS. Peter and Paul Middle School
Sharp Lane
Belle Isle
Tel: 0532 704890
p91 CC16

Sandforth Middle School
Landseer Mount
Bramley
Tel: 0532 755708
p35 W9

Scott Hall Middle School
Stainbeck Lane
Chapel Allerton
Tel: 0532 687355
p37 AA8

Seacroft Park Middle School
Dufton Approach
Seacroft
Tel: 0532 645911
p40 GG9

Shakespeare Middle School
Stoney Rock Lane
Leeds
Tel: 0532 482194
p56 CC10

Swarcliffe Middle School
Swarcliffe Drive
Seacroft
Tel: 0532 733262
p41 HH8

Swinnow Middle School
Swinnow Road
Pudsey
Tel: 0532 564832
p52 U11

Thornhill Middle School
Hayfield Terrace
Armley
Tel: 0532 637887
p54 Y12

Tinshill Middle School
Wood Nook Drive
Leeds
Tel: 0532 679467
p17 W5

Vesper Gate Middle School
Cragside Walk
Leeds
Tel: 0532 587727
p35 W7

Victoria Middle School
Raincliffe Road
Leeds
Tel: 0532 480890
p57 DD11

Whinmoor Middle School
White Laith Approach
Leeds
Tel: 0532 732823
p22 GG6

FURTHER EDUCATION

Airedale and Wharfedale College of Further Education
Calverley Lane
Horsforth
Tel: 0532 581723
p34 T7

Bradford & Ilkley Community College
Great Horton Road
Bradford
Tel: 0274 734844
p48 M12

Bramley Grange College
Skeltons Lane
Thorner
Tel: 0532 892202
p23 HH6

City of Leeds College of Music
Cookridge Street
Leeds
Tel: 0532 452069
p55 AA10

Jacob Kramer College
Vernon Street
Leeds
Tel: 0532 439931
p55 AA10

Kitson College of Technology
Cookridge Street
Leeds
Tel: 0532 430381
p55 AA10

Leeds College of Building
North Street
Leeds
Tel: 0532 30765
p56 BB10

Leeds Polytechnic
Beckett Park
Leeds
Tel: 0532 759061
p55 AA10

Park Lane College of Further Education
Park Lane
Leeds
Tel: 0532 443011
p55 AA11

Percival Whitley College of Further Education
Francis Street
Halifax
Tel: 0422 58221
p94 E20

Shipley College
Exhibition Road
Shipley
Tel: 0274 595731
p29 K7

Thomas Danby College
Roundhay Road
Leeds
Tel: 0532 494912
p56 BB10

Trinity and All Saints College
Brownberrie Lane
Horsforth
Tel: 0532 584341
p16 U5

University of Bradford
Great Horton Road
Bradford
Tel: 0274 733466
p48 M12

University of Leeds
University Road
Leeds
Tel: 0532 431751
p55 AA10

TRAVEL INFORMATION

AIR

Leeds and Bradford Airport (Yeadon)
Flight Enquiries and Reservations Tel: 0532 503431
p1 T3

BUS

Bradford Metro Travel Interchange
Bridge Street
Tel: 0274 720505
p49 N12

Brighouse Bus Station
Elland Road
Tel: 0484 716472
p101 L22

Halifax Bus Station
Broad Street
Tel: 0422 65985
p94 F19

Leeds Central Bus Station
New York Street
Tel: 0532 456308
P56 BB11

Leeds Wellington Street Bus Station
Wellington Street
Tel: 0532 460011
p55 AA11

RAIL

BRITISH RAIL

Passenger Train Enquiries: Bradford Area 0274 733994
Leeds Area 0532 448133

STATIONS

Baildon
p13 N5

Bingley
p10 G5

Halifax
p94 F20

Headingley
p36 X9

Horsforth
p17 V5

Bradford Interchange
p49 N12

Bradford, Forster Square
p49 N11

Leeds
p55 AA11

Morley
p89 Y16

New Pudsey
p51 S10

Bramley
p52 U10

Cross Gates
p59 HH10

Shipley
p30 M7

Sowerby Bridge
p93 C21

Woodlesford
p77 HH15

KEIGHLEY AND WORTH VALLEY RAILWAY
Timetable Enquiries 0535 43629

Damems
p7 B6

Haworth
p24 ZZ7

Ingrow
p7 B5

Oakworth
p6 ZZ6

Oxenhope
p24 ZZ9

TOURISM

LEISURE AND ENTERTAINMENT

THEATRES AND MUSIC HALLS

Alhambra Theatre
Bradford
Tel: 0274 752000
p49 N12

Bingley Little Theatre
Main Street
Bingley
Tel: 0274 564049
p10 G5

Bradford Playhouse
Chapel Street
Bradford
Tel: 0274 720329
p49 N11

City Varieties Music Hall
The Headrow
Leeds
Tel: 0532 430808
p56 BB11

Grand Theatre
New Briggate
Leeds
Tel: 0532 459351
p56 BB11

Halifax Civic Theatre
Fountain Street
Halifax
Tel: 0422 63299
p94 F20

Halifax Playhouse
King Cross Road
Halifax
Tel: 0422 65998
p93 D20

Leeds Civic Theatre
Cookridge Street
Leeds
Tel: 0532 455505
p55 AA10

Leeds Playhouse
Calverley Street
Leeds
Tel: 0532 442111
p55 AA10

Library Theatre
Prince's Way
Bradford
Tel: 0274 752375
p49 N12

CINEMAS

Cannon Cinema
Broadway
Bradford
Tel: 0274 723678
p49 N11

Cannon Cinema
Wards End
Halifax
Tel: 0422 52000
p94 F20

Cannon Cinema
Vicar Lane
Leeds
Tel: 0532 451013
p56 BB11

Lyric
Tong Road
Leeds
Tel: 0532 638154
p54 X11

Odeon
New Briggate
Leeds
Tel: 0532 430031
p56 BB11

Odeon
Prince's Way
Bradford
Tel: 0274 722442
p49 N12

Unit 4
Bradford Road
Shipley
Tel: 0274 583429
p30 L8

OTHER ENTERTAINMENTS

**Bradford City
Football Club**
Valley Parade
Bradford
p48 M10

**Bradford Northern
Rugby League Club**
Rooley Avenue
Bradford
p67 N15

**Headingley County
Cricket Ground**
Kirkstall Lane
Leeds
p36 Y9

Ice Rink
Little Horton Lane
Bradford
p49 N12

Leeds Bowl
Merrion Centre
Leeds
p56 BB10

**Leeds Rugby League
Club**
St. Michael's Lane
Leeds
p36 Y9

**Leeds United Football
Club**
Elland Road
Leeds
p73 Z13

SPORTS CENTRES AND SWIMMING POOLS

Armley Leisure Centre
Carr Crofts
Armley
p54 X11

**Baildon Recreation
Centre**
Green Lane
Baildon
p12 L6

Bramley Baths
Broad Lane
Bramley
p34 U9

**Bramstan Recreation
Centre**
Calverley Lane
Pudsey
p34 T9

**Brighouse Swimming
Pool**
Millroyd Street
Brighouse
p101 L22

**Carlton Bolling Sports
Centre**
Undercliffe Lane
Bradford
p49 O10

Eccleshill Upper School
Harrogate Road
Bradford
p32 P8

Fearnville Sports Centre
Oakwood Lane
Leeds
p39 EE9

Grange Sports Centre
Haycliffe Lane
Bradford
p66 L14

Halifax Swimming Pool
Skircoat Road
Halifax
p94 F20

Hanson Sports Centre
Sutton Avenue
Bradford
p31 N8

Holt Park Sports Centre
Holt Road
Leeds
p18 X4

International Pool
Westgate
Leeds
p55 AA11

**John Smeaton Sports
Centre**
Barwick Road
Seacroft
p41 JJ9

**Manningham Sports
Centre**
Carlisle Road
Bradford
p48 L10

Nab Wood Sports Centre
Cottingley New Road
Bingley
p29 J7

**North Bridge Leisure
Centre**
North Bridge
Halifax
p94 F19

Pudsey Pool
Market Place
Pudsey
p52 T11

Queensbury Baths
Station Road
Queensbury
p64 G14

Rhodesway Baths
Oaks Lane
Allerton
p47 J11

**Richard Dunn Sports
Centre**
Rooley Avenue
Bradford
p66 M15

**Richmond Hill
Recreation Centre**
Aysgarth Mount
Leeds
p56 CC11

Scatcherd Sports Centre
Queensway
Morley
p89 X17

Scott Hall Sports Centre
Scott Hall Road
Leeds
p37 AA8

**Seacroft Recreation
Centre**
Dufton Approach
Seacroft
p40 GG9

Shipley Baths
Alexandra Road
Shipley
p30 L7

**South Leeds Sports
Centre**
Beeston Road
Leeds
p55 AA12

**Sowerby Bridge
Swimming Pool**
Hollins Mill Lane
Sowerby Bridge
p92 B21

Thornton Baths
Thorton Road
Thornton
p46 G12

**Thornton Recreation
Centre**
Leaventhorpe Lane
Thornton
p46 H12

GOLF COURSES

Alwoodley Golf Course
Wigton Lane
Leeds
p21 DD4

Baildon Golf Course
Bingley Road
Baildon
p12 L4

**Bradford Moor Golf
Course**
Killinghall Road
Bradford
p50 P10

Bradley Hall Golf Course
Bradley Hall Lane
Greetland
p98 E24

Brandon Golf Course
Holywell Lane
Shadwell
p21 EE4

Branshaw Golf Course
Occupation Lane
Oakworth
p6 ZZ5

Clayton Golf Course
Thornton View Road
Bradford
p65 J13

Cleckheaton Golf Course
Bradford Road
Cleckheaton
p84 O18

East Bierley Golf Course
South View Road
Bradford
p88 Q15

Elland Golf Course
Hammerstone Leach Lane
Elland
p98 F24

Fulneck Golf Course
Fulneck
Leeds
p69 S13

**Gotts Park Municipal
Golf Course**
Stanningley Road
Armley
p54 X10

Headley Golf Course
Lower Kipping Lane
Thornton
p45 F12

Horsforth Golf Course
Layton Road
Horsforth
p16 T5

Leeds Golf Course
Elmete Lane
Roundhay
p39 EE7

Lightcliffe Golf Course
Knowle Top Road
Halifax
p96 K19

**Middleton Park
Municipal Golf Course**
Middleton Park
Leeds
p90 AA15

Moortown Golf Course
Harrogate Road
Leeds
p20 BB4

Northcliffe Golf Course
Long Lane
Shipley
p29 K8

**Phoenix Park Golf
Course**
Dick Lane
Bradford
p50 Q11

Queensbury Golf Course
Queensbury
Bradford
p64 G15

Rawdon Golf Course
Buckstone Drive
Leeds
p15 R5

**Roundhay Municipal
Golf Course**
Park Lane
Leeds
p21 EE6

Saint Ives Municipal Golf Course
Cross Gates Lane
Bingley
p9 F5

Sand Moor Golf Course
Alwoodley Lane
Leeds
p5 BB3

Shipley Golf Course
Beck Foot
Shipley
p10 G6

South Bradford Golf Course
Odsal
Leeds
p67 N15

South Leeds Golf Course
Gipsy Lane
Leeds
p73 AA15

Temple Newsam Municipal Golf Course
Temple Newsam Park
Leeds
p58 GG12

West Bowling Golf Course
West Bowling
Leeds
p67 N15

West Bradford Golf Course
Chellow Lane
Bradford
p29 J9

West End Golf Course
Paddock Lane
Halifax
p93 C19

Woodhall Hills Golf Course
Woodhall Road
Pudsey
p32 Q9

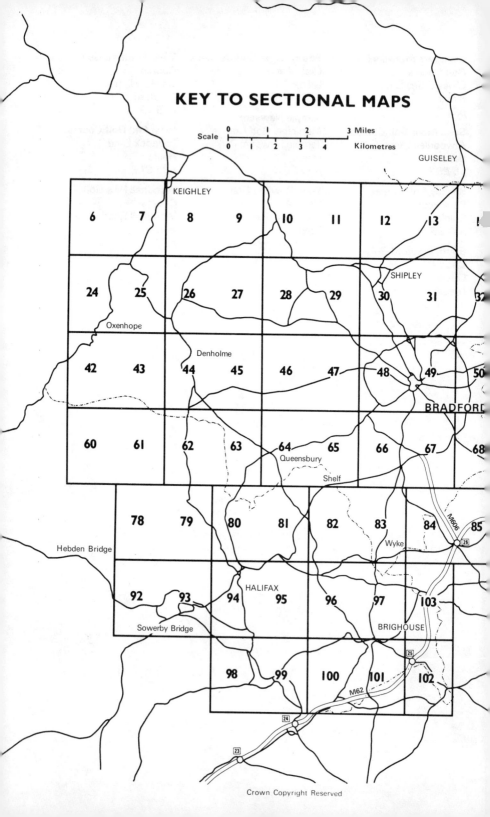

KEY TO SECTIONAL MAPS

Scale

0   1   2   3 Miles

0 1 2 3 4 Kilometres

GUISELEY

KEIGHLEY

| 6 | 7 | 8 | 9 | 10 | 11 | 12 | 13 | |

SHIPLEY

| 24 | 25 | 26 | 27 | 28 | 29 | 30 | 31 | 32 |

Oxenhope

Denholme

| 42 | 43 | 44 | 45 | 46 | 47 | 48 | 49 | 50 |

BRADFORD

| 60 | 61 | 62 | 63 | 64 | 65 | 66 | 67 | 68 |

Queensbury

Shelf

| 78 | 79 | 80 | 81 | 82 | 83 | 84 | 85 |

Hebden Bridge

Wyke

M606

26

HALIFAX

| 92 | 93 | 94 | 95 | 96 | 97 | 103 |

Sowerby Bridge

BRIGHOUSE

25

| 98 | 99 | 100 | 101 | 102 |

M62

24

23

Crown Copyright Reserved

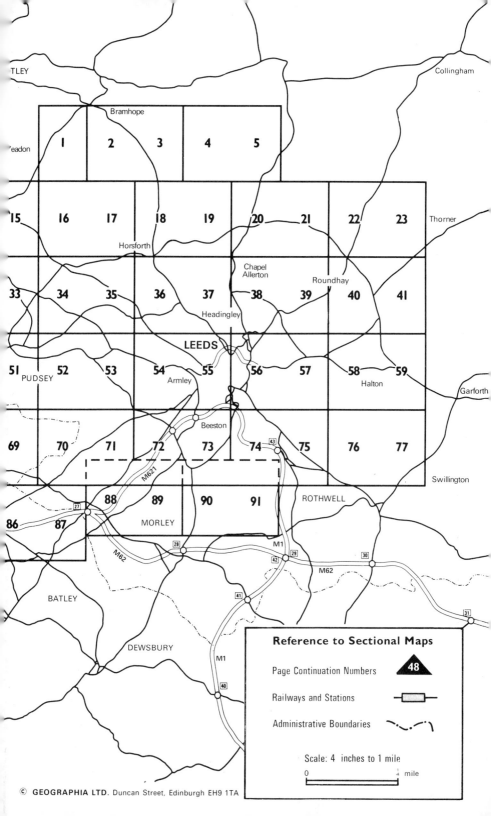

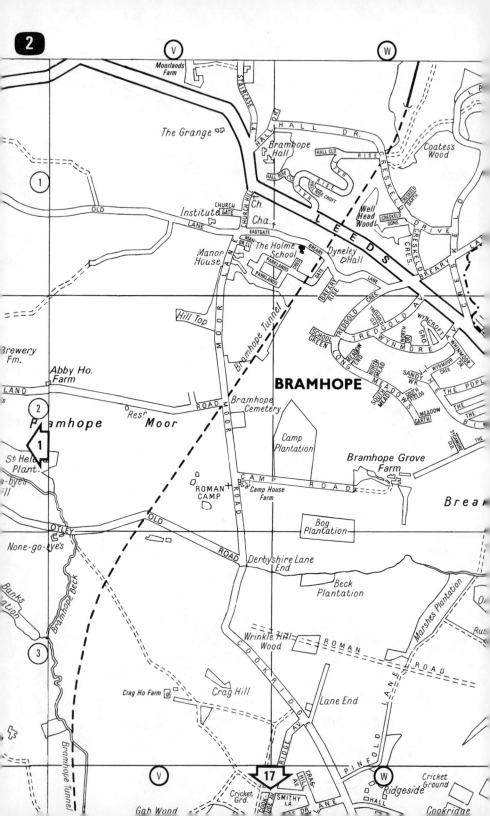

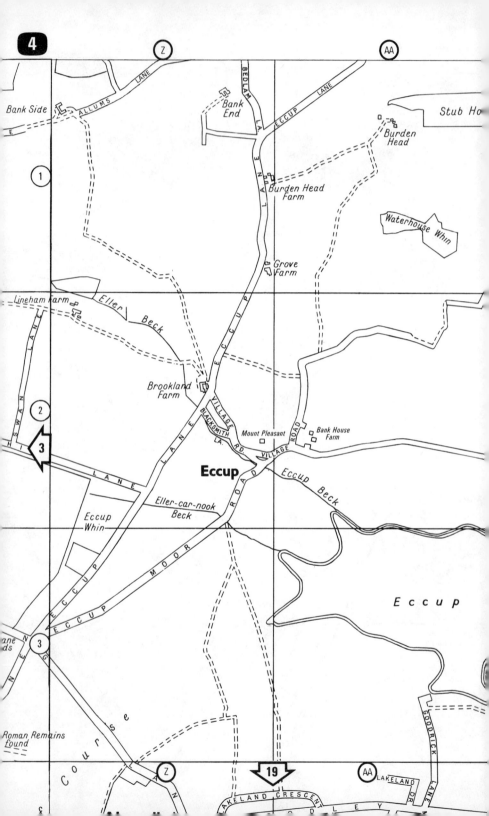

BB
CC

Carr House

CARR HOUSE PARK

ntation

Long Ing Pond

Weir Rough Bridge

Piper

Wood

Weir

Lodge Hills

Stub House Farm

1

Stub House Beck

New Bridge

Old Quarry

Swan Bushes

Grey Stone Pasture

Hazelwood Leys

Grey Stone Whin

2

Wikefield Farm

Eccup Filtration Works

Herd Farm

Owlet Hall

Sturdy

High Wood

ROAD

eservoir

Wigton Knowle

Millfield Farm

3

ALWOODLEY OLD HALL

Manor House

Golf Course

Wigton Knowle

GATE

BB

20

CC

WIGTON GR.

Moss Hall

Grove House

Meth Cha

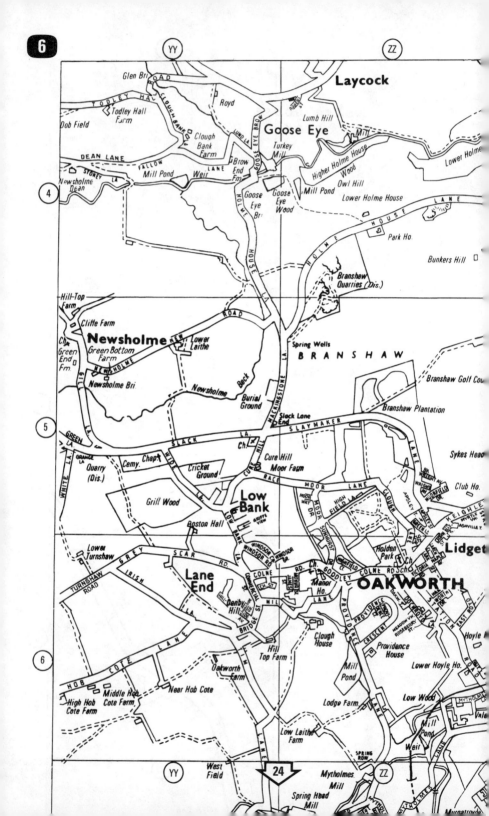

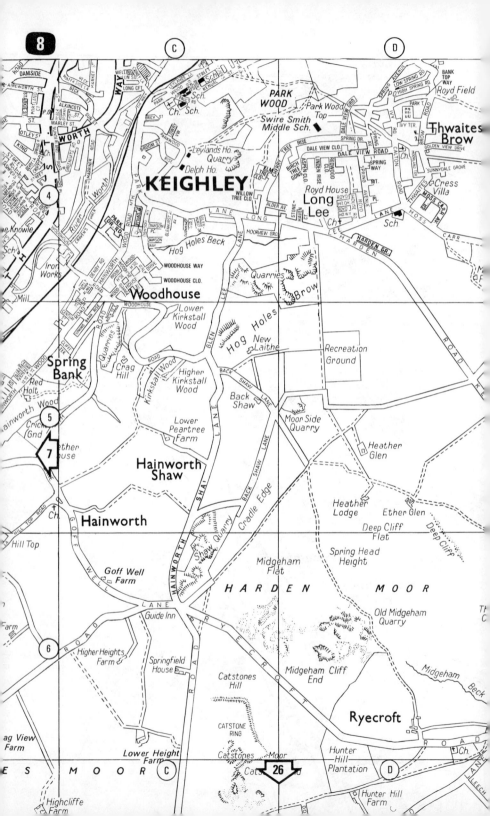

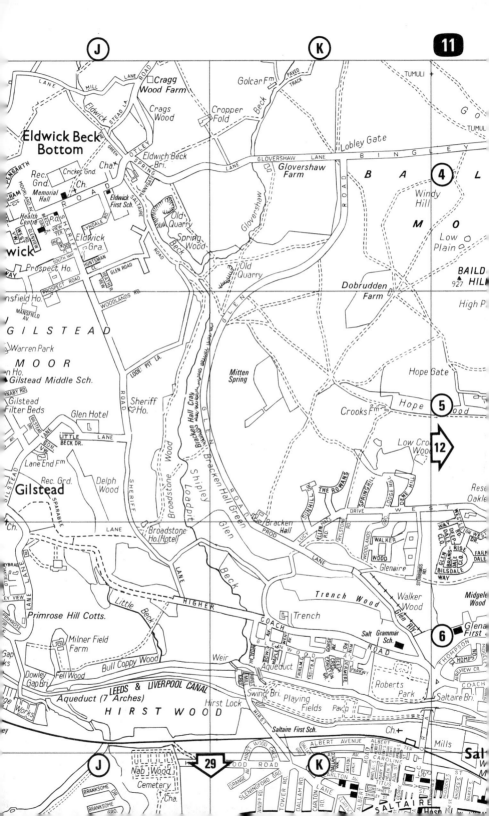

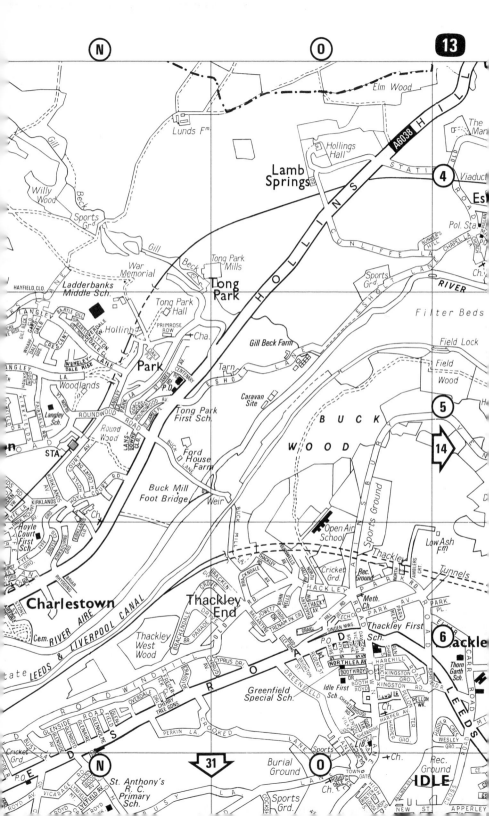

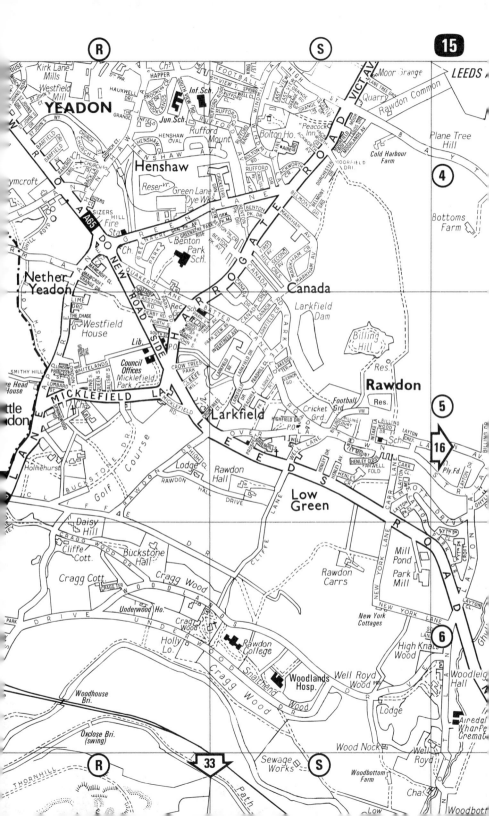

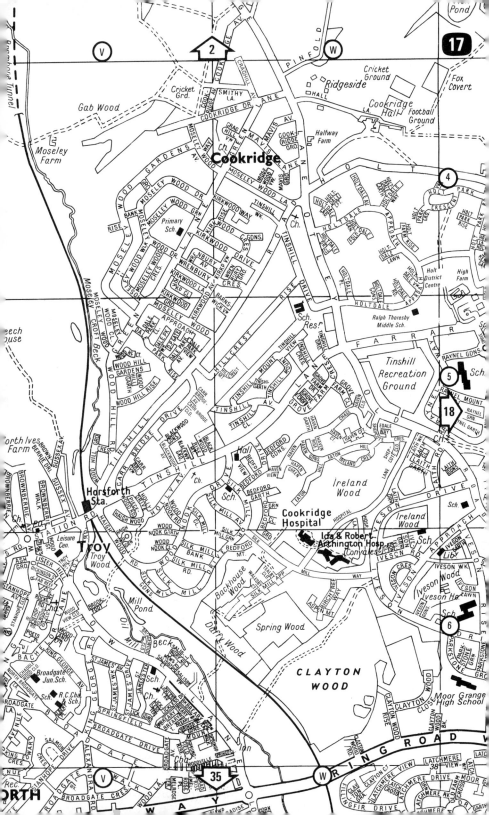

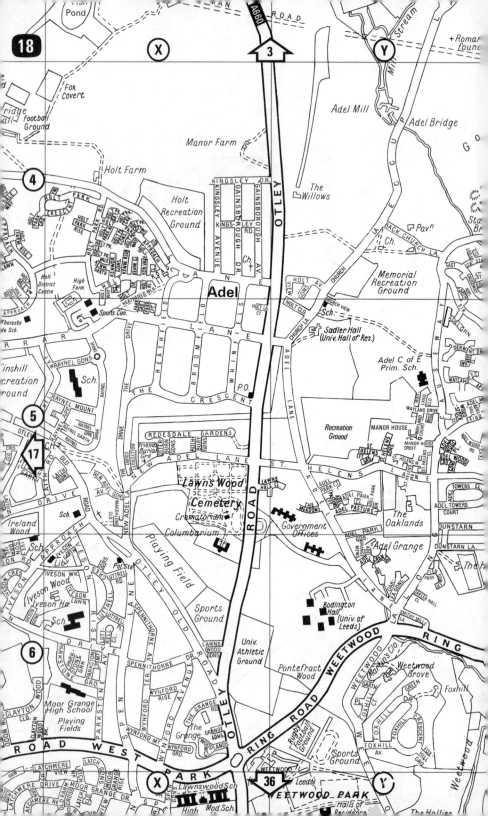

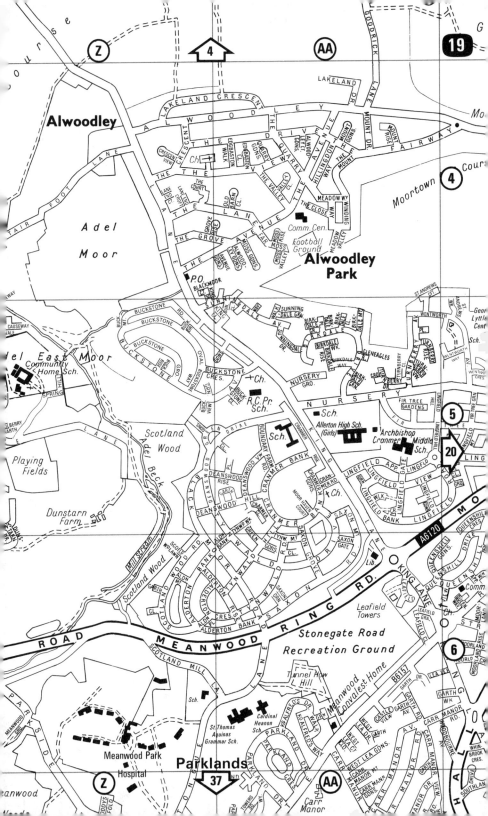

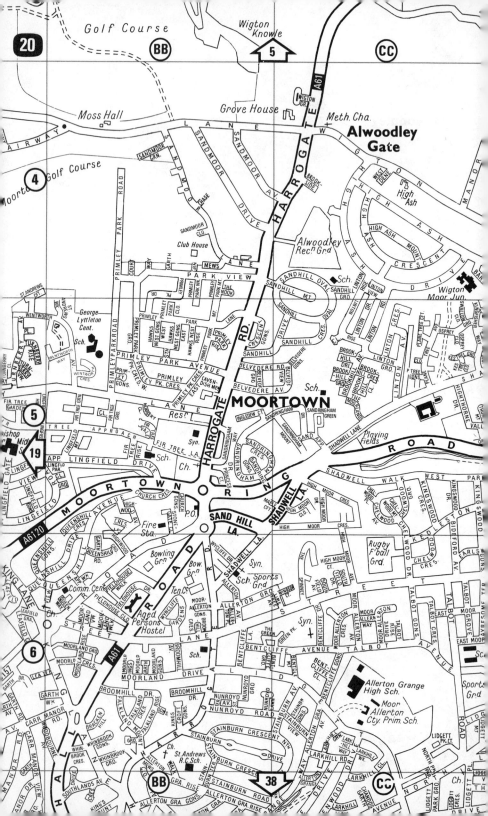

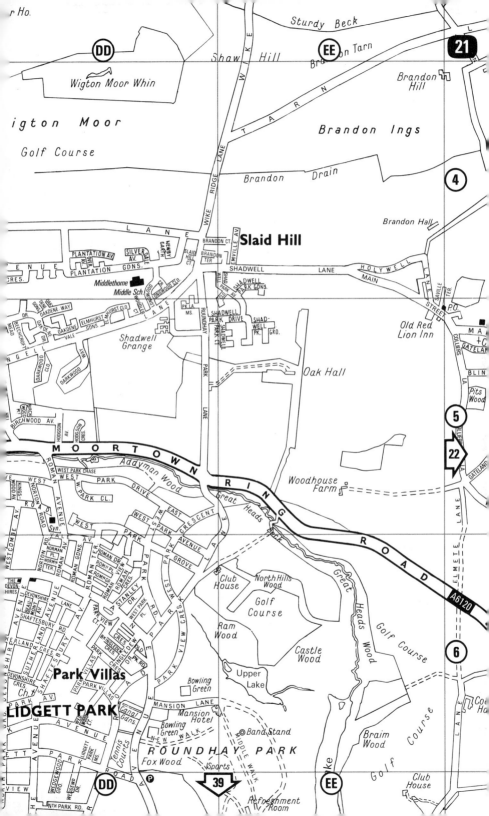

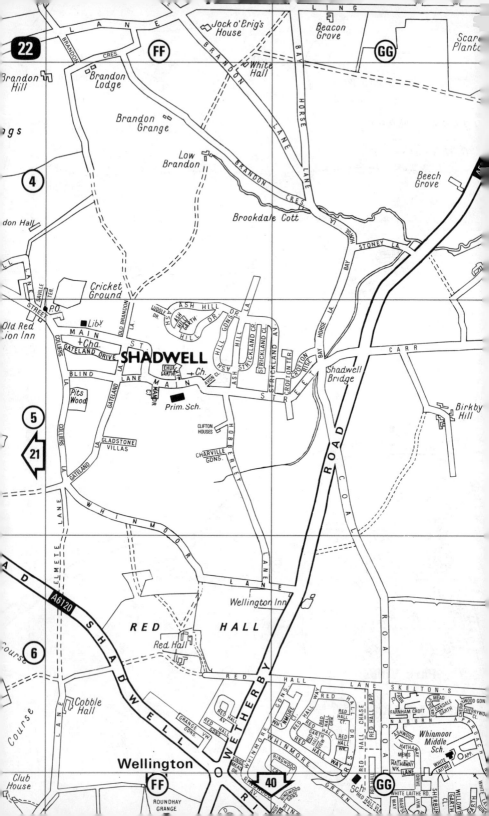

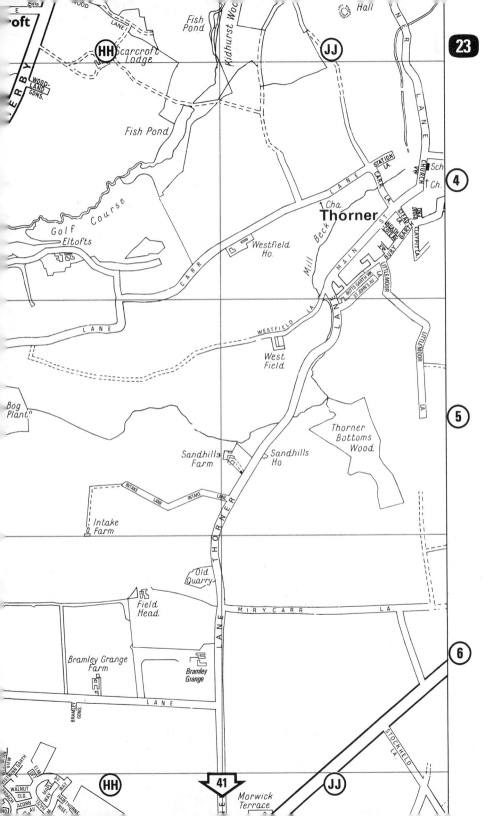

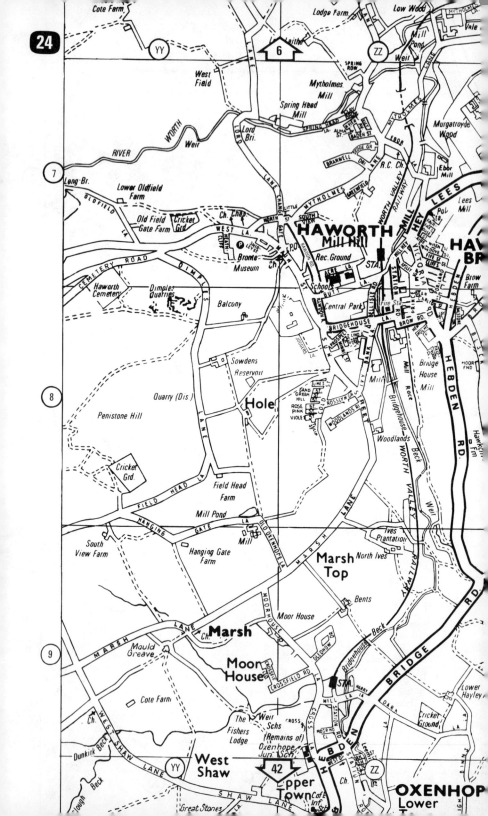

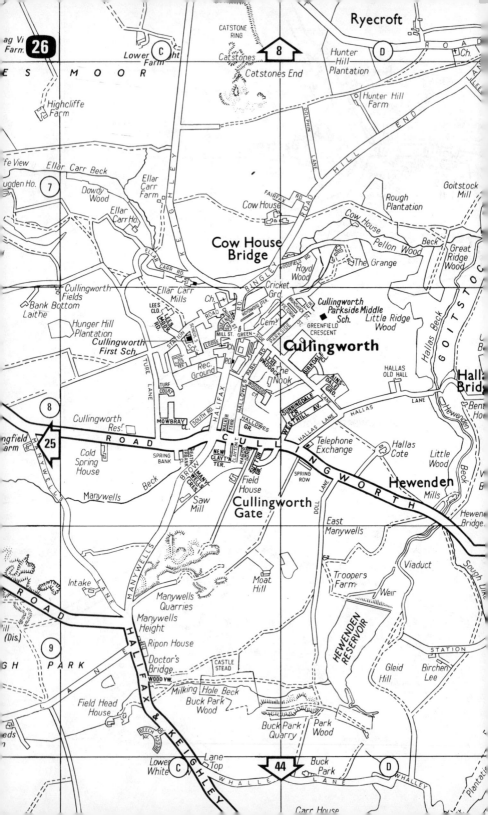

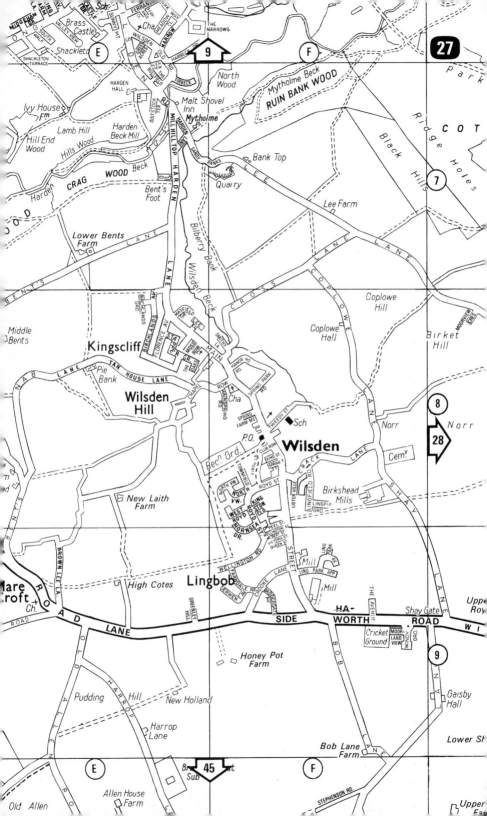

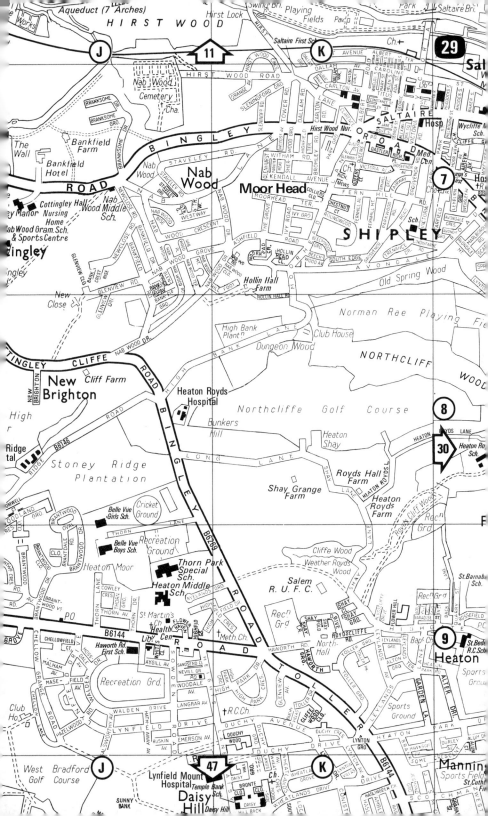

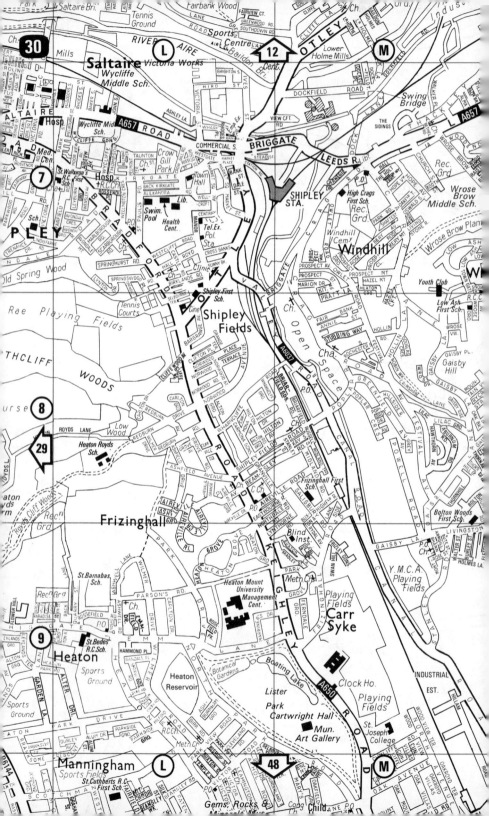

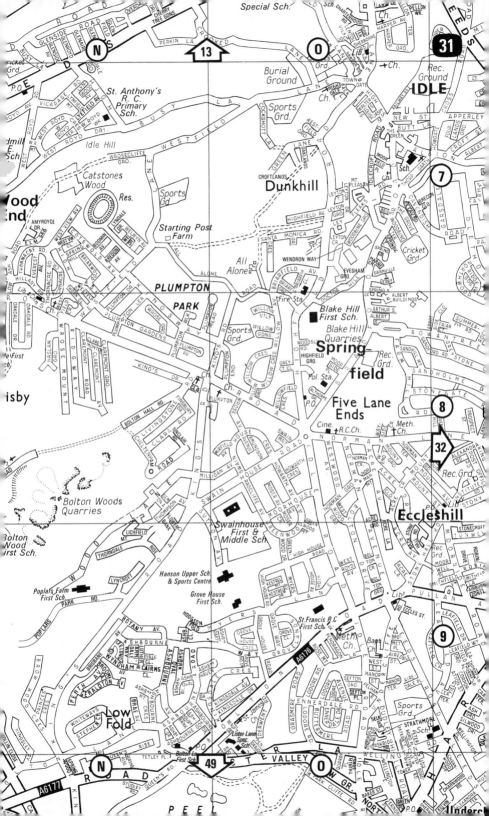

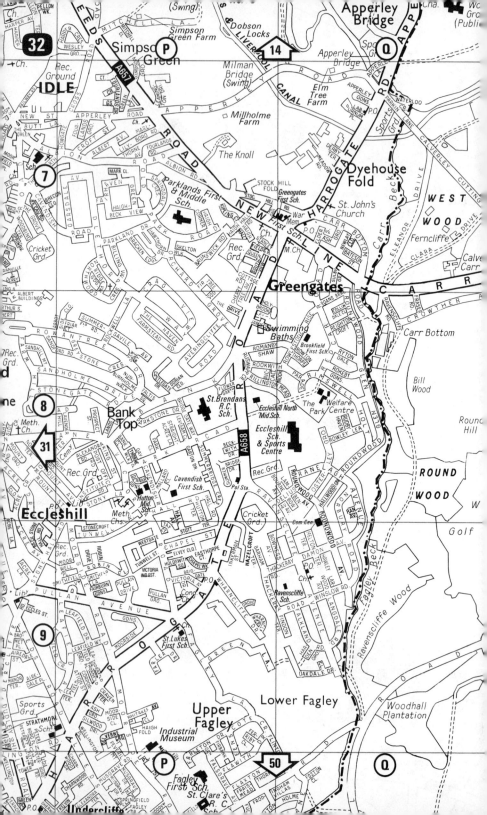

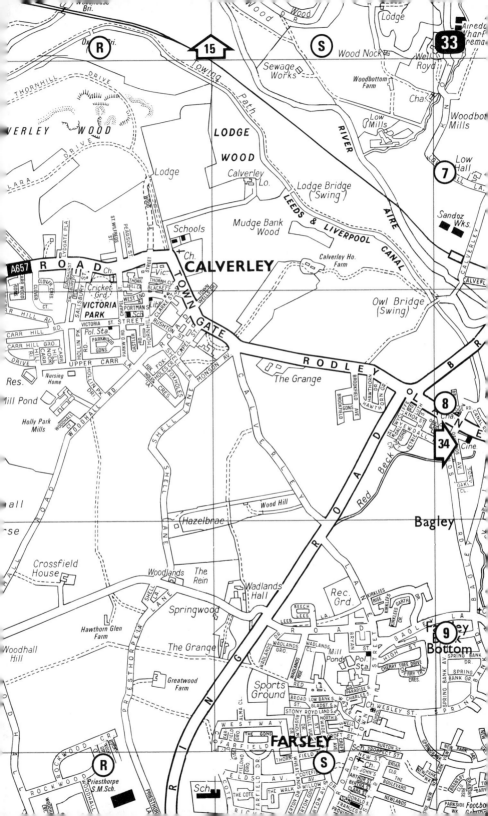

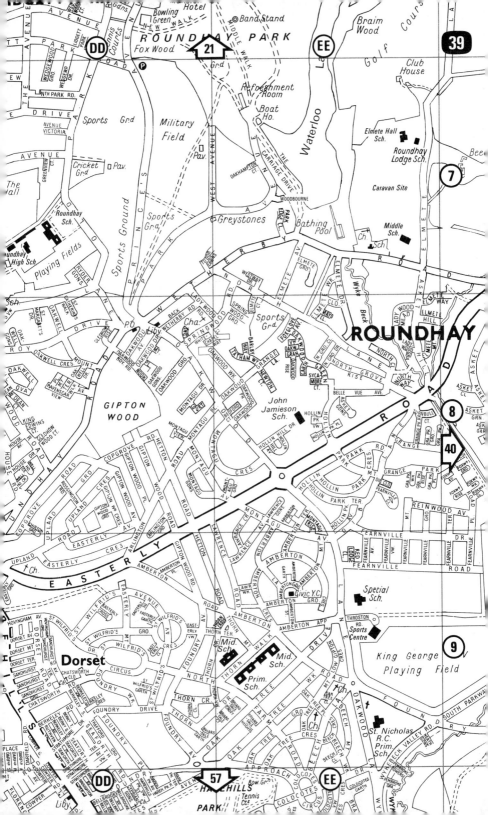

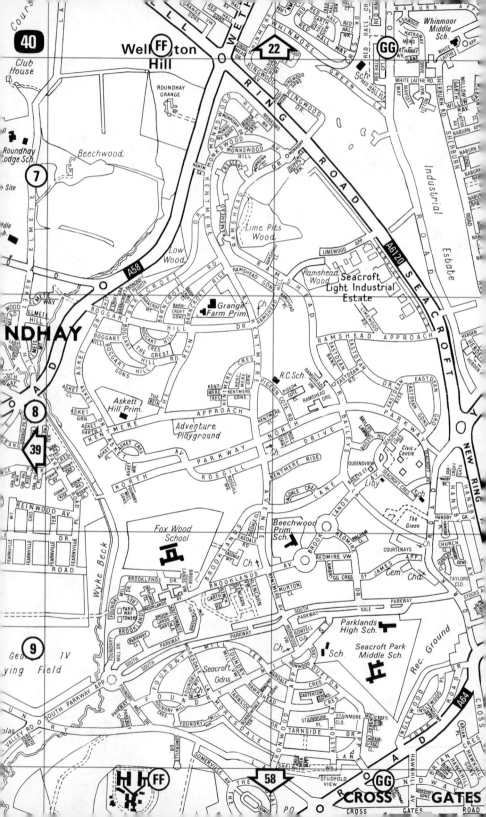

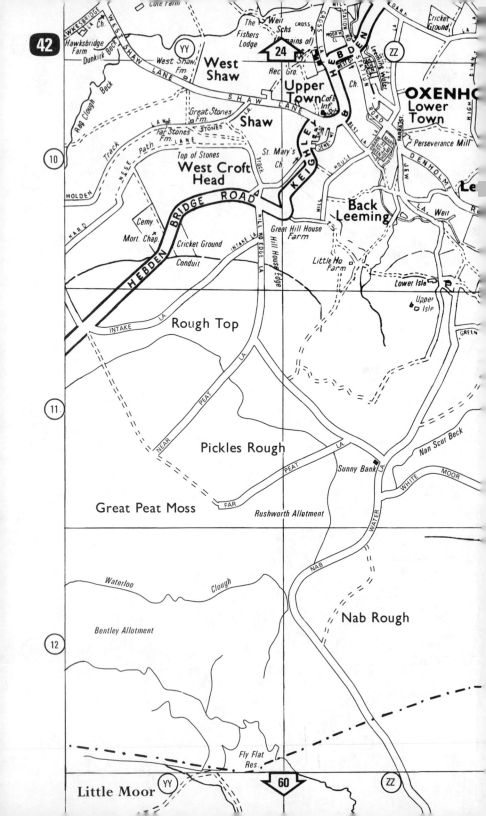

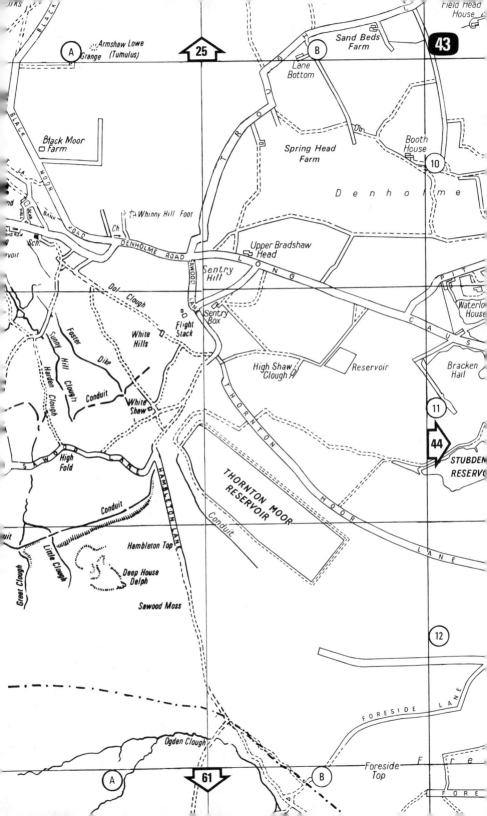

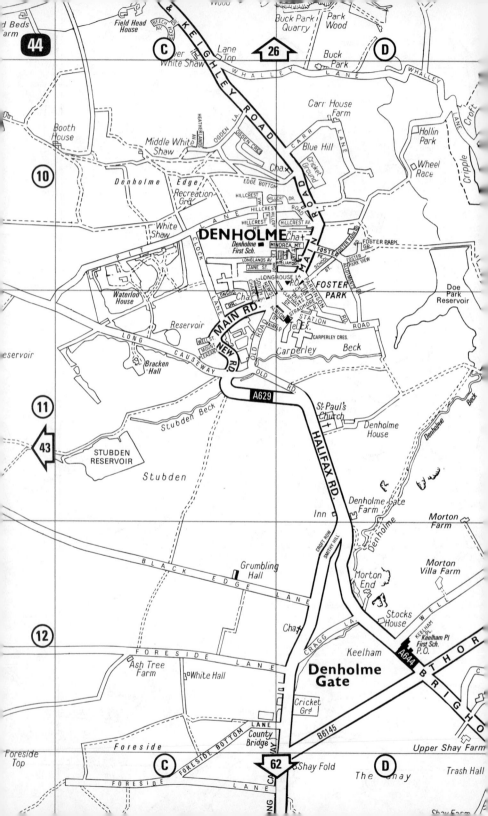

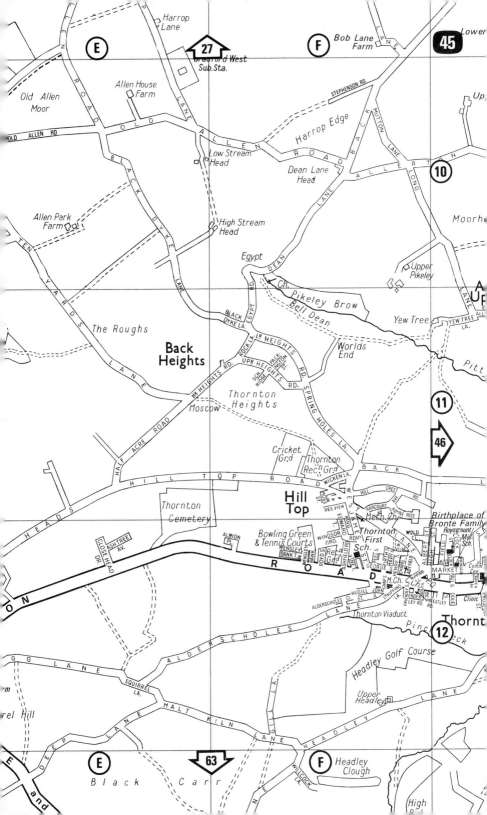

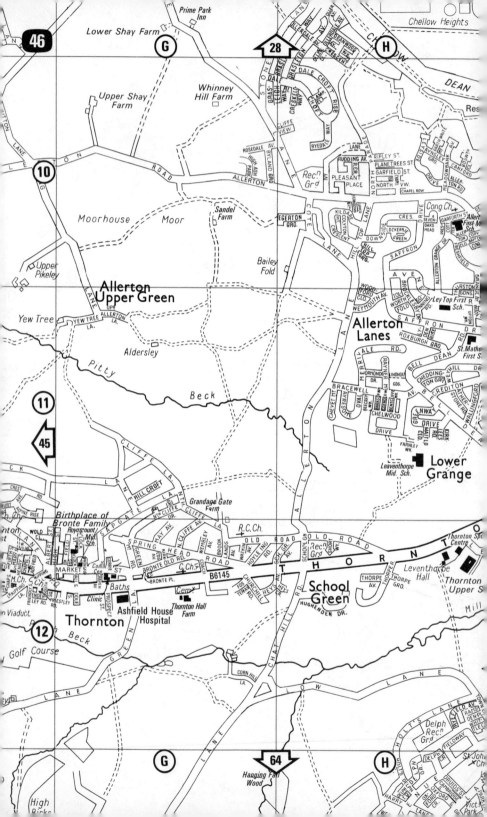

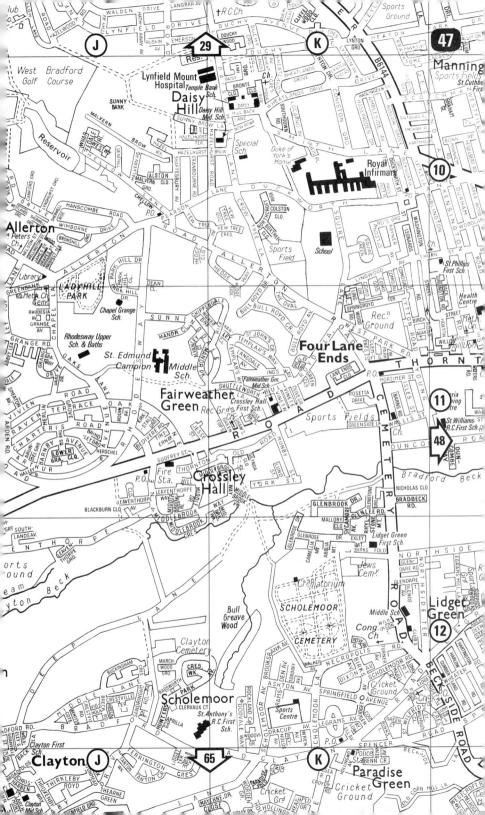

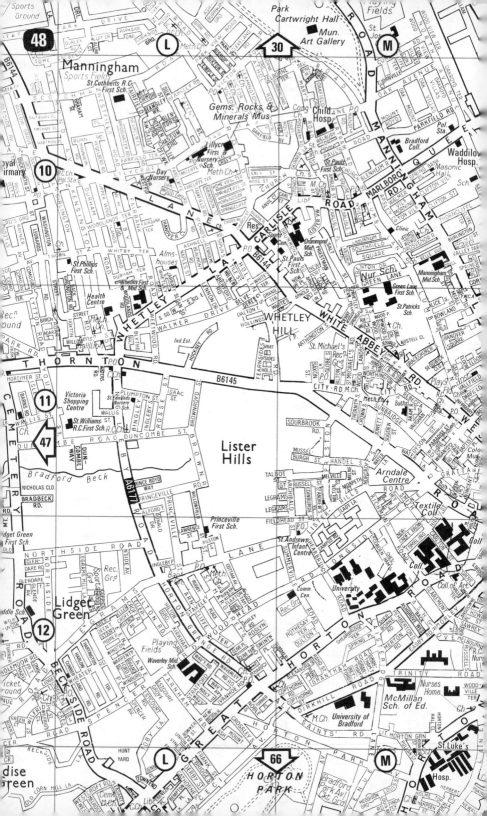

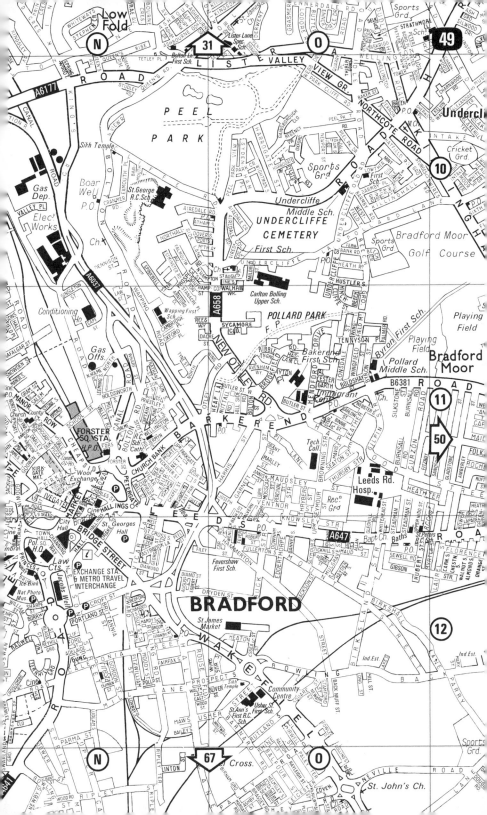

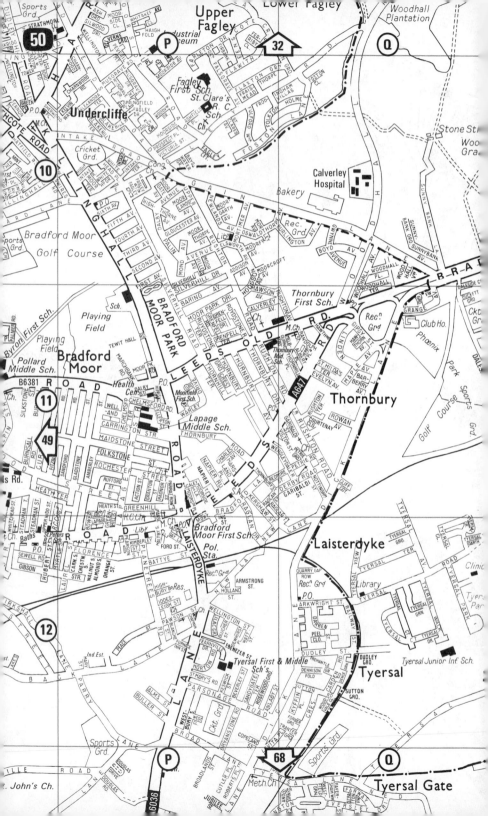

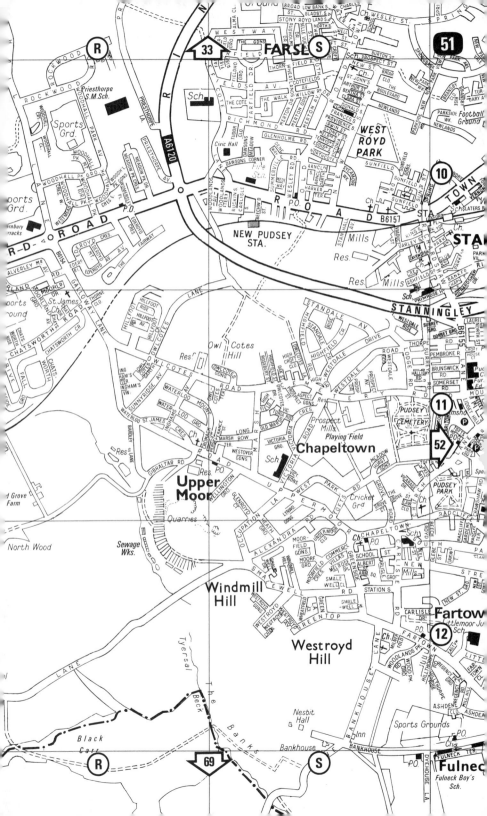

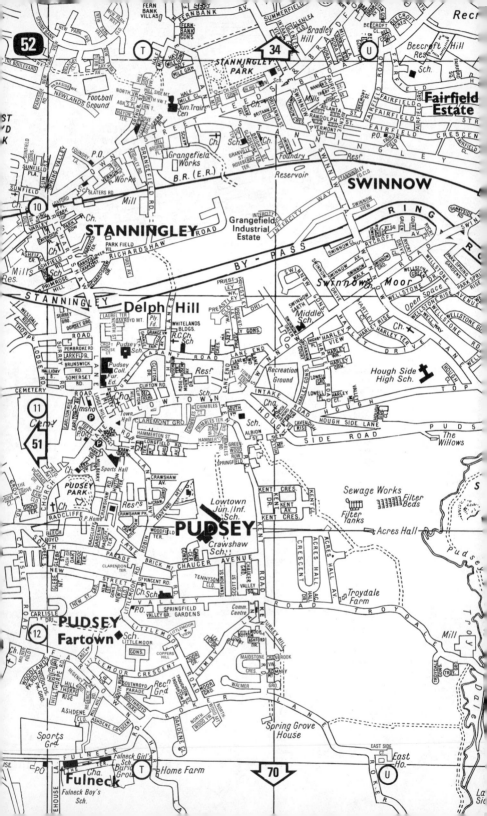

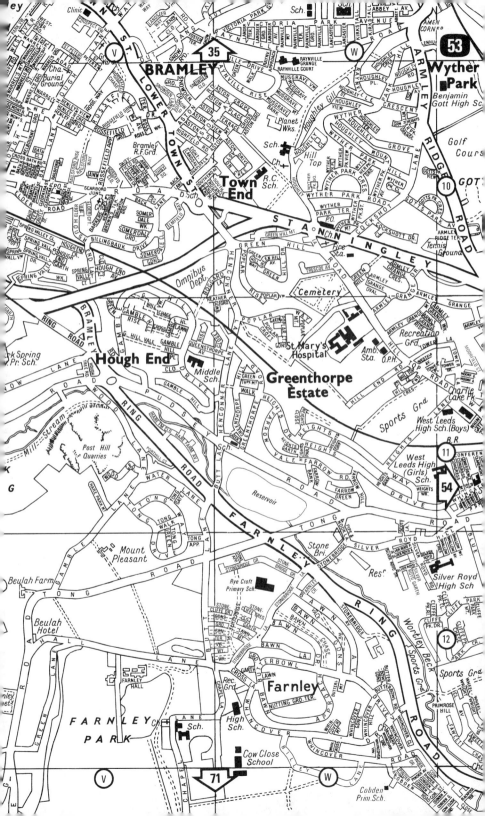

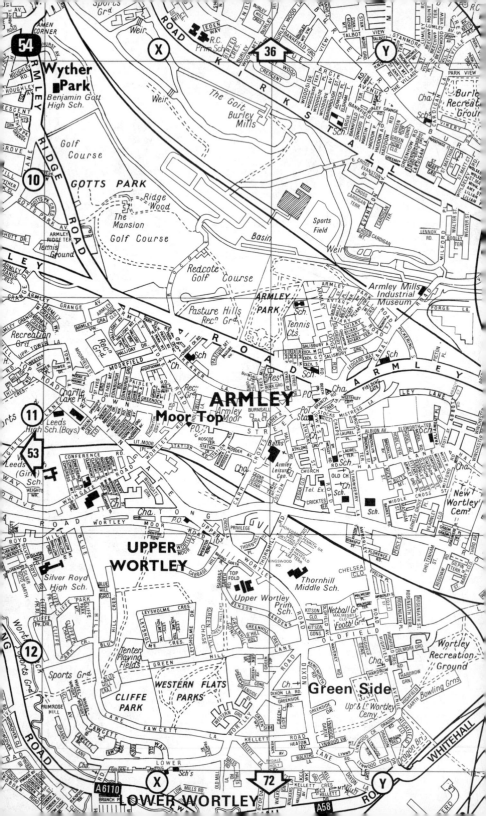

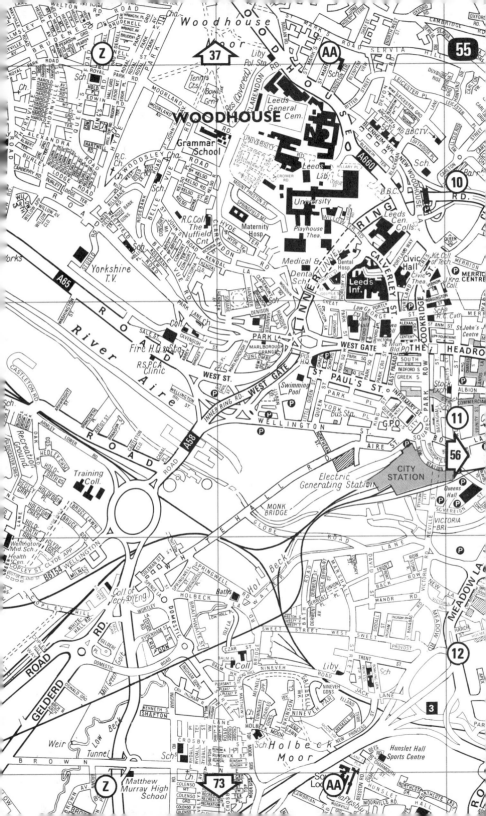

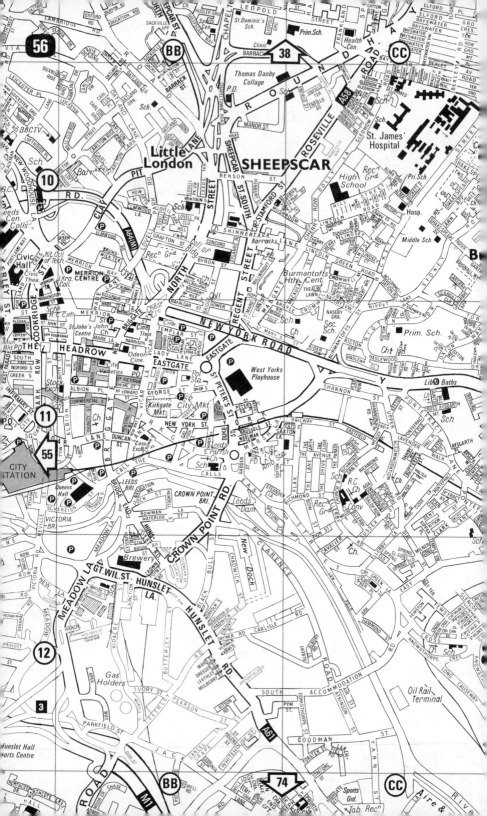

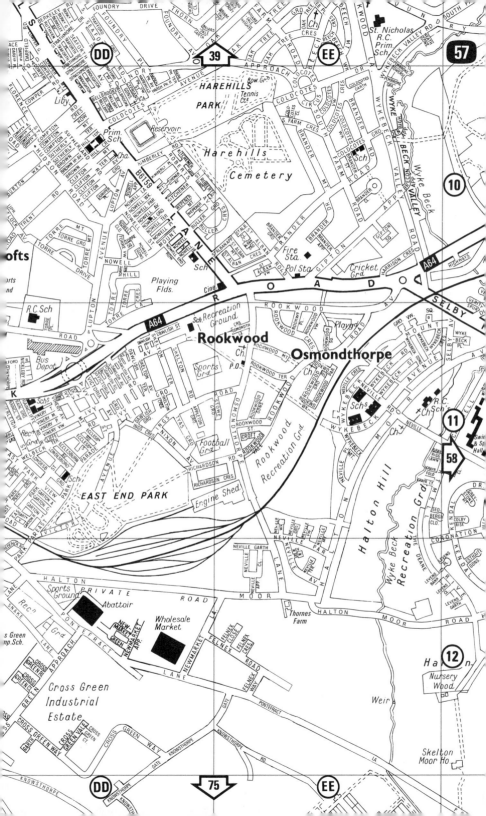

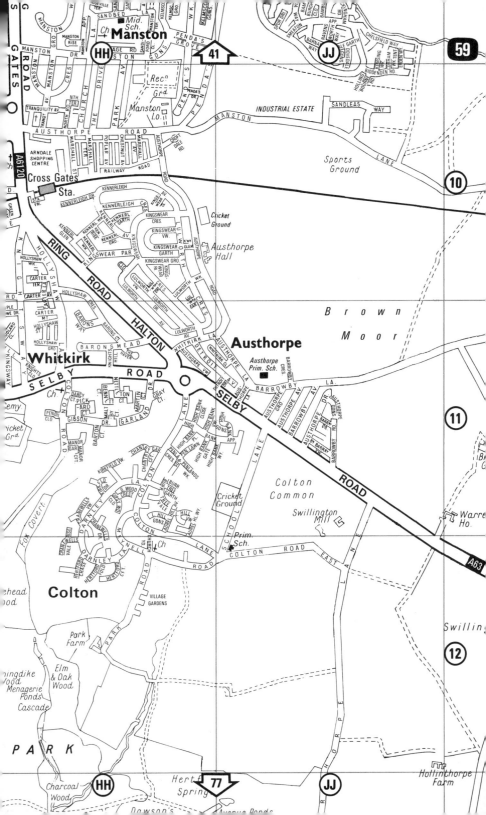

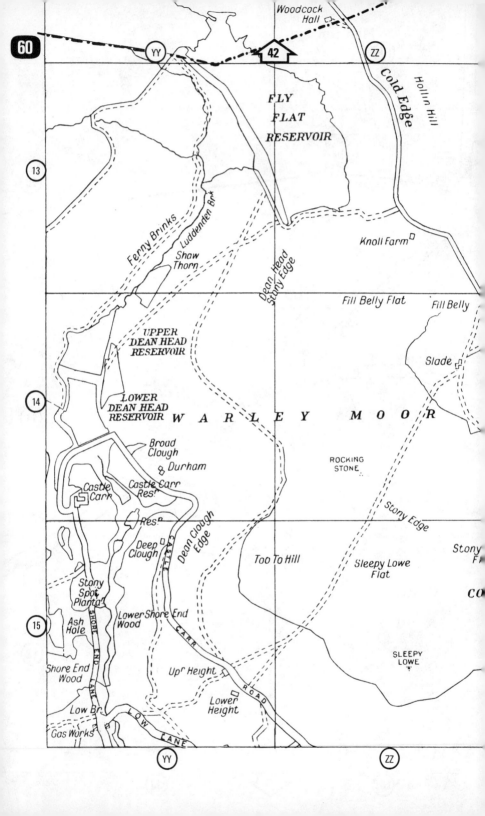

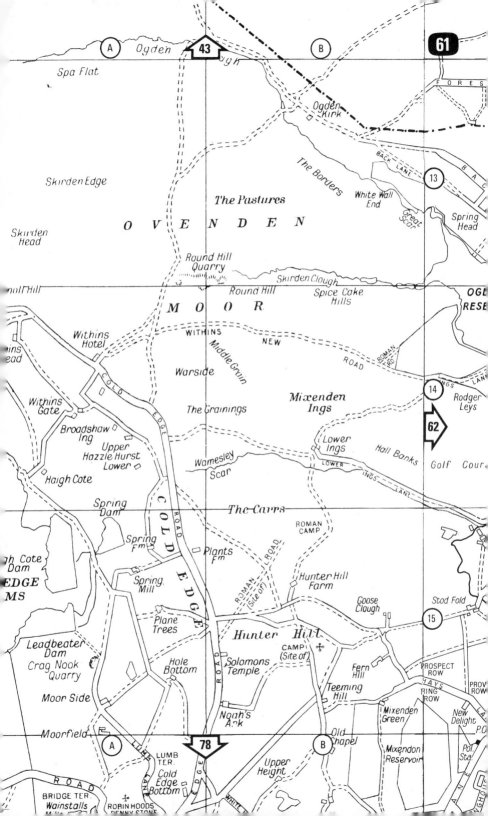

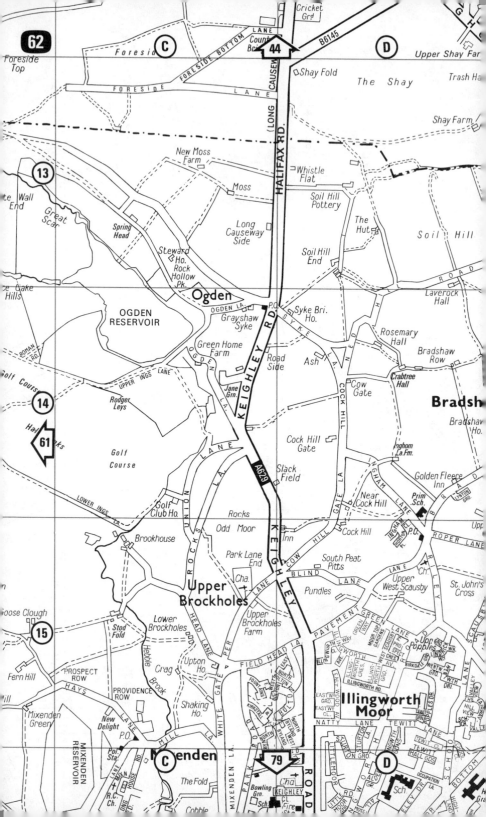

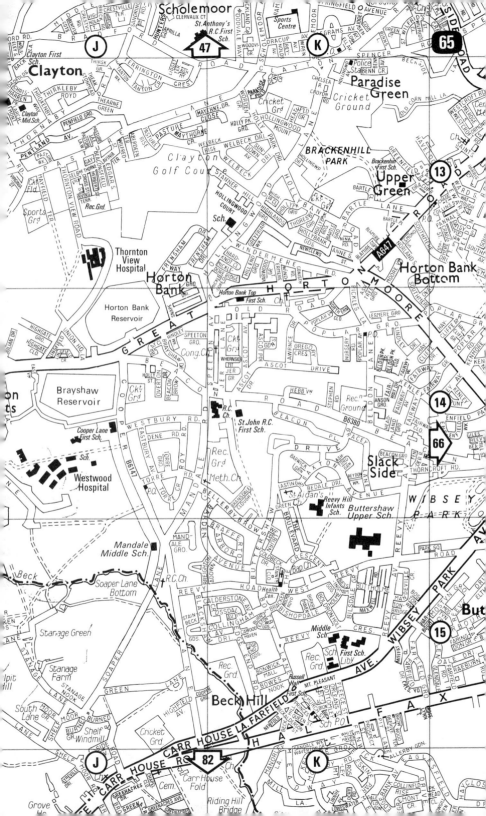

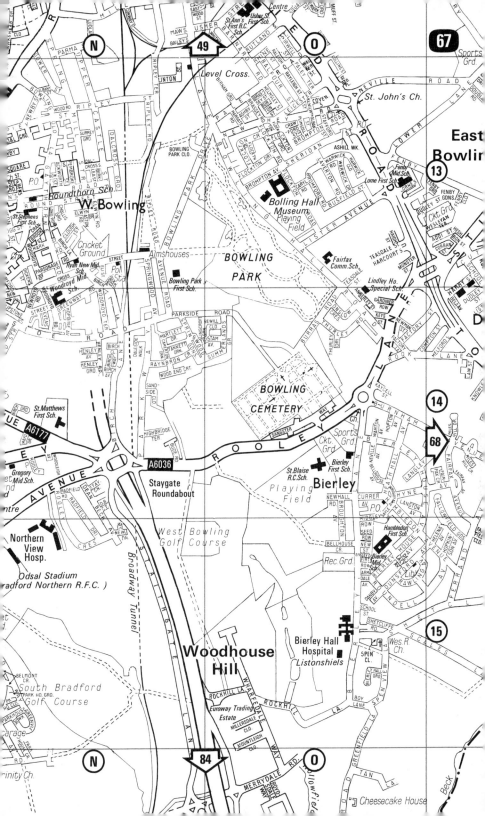

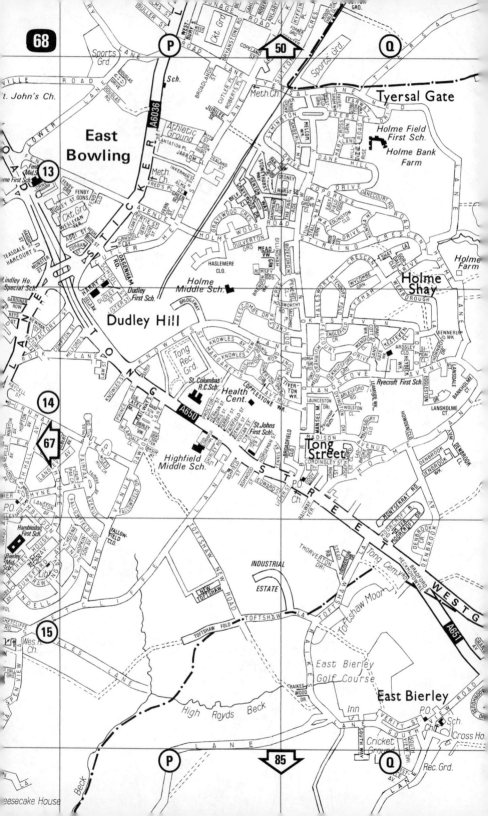

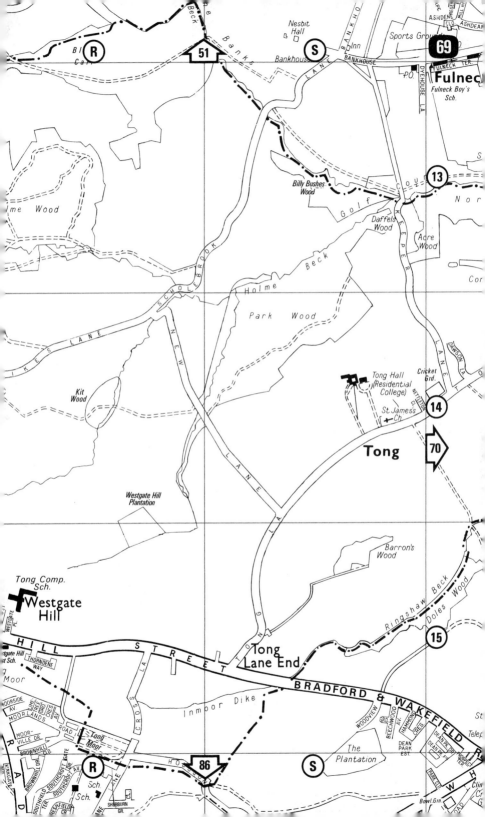

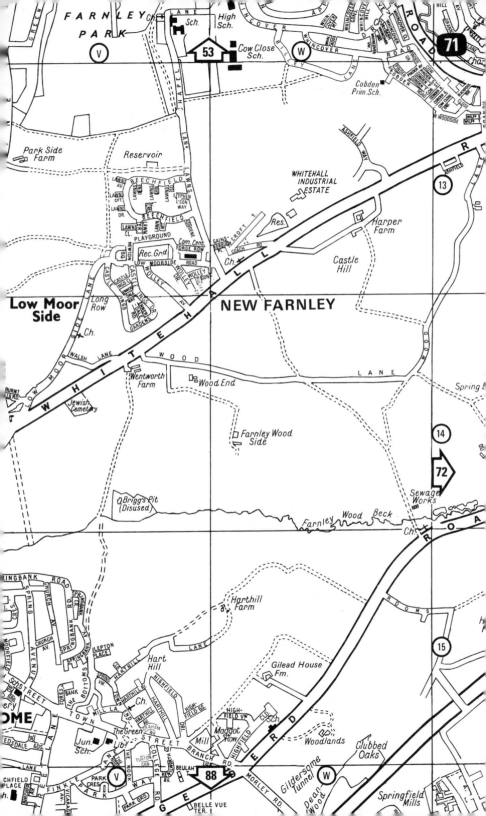

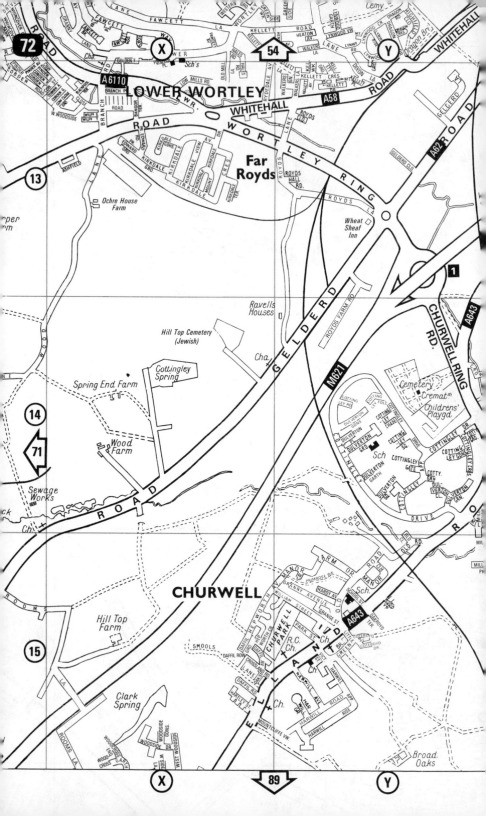

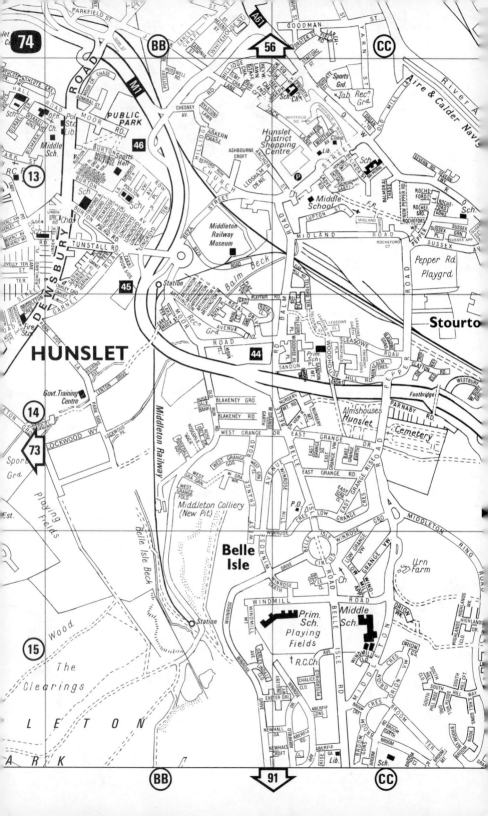

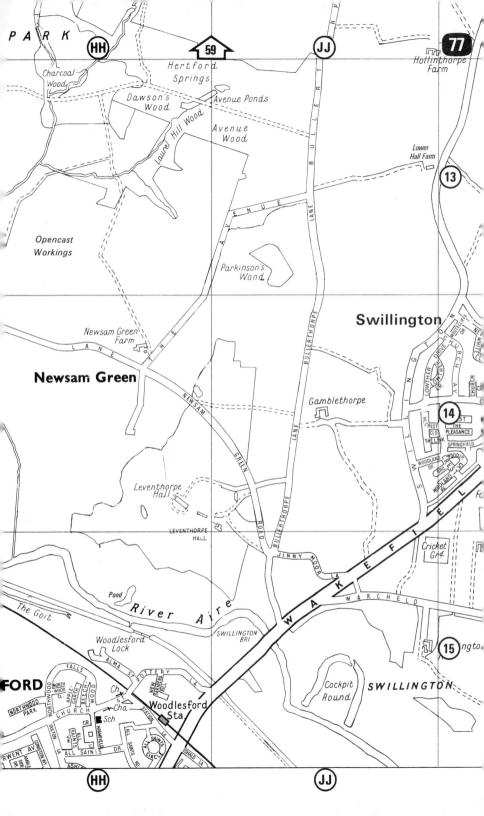

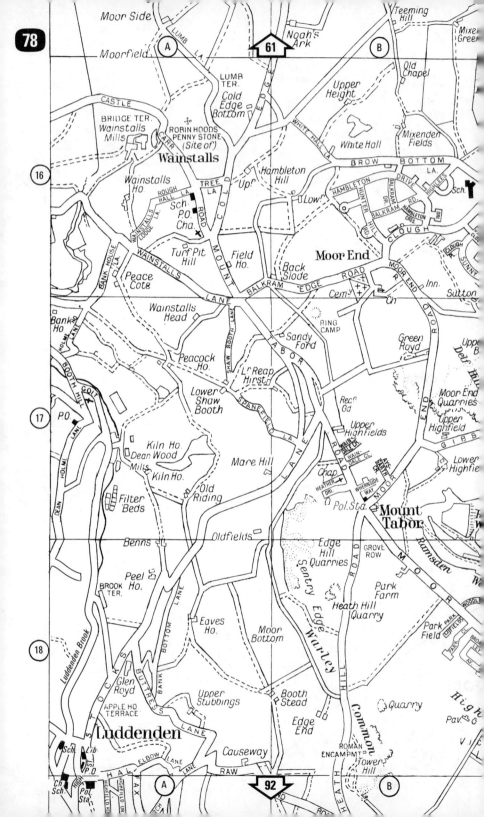

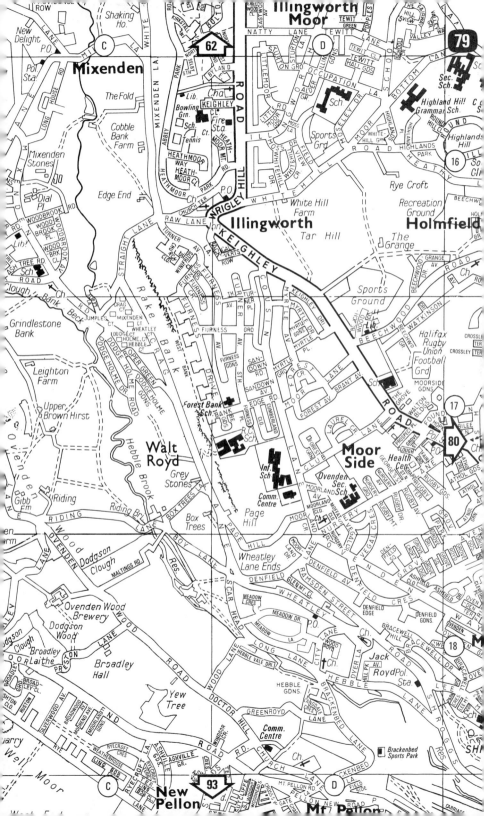

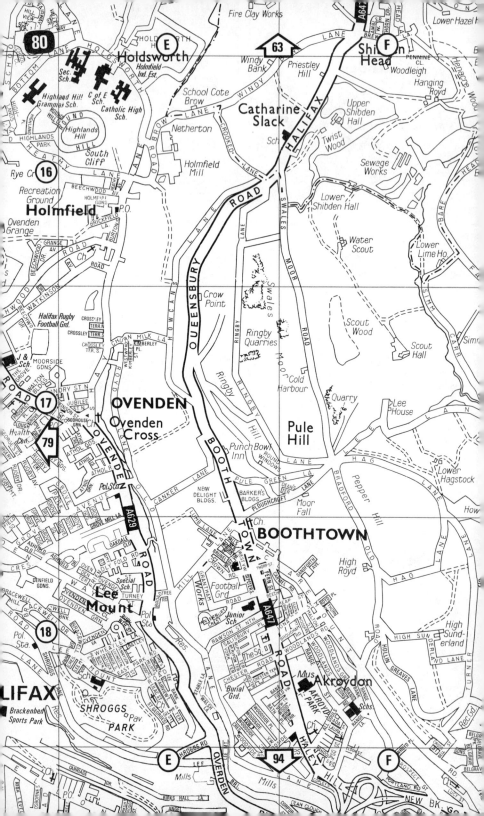

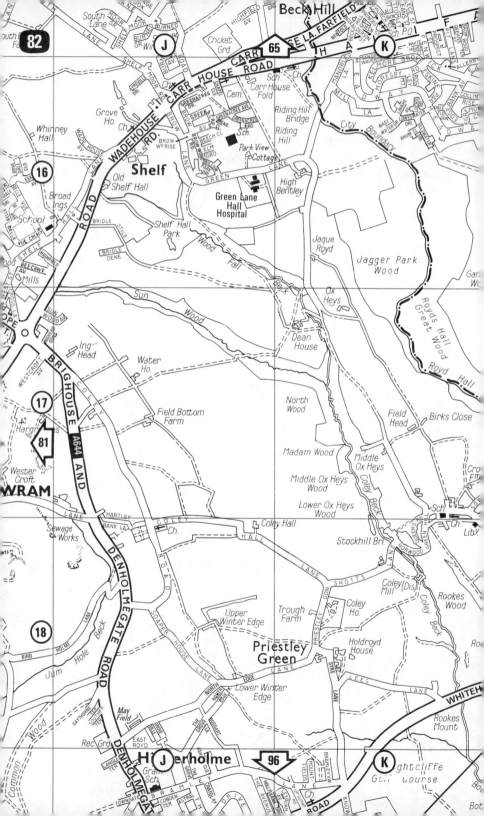

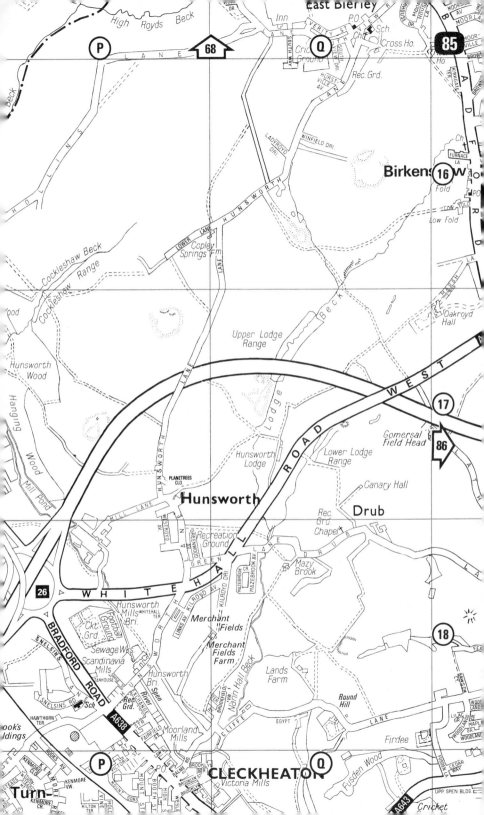

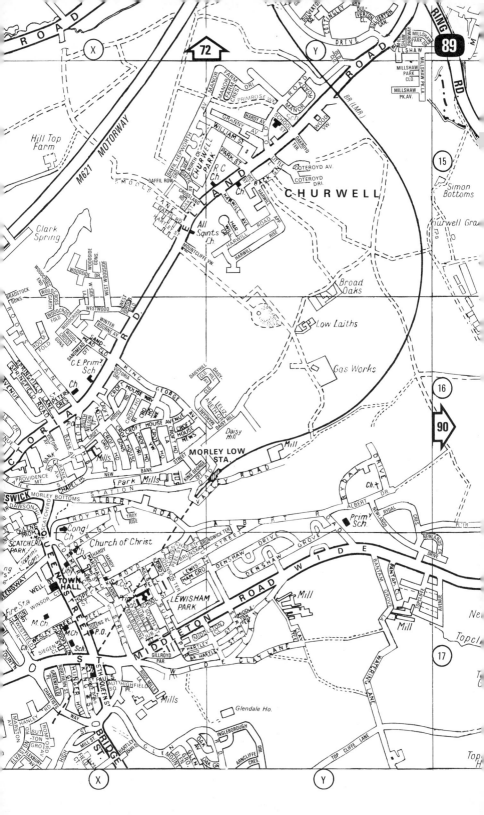

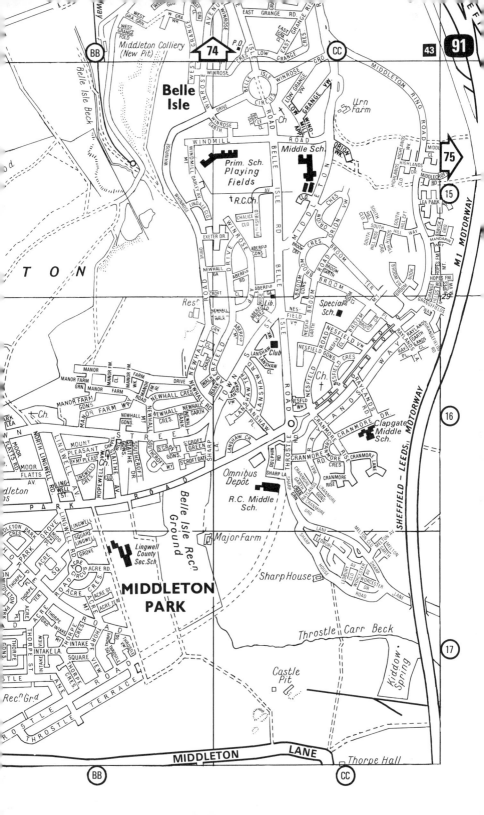

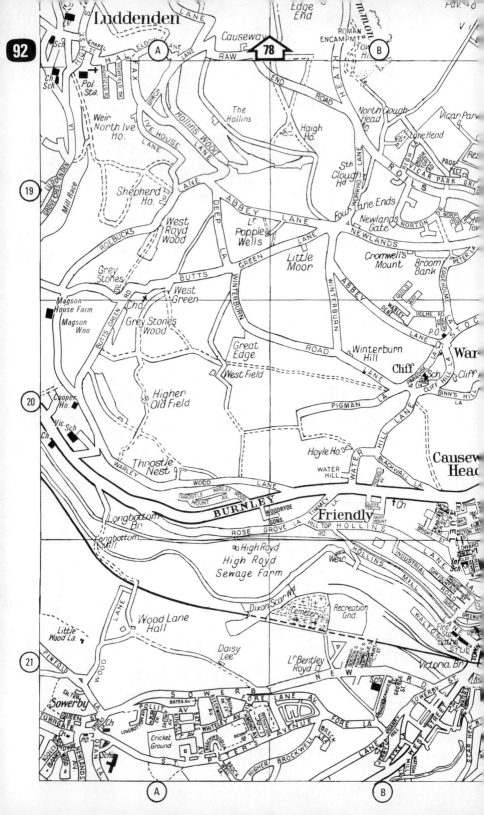

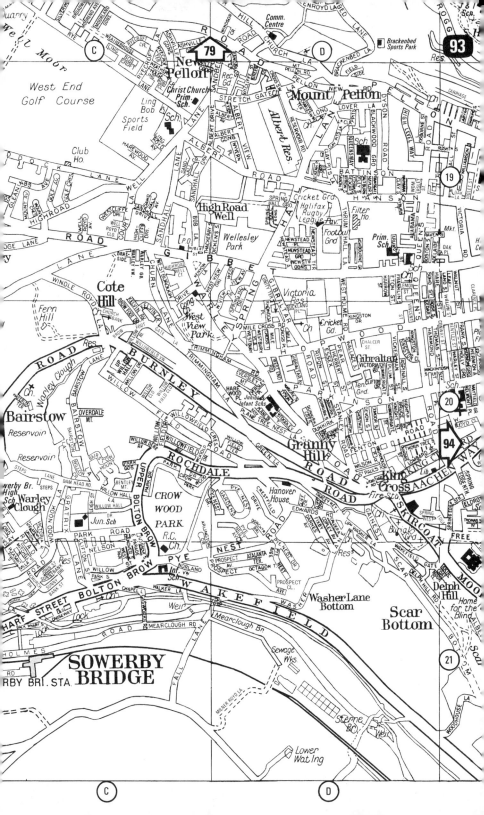

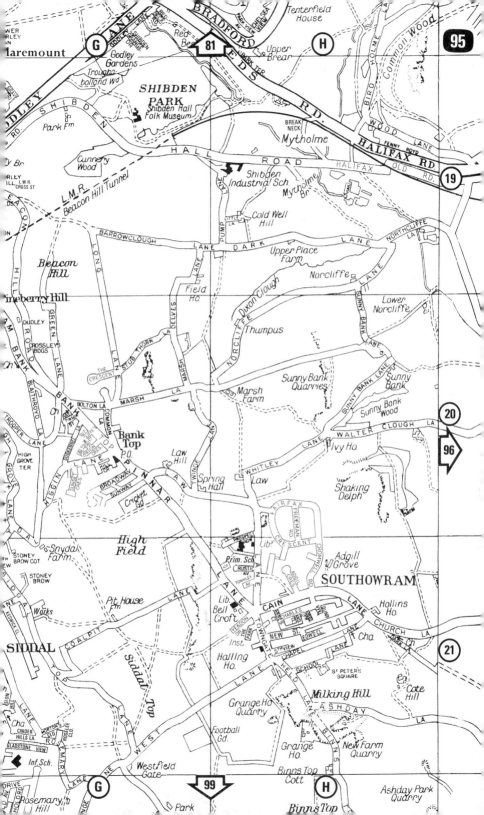

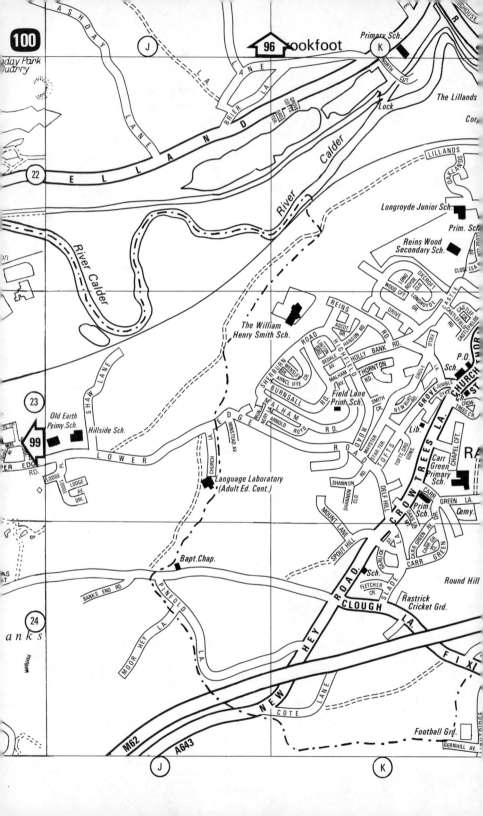

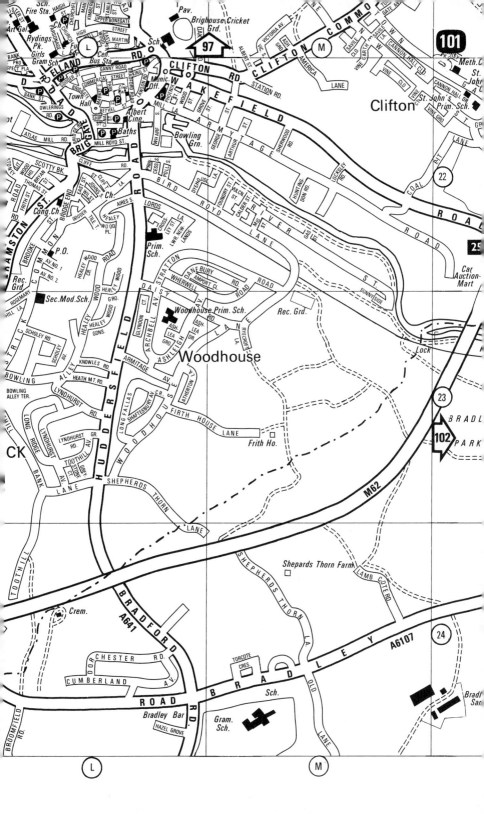

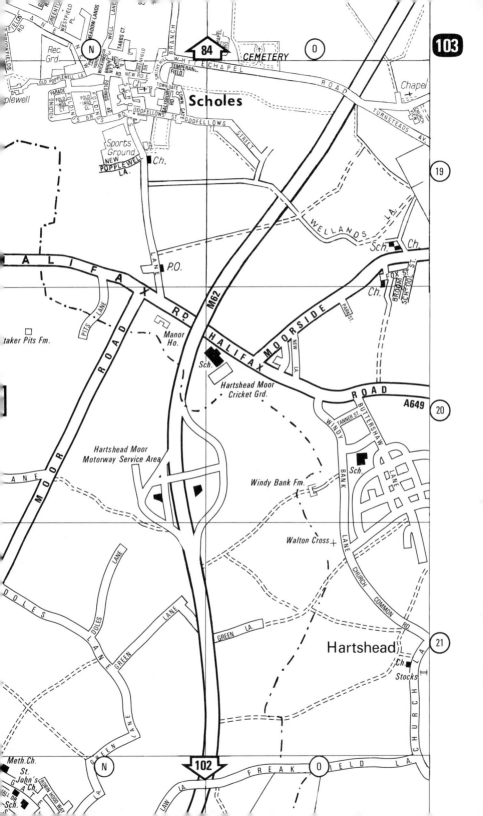

INDEX TO STREETS

General Abbreviations

All. —Alley
App. —Approach
Arc. —Arcade
Av. —Avenue
Bldgs. —Buildings
Boul. —Boulevard
Bri. —Bridge
Circ. —Circus
Cft. —Croft
Clo. —Close
Cor. —Corner
Cotts. —Cottages
Cres. —Crescent
Ct. —Court
Dr. —Drive
E. —East
Est. —Estate

Esp. —Esplanade
Gdns. —Gardens
Gra. —Grange
Grn. —Green
Gro. —Grove
Ho. —House
Ind. —Industrial
La. —Lane
Lo. —Lodge
Mans. —Mansions
Mkt. —Market
Ms. —Mews
Mt. —Mount
N. —North
Par. —Parade
Pass. —Passage
Pk. —Park

Pl. —Place
Prom. —Promenade
Quad. —Quadrant
Ri. —Rise
Rd. —Road
S. —South
Sq. —Square
Sta. —Station
St. —Street
Ter. —Terrace
Vills. —Villas
Vw. —View
W. —West
Wf. —Wharf
Wk. —Walk
Yd. —Yard

NOTES

The figures and letters following a street name indicate the postal district for that street with the square and page number where it will be found in the atlas. Thus Aachen Way is in the Halifax postal district 1, and in map square E20 on page 94. Street names followed by the letters LS are within a Leeds postal district, and those followed by the letters BD are within a Bradford postal district.

A street name followed by the name of another street in italics does not appear on the map, but will be found adjoining or near the latter.

District Abbreviations

Barwk. —Barwick-in-
   Elmet
Birs. —Birstal
Brad. —Bradford
Bram. —Bramhope
Brig. —Brighouse
Chur. —Churwell
Clay. —Clayton

Gild. —Gildersome
Greet. —Greetland
Hal. —Halifax
Hor. —Horsforth
Mor. —Morley
Pud. —Pusdey
Queens. —Queensbury
Raw. —Rawdon

Rod. —Rodley
Roth. —Rothwell
S.B. —Sowerby Bridge
Sea. —Seacroft
Stan. —Stanningley
Swi. —Swinnow
Wood. —Woodlesford
Yea. —Yeadon

Aachen Way HX1 E20 94
Abb Scott La. BD12 L16 83
Abb Scott La. BD6 L16 83
Abbey Av. LS5 W 9 35
Abbey Ct., Hor. LS13 U 8 34
Abbey La. HX2 A19 92
Abbey La. LS19 R 4 15
Abbey Lea BD15 J11 47
Abbey Mt. LS5 W 9 35
Raynville Rd.
Abbey Park Rd. HX2 C15 62
Abbey Rd. LS5 V 8 35
Abbey St. LS3 Z11 55
Abbey Ter. LS5 W·9 35
Abbey Vw. LS5 X 8 36
Abbey Gorse
Abbey Wk. HX3 F21 94
Abbey Wk. LS5 W 8 35
Abbey Wk. S. HX3 F21 94
Abbeydale Garth LS5 W 8 35
Abbeydale Gdns. LS5 W 8 35
Abbeydale Oval
Abbeydale Gro. LS5 W 8 35
Abbeydale Mt. LS5 W 8 35
Abbeydale Oval LS5 W 8 35
Abbeydale Vale LS5 W 8 35
Abbeydale Way LS5 W 8 35
Abbeydale Mt.
Abbotside Clo. BD10 O 8 31
Abbott Ct. LS12 Y11 54
Abbott Rd. LS12 Y11 54
Abbott Vw. LS12 Y11 54
Abel St. HX1 E19 94
Abelia Mt. BD7 K12 47
Abercorn Pl. LS11 AA13 73
Chester Pl.
Abercorn St. LS12 Y11 54
Armley Rd.
Abercorn Ter. LS12 Y11 54
Aberdeen Dr. LS12 X11 54
Aberdeen Gro. LS12 X11 54
Aberdeen Pl. BD7 L12 48
Aberdeen Rd. LS12 X11 54
Aberdeen Ter. BD14 J13 65
Aberdeen Ter. BD7 L12 48
Aberdeen Wk. LS12 X11 54
Aberfield Bank LS10 BB16 91
Aberfield Clo. LS10 CC15 74
Aberfield Cres. LS10 CC16 91
Aberfield Dr. LS10 CC16 91
Aberfield Garth LS10 CC15 74
Aberfield Gate LS10 CC15 54
Aberfield Gdns. LS10 CC15 74
Aberfield Mt. LS10 CC16 91
Aberfield Rd. LS10 CC15 74
Aberfield Ri. LS10 CC16 91
Aberfield Wk. LS10 BB16 91
Aberford Rd. BD8 L11 48
Abingdon St. BD8 L10 48
Abingdon Vills. BD8 L10 48
Toller La.
Abyssinia Gro. LS3 Z10 55
St. Johns Rd.
Abyssinia Rd. LS3 Z10 55
Abyssinia St. LS3 Z10 55
Abyssinia Ter. LS3 Z10 55
Acacia Dr. BD15 H 9 28
Acacia Park Cres. BD10 Q 6 14
Acacia Park Dr. BD10 Q 6 14
Acacia Park Ter. BD10 R 6 15
Academy St. LS10 BB12 56
Acaster Dr. BD12 M16 83
Accommodation Rd. LS9 CC10 56
Ackroyd Ct. BD13 F12 45
Market Rd.
Ackroyd Sq. BD13 H14 64
Highgate Rd.
Ackroyd St. BD14 H13 64
Clayton La.
Ackroyd St., Mor. LS27 X17 89
Ackworth Av. LS19 S 4 15
Ackworth Cres. LS19 S 4 15
Ackworth Dr. LS19 S 4 15
Ackworth St. BD5 N13 67
Acorn St. BD21 B 4 7
Acorn St. BD3 O12 49
Leeds Rd.
Acorn St. HX1 E19 94
Hanson La.
Acre Av. BD2 O 8 31
Acre Circus LS10 AA17 90
Acre Clo. BD2 O 8 31
Acre Cres. BD2 O 8 31
Acre Cres. LS10 BB17 91
Acre Dr. BD2 O 8 31
Acre Gro. BD2 O 9 31
Acre Gro. LS10 BB17 91
Acre Howe Ri. BD17 N 5 13

Acre La. BD2 O 9 31
Acre La. BD6 M14 66
Acre La., Haworth ZZ 7 24
Acre Mt.10 BB17 91
Acre Pl. BD6 M14 66
Acre La.
Acre Pl. LS10 BB17 91
Acre Rd. LS10 AA17 90
Acre Ri. BD17 M 5 12
Acre Sq. LS10 BB17 91
Acre St. LS10 BB17 91
Acre Ter. LS10 BB17 91
Acre, The BD12 L16 83
Acres Hall Av., Pud. LS28 U12 52
Acres Hall Cres., Pud. U12 52
LS28
Acres Hall Dr., Pud. LS28 U12 52
Acres St. BD21 B 4 7
Acton St. BD3 P11 50
Acton St. LS11 AA13 73
Kiln St.
Ada Cres. LS9 CC11 56
Ada St. BD13 F14 63
Ada St. BD17 N 6 13
Otley Rd.
Ada St. BD18 K 7 29
Ada St. HX3 F18 80
Ada Vw. LS9 CC11 56
Adam St. BD6 L14 66
Adams St. LS11 AA12 55
Canning St.
Adams Wk. LS6 Z10 55
Moorland Rd.
Adas Pl., Stan. LS28 T10 52
Arthur St.
Addi St. BD4 P13 68
Addison Av. BD3 P10 50
Adel Garth LS16 Y 4 18
Adel Grange Clo. LS16 Y 6 18
Adel Grange Ms. LS16 Y 6 18
Adel Grn. LS16 Y 5 18
Adel La. LS16 Y 5 18
Adel Mead LS16 Y 5 18
Adel Park Clo. LS16 Y 5 18
Adel Park Ct. LS16 Y 5 18
Adel Park Dr. LS16 Y 5 18
Adel Park Gdns. LS16 Y 5 18
Adel Pasture Cft. LS16 Y 5 18
Adel Pasture Dr. LS16 Y 5 18
Adel Pasture LS16 Y 5 18
Adel Towers Clo. LS16 Y 5 18
Adel Towers Ct. LS16 Y 5 18
Adel Vale LS16 Y 5 18
Adel Wood Clo. LS16 Y 5 18
Adel Wood Dr. LS16 Y 5 18
Adel Wood Gdns. LS16 Y 5 18
Adel Wood Gro. LS16 Y 5 18
Adel Wood Pl. LS16 Y 5 18
Adel Wood Rd. LS16 Y 5 18
Adelaide St. BD5 N12 49
Adelaide St. HX1 D19 93
Adgil Cres. HX3 H21 95
Admiral St. LS11 BB13 74
Adolphus St. BD1 N12 49
Eastbrook La.
Adwalton St. BD4 O12 49
Wakefield Rd.
Adwick Pl. LS4 Y10 54
Agar St. BD8 K11 47
Agar Ter. BD8 K11 47
Ainley Bottom, Elland H24 99
HX5
Ainley St., Elland HX5 G24 99
Ainsbury Av. BD10 O 6 13
Ainsdale Gro. BD13 D 8 26
Air St. LS10 CC12 56
Airdale Prospect LS13 U 9 34
Aire Clo. BD17 L 6 12
Aire Gro. LS19 S 4 15
Aire St. BD10 O 6 13
Aire St. BD16 G 4 10
Aire St. HD6 L22 101
Aire St. LS1 AA11 55
Aire St., Haworth ZZ 7 24
Aire Vw. Av. BD16 H 7 28
Aire Vw. St. LS19 S 4 15
Aire Way BD17 L 6 12
Airebank BD16 G 5 10
Airedale Av. BD16 H 7 28
Airedale Cft. LS18 T18 34
Airedale St.
Airedale Cliff LS13 V 8 35
Airedale College Mt. BD3 O10 49
Airedale College Rd.
Airedale College Ter. BD3 O10 49
Airedale Cres. BD3 O10 49
Airedale Dr. HX3 H16 80

Airedale Dr., Hor. LS18 T 7 34
Airedale Gdns., Rod. LS13 T 8 34
Airedale Gro., Hor. LS18 T 7 34
Airedale Mt. BD3 O10 49
Undercliffe La.
Airedale Mt. LS13 T 8 34
Airedale Pl. BD17 L 6 12
Green La.
Airedale Pl. BD2 N 6 13
Airedale Pl. BD2 O 9 31
Airedale Pl. LS1 Z11 55
West St.
Airedale Rd. BD3 N10 49
Airedale Sq. BD3 N11 49
Otley Rd.
Airedale St. BD16 G 5 10
Queen St.
Airedale St. BD2 O 9 31
Airedale Ter. BD17 M 6 12
Airedale Ter. LS10 DD14 75
Wakefield Rd.
Airedale Ter., Hor. LS18 U 7 34
Airedale Vw. BD13 G14 64
Thornton Rd.
Airedale Vw., Rod. LS13 T 8 34
Town St.
Aireview Cres. BD17 L 6 12
Aireville Av. BD18 L 8 30
Aireville Av. BD9 L 8 30
Aireville Clo. BD18 L 8 30
Aireville Cres. BD9 L 8 30
Aireville Dr. BD18 L 8 30
Aireville Grange BD18 L 8 30
Aireville Gro. BD18 L 8 30
Aireville Rd. BD9 L 8 30
Aireville Ri. BD9 L 8 30
Aireville Ter. BD9 M 8 30
Aireville Rd.
Aireworth St. BD21 B 4 7
Airlie Av. LS8 CC 9 38
Airlie Pl. LS8 CC 9 38
Airview Ter. LS18 U 9 34
Hill La.
Akam Rd. BD1 M11 48
Aked St. BD1 N11 49
Vicar La.
Akeds Rd. HX1 E20 94
Akeroyd Pk. BD4 Q12 50
Dick La.
Akroyd Pl. HX1 F19 94
Akroyd St. HX1 F19 94
Akroyd Ter. HX2 D20 93
Upper Washer La.
Alabama St. HX1 D19 93
Alan Cres. LS15 GG11 58
Alandale Rd. HD2 N24 102
Alaska Pl. LS7 CC 8 38
Alban St. BD4 O13 67
Plimsoll St.
Albany St. BD21 B 4 7
Catherine St.
Albany St. BD5 N13 67
Albany St. BD6 M14 66
Albany St. HX3 F20 94
Trooper La.
Albany St. LS12 X11 54
Albany Ter. LS12 X11 54
Albert Av. BD10 P 7 32
Albert Av. BD18 K 6 11
Albert Av. HX2 D19 93
Albert Bldgs. BD10 O 8 31
Albert Cres. BD11 R17 86
Albert Dr. HX2 C19 93
Albert Dr., Mor. LS27 Y16 89
Albert Edward St. BD13 G14 64
Alexandra St.
Albert Gdns. HX2 D19 93
Albert Gro. LS6 Y 8 36
Albert Pl. BD3 Q11 50
Albert Pl., Hor. LS18 V 6 17
Albert Promenade E21 94
HX3
Albert Rd. BD13 F14 63
Albert Rd. HX2 K 7 29
Albert Rd. HX2 C19 93
Albert Rd., Mor. LS27 X16 89
Albert Rd., S.B. HX6 C20 93
Albert St. BD10 O 8 31
Albert St. BD12 M18 83
Albert St. BD13 F12 45
Albert St. BD13 G14 64
Brunswick St.
Albert St. BD15 F 9 27
Albert St. BD16 G 5 10
Hillside Rd.
Albert St. BD17 M 6 12
Albert St. BD3 O11 49
Albert St. BD6 L15 66

Street	Grid	Page
Albert St. BD6	M14	66
Prospect St.		
Albert St. HX1	M21	97
Albert St. LS10	CC12	56
Albert St. LS28	S12	51
Albert St. LS6	AA 9	37
Albert St. N. HX1	F19	94
Albert St., Elland HX5	G24	99
Albert Ter. BD12	M18	83
Town Gate		
Albert Ter. BD12	N16	84
Albert Ter. BD13	F12	45
Albert St.		
Albert Ter. BD18	K 6	11
Albert Ter. BD19	M18	83
Craiglea Dr.		
Albert Ter. LS6	Z10	55
Albert Vw. HX2	D19	93
Albert Way BD11	S17	86
Albert Wk. BD18	K 7	29
Alberta Av. LS7	CC 7	38
Alberta Dr. LS7	BB 8	38
Montreal Av.		
Albion Av. LS12	Y11	54
Albion Ct. BD1	N11	49
Kirkgate		
Albion Ct., HX1	F19	94
Great Albion St.		
Albion Fold BD15	F 8	27
Main St.		
Albion Pl. BD13	F12	45
Albion Pl. LS1	BB11	56
Albion Rd. BD10	O 7	31
Albion Rd. LS28	T10	52
Town St.		
Albion St. BD1	M11	48
Gratton Rd.		
Albion St. BD13	C11	44
Albion St. BD13	F14	63
New Pk. Rd.		
Albion St. BD17	N 6	13
Oxford Pl.		
Albion St. BD18	M 7	30
Phoenix Ln.		
Albion St. BD6	K15	65
Albion St. HD6	L21	97
Piggott St.		
Albion St. HX1	F19	94
Albion St. LS1	BB11	56
Albion St., Haworth	A 7	25
Albion St., Mor. LS27	X17	89
Albion St., Pud. LS28	T11	52
Albion Ter. BD12	M18	83
Griffe Rd.		
Albion Wk. LS1	BB11	56
Albion St.		
Albion Yd. BD1	N11	49
Ivegate		
Albury Rd. LS10	CC12	56
Albury Ter. LS28	R11	51
Bradley La.		
Alcester Garth BD3	O11	49
Alcester Pl. LS8	CC 9	38
Hill Top Av.		
Alcester Rd. LS8	CC 9	38
Alcester Ter. LS8	CC 9	38
Hill Top Av.		
Alder Av. BD21	C 4	8
Alder Carr BD17	L 5	12
Alder Clo. WF17	T18	87
Alder Gro. HX2	D16	79
Alder Hill Av. LS7	AA 7	37
Alder Hill Gro. LS7	AA 7	37
Aldermanbury BD1	N12	49
Alderon St. LS12	Z12	55
Lord St.		
Alderscholes Clo. BD13	F12	45
Alderscholes La. BD13	E12	45
Alderston St. BD6	K15	65
Aldersyde Av. WF17	T18	87
Alderton Bank LS17	Z 6	19
Alderton Cres. LS17	Z 6	19
Alderton Mt. LS17	Z 6	19
Alderton Pl. LS17	Z 6	19
Alderton Ri. LS17	Z 6	19
Alexander Av. LS15	FF11	58
Alexander Sq. BD14	H13	64
Alexander St. HX1	F19	94
Alexander St. LS1	AA11	55
Alexander Ter. HX1	D19	93
Hanson La.		
Alexandra Av. WF17	T18	87
Leeds Rd.		
Alexandra Cres., Elland HX5	H23	99
Alexandra Gro. LS28	S12	51
Alexandra Rd.		
Alexandra Gro. LS6	Z10	55
Alexandra Rd. BD18	L 7	30
Alexandra Rd. BD2	P 8	32
Alexandra Rd. LS28	S12	51
Alexandra Rd. LS6	Z10	55
Alexandra Rd., Hor. LS18	V 6	17
Alexandra Sq. BD13	F14	63
Alexandra St. BD7	M12	48
Alexandra St. HX1	F20	94
Alexandra Ter. BD2	P10	50
Alford Ter. BD7	L11	48
Camp Rd.		
Alfred Pl. LS7	BB10	56
Alfred St.	D19	93
Alabama St.		
Alfred St. E. HX1	F20	94
Church St.		
Alfred St. HX1	D19	93
Hanson La.		
Alfred St., Greet. HX4	F23	98
Alfred Ter., Mor. LS27	X17	89
Algot Gro. LS10	CC14	74
Springfield Av.		
Algot St. LS10	CC14	74
Springfield Av.		
Alice St. BD22	ZZ 8	24
Rosslyn Gro.		
Alice St. BD8	M11	48
Alkincote St. BD21	C 4	8
All Alone Rd. BD10	N 7	31
All Saints Av. LS9	CC11	56
York Rd.		
All Saints Circle, Wood. LS26	HH15	77
All Saints Pl. LS9	CC11	56
York Rd.		
All Saints Rd. BD7	M12	48
All Saints Ter. LS9	CC11	56
All Saints Vw., Wood. LS26	HH15	77
Allan St. BD3	O12	49
Allandale Rd. BD6	L15	66
Allen Cft. BD11	R16	86
Allenby Cres. LS11	AA11	73
Allenby Dr. LS11	AA15	73
Allenby Gdns. LS11	AA15	73
Allenby Gro. LS11	AA15	73
Allenby Pl. LS11	AA15	73
Allenby Rd. LS11	AA15	73
Allenby Vw. LS11	AA14	73
Allendale Av. BD6	L15	66
Allerby Gdns. BD6	K16	82
Allerton Av. LS17	BB 6	20
Allerton Clo. BD15	H10	46
Allerton Grange Av. LS17	CC 6	20
Allerton Grange Cft. LS8	CC 7	38
Allerton Grange Clo. LS17	BB 7	38
Allerton Grange Cres. LS17	BB 7	38
Allerton Grange Dr. BD15	H10	46
Allerton Grange Dr. LS17	BB 7	38
Allerton Grange Gdns. LS17	BB 7	38
Allerton Grange LS17	BB 6	20
Allerton Grange Ri. LS17	BB 7	38
Allerton Grange Vale LS17	BB 7	38
Allerton Grange Way LS17	BB 7	38
Allerton Grange Wk. LS17	BB 7	38
Allerton Gro. LS17	BB 6	20
Allerton Hill LS7	BB 7	38
Allerton La. BD13	H11	46
Allerton La. BD15	H11	46
Allerton Ms. LS17	BB 6	20
Allerton Pk. LS7	BB 7	38
Allerton Pl. HX1	E19	94
Allerton Pl. LS17	BB 6	20
Allerton Rd. BD15	F10	45
Allerton Rd. BD8	K11	47
Allison La. BD2	M 9	30
Livingstone Rd.		
Alloe Field Vw. HX2	D16	79
Allotments Rd. BD13	D11	44
Allums La., Eccup LS17	Z 1	4
Alma Clo. LS28	S 9	33
Alma Cotts. LS6	Y 8	36
Alma Gro. BD18	M 7	30
Alma Gro. LS9	CC10	56
Alma Pl. BD21	C 4	8
Woodhouse Rd.		
Alma Pl. BD3	P11	50
Leeds Old Rd.		
Alma Pl. LS9	CC10	56
Alma Rd. HX3	F19	94
Alma Rd. LS6	Y 8	36
Alma Row BD17	N 6	13
Alma St. BD13	F14	63
Alma St. BD18	M 7	30
Alma St. BD21	C 4	8
Alma St. BD4	P12	50
Alma St., Haworth	ZZ 7	24
Alma St., Wood. LS26	HH15	77
Alma Ter. BD21	C 4	8
Almond St. BD3	P12	50
Almscliffe Pl. BD2	P 8	32
Victoria Rd.		
Aloe St. LS10	CC12	56
Orchard St.		
Alpha St. BD21	C 4	8
Park Wood St.		
Alpine Ri. BD13	F11	45
Alston La. LS14	GG 9	40
Alstone Clo. BD9	J10	47
Altar La. BD16	F 5	9
Alter Dr. BD9	L 9	30
Althorpe Gro. BD10	O 8	31
Altofts St. LS11	AA13	73
Cambrian Rd.		
Alton Gro. BD18	L 8	30
Alton Gro. BD9	K 9	29
Alton Ter. LS10	BB13	74
Alum Ct. BD9	L 9	30
Alum Dr. BD9	L 9	30
Alvanley Ct. BD8	J11	47
Alverley Moor Av. LS28	R10	51
Alwoodley Court Gdns. LS17	AA 4	19
Alwoodley Gdns. LS17	AA 4	19
Alwoodley La. LS17	Z 4	19
Amams Gro. LS15	JJ 9	41
Amberley Ct. BD3	P12	50
Amberley St.		
Amberley Gdns. LS12	Y12	54
Amberley Rd.		
Amberley Rd. LS12	Y11	54
Amberley St. BD3	P12	50
Amberley St. LS12	Y12	54
Amberton App. LS8	EE 9	39
Amberton Clo. LS8	EE 8	39
Amberton Cres. LS8	EE 9	39
Amberton Garth LS8	EE 9	39
Amberton Gdns. LS8	EE 9	39
Amberton Gro. LS8	EE 9	39
Amberton La. LS8	EE 9	39
Amberton Mt. LS8	EE 9	39
Amberton Pl. LS8	DD 9	39
Amberton Rd. LS8	DD 9	39
Amberton St. LS8	EE 9	39
Amberton Ter. LS8	EE 9	39
Ambler St. BD8	M10	48
Ambler Thorne BD11	R16	86
Ambler Way BD13	F15	63
Amblers Cft. BD10	O 6	13
Ambleside Av. BD9	K10	47
Amelia St. BD18	K 7	29
Amen Corner LS12	W 9	35
America La. HD6	M22	101
America Sq. BD4	O14	67
Rooley La.		
Amisfield Rd. HX3	J19	96
Amos St. HX1	D19	93
Alabama St.		
Amundson Av. BD2	O 8	31
Amy St. BD16	H 5	10
Amy St. HX3	E18	80
Amy St. LS4	Y10	54
Amyroyce Dr. BD18	N 7	31
Ancaster Cres. LS16	X 7	36
Ancaster Rd. LS16	X 7	36
Ancaster Vw. LS16	X 7	36
Anchor Ct. BD8	M11	48
Jervaulx Cres.		
Anchor Rd. LS10	BB13	74
Anchor St. LS10	BB13	74
Anderson Av. LS9	CC10	56
Dolly La.		
Anderson Mt. LS8	CC10	56
Anderson St. BD8	M10	48
Andover Grn. BD4	Q13	68
Andrew Clo. HX3	H21	95
Andrews Sq. LS28	S 9	33
Town St.		
Andrews St. LS28	S10	51
Old Rd.		
Anerley St. BD4	O13	67
Bowling Hall Rd.		
Angel Ct. BD12	M16	83
Bolton St.		
Angel Inn Yd. LS1	BB11	56
Briggate		
Angel St. BD7	M 5	12
Angerton Way BD6	L16	83
Angus Av. BD12	M18	83
Anlaby St. BD4	P12	50
Ann Pl. BD5	N12	49
Ann St. BD21	B 4	7
Fanny St.		

Street	Ref	Page
Ann St. HX1	F19	94
Anne St. BD13	D10	44
Anne St. BD7	K13	65
Annerley St. BD4	O14	67
Annes Ct. HX3	H21	95
Annie St. BD18	M 8	30
Annie St. LS27	X17	89
Annie Vills. BD4	N12	49
Bailey St.		
Annison St. BD3	O11	49
Anorl Rd. HX1	E19	94
Anson Gro. BD7	K14	65
Beldon La.		
Anthony La. BD16	E 6	9
Moor Edge Low Side		
Anvil Ct. BD8	L10	48
Anvil St. HD6	L21	97
Apex Way LS11	BB12	56
Apperley Gdns. BD10	Q 7	32
Apperley La. BD10	Q 6	14
Apperley La. LS19	Q 6	14
Apperley Rd. BD10	P 7	32
Apple Clo. WF17	U18	87
Apple St. BD21	B 5	7
Damems Rd.		
Appleby Pl. LS15	FF11	58
Appleby Wk. LS15	FF11	58
Applegarth, Wood. LS26	HH11	59
Appleton Clo. LS9	CC11	56
Appleton Ct. LS9	CC11	56
Appleton Garth LS9	CC11	56
Appleton Gro. LS9	DD11	57
Appleton Sq. LS9	CC11	56
Appleton Way LS9	CC11	56
Appleyard La. LS12	X11	54
Town St.		
Approach, The LS15	JJ 7	41
Apricot St. BD21	B 5	7
Damems Rd.		
Aprilla Ct. BD7	J12	47
Apsley Cres. BD8	M10	48
Apsley St. BD21	B 4	7
Apsley St., Haworth	ZZ 7	24
Apsley Ter., Oakworth	ZZ 5	6
Apsley Vills. BD8	M10	48
Apsley Cres.		
Arcadia St. BD21	B 4	7
Queens Rd.		
Arch Rd. LS12	Z12	55
Arch Ter. LS12	Z12	55
Archbell Av. HD6	L23	101
Archer St. BD3	Q11	50
Archery Pl. LS2	AA10	55
Archery Rd.		
Archery Rd. LS2	AA10	55
Archery Rd. LS7	BB10	56
Hawkins Dr.		
Archery St. LS2	AA10	55
Archery Rd.		
Archery Ter. LS2	AA10	55
Archery Rd.		
Arches St. HX1	E20	94
Paradise St.		
Archibald St. BD7	M11	48
Arctic Par. BD7	L13	66
Arctic St., Haworth	A 7	25
Arden Rd. BD8	J11	47
Arden Rd. HX1	E20	94
Ardsley Clo. BD4	Q14	68
Argie Av. LS4	X 9	36
Argie Gdns. LS4	Y10	54
Burley Rd.		
Argie Rd. LS4	Y10	54
Argie Ter. LS4	Y10	54
Argyle Clo. BD17	N 6	13
Argyle Clo., Troy LS18	U 5	16
Argyle Rd. LS9	BB11	56
Argyle St. BD18	L 8	30
Valley Rd.		
Argyle St. BD4	O13	67
Lorne St.		
Ark St. LS9	CC12	56
Arkwright St. BD14	H13	64
Oak St.		
Arkwright St. BD4	Q12	50
Arkwright St. LS12	Z11	55
Arlesford Rd. BD4	Q14	68
Arley Gro. LS12	Y11	54
Aviary Rd.		
Arley Pl. LS12	Y11	54
Arley St. LS12	Y12	54
Arley Ter. LS12	Y11	54
Arlington Cres. HX2	C20	93
Arlington Gro. LS8	DD 8	39
Arlington Rd. LS8	DD 9	39
Arlington St. BD3	O12	49
Armadale Av. BD4	O15	67
Armgill La. BD2	M 9	30
Armidale Way BD2	N 9	31
Armitage Av. HD6	L23	101
Armitage Rd. BD12	N17	84
Armitage Rd. HX1	D20	93
Warley Rd.		
Armitage Sq. LS28	S12	51
Greenside		
Armley Grange Av. LS12	W10	53
Armley Grange Cres. LS12	W10	53
Armley Grange Dr. LS12	W11	53
Armley Grange Mt. LS12	W11	53
Armley Grange Oval LS12	W10	53
Armley Grange Ri. LS12	W11	53
Armley Grange Vw. LS12	X11	54
Armley Grange Wk. LS12	X11	54
Armley Grove Pl. LS12	Y11	54
Armley Lodge Rd. LS12	Y10	54
Armley Lower Rd. LS12	Z11	55
Armley Park Rd. LS12	Y10	54
Armley Rd. LS12	Y11	54
Armley Ridge Clo. LS12	X11	54
Armley Ridge Rd. LS12	W 9	35
Armley Ridge Rd. LS12	X11	54
Armley Ridge Ter. LS12	X10	54
Armoride St. BD4	P14	68
Rook La.		
Armscliffe Pl. BD2	P 9	32
Victoria St.		
Armstrong St. BD4	P12	50
Armstrong St. LS28	S10	51
Old Rd.		
Armytage Rd. HD6	M22	101
Arncliffe Av. BD21	B 4	7
Oakworth Rd.		
Arncliffe Cres. HD6	K23	100
Arncliffe Cres., Mor. LS27	Y17	89
Arncliffe Garth LS28	S10	51
Arncliffe Gro. BD21	B 4	7
Oakworth Rd.		
Arncliffe Path BD21	B 4	7
Arncliffe Rd.		
Arncliffe Pl. BD21	B 4	7
Arncliffe Rd. BD21	B 4	7
Arncliffe Rd. LS16	X 7	36
Arncliffe St. LS28	S10	51
Arncliffe Ter. BD7	L12	48
Arndale Shopping Centre LS15	HH10	59
Arnford Clo. BD3	N11	49
Arnold Pl. BD8	M11	48
Arnold Rd. HX1	E19	94
Arnold St. BD8	M11	48
Arnold St. HX1	E19	94
Arnside Rd. BD5	N14	67
Arran Dr., Troy LS18	U 5	16
Arskey Ter. LS12	Y11	54
Aviary Rd.		
Arthington Av. LS10	BB14	74
Arthington Gro. LS10	BB14	74
Arthington Rd. LS10	BB14	74
Arthington Rd., Bram.	Y 3	3
Arthington Rd., Bram. & LS16	X 1	3
Arthington St. BD8	M11	48
Arthington St. LS10	BB14	74
Arthington Ter. LS10	BB13	74
Arthington Vw. LS10	BB13	74
Arthur Av. BD8	J11	47
Arthur St. BD10	O 8	31
Arthur St. BD16	G 5	10
Hill Side Rd.		
Arthur St. HD6	M22	101
Arthur St. HX1	D19	93
Alabama St.		
Arthur St. LS28	S10	51
Arthur St., Oakworth	ZZ 6	6
Arthur St., Stan. LS28	T10	52
Arthursdale Clo. LS15	JJ 7	41
Arthursdale Dr. LS15	JJ 7	41
Arthursdale Grange, Scholes	JJ 7	41
Artillery Ter. LS7	CC 9	38
Roundhay Rd.		
Artist St. LS12	Z11	55
Arum St. BD5	M13	66
Arundel Clo. WF17	U18	87
Near Windsor Rd.		
Arundel Gro. LS8	CC10	56
Arundel Mt. LS8	CC10	56
Arundel St. HX1	D19	93
Arundel St. LS28	CC10	56
Arundel Wk. WF17	U18	87
Ascot Av. BD7	K14	65
Ascot Cres. HD6	K23	100
Ascot Dr. BD7	K14	65
Ascot Gdns. BD7	K14	65
Ascot Par. BD7	K14	65
Ascot Ter. LS9	CC11	56
Ash Clo. HX3	J19	96
Bramley La.		
Ash Cres. LS6	Y 8	36
Ash Down Clo. BD6	L14	66
High St.		
Ash Gdns. LS6	Y 8	36
Ash Gro. BD10	Q 7	32
Ash Gro. BD11	R16	86
Old Rd.		
Ash Gro. BD16	H 6	10
Ash Gro. BD19	R18	86
Ash Gro. BD2	P 9	32
Ash Gro. BD21	B 5	7
Ash Gro. HD6	M21	97
Ash Gro. LS28	T12	52
Ash Gro. LS6	Z 9	37
Ash Gro., Troy LS18	V 6	17
Ash Hill Dr. LS17	FF 5	22
Ash Hill Garth LS17	FF 5	22
Ash Hill Gdns. LS17	FF 5	22
Ash Hill La. LS17	FF 5	22
Ash Mt. BD14	J13	65
Ash Mt. BD21	B 4	7
Ash Mt. BD7	L12	48
Ash Rd. LS6	Y 8	36
Ash St.	ZZ10	42
Ash St. BD3	N11	49
Dacre St.		
Ash Ter. BD16	G 6	10
Ash Ter. LS6	Y 8	36
Ash Tree App. LS14	HH 9	41
Ash Tree Bank LS14	HH 8	41
Ash Tree Clo. LS14	HH 8	41
Ash Tree Gdns. HX2	C16	79
Ash Tree Gdns. LS14	HH 8	41
Ash Tree Gro. BD7	K14	65
Ash Tree Gro. LS14	HH 8	41
Ash Tree Rd. HX2	C16	79
Ash Tree Vw. LS14	HH 8	41
Ash Tree Wk. LS14	HH 8	41
Ash Vw. LS6	Y 8	36
Ashbourne Av. BD2	N 9	31
Ashbourne Bank BD2	N 9	31
Ashbourne Cft. LS10	BB13	74
Ashbourne Clo. BD2	N 9	31
Ashbourne Cres. BD13	F14	63
Ashbourne Cres. BD2	N 9	31
Ashbourne Dr. BD2	N 9	31
Ashbourne Garth BD2	O 9	31
Ashbourne Gdns. BD2	N 9	31
Ashbourne Gro. BD2	N 9	31
Ashbourne Gro. HX1	D19	93
Ashbourne Haven BD2	N 9	31
Ashbourne Mt. 2	N 9	31
Ashbourne Oval BD2	N 9	31
Ashbourne Rd. BD2	N 9	31
Ashbourne Rd. BD21	B 4	7
Ashbourne Ri. BD2	N 9	31
Ashbourne Way BD2	N 9	31
Ashburn Gro. BD17	M 5	12
Ashburnham Gro. BD9	L 9	30
Ashby Av. LS13	V10	53
Ashby Cres. LS13	V10	53
Ashby Sq. LS13	V10	53
Ashby St. BD4	O13	67
Ashby Ter. LS13	V10	53
Ashby Vw. LS13	V10	53
Ashday La. HX3	H21	95
Ashdene Clo., Pud. LS28	T12	52
Ashdene Cres., Pud. LS28	T12	52
Ashdene LS12	V13	71
Ashdon Ct. BD18	L 7	30
Rossendale Pl.		
Ashdowne Pl. BD8	M10	48
East Squire La.		
Ashfield Av. BD18	L 8	30
Ashfield Clo. HX3	D18	79
Ashfield Clo. LS15	HH 9	41
Ashfield Cres. BD16	H 6	10
Ashfield Cres. LS28	S10	51
Ashfield Ct. BD16	H 6	10
Ashfield Dr. BD17	M 5	12
Ashfield Dr. BD9	L 8	30
Ashfield Gro., Pud. LS28	T10	52
Ashfield LS12	X13	72
Ashfield Pl. BD2	P 8	32
Ashfield Pl. BD2	P10	50
Ashfield Rd. BD10	O 6	13
Ashfield Rd. BD11	U18	87
Leeds Rd.		
Ashfield Rd. BD13	F12	45
Ashfield Rd. BD18	K 7	29
Ashfield Rd. HX4	E23	98

Back Chestnut Av. LS15 HH10 59
Chestnut Av.
Back Church La. LS16 Y 4 18
Back Church La. LS5 X 9 36
Hesketh Rd.
Back Clarence Pl. HX1 E20 94
Hopwood La.
Back Clarence St. HX1 E19 94
Lister La.
Back Clarendon St. E. BD8 M11 48
Near Clarendon Pl.
Back Clarendon St. W. BD8 M11 48
Near Clarendon Pl.
Back Clough HX3 H18 81
Back Colton Rd. LS12 Y11 54
Church Rd.
Back Cowper St. LS7 BB 9 38
Cowper St.
Back Cragg Wood Rd. LS18 V 7 35
Cragg Wood Rd.
Back Craven St. LS6 AA 9 37
Back Cromwell Ter. HX1 E19 94
West Hill St.
Back Cross Flatts Mt. AA14 73
LS11
Theodore St.
Back Dargai St. LS7 BB 9 38
Penraevon Av.
Back Derwent St. LS11 AA12 55
Back Dudley Hill Rd. BD2 O10 49
Tower St.
Back Ebenezer St. BD1 N12 49
Vicar La.
Back Edmond Ter. LS12 Y11 54
Hall Rd.
Back Elizabeth St. BD5 N12 49
Grafton
Back Elmfield Ter. HX1 E20 94
Back Erick St. LS13 V 8 35
Back Field BD13 G12 46
Market St.
Back Fold BD14 H12 46
Back Foster Rd. BD21 B 4 7
Back Francis St. LS7 BB 9 38
Back Garden Field BD12 M17 83
Town Gate
Back George St. LS2 BB11 36
Back Gerrard St. HX1 E19 94
Lister La.
Back Giles St. N. BD5 M12 48
Near Lit. Horton La.
Back Giles St. S. BD5 M12 48
Near Lit. Horton La.
Back Girlington BD8 L11 48
Back Glen Mt. BD8 M10 48
Blenheim Rd.
Back Glen Ter. HX1 E20 94
Back Great Russell St. M11 48
BD7
Preston St.
Back Greaves St. BD5 M13 66
Roundhill St.
Back Green St. BD12 O16 84
Mill Carr Hill Rd.
Back Greenmount Ter. AA13 73
LS11
Lady Pit La.
Back Grn., Chur. LS27 Y15 72
Back Grosvenor Ter. LS6 Z 9 37
Back Grovehall Dr. LS11 Z14 73
Grovehall Dr.
Back Hallfield Pl. BD1 N11 49
Trafalgar St.
Back Hampshire Ter. LS7 BB10 56
Claypit La.
Back Hanover Sq. LS1 AA10 55
Hanover Sq.
Back Harrison St. LS1 BB11 56
Harrison St.
Back Hartley St., Mor. X17 89
LS27
Vesper Rd.
Back Hawksworth Gro. LS5 V 8 35
Vesper Rd.
Back Heights Rd. BD13 E11 45
Back Hill St. BD21 B 4 7
Aireworth St.
Back Hird St. BD21 B 4 7
Lister La.
Back Hollyshaw Ter. LS15 HH11 59
Hollyshaw Gro.
Back Hubert St. BD3 O12 49
Hubert St.
Back Hyde Ter. LS2 AA10 55
Back Ingledew Cres. LS8 DD 6 21
Back Jewell St. BD4 O12 49
Bowling Back La.
Back John St. BD13 F12 45
Chapel La.

Back Kelso Rd. LS2 Z10 55
Back Kensington St. BD8 L11 48
Thornton Rd.
Back King St. BD12 M16 83
King St.
Back Kirkgate BD18 L 7 30
Back Kirkstall Av. LS5 W 9 35
Kirkstall Av.
Back La. BD10 O 7 31
Back La. BD13 F11 45
Back La. BD13 H14 64
Back La. BD14 J13 65
Back La. BD15 F10 45
Back La. BD9 L 9 30
Back La. HX2 C13 62
Back La. HX2 C16 79
Back La. LS11 Z14 73
Back La. LS12 V14 71
Back La. LS13 V10 53
Back La. LS19 R 4 15
Back La. LS28 S 9 33
Back La., Hor. LS18 U 7 34
Great Horton Rd.
Back Lane Dr. LS27 T15 70
Back Lascelles Ter. LS8 CC 9 38
Back Lily St. BD8 L10 48
Lily St.
Back Lime St. BD21 B 5 7
Hainworth Wood Rd.
Back Lombard St. LS19 R 5 15
Micklefield La.
Back Lord St. HX1 F19 94
Lord St.
Back Low La., Hor. LS18 V 6 17
Back Lyon St. BD13 G14 64
Highgate Rd.
Back Mannville Rd. BD21 B 4 7
Mannville Rd.
Back Manor Gro. LS7 BB 8 38
Back Manor St. BD2 O 9 31
Undercliffe Rd.
Back Market St. BD6 M14 66
High St.
Back Marshall Av. LS15 HH10 59
Marshall Av.
Back Middle Cross St. Y11 54
LS12
Middle Cross St.
Back Middleton Vw. LS11 AA13 73
Back Moorfield St. HX1 E20 94
Back Morning St. BD21 B 5 7
Hainworth Wood Rd.
Back Mount Pleasant LS10 BB16 91
Back Muff St. BD4 O12 49
Back Myrtle Av. BD16 G 6 10
New Briggate
Back New St. BD12 O16 84
New St.
Back Newton Gro. LS7 BB 9 38
Back Nile St. LS2 BB10 56
Back North St. BD12 O17 84
Green Side
Back Northbrook St. LS7 BB 7 38
Back Northfield Pl. BD8 M10 48
Carlisle Rd.
Back o'the Mill BD16 E 6 9
Effingham Rd.
Back Outward La. LS18 V 7 35
Oxford Row
Back Oxford Pl. LS1 AA11 55
Back Park Ter. HX1 E20 94
Hopwood La.
Back Pasture Gro. LS7 BB 7 38
Pasture Av.
Back Pleasant St., S.B. C20 93
Back Pollard La. LS13 V 8 35
Back Poplar Av. LS15 HH10 59
Poplar Av.
Back Potternewton La. LS7 BB 8 38
Back Potters St. LS7 BB 8 38
St. Martins Dr.
Back Proctor St. BD4 P14 68
Proctor St.
Back Raglan St. HX1 E19 94
Lockwood St.
Back Railway Ter. BD12 N16 84
Amberley St.
Back Regent Park Ter. Z 9 37
LS7
Regent Park Av.
Back Rhodes St. HX1 E19 94
Back Richardson St. O17 84
BD12
Wyke La.

Back Richmond Vw. LS12 Y11 54
Church Rd.
Back Ridge Vw. LS7 AA 8 37
Back Ripon Ter. HX3 E18 80
Back Rockingham St. LS2 Z 9 37
Woodhouse La.
Back Roman Gro. LS8 DD 6 21
Roman Vw.
Back Row LS11 AA12 55
Back Russell St. BD5 M12 48
Melbourne Pl.
Back Shaw La. BD21 C 5 8
Back Sholebroke Av. LS7 BB 8 38
Back Sholebroke Ter. LS7 BB 8 38
Back Sidlaw Ter. LS8 CC 9 38
Markham Av.
Back Southfield Sq. BD8 M10 48
Lumb La.
Back Springfield Pl. LS2 AA10 55
Little Woodhouse St.
Back St. BD5 N12 49
Manchester Rd.
Back St. BD8 M10 48
Manningham La.
Back St. Marks Rd. LS2 AA10 55
St. Marks La.
Back Stanmore Pl. LS4 Y 9 36
Michaels La.
Back Stone Hall Rd. BD2 O 9 31
Stone Hall Rd.
Back Stonegate Rd. LS6 Z 7 37
Back Storey Pl. LS14 FF10 58
Back Sunny Rd., Hor. LS18 U 7 34
Back Sunnydene LS14 FF10 58
Watson Rd.
Back Sutton App. LS14 FF10 58
Sutton App.
Back Swinton St. HX6 D20 93
Dunkirk La.
Back Victoria Pl. LS7 BB10 56
Camp Rd.
Back Victoria St. HX1 F19 94
Pellon La.
Back Walnut St. BD21 B 5 7
Hainworth Wood Rd.
Back Welton Av. LS6 Z 9 37
Back Wesley Rd. LS12 Y11 54
Back Wetherby Rd. LS8 DD 8 39
Back Wharf St., S.B. C21 93
HX6
Back Wheat St. BD21 B 5 7
Wheat St.
Back Wolseley Ter. HX1 D19 93
Hanson La.
Back Wood St. BD8 M11 48
Back Wright Av. ZZ 5 6
Back York St. LS2 BB11 56
Church St.
Backhold Av. HX3 G22 99
Backhold Dr. HX3 G22 99
Backhold La. HX3 F22 98
Backhold Rd. HX3 G22 99
Baddeley Gdns. BD10 O 6 13
Baden St., Haworth ZZ 7 24
Badgergate Av. BD15 F 9 27
Badgers Mt. LS15 JJ 9 41
Tenterden Way
Badminton Ter. LS7 CC10 56
Badsworth Ct. BD14 J12 47
Bagby Pl. LS2 AA10 55
Kingston Rd.
Bagby Rd. LS2 AA10 55
Bagby Sq. LS2 AA10 55
St. Marks Rd.
Bagby Ter. LS2 AA10 55
Bagby St.
Bagby Vw. LS2 AA 9 37
Devon Rd.
Bagley La. LS13 S 9 33
Bagley La. LS13 S 9 33
Bagley La., Rod. LS13 T 9 34
Bagnall Ter. BD6 L14 66
Baildon Chase LS14 HH 7 37
Baildon Dr. LS14 HH 8 37
Baildon Grn. LS14 HH 7 41
Baildon Holmes BD17 HH 8 37
Baildon Pl. LS14 GG 8 40
Baildon Rd. BD17 GG 7 40
Baildon Rd. LS14 GG 8 40
Baildon St. LS14 GG 7 40
Baildon Wood BD17 M 6 12
Bailes Rd. LS7 AA 8 37
Meanwood Rd.
Bailey Fold BD15 H10 46
Bailey Hall Rd. HX3 F20 94
Bailey Hills Rd. BD16 G 5 10
Bailey St. BD4 N12 49

Street	Ref	Page
Bailey Wells Av. BD5	M13	66
Baileys Ct. LS14	GG 8	40
Baileys Hill LS14	GG 8	40
Baileys La. LS14	GG 8	40
Baileys Lawn LS14	GG 8	40
Bainbridge Rd. LS6	Y 9	36
Baines St. HX1	E19	94
Oak La.		
Baird St. BD5	N13	67
Bairstow HX6	C20	93
Bairstow La., S.B. HX6	C20	93
Bairstow Mt., S.B. HX6	C20	93
Bairstow St. BD15	H 9	28
Baker Cres., Mor. LS27	X17	89
Baker Rd., Mor. LS27	W17	88
Baker St. BD18	L 7	30
Baker St. BD2	O10	49
Baker St. N. HX2	E16	80
Beechwood Rd.		
Baker St., Mor. LS27	X17	89
Bakers Fold HX1	E19	94
Crossley Gdns.		
Balbec Av. LS6	Z 8	37
Balbec St. LS6	Z 8	37
Balcombe Gro. LS10	CC13	74
Low Rd.		
Balcombe Pl. LS10	CC13	74
Low Rd.		
Balcombe St. LS10	CC13	74
Low Rd.		
Balcombe Ter. LS10	CC13	74
Low Rd.		
Balcony Cotts. BD13	G15	64
Baldovan Mt. LS8	CC 9	38
Baldovan Ter. LS8	CC 9	38
Baldovan Mt.		
Baldwin La. BD13	H14	64
Baldwin La. BD14	H14	64
Baldwin La., Clay. HX1	F19	94
Baldwin Ter. HX3	F19	94
Balfour St. BD16	G 6	10
Ash Ter.		
Balfour St. BD21	B 4	7
Lister St.		
Balfour St. BD4	O13	67
Balk La. BD7	L13	66
Balkcliffe La. LS10	AA16	90
Balkram Dr. HX2	B16	78
Balkram Edge HX2	B16	78
Balkram Edge Rd. HX2	A16	78
Ball St. BD13	G12	46
Ballantyne Rd. BD10	O 6	13
Balm Pl. LS11	AA12	55
Balm Rd. LS10	CC14	74
Balm Wk. LS11	Z12	55
Balme La. BD12	M17	83
Balme St. BD1	N11	49
Balme St. BD12	M17	83
Balmoral Chase LS10	CC13	74
Balmoral Pl. HX1	F20	94
Balmoral Rd. BD4	P13	68
Broad La.		
Balmoral St. LS10	CC13	74
Bamburgh Clo. LS15	JJ 9	41
Bamburgh Rd. LS15	JJ 9	41
Bancroft St. BD13	C 8	26
Mill St.		
Bangor Gro. LS12	X13	72
Cow Close Rd.		
Bangor Pl. LS12	X13	72
Cow Close Rd.		
Bangor St. HX1	E19	94
Bangor St. LS12	X13	72
Branch Rd.		
Bangor St. LS28	S10	51
Sun Field		
Bangor Ter. LS12	W12	53
Cow Close Rd.		
Bangor Ter. LS12	X13	72
Bangor Vw. LS12	X13	72
Cow Close Rd.		
Bank Av., Mor. LS27	X16	89
Bank Av., Hor. LS18	U 7	34
Bank BD10	P 8	32
Bank Bottom HX3	F19	94
Bank Bottom La. HX2	A18	78
Bank Clo. BD10	P 8	32
Bank Crest BD17	M 5	12
Bank Crest Ri. BD18	J 7	29
Bank Dr. BD6	M15	66
Bank Edge Gdns. HX2	D17	79
Bank Edge Rd. HX2	D17	79
Bank Foot BD6	M14	66
Bank Gdns., Hor. LS18	U 7	34
Bank House Clo., Mor. LS27	X16	89
Bank House La. HX3	A16	78
Moor End		
Bank Pl. HX3	E17	80
Nursery La.		
Bank Rd. BD3	O10	49
Bank St. BD1	N11	49
Bank St. BD18	L 7	30
Bank St. BD6	M14	66
Bank St. HD6	L22	101
Bank St., Haworth	ZZ 7	24
Main St.		
Bank St., Mor. LS27	X16	89
Bank Top BD6	M14	66
Bank Top HX3	G20	95
Bank Top La., Eccup LS17	Y 1	3
Bank Top Way BD21	D 4	8
Bank Top, Greet. HX4	F23	98
Bank Vw. BD17	L 6	12
Bank Wk. BD17	M 5	12
Bank, The BD6	M14	66
Holroyd Hill		
Banke End Rd. HD6	J24	100
Bankfield Av. BD18	J 7	29
Bankfield Dr. BD18	J 7	29
Bankfield Gdns. HX3	G20	95
Bolton La.		
Bankfield Gdns. LS4	Y10	54
Bankfield Ter.		
Bankfield Gro. BD18	J 8	29
Bankfield Gro. LS4	Y 9	36
Bankfield Rd. BD18	J 7	29
Bankfield Rd. LS4	Y10	54
Bankfield Ter. BD17	M 6	12
Bankfield Ter. LS4	Y10	54
Bankfield Ter., Pud. LS28	T10	52
Bankfield Vw. HX3	E18	80
Bankholme Ct. BD4	Q14	68
Bankhouse La. HX3	F22	98
Bankhouse La. LS28	S12	51
Bankhouse LS28	S12	51
Bankside St. LS8	CC 9	38
Bankside Ter. BD17	L 6	12
Green Rd.		
Bankwell Fold BD6	M14	66
Banner St. BD3	O12	49
Bannerman St. BD12	O16	84
Banstead St. LS8	CC 9	38
Banstead Ter. LS8	CC 9	38
Bantam Clo., Mor. LS27	Y17	89
Bantam Grove La., Mor. LS27	Y17	89
Baptist Pl. BD1	M11	48
Baptist St. LS12	Z12	55
Wellington Rd.		
Bar La., Hor. LS18	T 7	34
Bara St., Oxenhope	ZZ10	42
Barberry Av. BD3	Q11	50
Barclay Clo. BD13	C 8	26
Greenside La.		
Barclay St. LS7	BB10	56
North St.		
Barcroft, Haworth	A 7	25
Barden Av. BD6	K14	65
Barden Clo. LS12	X11	54
Whingate Grn.		
Barden Grn. LS12	X11	54
Whingate Rd.		
Barden Gro. LS12	X11	54
Whingate Rd.		
Barden Mt. LS12	X11	54
Barden Pl. LS12	X11	54
Barden St. BD8	L10	48
Carlisle Rd.		
Barden Ter. LS12	X11	54
Barfield Av. LS19	R 4	15
Barfield Cres. LS17	CC 4	20
Barfield Dr. LS19	R 4	15
Barfield Gro. LS17	DD 4	21
High Ash Av.		
Barfield Mt. LS17	DD 4	21
High Ash Av.		
Barfield Rd. HX3	J19	96
Brighouse Rd.		
Bargrave Av. BD18	L 8	30
Barham Ter. BD10	P 9	32
Baring Av. BD3	P11	50
Barker Clo. HX3	G21	95
Barker Hill, Gild. LS27	U14	70
Barker Pl. LS13	V10	53
Barkerend Rd. BD3	N11	49
Barkers Bldgs. HX3	E17	80
Barkly Av. LS11	AA14	73
Barkly Dr. LS11	AA14	73
Barkly Gro. LS11	AA14	73
Barkly Par. LS11	AA14	73
Barkly Pl. LS11	Z14	73
Barkly Rd. LS11	AA14	73
Barkly St. LS11	AA14	73
Barkly Ter. LS11	AA14	73
Barkston Wk. BD15	H11	46
Barlby Way LS8	EE 8	39
Barley St. BD22	B 5	7
Barleycorn St. LS11	Z12	55
Whitehall Rd.		
Barlow St. BD3	O11	49
Barmby Pl. BD2	O10	49
Barmby Rd. BD2	O10	49
Barmby St. BD12	M17	83
Barmby St. BD2	O10	49
Undercliffe Old Rd.		
Barmouth Ter. BD3	N10	49
Barn St. BD22	ZZ10	42
Barnaby Rd. BD16	J 5	11
Barnard Clo. LS15	JJ 9	41
Barnard Way		
Barnard Rd. BD4	O12	49
Barnard Way LS15	JJ 9	41
Barnborough St. LS4	Y10	54
Barnby Av. BD8	J11	47
Barncroft Clo. LS14	FF 7	40
Barncroft Ct. LS14	FF 8	40
Barncroft Dr. LS14	FF 7	40
Barncroft Gdns. LS14	FF 8	40
Barncroft Grange LS14	FF 8	40
Barncroft Heights LS14	FF 7	40
Barncroft Mt. LS14	FF 8	40
Barncroft Rd. LS14	FF 8	40
Barncroft Ri. LS14	FF 8	40
Barncroft Towers LS14	FF 8	40
Barnes Rd. BD8	K11	47
Barnet Mt. LS12	Y11	54
Strawberry Rd.		
Barnet Rd. LS12	Y11	54
Barnsley Beck Gro. BD17	M 5	12
Barnstaple Way BD4	P14	68
Knowles La.		
Barnswick Vw. LS16	W 4	17
Barnthorpe Cres. LS17	BB 7	38
Baron Clo. LS11	AA13	73
Barons Ct. LS15	HH11	59
Barons Way LS15	HH11	59
Baronscourt LS15	HH11	59
Baronsmead LS15	HH11	59
Barrack Rd. LS7	BB 9	38
Barrack St. LS7	BB10	56
Barraclough Bldgs. BD10	Q 7	32
Carr Bottom Rd.		
Barraclough Sq. BD12	M17	83
Barraclough St. BD12	L16	83
Moor Top Rd.		
Barran St. BD16	H 5	10
Mornington Rd.		
Barras Garth Pl. LS12	X12	54
Barras Garth Rd. LS12	X12	54
Barras Pl. LS12	X11	54
Upper Wortley Rd.		
Barras St. LS12	X11	54
Upper Wortley Rd.		
Barras Ter. LS12	X11	54
Upper Wortley Rd.		
Barrington Clo. HX3	H21	95
Towngate		
Barrowby Av. LS15	JJ11	59
Barrowby Cres. LS15	JJ11	59
Barrowby Dr. LS15	JJ11	59
Barrowby La. LS15	JJ11	59
Barrowby Rd. LS15	JJ11	59
Barrowclough La. HX3	G19	95
Barry St. BD1	N11	49
Barstow St. LS11	BB12	56
Bartholomews Clo. LS12	Y11	54
Church Rd.		
Barthorpe Av. LS17	AA 7	37
Bartle Clo. BD7	K13	65
Bartle Gill Dr. BD17	N 5	13
Bartle Gill Ri. BD17	N 5	13
Bartle Gill Vw. BD17	N 4	13
Bartle Gro. BD7	K13	65
Bartle La. BD7	K13	65
Bartle Pl. BD7	K13	65
Barton Ct. LS15	HH11	59
Barton Gro. LS11	AA13	73
Barton Mt. LS11	AA13	73
Barton Rd.		
Barton Pl. LS11	AA13	73
Barton Rd.		
Barton Rd. LS11	AA13	73
Barton St. BD7	L13	66
Barton St. HD6	L21	97
Manley St.		
Barton Ter. LS11	AA13	73
Barton Vw. LS11	AA13	73
Barton Rd.		
Barum Top HX1	F19	94
Barwick Grn. BD6	K14	65
Barwick Rd., Scholes LS15	HH 9	41
Basil St. BD5	L13	66

Belgrave St. HX6	B21	92
Wallis St.		
Belgrave St. LS2	BB10	56
Belgrave Ter. LS2	BB10	56
Belgrave St.		
Belina Ct. BD21	B 4	7
South St.		
Belinda St. LS13	CC13	74
Bell Bank Vw. BD16	G 5	10
Bell Dean Rd. BD15	H11	46
Bell Dean Rd. BD8	H11	46
Bell Hall Ter. HX1	E20	94
Bell La. LS13	V 9	35
Bell La. LS7	BB 9	38
Bell Mt. LS13	V 9	35
Bell La.		
Bell Rd. LS13	V 9	35
Bell St. HX3	F19	94
Bell St. LS2	BB11	56
Bellbrooke Av. LS9	DD10	57
Bellbrooke Gro. LS9	DD10	57
Bellbrooke Pl. LS9	DD10	57
Bellbrooke St. LS9	DD10	57
Belle Isle Circ. LS10	CC15	74
Belle Isle Par. LS10	CC14	74
Belle Isle Rd.		
Belle Isle Rd. LS10	CC14	74
Belle View Av., Scholes LS15	JJ 8	41
Belle Vue Av. LS8	EE 8	39
Belle Vue BD2	P 8	32
Victoria Rd.		
Belle Vue BD8	M10	48
Belle Vue Cres. HX3	H16	81
Belle Vue Dr. LS28	S 9	33
Belle Vue Est., Scholes LS15	JJ 8	41
Belle Vue Lawn LS3	Z10	55
Belle Vue Rd.		
Belle Vue Pl. HX1	E19	94
Belle Vue Pl. LS11	AA13	73
South Ridge St.		
Belle Vue Rd. LS3	Z10	55
Belle Vue Cres.		
Belle Vue Rd. HX3	H16	81
Belle Vue Rd. LS8	JJ 8	41
Belle Vue Rd. LS3 & LS6	Z10	55
Belle Vue Ri. HX3	H16	82
Belle Vue St. LS3	Z10	55
Belle Vue Rd.		
Belle Vue Ter. HX3	G20	95
Trooper La.		
Bellerby Brow BD6	J14	65
Bellhouse Av. BD4	O14	67
Bellhouse Cres. BD4	O15	67
Bellisle Rd., Oxenhope	ZZ 8	24
Bellmount Gdns. LS13	V 9	35
Bellmount Grn. LS13	V 9	35
Bellmount Pl. LS13	V 9	35
Broad La.		
Bellmount Vw. LS13	V 9	35
Belloe St. BD5	M13	66
Little Horton La.		
Bellshaw St. BD8	K11	47
Belmont Av. BD12	M15	66
Belmont Av. BD17	L 5	12
Belmont Clo. BD12	L 5	12
Belmont Cres. BD12	N15	67
Belmont Cres. BD18	L 7	30
Belmont Cres. LS10	CC13	74
Spring Grove St.		
Belmont Gdns. BD6	M15	66
Belmont Gro. BD6	M15	66
Belmont Gro. LS19	S 4	15
Belmont Gro. LS2	AA10	55
Woodhouse Sq.		
Belmont Mt. LS10	CC13	74
Spring Grove St.		
Belmont Pl. HX1	E20	94
Belmont Pl. LS13	V 9	35
Belmont Rd. LS10	CC13	74
Spring Grove St.		
Belmont Ri. BD12	N15	67
Belmont Ri. BD17	L 5	12
Belmont St. BD2	P 9	32
Institute St.		
Belmont St. BD3	O11	49
Barkerend Rd.		
Belmont St. HX3	G19	95
Belgrave Dr.		
Belmont Ter. BD18	L 7	30
Belmont Vw. LS10	CC13	74
Spring Grove St.		
Belmount Grn. LS13	V 9	35
Belton Clo. BD7	L13	66
Belvedere Av. LS11	AA14	73
Harlech Rd.		
Belvedere Av. LS17	BB 5	20
Belvedere Gdns. LS17	CC 5	20
Belvedere Gro. LS17	BB 5	20
Belvedere Gro., Bram. LS16	V 9	35
Bell La.		
Belvedere Rd. LS17	BB 5	20
Belvedere Ter. BD8	L11	48
Belvedere Ter. LS11	AA14	73
Harlech Rd.		
Belvedere Vw. LS17	CC 5	20
Belvidere Rd. BD8	J11	47
Belvoir Gdns. HX3	F21	94
Bempton Ct. BD7	L13	66
Bempton Pl.		
Bempton Pl. BD7	L13	66
Benbow Av. BD10	Q 8	32
Benfield Cotts. BD14	J12	47
Benn Av. BD7	K13	65
Benn Cres. BD7	K13	65
Bennett Ct. LS15	HH11	59
Bennett Rd. LS6	Y 8	36
Bennett St. HX3	G20	95
Benson Gdns. LS12	X12	54
Benson Pl. LS10	CC14	74
Woodhouse Hill Rd.		
Benson St. LS7	BB10	56
Bent Lea HD2	N24	102
Bentcliffe Av. LS17	BB 6	20
Bentcliffe Clo. LS17	CC 6	20
Bentcliffe Ct. LS17	BB 6	20
Bentcliffe Gro.		
Bentcliffe Dr. LS17	CC 6	20
Bentcliffe Av.		
Bentcliffe Dr. BD17	CC 6	20
Bentcliffe Gdns. LS17	CC 6	20
Bentcliffe Gro. LS17	CC 6	20
Bentcliffe La. LS17	BB 6	20
Bentcliffe Mt. LS17	CC 6	20
Bentcliffe Wk. BD15	H11	46
Bentinck St. BD16	H 5	10
Ferrand St.		
Bentley Av. HX3	L19	97
Bentley Clo. BD17	L 5	12
Bentley Gro. LS6	Z 8	37
Bentley La. LS6	Z 8	37
Bentley La. LS7	Z 8	37
Bentley Mt. LS6	Z 8	37
Bentley Mt., S.B.	C20	93
Bentley Par. LS6	Z 8	37
Bentley St. BD12	M17	83
Temperance Field		
Bentley St. HX1	E20	94
Benton Park Av. LS19	S 4	15
Benton Park Cres. LS19	S 4	15
Benton Park Dr. LS19	S 4	15
Bents La. BD15	E 8	27
Benyon Park Way LS12	Y13	72
Beresford Rd. BD6	L15	66
Beresford St. BD12	O16	84
Berkeley Av. LS8	DD 9	39
Berkeley Cres. LS8	DD 9	39
Berkeley Gro. LS8	DD 9	39
Berkeley Mt. LS8	DD 9	39
Strathmore Dr.		
Berkeley Rd. LS8	DD 9	39
Berkeley St. LS8	DD 9	39
Berkeley Ter. LS8	DD 9	39
Berkeley Vw. LS8	DD 9	39
Berkine Av. LS9	CC11	56
Berkine Row LS9	CC11	56
Berkine Av.		
Bernard St. LS2	BB11	56
Union St.		
Berry La. BD21	B 4	7
Berry La. HX1	F19	94
Berrys Bldgs. HX2	D17	79
Keighley Rd.		
Bertha St. LS28	S10	51
Bertie St. BD4	P13	68
Bertram Dr. BD17	L 6	12
Bertram Rd. BD8	M10	48
Berwick St. HX1	F19	94
Dispensary Wk.		
Besha Av. BD12	M16	83
Besha Gro. BD12	M16	83
Bessingham Gdns. BD6	K15	65
Best La., Oxenhope	ZZ10	42
Beta St. BD21	C 4	8
Bethel Rd. BD18	M 7	30
Bethel St. HD6	L22	101
Bethel St. HX3	E18	80
Friendly Fold Rd.		
Beulah Gro. LS6	AA 9	37
Beulah Ter.		
Beulah Mt. LS6	AA 9	37
Christopher Rd.		
Beulah St. LS6	AA 9	37
Beulah Ter.		
Beulah Ter. LS15	HH10	59
Austhorpe Rd.		
Beulah Ter. LS6	AA 9	37
Beulah Ter., Gild. LS27	V15	71
Beulah Vw. LS6	AA 9	37
Christopher Rd.		
Beverley Av. BD12	M18	83
Beverley Av. LS11	AA13	73
Beverley Clo., Elland HX5	H23	99
Beverley Dr. BD12	M18	83
Beverley Gdns. WF17	U18	87
Beverley Mt. LS11	AA13	73
Beverley Pl. HX3	E18	80
Chester Rd.		
Beverley St. BD4	P12	50
Beverley Ter. LS11	AA13	73
Beverley Vw. LS11	AA13	73
Bevers Ter. LS11	AA13	73
Hill St.		
Bewerley Cres. BD6	L16	83
Bewick Gro. LS26	CC15	91
Bexley Av. LS8	CC 9	38
Bexley Gro. LS8	CC10	56
Bexley Mt. LS8	CC10	56
Bexley Pl. LS8	CC10	56
Bexley Rd. LS8	CC10	56
Bexley Ter. LS8	CC10	56
Bexley Vw. LS8	CC10	56
Bexley Gro.		
Beza Rd. LS10	BB13	74
Beza St. LS10	BB13	74
Biddenden Rd. LS15	JJ 9	41
Bideford Av. LS8	CC 6	20
Bideford Mt. BD4	Q13	68
Bierley Hall Gro. BD4	O15	67
Bierley House Av. BD4	O14	67
Bierley La. BD4	O15	67
Bierley Vw. BD4	P14	68
Billey La. LS12	W12	53
Billing Ct. LS19	S 5	15
Billing Dr., Raw. LS19	T 5	16
Billing Vw. BD10	P 7	32
Billing Vw. LS19	S 5	15
Billingbauk Dr. LS13	V10	53
Billingbauk Ter. LS13	V10	53
Brighton Gro.		
Billingsley Ter. BD4	O13	67
Wakefield Rd.		
Billingwood Dr. LS19	S 5	15
Bilsdale Gro. BD6	K15	65
Bilsdale Way BD17	L 6	12
Bilton Pl. BD8	M11	48
Bingley Rd. BD13	C 7	26
Bingley Rd. BD17	K 4	11
Bingley Rd. BD18	J 7	29
Bingley Rd. BD21	B 7	25
Bingley Rd. BD9	J 8	29
Bingley Rd., Haworth	A 7	25
Bingley St. BD8	L11	48
Bingley St. LS3	Z11	55
Bingley Sta. BD16	G 5	10
Binks Fold BD12	M18	83
Wyke La.		
Binks St. LS12	Z11	55
Binnie St. BD3	O11	49
Binns Hill La. HX2	B20	92
Binns La. BD7	K12	47
Binns St. BD16	H 5	10
Binns Ter. HX2	D17	79
Nursery La.		
Binns Top La. HX3	H21	95
Birch Av. BD5	N14	67
Birch Av. LS15	GG11	58
Birch Clo. BD5	N14	67
Birch Cres. LS15	GG11	58
Birch Gro. BD21	B 5	7
Ash Gro.		
Birch Gro. BD5	N14	67
Birch Hill Ri. LS5	W 7	35
Birch La. BD5	N14	67
Birch La. HX2	A19	92
Birch St. BD8	K11	47
Birch Tree Gdns. BD21	D 4	8
Birchdale BD16	G 4	10
Birches, The, Bram. LS16	W 2	3
Birchfield Av., Mor. LS27	V16	88
Birchfields Av. LS14	HH 7	41

Name	Grid	Pg
Birchfields Clo. LS14	HH 7	41
Birchfields Ri.		
Birchfields Cres. LS14	HH 7	41
Birchfields Ri. LS14	HH 7	41
Birchfields Ri.		
Birchfields Garth LS14	HH 7	41
Birchfields Ri. LS14	HH 7	41
Birchlands Av. BD15	E 8	27
Birchlands Gro. BD15	E 8	27
Birchtree Way LS16	W 6	17
Birchway BD5	N14	67
Birchwood Av. LS17	DD 5	21
Birchwood Av. WF17	T18	87
Sandal Way		
Birchwood Hill LS17	DD 5	21
Birchwood Mt. LS17	DD 5	21
Bird Holme La. HX3	H19	95
Birdcage Hill HX3	E21	94
Birdcage La. HX3	E21	94
Birdroyd La. HD6	L22	101
Birdswell Av. HD6	M21	97
Birfed Cres. LS4	X 9	36
Birk Hill Cres. BD11	R16	86
Birk La., Mor. LS27	W17	88
Birkby Haven BD6	K15	65
Birkby La. HD6	M19	97
Birkby St. BD12	M17	83
Birkdale Clo. BD13	D 8	26
Birkdale Clo. LS17	AA 5	19
Birkdale Dr. LS17	AA 5	19
Birkdale Grn. LS17	AA 5	19
Birkdale Gro. HX2	D15	62
Birkdale Gro. LS17	AA 5	19
Birkdale Mt. LS17	AA 5	19
Birkdale Pl. LS17	AA 5	19
Birkdale Ri. LS17	AA 5	19
Birkdale Way LS17	AA 5	19
Birkdale Wk. LS17	AA 5	19
Birkenshaw La. BD11	R16	86
Birkhouse La. HD6	M20	97
Birklands Moor BD11	S17	86
Birklands Rd. BD18	L 7	30
Birklands Ter. BD18	L 7	30
Hall Royd		
Birklea St. BD5	N13	67
Birks Av. BD7	K12	47
Birks Fold BD7	K12	47
Birks Hall La. HX1	E19	94
Birks Hall Ter. HX1	E19	94
Pellon La.		
Birkshall La. BD3	O12	49
Birkshall La. BD4	O12	49
Birksland St. BD3	O12	49
Birksland St. BD4	O12	49
Birkwith Clo. LS14	GG 7	40
Litton Way		
Birlands Ter. BD18	L 7	30
Castle Rd.		
Birnam Gro. BD4	O13	67
Birr Rd. BD9	L 9	30
Bischoffs Yd. LS2	BB10	56
North St.		
Bishop St. BD9	L 9	30
Bishopdale Holme BD6	K15	65
Bishopgate St. LS1	AA11	55
Bismarck Dr. LS11	AA13	73
Bismarck St. LS11	AA13	73
Black Bull St. LS10	BB12	56
Black Dyke BD13	E10	45
Black Dyke La. BD13	E10	45
Black Edge La. BD13	C12	44
Black Hill La. LS16	Y 2	3
Black Moor Rd. LS17	Z 5	19
Black Moor Rd., Oxenhope	A10	43
Black Moor Rd., Haworth	ZZ 8	24
Black Swan Ginnell HX1	F19	94
Silver St.		
Black Swan Pass. HX1	F19	94
Silver St.		
Blackburn Clo. BD8	J12	47
Blackburn Rd. HD6	L21	97
Blackburn Rd. WF17	T18	87
Blackett St. LS28	R 7	33
Blackledge HX1	F20	94
Blackley Rd., Elland HX5	F24	98
Blackman La. LS2	AA10	55
Blackmire St. HX2	E16	80
Blackmoor Ct. LS17	Z 4	19
Blackpool Gro. LS12	X13	72
Cow Close Rd.		
Blackpool Rd. LS12	X13	72
Blackpool Ter.		
Blackpool Ter. LS12	X13	72
Blackpool Vw. LS12	X13	72
Cow Close Rd.		
Blackshaw Beck La. BD13	H15	64
Blackshaw Dr. BD6	J15	65
Blacksmith La. LS16	Z 2	4
Blackstone Av. BD12	M18	83
Blackwall HX1	F20	94
Blackwall La. HX6	B20	92
Blackwood Av. LS16	V 5	17
Blackwood Gdns. LS16	V 5	17
Blackwood Gro. HX1	D19	93
Blackwood Gro. LS16	V 5	17
Blackwood Mt. LS16	V 5	17
Blackwood Ri. LS16	V 5	17
Blairsville Gdns. LS13	U 9	34
Blairsville Gro. LS13	V 9	35
Blaithroyd La. HX3	G20	95
Blake Gro. LS7	BB 8	38
Blake Hill HX3	G17	81
Blakehill Av. BD2	P10	50
Blakehill Ter. BD2	P10	50
Blakelaw La. HD2	N22	102
Blakeney Gro. LS10	BB14	74
Blakeney Rd. LS10	BB14	74
Blamires Pl. BD7	K13	65
Blamires St. BD7	K13	65
Blanche St. BD4	P12	50
Blayds St. LS9	CC11	56
Blayds Yd. LS1	BB11	56
Blencarn Clo. LS14	FF 9	40
Blencarn Garth LS14	FF 9	40
Blencarn Lawn LS14	FF 9	40
Blencarn Clo.		
Blencarn Path LS14	FF 9	40
Brooklands Av.		
Blencarn Rd. LS14	FF 9	40
Blencarn Vw. LS14	FF 9	40
Blenheim Av. LS2	AA10	55
Blenheim Cres. LS2	AA10	55
Blenheim Av.		
Blenheim Gro. LS7	AA10	55
Blenheim Mt. LS7	AA10	55
Blenheim Pl. BD10	O 6	13
Town La.		
Blenheim Rd. BD8	M10	48
Blenheim Sq. LS2	AA10	55
Blenheim St. BD21	B 4	7
Apsley St.		
Blenheim Ter. LS2	AA10	55
Blenheim Vw. LS2	AA10	55
Blenheim Wk. LS2	AA10	55
Blezard Ct. LS11	BB12	56
Meadow La.		
Blind La. BD16	F 5	9
Biind La. Dr. BD4	T15	70
Blind La. HX2	D15	62
Blind La. LS17	FF 5	22
Bloody Row HX3	G16	81
Bloomfield Mt. LS6	AA 9	37
Holborn St.		
Bloomfield Pl. LS6	AA 9	37
Holborn St.		
Bloomfield Ter. LS6	AA 9	37
Holborn St.		
Blucher St. BD4	P12	50
Blucher St. LS12	Z11	55
Blue Hill Cres. LS12	X12	54
Blue Hill Grange LS12	X12	54
Blue Hill Gro. LS12	X12	54
Blue Hill La. LS12	X12	54
Bluebell Ct. WF17	T18	87
Blundell St. LS2	AA10	55
Blundell Ter. LS1	AA10	55
Caledonian Rd.		
Blythe Av. BD8	L11	48
Blythe St. BD7	M11	48
Boar La. LS1	AA11	55
Bob La. BD15	F 9	27
Bob La. HX2	C19	93
Bodley Ter. LS4	Y10	54
Bodmin App. LS10	AA16	90
Bodmin Av. BD18	N 7	31
Bodmin Clo. LS10	AA17	90
Bodmin Cres. LS10	AA16	90
Bodmin Croft LS10	AA16	90
Bodmin Garth LS10	AA17	90
Bodmin Gdns. LS10	AA16	90
Bodmin Pl. LS10	AA17	90
Bodmin Rd. LS10	Z16	90
Bodmin Sq. LS10	AA17	90
Bodmin St. LS10	AA17	90
Bodmin Ter. LS10	AA17	90
Bog St. HX6	B21	92
Boggard La. LS13	V10	53
Boggart Hill Cres. LS14	FF 8	40
Boggart Hill Dr. LS14	FF 8	40
Boggart Hill Gdns. LS14	FF 8	40
Boggart Hill La. LS14	FF 8	40
Boggart Hill Rd. LS14	FF 8	40
Boggart La. HX3	J19	96
Bold St. LS12	Z12	55
Whitehall Rd.		
Boldmere Rd. LS15	FF11	58
Boldron Holt BD6	K15	65
Boldshay St. BD3	O11	49
Bolehill Pk. HD6	K20	96
Bolingbroke St. BD5	M14	66
Bolland St. BD12	N16	84
Bolland St. LS6	AA 9	37
Bollands Ct. LS6	AA 9	37
Pennington St.		
Bolling Rd. BD4	N12	49
Boltby La. BD6	K15	65
Bolton Brow, S.B. HD6	C21	93
Bolton Cres. BD2	O 9	31
Bolton Dr. BD2	O 8	31
Bolton Gro. BD2	O 9	31
Bolton Hall Rd. BD2	M 8	30
Bolton Hall Rd. BD8	M 8	30
Bolton La. BD2	N10	49
Bolton La. HX3	G20	95
Bolton Rd. BD1	N11	49
Bolton Rd. BD2	N10	49
Bolton Rd. BD3	N10	49
Bolton Rd. LS19	S 4	15
Bolton St. BD12	M16	83
Bolton St. BD13	O11	49
Bolton Zone HX2	D15	62
Bond St. BD13	D10	44
Main Rd.		
Bond St. HD6	E20	94
Bond St. LS1	AA11	55
Bond St. WF17	T18	87
Bonegate Av. HD6	L21	97
Bonegate Rd.		
Bonegate Rd. HD6	L21	97
Bonn Rd. BD9	L10	48
Bonwick Mall BD6	K15	65
Booth Hill HX2	A17	78
Booth Pl. LS6	AA 9	37
North West St.		
Booth Royd BD10	O 6	13
Booth St. BD10	O 7	31
Bradford Rd.		
Booth St. BD13	F15	63
Lee St.		
Booth St. BD18	M 7	30
Booth St. LS11	AA12	55
Sweet St.		
Boothman Wk. BD21	B 4	7
Broomhill Gro.		
Boothroyd Dr. BD10	O 6	13
Booths Yd. LS28	T11	52
Lowtown		
Borrins Way BD17	M 5	12
Borrough Av. LS8	CC 7	38
Borrough Vw. LS8	CC 7	38
Borrowdale Ter. LS14	FF 9	40
Bosnia Pl. LS12	X11	54
Whingate Rd.		
Bosphorous St. LS12	X11	54
Boston Av. LS5	W 9	35
Boston St. HX1	D19	93
Boston St., S.B. HX6	B21	92
Boston Wk. BD6	K15	65
Bosworth Clo. BD15	H10	46
Botany Av. BD2	N 9	31
Bottomley St. BD5	M13	66
Newstead Av.		
Bottomley St. BD6	K15	65
Bottomleys Bldgs. LS6	AA 9	37
Shay St.		
Bottoms HX3	F21	94
Bottoms La. BD11	R17	86
Bottoms, The, Gild. LS27	V15	71
Boulevard, The BD18	L 6	12
Central Av.		
Boulevard, The BD6	K15	65
Boundary Farm Rd. LS17	AA 5	19
Boundary St. LS7	CC 9	38
Roundhay Rd.		
Bourbon Clo. BD6	L15	66
Bourne St. BD10	O 6	13
Bow Bridge Rd. BD5	N13	67
Bow St. LS9	CC11	56
Bower Grn. BD3	P12	50
Bower Rd. LS10	CC13	74
Bower Rd. LS15	JJ 9	41
Bower Rd., Elland HX5	H23	99
Bower St. LS10	CC13	74
Low Rd.		
Bower Yd. LS10	CC14	74
Woodhouse Hill Rd.		
Bowes Nook BD6	K15	65
Bowes Yd., Greet.	F23	98
Bowfell Clo. LS14	GG 9	40
Bowker St. BD7	L12	48
Bowl Shaw La. HX3	G16	81

Street	Grid	Page
Bowland Av. BD17	K 6	11
Bowland Clo. LS15	FF11	58
Bowland St. BD1	M11	48
Bowler Clo. BD12	M16	83
Union Rd.		
Bowling Alley HD6	L23	101
Bowling Alley Ter. HD6	L23	101
Bowling Back La. BD4	O12	49
Bowling Dyke HX1	F19	94
North Bridge St.		
Bowling Green Ter. LS11	AA12	55
Bowling Hall Rd. BD4	O13	67
Bowling Old La. BD5	M14	66
Bowling Park Clo. BD5	N13	67
Bowling Park Dr. BD4	N13	67
Bowman Av. BD6	L15	66
Bowman Gro. HX1	E19	94
Bowman La. LS10	BB11	56
Bowman Pl. HX1	E19	94
Bowman Gro.		
Bowman Rd. BD6	L15	66
Bowman St. HX1	E19	94
Bowman Gro.		
Bowman Ter. HX1	E19	94
Bowness Av. BD10	P 9	32
Bowness St. LS11	AA13	73
Cambrian Rd.		
Bowood Av. LS7	AA 7	37
Bowood Cres. LS7	AA 7	37
Bowood Gro. LS7	AA 7	37
Bowood Rd., Elland HX5	G24	99
Box Trees La. HX2	C17	79
Boxhall Rd., Elland	G23	99
Boxtree Clo. BD8	K10	47
Boy La. BD4	O15	67
Boy La. HX3	C18	79
Boyd Av. BD3	Q10	50
Boyle St. LS12	X11	54
Boyne Pl. LS10	BB12	56
Boyne St. HX1	E19	94
Boynton St. BD5	M13	66
Boynton Ter. BD5	M13	66
Boxandall St.		
Boys La. HX3	F20	94
Bracewell Av. BD15	H11	46
Bracewell Bank HX3	D18	79
Bracewell Dr. HX3	D18	79
Bracewell Gro. HX3	E18	80
Bracewell Hill HX3	D18	79
Bracewell Mt. HX3	D18	79
Bracewell Dr.		
Bracewell Ter. HX3	D18	79
Ramsden Street Rd.		
Bracken Av. HD6	L20	97
Bracken Bank Av. BD22	B 5	7
Bracken Bank Av., Keighley	A 5	7
Bracken Bank Cres., Keighley	B 5	7
Bracken Bank Gro. BD22	B 5	7
Bracken Bank Gro., Keighley	A 5	7
Bracken Bank Way BD22	B 5	7
Bracken Bank Way, Keighley	A 5	7
Bracken Clo. HD6	L20	97
Bracken Ct. LS17	BB 6	20
Bracken Hill		
Bracken Edge BD10	P 7	32
Bracken Edge Grange LS8	CC 8	38
Bracken Edge LS8	CC 8	38
Bracken Hall Dr. BD17	K 6	11
Bracken Hill LS17	BB 6	20
Bracken Holme Royd BD6	K15	65
Bracken Rd. BD21	B 5	7
Ingrown La.		
Bracken Rd. HD6	L20	97
Bracken St. BD21	B 5	7
Brackenbed La. HX2	D18	79
Brackendale Av. BD10	O 6	13
Brackendale BD10	O 6	13
Brackendale Dr. BD10	N 6	13
Brackendale Gro. BD10	N 6	13
Brackendale Par. BD10	N 6	13
Brackens La. HX3	H15	64
Brackenwood Clo. LS8	CC 7	38
Brackenwood Dr. LS8	CC 7	38
Brackenwood Gro. LS8	CC 7	38
Bradbeck Rd. BD7	K11	47
Bradford & Heckmondwyke Rd. BD4	Q15	68
Bradford & Wakefield Rd. BD11	S15	69
Bradford La. BD3	P11	50
Bradford Old Rd. BD16	H 7	28
Bradford Old Rd. HX3	F17	80
Bradford Rd. BD10	O 8	31
Bradford Rd. BD11	U16	87
Bradford Rd. BD12	O17	84
Bradford Rd. BD14	J12	47
Bradford Rd. BD16	G 6	10
Bradford Rd. BD18	L 7	30
Bradford Rd. BD19	O17	84
Bradford Rd. BD4	R15	69
Bradford Rd. HD2	L22	101
Bradford Rd. HD2	L24	101
Bradford Rd. HD6	L21	97
Bradford Rd. HX3	G18	81
Bradford Rd. LS28	R10	51
Bradford Rd. WF17	S18	86
Bradgate Ri., Hor. LS18	V 7	35
Bradlaugh Rd. BD6	L14	66
Bradlaugh Ter. BD6	M14	66
High St.		
Bradley Grange Gdns.	O24	102
Bradley Hall La., Greet. HX4	E24	98
Bradley La. LS28	R11	51
Bradley La., Greet. HX4	E24	98
Bradley Rd. HD6	M24	101
Bradley St. BD16	G 5	10
Bradley St. BD8	M 9	30
Bradshaw La. HX2	D14	62
Bradstock Gdns., Mor. LS27	X16	89
Brae Av. BD2	N 9	31
Brae Head La. HX3	F16	80
Braeside HX2	C19	93
Brafferton Arbor BD6	K15	65
Braithwaite Row LS10	CC14	74
Belle Rd.		
Braithwaite St. LS11	Z12	55
Bramble Clo. BD14	J13	65
Bramham Dr. BD17	M 5	12
Bramham Rd. BD16	H 5	10
Bramley Av. LS13	V10	53
Stanningley Rd.		
Bramley Gdns. LS14	HH 6	23
Bramley Gro. LS13	V10	53
Bramley La. HX3	J19	96
Bramley Mt. LS13	V10	53
Bramley Pl. LS13	V10	53
Bramley St. BD6	N12	49
Bramley St. LS13	V10	53
Bramley Vw. HX3	K19	96
Bramley Vw. LS13	V10	53
Stanningley Rd.		
Bramstan Av. LS13	U 9	34
Bramstan Clo. LS13	U 9	34
Bramstan Gdns. LS13	U 9	34
Bramston St. HD6	L22	101
Bran St. BD21	B 5	7
Corn St		
Brancepeth Pl. LS12	Z11	55
Branch Church St. LS10	CC13	74
Waterloo Rd.		
Branch Pl. LS12	X13	72
Branch Rd. BD19	N18	84
Branch Rd. LS12	X13	72
Branch Rd., Gild. LS27	V15	71
Branch St. LS12	X13	72
Branch Rd.		
Brander App. LS9	EE10	57
Brander Clo. LS9	EE10	57
Brander Dr. LS9	EE10	57
Brander Gro. LS9	EE10	57
Brander Mt. LS9	EE10	57
Brander Rd. LS9	EE10	57
Brander St. LS9	EE10	57
Brandford St. BD7	L12	48
Branding Pl. LS10	BB13	74
Longwood Pl.		
Brandon Cres., Thorner	FF 4	22
Brandon Ct. LS17	DD 4	20
Brandon Gro. LS7	BB 8	38
Brandon La., Wike & Sha.	FF 4	22
Brandon Rd. LS3	AA10	55
Brandon St. LS12	Z11	55
Brandon Ter. LS17	DD 4	21
Brandon Way LS7	BB 8	38
Branksome Cres. BD9	K 9	29
Branksome Dr. BD16	J 7	29
Branksome Gro. BD16	J 7	29
Branksome Pl. LS6	Z10	55
Queens Rd.		
Branksome Ter. LS6	Z10	55
Queens Rd.		
Bransby Clo. LS18	T 9	34
Bransby Ct. LS18	T 9	34
Springbank Clo.		
Bransby Ri. LS18	T 9	34
Springbank Clo.		
Bransdale Clo. BD17	L 6	12
Bransdale Clough BD6	K14	65
Branshaw Dr., Keighley	A 4	7
Branshaw Gr., Keighley	A 4	7
Branshaw Mt., Keighley	A 4	7
Branston Clo. LS18	U 9	34
Bradford Rd.		
Brant Av. HX2	D17	79
Brantcliffe Dr. BD17	M 5	12
Brantdale Clo. BD9	J 9	29
Brantdale Rd. BD9	J 9	29
Brantford St. LS7	BB 8	38
Brantwood Av. BD9	J 9	29
Brantwood Clo. BD9	J 9	29
Brantwood Cres. BD9	H 9	28
Brantwood Dr. BD9	J 9	29
Brantwood Gro. BD8	J 9	29
Brantwood Oval BD9	J 8	29
Brantwood Rd. BD9	H 9	28
Brantwood Vills. BD9	J 9	29
Branwell Av. WF17	T17	87
Branwell Dr., Haworth	ZZ 7	24
Brassey Rd. BD4	O13	67
Brassey St. BD4	O13	67
Brassey St. HX1	E20	94
Brathay Gdns. LS14	FF 9	40
Bray Clo. BD7	J14	65
Braybrook Ct. BD8	M 9	30
Keighley Rd.		
Brayshaw Dr. BD7	J14	65
Brayshaw St. LS28	S12	51
New St.		
Brayton App. LS14	HH 8	41
Brayton Clo. LS14	HH 8	41
Brayton Garth LS14	HH 8	41
Brayton Grn. LS14	HH 8	41
Brayton Gro. LS14	HH 8	41
Brayton Pl. LS14	HH 8	41
Brayton Sq. LS14	HH 8	41
Brayton Ter. LS14	HH 8	41
Brayton Wk. LS14	HH 8	41
Break Lea HX6	B21	92
Break Neck HX3	H19	95
Breaks Fold BD12	M18	83
Breaks Rd. BD12	M16	83
Brearcliffe Clo. BD6	L15	66
Brearcliffe Dr. BD6	L15	66
Brearcliffe Rd. BD6	L15	66
Brearcliffe St. BD6	L15	66
Brearton St. BD1	N11	49
Breary Av., Hor. LS18	W 6	17
Breary La., Bram. LS16	V 1	2
Breary Ri., Bram. LS16	W 2	2
Breary Ter., Hor. LS18	V 6	17
Breary Wk., Hor. LS18	V 6	17
Breck Rd. BD14	J12	47
Breck St. BD14	J12	47
Brecon App. LS9	EE10	57
Brecon Clo. BD10	O 7	31
Bredon Av. BD18	N 7	31
Breighton Adown BD6	J15	65
Brendon Wk. BD4	P13	68
Brentford Rd. BD12	M16	83
Brentford Rd. BD15	M15	66
Brentwood Gdns. BD6	M15	66
Brentwood Gro. LS12	Y11	54
Brooklyn Ter.		
Brett Gdns. LS11	AA13	73
Brewerley St. LS11	AA12	55
Brewery La. BD13	F15	63
Brewery Rd. BD21	B 5	7
Damems Rd.		
Brewery St. HX3	F18	80
Brian Cres. LS15	GG 9	40
Brian Pl. LS15	GG 9	40
Brian Vw. LS15	GG 9	40
Briar Clo. LS28	S10	51
Briar Clo., Elland HX5	G24	99
Briardale Rd. BD9	H 9	28
Briarfield Av. BD10	O 7	31
Briarfield Clo. BD10	O 7	31
Briarfield Gdns. BD18	M 8	30
Briarfield Gro. BD10	O 7	31
Briarfield Rd. BD18	M 8	30
Briarlee Clo. LS19	Q 4	14
Briarmains Rd. WF17	T18	87
Briarsdale Cft. LS8	EE 9	39
Briarsdale Ct. LS8	EE 9	39
Briarsdale Garth LS8	DD 9	39
Briarsdale Hts. LS8	EE 9	39
Briarwood Av. BD6	L14	66
Briarwood BD18	N 7	31
Briarwood Dr. BD6	L14	66
Brearcliffe Clo. BD6	L15	66
Brearcliffe Dr. BD6	L15	66
Brearcliffe Gro. BD6	L15	66
Brearcliffe Rd. BD6	L15	66
Brearton St. BD1	N11	49
Breary Av., Hor. LS18	W 6	17

Breary La., Bram. LS16	W 1	2
Breary Ri., Bram. LS16	W 2	2
Breary Ter., Hor. LS18	V 6	17
Breary Wk., Hor. LS18	V 6	17
Breck Rd. BD14	J12	47
Breck St. BD14	J12	47
Brecon App. LS9	EE10	57
Brecon Clo. BD10	O 7	31
Bredon Av. BD18	N 7	31
Breighton Adown BD6	J15	65
Brendon Wk. BD4	P13	68
Brentford Rd. BD12	M16	83
Brentford Rd. BD15	M15	66
Brentwood Gdns. BD6	M15	66
Brentwood Gro. LS12	Y11	54
Brooklyn Ter.		
Brett Gdns. LS11	AA13	73
Brewerley St. LS11	AA12	55
Brewery La. BD13	F15	63
Brewery Rd. BD21	B 5	7
Damems Rd.		
Brewery St. HX3	F18	80
Brian Cres. LS15	GG 9	40
Brian Pl. LS15	GG 9	40
Brian Vw. LS15	GG 9	40
Briar Clo. LS28	S10	51
Briar Clo., Elland HX5	G24	99
Briar-rhydding BD17	N 6	13
Briardale Rd. BD9	H 9	28
Briarfield Av. BD10	O 7	31
Briarfield Clo. BD10	O 7	31
Briarfield Gdns. BD18	M 8	30
Briarfield Gro. BD10	O 7	31
Briarfield Rd. BD18	M 8	30
Briarlee Clo. LS19	Q 4	14
Briarmains Rd. WF17	T18	87
Briarsdale Cft. LS8	EE 9	39
Briarsdale Ct. LS8	EE 9	39
Briarsdale Garth LS8	DD 9	39
Briarsdale Hts. LS9	EE 9	39
Briarwood Av. BD6	L14	66
Briarwood BD18	N 7	31
Briarwood Dr. BD6	L14	66
Briarwood Gro. BD6	L14	66
Brick Mill Rd., Pud. LS28	T12	52
Brick Row BD12	M17	83
Brick Row LS6	Z 7	37
Green Rd.		
Brick St. BD21	C 4	8
Brick Wood St. LS18	T 8	34
Town St.		
Brickfield Gro. HX2	E16	80
Brickfield La.		
Brickfield La. HX2	E16	80
Brickfield Ter. HX2	E16	80
Brickfield La.		
Bridge End HD2	L22	101
Bridge End LS1	BB11	56
Bridge Fold LS5	X 9	36
Bridge Gate Way BD10	P 8	32
Bridge La. HX1	H16	81
Bridge Rd. HD2	L22	101
Bridge Rd. LS11	AA12	55
Bridge Rd. LS5	X 9	36
Bridge Rd., Rood. LS13	T 8	34
Bridge St. BD1	N12	49
Bridge St. BD13	G12	46
Market St.		
Bridge St. BD16	G 4	10
Micklethwaite La.		
Bridge St. HD6	B21	92
Bridge St. HX1	F19	94
North Bridge		
Bridge St. LS2	BB11	56
Bridge St., Mor. LS27	X17	89
Bridge St., Oakworth	YY 6	6
Bridge Ter. HX2	A16	78
Bridge Ter. LS17	GG 5	22
Bay Horse La.		
Bridge Vw. LS9	BB12	56
South Accommodation Rd.		
Bridge Vw., Rood. LS12	T 8	34
Bridge Wood Clo. LS18	V 6	17
Bridgefield Pl. LS9	BB12	56
South Accommodation Rd.		
Bridgehouse La.,	ZZ 8	24
Haworth		
Bridgewater Rd. BD9	J10	48
Bridle Dene HX3	J16	82
Bridle Path Cres. LS15	GG10	58
Bridle Path La. BD15	GG10	58
Bridle Path Rd. LS15	GG10	58
Bridle Path Sq. LS15	GG10	58
Bridle Path Wk. LS15	GG10	58
Bridle St. HX3	J16	82
Bridle Stile HX3	J16	82
Bridle Stile La. BD13	G14	64
Brier La. HD6	J21	96

Brierfield Gdns., Mor.	V16	88
LS27		
Brierley Hill HX3	G19	95
Briery Field BD18	L 8	30
Bradford Rd.		
Brigate HD6	L22	101
Brigg St. BD16	G 4	10
Briggate BD17	L 7	30
Briggate BD2	P 9	32
Briggate Crag Rd. BD18	L 8	30
Briggate LS1	BB11	56
Briggate, Elland HX5	G23	99
Briggs Av. BD6	L14	66
Briggs Gro. BD6	L14	66
Briggs Pl. BD6	L14	66
Briggs St. BD13	F14	63
Brighouse & Denholme Rd.	D12	44
BD13		
Brighouse & Denholme Rd.	G15	64
HX3		
Brighouse & Denholme Rd.	G15	64
BD13		
Brighouse & Denholmegate	H17	81
Rd. HX3		
Brighouse Rd. BD12	M16	83
Brighouse Rd. HX3	J19	96
Brighouse Wood La. HD6	K21	96
Bright St. BD10	O 7	31
Bright St. BD11	R16	86
Allen Cft.		
Bright St. BD13	G14	64
Bright St. BD15	H10	46
Bright St. BD4	P14	68
Bright St., Mor. LS27	W17	88
Bright St., S.B. HX6	B20	92
Bright St., Stan. LS28	T10	52
Brighton Av., Mor. LS27	W17	88
Brighton Gro. HX1	E19	94
Pellon La.		
Brighton Gro. LS13	V10	53
Brighton St. BD10	O 6	13
Brighton St. BD17	L 7	30
Brighton St. HX3	E18	80
East Park Rd.		
Brighton Ter. BD19	N19	103
Brignall Cft. LS9	CC10	56
Brignall Garth LS9	CC10	56
Brignall Way LS9	CC10	56
Brindley Gro. BD8	J11	47
Brisbane Av. BD2	N 9	31
Briscoe La., Greet. HX4	E23	98
Bristol St. HX3	F21	94
Huddersfield Rd.		
Britania Cotts. WF17	T18	87
Britannia Clo., Stan.	T10	52
LS28		
Britannia St. BD16	H 5	10
Britannia St. BD21	B 4	7
Aireworth St.		
Britannia St. BD5	N12	49
Britannia St. LS1	Z11	55
Wellington St.		
Britannia St., Stan. LS28	T10	52
Brittania Ct. LS13	U11	52
Broad La. BD4	P12	50
Broad La. LS28	U10	52
Broad La., Stan. LS13	W 9	35
Broad St. BD1	N11	49
Broad St. HX1	F19	94
Broad St. LS28	S 9	33
Broadfield Clo. BD4	Q14	68
Broadfolds BD14	J13	65
Broadgate Av., Hor. LS18	V 6	17
Broadgate Cres., Hor.	V 7	35
LS18		
Broadgate Dr., Hor. LS18	V 6	17
Broadgate La., Hor. LS18	V 6	17
Broadgate Wk., Hor. LS18	V 7	35
Broadlands St. BD4	P13	68
Broadlea Av. LS13	W 9	35
Broadlea Clo. LS13	W 9	35
Broadlea Cres. BD5	N13	67
Broadlea Cres. LS13	W 9	35
Broadlea Gdns. LS13	W 9	35
Broadlea Gro. LS13	W 9	35
Broadlea Hill LS13	W 9	35
Broadlea Mt. LS13	W 9	35
Broadlea Oval LS13	V 9	35
Broadlea Pl. LS13	W 9	35
Broadlea Rd. LS13	W 9	35
Broadlea Ter. LS13	W 9	35
Broadlea Vw. LS13	V 9	35
Broadley Av. HX2	B18	78
Broadley Clo. HX2	C18	79
Broadley Cres. HX2	B18	78
Broadley Gro. HX2	C18	79
Broadley Rd. HX2	B18	78
Broadstone Way BD4	Q14	68

Broadtree Rd. HX3	E18	80
Broadway Av. BD5	M14	66
Broadway BD1	N11	49
Broadway BD16	H 5	10
Broadway BD22	A 5	7
Broadway Clo. BD5	M14	66
Broadway Dr., Hor. LS18	U 7	34
Stoney La.		
Broadway HX3	G20	95
Broadway HX6	A21	92
Broadway LS15	FF11	58
Broadway, Hor. LS18	T 8	34
Broadway, Hor. LS18	W 7	35
Broadwood Av. HX2	C18	79
Brock Well La. HX6	A21	92
Brocklesby Dr. BD15	H10	46
Brodlea St. LS13	W 9	35
Bromely Rd. BD16	G 5	10
Bromet Pl. BD2	O 9	31
Bromford Rd. BD4	O13	67
Bromley Gro., Keighley	A 4	7
Bromley Rd. BD18	K 7	29
Brompton Av. BD4	O13	67
Brompton Gro. LS11	AA13	73
Stratford Ter.		
Brompton Mt. LS11	AA13	73
Stratford Ter.		
Brompton Rd. BD4	O13	67
Brompton Row LS11	AA13	73
Straftord Ter.		
Brompton Ter. LS11	AA13	73
Stratford Ter.		
Brompton Vw. LS11	AA13	73
Stratford Ter.		
Bronshill Gro. BD15	J10	47
Bronte Clo. BD9	K10	47
Bronte Dr., Keighley	A 5	7
Bronte Old Rd. BD13	G12	46
Bronte Pl. BD13	G12	46
Bronte Rd. WF17	T18	87
Bronte St., Haworth	YY 7	24
West La.		
Brook Hill BD17	M 5	12
Brook La. BD14	H13	64
Brook Royd Av. HD6	L20	97
Brook St. BD12	O17	84
Brook St. BD21	B 4	7
South St.		
Brook St., Elland HX5	H24	99
Brook Ter. HX2	A18	78
Brookdale Ter. LS11	AA13	73
Malvern Ter.		
Brooke St. HD6	L22	101
Brookfield Av. BD18	M 7	30
Brookfield Av. BD18	Q18	85
Brookfield Av. LS13	S 8	33
Brookfield Av. LS8	CC 9	38
Brookfield Gdns. LS13	S 8	33
Brookfield Pl. LS6	Z 8	37
Brookfield Rd.		
Brookfield Rd. BD18	M 7	30
Brookfield Rd. BD3	O11	49
Brookfield Rd. LS6	Z 8	37
Brookfield Rd. LS10	BB12	56
Brookfield Ter. BD19	Q18	85
Brookfield Ter. LS6	Z 8	37
Monk Bridge Rd.		
Brookfield Vw. BD19	Q18	85
Brookfields Av. BD12	N18	84
Brookfields Rd. BD12	N18	84
Brookfoot Av. BD11	R16	86
Old Rd.		
Brookfoot La. HD6	J21	96
Brookfoot, Hor. LS18	V 6	17
Brookgrain Hill HD6	L23	101
Brookhill HX3	J10	96
Brookhill Clo. LS17	CC 5	20
Brookhill Cres. LS17	CC 5	20
Brookhill Dr. LS17	CC 5	20
Brookhill Gro. LS17	CC 5	20
Brooklands Av. BD13	G12	46
Brooklands Av. LS14	FF 9	40
Brooklands Clo. LS14	FF 9	40
Brooklands Cres. LS14	FF 9	40
Brooklands Cres. LS19	R 4	15
Brooklands Dr. LS14	FF 9	40
Brooklands Garth LS14	FF 9	40
Brooklands HD2	N24	102
Brooklands La. LS14	FF 9	40
Brooklands Pl. LS14	FF 9	40
Brooklands Rd. BD18	L 7	30
Manor La.		
Brooklyn Av. LS14	FF 9	40
Brooklyn Av. LS12	Y11	54
Brooklyn Pl. LS12	Y11	54
Brooklyn St. LS12	Y11	54

Street	Grid	Page
Brooklyn Ter. LS12	Y11	54
Brooklyn Ter., Brig.	K20	96
Brookroyd La. WF17	T18	87
Brooks Ter. BD13	H14	64
Highgate Rd.		
Brooksbank Av. BD7	K12	47
Brooksbank Dr. LS15	GG11	58
Brooksbank Gdns.,	G24	99
Elland HX5		
Brookside LS17	CC 4	20
Broom Cres. LS10	CC15	74
Broom Ct. LS10	CC15	74
Broom Garth LS10	CC15	74
Broom Gdns. LS10	CC15	74
Broom Gro. LS10	CC16	91
Broom Lawn LS10	CC16	91
Broom Rd.		
Broom Mt. LS10	CC16	91
Broom Nook LS26	CC15	91
Broom Pl. LS10	CC15	74
Broom Rd. LS10	CC16	91
Broom St. BD21	C 4	8
Broom St. BD4	N12	49
Broom Ter. LS10	CC15	74
Broom Way LS26	CC15	74
Broomcroft BD14	J13	65
Broome Av. BD2	N 9	31
Broomfield Av. HX3	E21	94
Broomfield Cotts. BD14	H13	64
Broomfield Pl.		
Broomfield Cres. LS6	Y 9	36
Broomfield LS16	X 5	18
Broomfield Pl. BD14	H13	64
Broomfield Pl. LS6	Y 9	36
Broomfield Rd. HD2	L24	101
Broomfield Rd. LS6	Y 9	36
Broomfield St. BD13	G14	64
High St.		
Broomfield St. LS6	Y 9	36
Broomfield Ter. LS6	Y 9	36
Broomfield Vw. LS6	Y 9	36
Chapel La.		
Broomfield, Greet. HX4	F24	98
Broomhill Av. BD21	B 4	7
Broomhill Av. LS17	BB 6	20
Broomhill Cres. LS17	BB 6	20
Broomhill Dr. BD21	B 4	7
Broomhill Dr. LS17	BB 6	20
Broomhill Gro. BD21	B 4	7
Broomhill Mt. BD21	B 4	7
Broomhill St. BD21	B 4	7
Broomhill Way BD21	B 4	7
Broomhill Wk. BD21	B 4	7
Brougham Rd. HX3	F18	80
Brougham St. BD4	O12	49
Rhine St.		
Brougham St. HX3	F18	80
Brougham Rd.		
Brougham Ter. HX3	F18	80
Brougham Rd.		
Broughton Av. BD4	O14	67
Broughton Av. LS9	DD10	57
Broughton Ter. LS28	T11	52
North St.		
Broughton Ter. LS9	DD10	57
Brow Bottom La. HX2	B16	78
Brow Foot Dr. HX2	C20	93
Brow Foot Gate La.	C20	93
HX2		
Brow Gate BD17	M 5	12
Brow Hill Rd.	ZZ 8	24
Prince St.		
Brow La. BD14	G13	64
Brow La. HX2	E16	80
Brow La. HX3	G17	81
Brow La., Shelf HX3	J16	82
Brow Rd., Haworth	ZZ 8	24
Brow St. BD21	C 4	8
Brow Top BD13	H14	64
Brow Top Rd., Haworth	ZZ 8	24
Brow Top, Haworth	A 7	25
Brow Wood Av. HX3	J16	82
Brow Wood Cres. BD2	N 9	31
Brow Wood Rd. HX3	J16	82
Brow Wood Ri. HX3	J16	82
Brow Wood Ter. BD6	K15	65
Brow, The, Greet. HX4	F23	98
Browfoot BD18	M 7	30
Brown Av. LS11	Z13	73
Brown Hill Av. LS9	DD10	57
Brown Hill Cres. LS9	DD10	57
Brown Hill Ter. LS9	DD10	57
Brown La. LS11	Z12	55
Brown La. LS12	Z12	55
Brown Lee La. BD15	E 9	27
Brown Pl. LS11	Z13	73
Brown Rd. LS11	Z13	73
Brown St. HX3	F19	94
Brownberrie Av., Troy	V 5	17
LS18		
Brownberrie Cres., Troy	U 5	16
LS18		
Brownberrie Dr., Troy	V 5	17
LS18		
Brownberrie Gdns., Troy	U 5	16
LS18		
Brownberrie La., Troy	T 5	16
LS18		
Brownberrie Wk., Troy	V 5	17
LS18		
Brownhill Clo. BD11	R15	69
Brownhill Clo. WF17	T18	87
Brownhill Dr. BD11	R16	86
Brownhill Garth WF17	T18	87
Brownhill Rd. WF17	T18	87
Browning Av. HX3	F21	94
Browning St. BD3	O11	49
Brownlea Clo. LS19	Q 4	14
Brownroyd Fold BD5	L14	66
Carrbottom Rd.		
Brownroyd Hill Rd. BD6	L14	66
Brownroyd St. BD7	L11	48
Brownroyd St. BD8	L11	48
Brownroyd Wk. BD6	L14	66
Browns Sq. LS7	BB10	56
Skinner La.		
Browns Ter. LS13	V10	53
Brownsholme St. BD21	C 4	8
Bruce Gdns. LS12	Z11	55
Bruce Lawn LS12	Z11	55
Bruce St. HX1	D20	93
Brudenell Av. LS6	Z 9	37
Brudenell Gro. LS6	Z 9	37
Brudenell Mt. LS6	Z 9	37
Brudenell Rd. LS6	Z 9	37
Brudenell St. LS6	Z 9	37
Brudenell Vw. LS6	Z 9	37
Brunel Ct. HX3	E18	80
Brunswick Gdns. HX1	E19	94
Brunswick Pl. BD10	P 7	32
Stock Hill La.		
Brunswick Pl., Mor. LS27	X17	89
Brunswick Rd. BD10	P 7	32
Brunswick Rd., Pud. LS28	T11	52
Brunswick St. BD16	H 5	10
Brunswick St.,	D 8	26
Cullingworth BD13		
Brunswick St., Mor. LS27	X16	89
Brunswick St., Queens.	G14	64
BD13		
Brunswick Ter. BD12	M15	66
Brunswick Ter. LS2	BB10	56
Brunswick Ter. LS27	X17	89
Bruntcliffe Clo., Mor.	W17	88
LS27		
Bruntcliffe Dr., Mor.	W17	88
LS27		
Bruntcliffe La., Mor.	W17	88
LS27		
Bruntcliffe Rd., Mor.	V17	88
LS27		
Bruntcliffe Way LS27	V17	88
Brussels St. LS9	BB11	56
Bryan Rd., Elland HX5	F24	98
Bryan St. HD6	L22	101
Bryan St. LS28	S 9	33
Bryanstone Rd. BD4	P13	68
Buck La. BD17	N 5	13
Buck Mill La. BD10	O 5	13
Buck St. BD13	D11	44
Stradmore Rd.		
Buckingham Av. LS6	Z 9	37
Buckingham Cres.	J12	47
BD14		
Buckingham Dr. LS6	Z 9	37
Buckingham Gro. LS6	Z 9	37
Buckingham Mt. LS6	Z 9	37
Buckingham Rd. LS6	Z 9	37
Buckingham St. BD3	N10	49
Buckland Pl. HX1	D20	93
Buckland Rd. BD8	K11	47
Springroyd Ter.		
Buckley La. HX2	C18	79
Buckstone Av. LS17	Z 5	19
Buckstone Clo. LS17	AA 5	19
Buckstone Dr. LS17	Z 5	19
Buckstone Oval		
Buckstone Dr. LS19	R 5	15
Buckstone Gdns. LS17	AA 5	19
Buckstone Grn. LS17	Z 5	19
Buckstone Gro. LS17	Z 5	19
Buckstone Mt. LS17	Z 5	19
Buckstone Oval LS17	Z 5	19
Buckstone Rd. LS17	Z 5	19
Buckstone Ri. LS17	Z 5	19
Buckstone Vw. LS17	Z 5	19
Buckton Clo. LS11	AA13	73
Malvern St.		
Buckton Mt. LS11	AA13	73
Buckton Ter. LS11	AA13	73
Buckton Rd.		
Buckton Vw. LS11	AA13	73
Bude Rd. BD5	N14	67
Bude Rd. LS11	AA14	73
Bulgaria St. LS12	X11	54
Bull & Bell Yd. LS1	BB11	56
Briggate		
Bull Close La. HX1	F20	94
Bull Grn. HX1	F19	94
Bull Royd Av. BD8	K11	47
Bull Royd Cres. BD8	K11	47
Bull Royd Dr. BD8	K11	47
Bull Royd La. BD8	K11	47
Buller Cres. LS9	EE10	57
Buller St. BD4	P12	50
Bullerthorpe La. LS26	JJ14	77
Bullerthorpe La., Swil.	JJ12	59
LS15		
Bullfield, The BD16	E 7	27
Bullogh La., Roth. LS26	FF15	76
Bulmer St. LS7	Z 8	37
Meanwood Rd.		
Bummside Clo. WF17	U18	87
Bunkers Hill BD17	O 4	13
Bunkers Hill La.,	ZZ 4	6
Keighley		
Burchett Gro. LS6	AA 9	37
Burchett Pl. LS6	AA 9	37
Burchett Ter. LS6	AA 9	37
Hartley Av.		
Burdale Pl. BD7	L12	48
Burdett Ter. LS4	Y10	54
Adwick Pl.		
Burdock Way HX1	E19	94
Burleigh St. HX1	D20	93
Fenton Rd.		
Burley Grange Rd. LS4	Y10	54
Burley Hill Cres. LS4	X 9	36
Burley Hill Dr. LS4	X 9	36
Burley La., Hor. LS18	U 7	34
Burley Lodge Pl. LS6	Z10	55
Burley Lodge Rd.		
Burley Lodge Rd. LS6	Z10	55
Burley Lodge Ter. LS6	Z10	55
Burley Pl. LS4	Y10	54
Burley Rd. LS3	Y10	54
Burley Rd. LS4	Y10	54
Burley St. BD2	M 9	30
Burley St. LS3	Z11	55
Burley St., Elland HX5	G24	99
Burley Wood Cres. LS4	X 9	36
Burley Wood La. LS4	Y 9	36
Burley Wood Mt. LS4	X 9	36
Burley Wood Vw. LS4	Y 9	36
Burlington Av. BD3	Q10	50
Burlington Pl. LS11	AA13	73
Tempest Rd.		
Burlington Rd. LS11	AA14	73
Burlington St. BD8	M10	48
Burlington St. HX1	D19	93
Hanson La.		
Burmah St. HX1	D19	93
Battinson Rd.		
Burmantofts St. LS9	CC11	56
Burned Gro. HX3	J15	65
Burned Rd. HX3	J15	65
Burneston Gdns. BD6	K15	65
Burnett Av. BD5	M13	66
Burnett Pl. BD5	M13	66
Burnett St. BD1	N11	49
Burnham Av. BD4	O14	67
Burniston Clo. BD15	F 8	27
Royd St.		
Burnley Rd., S.B. HX2	D20	93
Burnley Ville BD19	R18	86
Reform St.		
Burns St. HX3	D17	79
Foundry St. N.		
Burnsall Clo. LS12	X11	54
Burnsall Gdns. LS12	X11	54
Burnsall Grange Ct. LS12	X11	54
Burnsall Rd. LS12	X11	54
Burnsall Rd. BD3	O11	49
Burnsall Rd. HD6	K23	100
Burnside Av. HX3	J16	82
Burnt Hills Rd. LS12	V14	71
Burnwells Av. BD10	O 6	13
Burr Tree Dr. LS15	HH11	59
Burr Tree Vale		
Burr Tree Gdns LS15	HH11	59
Burr Tree Vale LS15	HH11	59
Burrage St. BD16	G 5	10
Chapel La.		
Burras Rd. BD4	O14	67

Name	Ref	Page
Carmel Rd. HX3	E18	80
Carmona Av. BD18	L 8	30
Carmona Gdns. BD18	L 8	30
Carnaby Rd. BD7	K14	65
Speetan Av.		
Carnarvon St. BD3	N10	49
Carnation St. BD3	P12	50
Carnegie Dr. LS28	M 7	30
Carnoustie Gro. BD16	H 7	28
Caroline St. BD18	K 7	29
Carperley Cres. BD13	D11	44
Station Rd.		
Carr Bottom Rd. BD10	Q 7	32
Carr Bridge Av. LS16	V 5	17
Carr Bridge Clo. LS16	V 5	17
Carr Bridge Dr. LS16	V 5	17
Carr Bridge Vw. LS16	V 5	17
Carr Clo. LS9	S 5	15
Carr Crofts LS12	X11	54
Carr Crofts Ter. LS12	X11	54
Tong La.		
Carr Cross St. LS7	BB 9	38
Carr Green Av. HD6	K24	100
Carr Green Clo. HD6	K24	100
Carr Green La. HD6	K23	100
Carr Hall Rd. BD12	M17	83
Carr Hill Av. LS28	R 8	33
Carr Hill Dr. LS28	R 8	33
Carr Hill Gro. LS28	R 8	33
Carr Hill Nook LS28	R 8	33
Carr Hill Rd. LS28	R 8	33
Carr Hill Ri. LS28	R 8	33
Carr House Gate BD12	M17	83
Carr House Gro. BD12	M17	83
Carr House La. BD12	L16	83
Carr House La. HX3	J16	82
Carr House Mt. BD12	M17	83
Carr House Rd. HX3	J16	82
Carr La. BD12	M16	83
Carr La. BD13	D10	44
Carr La. BD18	M 7	30
Carr La. LS19	S 5	15
Carr La., Sha. LS14	GG 5	22
Carr La., Thorner LS14	GG 4	22
Carr La., Thorner LS14	JJ 4	23
Carr Manor Av. LS17	AA 7	37
Carr Manor Cft. LS7	AA 7	37
Carr Manor Cres. LS17	AA 6	19
Carr Manor Dr. LS17	AA 7	37
Carr Manor Garth LS17	AA 6	19
Carr Manor Gdns. LS17	AA 7	37
Carr Manor Gro. LS17	AA 7	37
Carr Manor Mt. LS17	AA 7	37
Carr Manor Par. LS17	AA 7	37
Carr Manor Pl. LS7	AA 7	37
Carr Manor Rd. LS17	AA 7	37
Carr Manor Vw. LS17	AA 6	19
Carr Manor Wk. LS7	AA 7	37
Carr Moor Side LS11	BB13	74
Carr Moor St. LS10	BB14	74
Carr Rd. BD12	M17	83
Carr Rd. LS28	Q 8	32
Carr Row BD12	M17	83
Carr St. HD6	L21	97
Carr St. WF17	T18	87
Carrbottom Av. BD5	L14	66
Carrbottom Fold BD5	M14	66
Carrbottom Gro. BD5	L14	66
Carrbottom Rd. BD5	L14	66
Carrholm Cres. LS7	AA 7	37
Carrholm Dr. LS7	AA 7	37
Carrholm Gro. LS7	AA 7	37
Carrholm Mt. LS7	AA 7	37
Carrholm Rd. LS7	AA 7	37
Carrholm Vw. LS7	AA 7	37
Carriage Dr.	E19	94
Carriage Dr., The LS8	EE 7	39
Carriage La., Greet.	F23	98
Carrier St. HX1	F19	94
Albion St.		
Carrington St. BD3	P11	50
Carrol St. BD3	O12	49
Cart Gate BD6	M14	66
Carter Av. LS15	HH11	59
Carter La. BD13	F14	63
Carter La. LS15	HH11	59
Carter Mt. LS15	HH11	59
Carter St. BD4	N12	49
Carter Ter. LS11	Z14	73
Town St.		
Carter Ter. LS15	HH10	59
Cartmell Dr. LS15	FF11	58
Caryl Rd. BD4	O13	67
Caster Rd. BD18	K 7	29
Casterton Gdns. LS14	GG 9	40
Castle Av. HD6	K23	100
Castle Clo. WF17	U18	87
Castle Fields La. BD16	F 4	9
Castle Grange LS19	S 4	15
Castle Gro. Av. LS6	Y 8	36
Castle Gro. BD16	E 6	9
Castle Gro. Dr. LS6	Y 8	36
Castle Ings Clo. LS12	V13	71
Castle Ings Dr. LS12	V13	71
Castle Ings Gdns. LS12	V13	71
Castle More Rd. BD17	M 6	12
Castle Rd. BD18	L 7	30
Castle St. BD5	N12	49
Castle Ter. HD6	K21	96
Castle Vw. LS17	AA 6	19
Castlefield Cres. HD6	K23	100
Castlefield Rd. HD6	K23	100
Castlefields Dr. HD6	K23	100
Castlefields Rd. BD16	G 4	10
Castlegate Dr. BD10	P 8	32
Castleton Clo. LS12	Z11	55
Castleton Rd. LS12	Z11	55
Castleton Ter. LS12	Y11	54
Armley Rd.		
Cater St. BD1	N11	49
Cath St. HD6	L21	97
Cathcart St. HX3	E18	80
Rawson St. N.		
Cathcart St. LS6	AA 9	37
Catherine Gro. LS11	AA13	73
Lodge La.		
Catherine Slack HD6	K20	96
Catherine St. BD21	B 4	7
Cato St. LS9	CC 9	56
Caukroger La. HX1	F20	94
Causeway HX1	F19	94
Causeway La. LS16	Y 6	18
Weetwood La.		
Cautley Pl. LS13	V10	53
Cautley Rd. LS9	CC12	56
Cautley St. LS13	V10	53
Cavalier St. LS9	CC12	56
Cave St. LS11	BB12	56
Cavendish Ct. BD2	P 8	32
Park Rd.		
Cavendish Dr. BD16	H 5	10
Cavendish Ms. LS17	BB 5	20
Cavendish Pl., Pud. LS28	T10	52
Cavendish Rd. BD10	O 7	31
Cavendish Rd. BD2	P 8	32
Cavendish Ri., Pud. LS28	U11	52
Cavendish St. BD7	M12	48
Lady La.		
Cavendish St. HX1	E19	94
West Hill St.		
Cavendish St. LS3	Z11	55
Cavendish St., Pud. LS28	T11	52
Cavendish Ter. HX1	E19	94
West Hill St.		
Cawcliffe Dr. HD6	L20	97
Cawcliffe Rd. HD6	L20	97
Cawood Haven BD6	K15	65
Cawood Yd. LS9	BB11	56
Caythorpe Rd. LS16	X 7	36
Cecil Av. BD17	M 5	12
Cecil Av. BD7	L13	66
Cecil Av. HX3	K19	96
Cecil Gro. LS12	Y11	54
Cecil Mt. LS12	Y11	54
Cecil Rd. LS12	Y11	54
Cecil St. LS12	Y11	54
Cedar Clo. LS12	Y11	54
Cedar Dr. BD12	N17	84
Cedar Gro. LS12	X11	54
Carr Crofts		
Cedar Gro., Greet. HX4	E23	98
Cedar Mt. LS12	X11	54
Cedar St. BD16	G 4	10
Canal Rd.		
Cedar St. BD21	B 5	7
Cedar St. HX1	D20	93
Cedar St. LS12	X11	54
Cedar Ter. LS12	X11	54
Cedars, The, Bram. LS16	W 2	2
Cemetery Pl. LS2	Z 9	37
Woodhouse La.		
Cemetery Rd. BD16	G 5	10
Cemetery Rd. BD6	L15	66
Cemetery Rd. BD7	K11	47
Cemetery Rd. BD8	K11	47
Cemetery Rd. LS11	AA13	73
Cemetery Rd. LS28	S11	51
Cemetery Rd., Haworth	YY 7	24
Centenary Rd. BD17	N 5	13
Centenary St. LS1	AA11	55
Central Av. BD17	L 6	12
Central Av. BD18	L 7	30
Central Av. BD5	M13	66
Central Av., Keighley	A 5	7
Central Dr., Keighley	A 5	7
Central Par. LS9	EE13	75
Central Pk. HX1	E20	94
Central Rd. LS1	BB11	56
Central St. LS1	AA11	55
St. Pauls St.		
Centre St. BD5	M13	66
Thornton La.		
Century Rd., Elland HX5	G23	99
Century St. BD21	C 5	8
Chadwick St. LS10	BB12	56
Chain St. BD1	M11	48
Chalfont Rd. LS16	X 7	36
Chalice Clo. LS10	CC15	91
Challis Gro. BD5	N13	67
Chancellor Pl. LS6	AA 9	37
Speedwell St.		
Chancellor St. LS6	AA 9	37
Ridge Rd.		
Chandos Av. LS8	CC 7	38
Chandos Fold LS8	CC 7	38
Chandos Garth LS8	CC 7	38
Chandos Gdns. LS8	CC 7	38
Chandos Grn. LS8	CC 7	38
Chandos Pl. LS8	CC 7	38
Chandos St. BD21	B 4	7
Chandos St. BD4	N12	49
Chandos Ter. LS8	CC 7	38
Chandos Wk. LS8	CC 7	38
Change Gate, Haworth	ZZ 7	24
Change La. HX3	G22	99
Chanler Clo. WF17	T18	87
Channing St. BD1	N12	49
Channing Way BD1	N12	49
Chantrell Gro. LS9	BB11	56
York Rd.		
Chantry Cft. LS15	HH11	59
Chantry Garth LS15	HH11	59
Chapel Cft. HD6	K23	100
Chapel Clo. HX3	J16	82
Chapel Ct. LS11	AA12	55
Marshall St.		
Chapel Fold BD12	L19	97
Chapel Fold BD6	L14	66
Chapel Fold LS6	Y 9	36
Cardigan La.		
Chapel Grn. LS28	S12	51
School Rd.		
Chapel Gro. BD16	G 4	10
Chapel Hill LS10	BB16	91
Chapel Hill, Mor. LS27	X16	89
Chapel House Rd. BD12	M15	66
Chapel La. BD13	F14	63
Chapel La. BD15	J11	47
Chapel La. BD16	G 5	10
Chapel La. BD17	P 4	14
Chapel La. HX3	F21	94
Huddersfield Rd.		
Chapel La. HX3	H21	95
Chapel La. LS12	V13	71
Chapel La. LS12	W12	53
Chapel La. LS12	Y11	54
Chapel La. LS6	Y 9	36
Chapel La. WF17	T18	87
Market Pl.		
Chapel La., S.B. HD6	C31	93
Chapel Pl. BD8	J11	47
Chapel Pl. LS6	Y 9	36
North La.		
Chapel Rd. BD12	M16	83
Chapel Rd. BD16	G 4	10
Chapel Rd. LS7	BB 8	38
Chapel Row LS11	AA12	55
Marshall St.		
Chapel Row, Allerton	H10	46
BD15		
Chapel Row, Wilsden BD15	E 8	27
Chapel Sq. LS6	Y 8	36
Chapel St.		
Chapel St. BD1	N11	49
Chapel St. BD16	G 4	10
Chapel Rd.		
Chapel St. BD2	P 9	32
Chapel St. BD5	M13	66
Hampden St.		
Chapel St. BD6	M14	66
Chapel St. HX3	K20	96
Chapel St. LS15	GG11	58
Chapel St. LS18	T 8	36
Rodley La.		
Chapel St. LS19	R 5	15
Chapel St. LS27	W17	88
Bruntcliffe Rd.		
Chapel St. LS28	P 8	32
Chapel St. LS6	Y 8	36
Chapel St. N. HX3	D17	79
Chapel St., Denholme	C10	44
BD13		
Chapel St., Pud. LS28	T10	52
Chapel St., Queens. BD13	G14	64

118

Name	Ref	Page
Chapel St., Thornton BD13	F12	45
Chapel Ter. BD13	F12	45
George St.		
Chapel Ter. BD15	H10	46
Chapel Vw., Hor. LS18	V 7	35
Chapel Vw. BD2	P 9	32
Chapel Yd. LS15	GG11	58
Chapel St.		
Chapeltown HX1	F19	94
Pellon La.		
Chapeltown LS28	S12	51
Chapeltown Rd. LS7	BB10	56
Chapman St. BD4	P12	50
Charing Cross Ms. LS6	AA 9	37
Shay St.		
Chariot St. LS1	AA11	55
Charles Av. BD3	P11	50
Charles Av. HX3	H21	95
Charles Av. LS9	CC12	56
Charles Clo. HX3	H21	95
Charles Gdns. LS11	AA12	55
Charles St.	F19	94
Charles St. BD1	N11	49
Charles St. BD16	H 5	10
Charles St. BD18	L 7	30
Stead St.		
Charles St. HD6	L21	97
Piggott St.		
Charles St. HX1	F19	94
Square Rd.		
Charles St. LS28	S 9	33
Charles St., Elland HX5	G24	99
Charles St., Hor. LS18	U 7	34
Charles St., Mor. LS27	X17	89
Charles St., Queens. HX1	F19	94
Charlestown Ter. HX3	F19	94
Charlesworth Ter. HX2	D19	93
Charlotte Clo. WF17	T17	87
Charlton Ct. HX2	D19	93
Long Lover La.		
Charlton Gro. LS9	CC11	56
Charlton Mt. LS9	CC11	56
Charlton Pl. LS9	CC11	56
Charlton Rd. LS9	CC11	56
Charlton St. LS9	DD11	57
Charmouth Pl. LS11	AA12	55
Charmouth St.		
Charmouth St. LS11	AA12	55
Charmouth Ter. LS11	AA13	73
Charnwood Clo. BD2	P10	50
Charnwood Rd.		
Charnwood Gro. BD2	P10	50
Charnwood Rd. BD2	O10	49
Charterhouse Rd. BD10	O 6	13
Charteris Rd. BD8	J11	47
Chartists Way, Mor. LS27	X17	89
Charville Gdns. LS17	FF 5	22
Chase, The, LS19	S 4	15
Chassum Gro. BD9	L10	48
Chat Hill Rd. BD13	G12	46
Chatham St.	E19	94
Chatham St. BD3	N10	49
Chatham St. HX1	E19	94
Hope St.		
Chatswood Av. LS11	Z15	73
Chatswood Cres. LS11	Z14	73
Chatswood Dr. LS11	Z14	73
Chatsworth Av. LS28	R11	51
Chatsworth Clo. LS8	DD 9	39
Chatsworth Cres. LS28	R11	51
Chatsworth Dr. LS28	R11	51
Chatsworth Fall LS28	R11	51
Chatsworth Pl BD8	L10	48
Chatsworth Rd. LS28	P11	50
Chatsworth Rd. LS8	DD 9	39
Chatsworth Ri. LS28	R11	51
Chatsworth St. LS12	Y12	54
Leamington Ter.		
Chatsworth Ter. LS12	Y12	54
Leamington Ter.		
Chaucer Av., Pud. LS28	T12	52
Chaucer Gdns., Pud. LS28	T12	52
Chaucer Gro., Pud. LS28	T12	52
Chaucer Pl BD3	O11	49
Chaucer St. HX1	D20	93
Cheapside BD1	N11	49
Cheapside HX1	F19	94
Cheapside HX3	J16	82
Shelf Moor Rd.		
Cheapside, Greet. HX4	F23	98
Checker Row, Pud. LS28	T10	52
Richardshaw La.		
Cheddington Gro. BD15	H11	46
Chedwell Springs BD16	H 7	28
Chellow Grange Rd. BD9	J 9	29
Chellow La. BD9	J10	47
Chellow St. BD5	M14	66
Chellow Ter. BD9	J10	47
Chellowfield Ct. BD9	J 9	29
Chelmsford Rd. BD3	P11	50
Chelmsford Ter. BD3	P11	50
Chelsea Clo. LS12	Y12	54
Chelsea Mans. HX3	H18	81
Chelsea Rd. BD7	K13	65
Chelsea St. BD21	B 4	7
Chelsea Vw. HX3	H18	81
Chelsfield Way LS15	JJ 9	41
Cheltenham Gdns. HX3	F21	94
Cheltenham Pl. HX3	F21	94
Cheltenham Rd. BD2	N 8	31
Cheltenham St. LS12	Y12	54
Chelwood Av. LS8	CC 5	20
Chelwood Cres. LS8	CC 6	20
Chelwood Dr. BD15	H11	46
Chelwood Dr. LS8	CC 5	20
Chelwood Gro. LS8	CC 5	20
Chelwood Mt. LS8	CC 5	20
Chelwood Pl. LS8	CC 5	20
Chenies Clo. LS14	FF10	58
Cherry Ct. LS9	CC10	56
Cherry Pl. LS9	CC10	56
Cherry Ri. LS14	HH 7	41
Cherry Row LS9	CC10	56
Cherry Tree Av. BD10	P 8	32
Cherry Tree Cres. LS28	S 9	33
Cherry Tree Dr. LS28	S 9	33
Cherry Tree Dr., Greet. HX4	E23	98
Cherry Tree Gdns. BD10	N 6	13
Cherry Tree Gro., Rod. LS13	T 9	34
Cherry Tree Ri. BD21	D 4	8
Cherry Tree Row BD15	E 7	27
Harden La.		
Cherrywood Clo. LS14	GG 6	22
Cherrywood Gdns. LS14	GG 6	22
Chesham St. BD7	M12	48
Chesney Av. LS10	BB13	74
Chester Clo. HX3	E18	80
Chester Ter.		
Chester Gro. HX3	E18	80
Chester St.		
Chester Pl. HX3	E18	80
Chester St.		
Chester Rd. HX3	E18	80
Chester St. BD7	N12	49
Chester St. HX3	E18	80
Chester Ter. HX3	E18	80
Chestnut Av. LS15	HH10	59
Chestnut Av. LS6	Z 9	37
Chestnut Clo., Greet. HX4	E23	98
Chestnut Ct. BD18	K 7	29
Chestnut Gro. BD2	M 9	30
Chestnut Gro. LS28	R 8	33
Clarke St.		
Chestnut St. BD16	G 4	10
Foster St.		
Chestnut St. BD3	P12	50
Chestnut St. HX1	D20	93
Chetwynd St. LS11	AA12	55
Chetwynd Ter. LS11	AA12	55
Meadow Rd.		
Chevet Mt. LS12	W10	53
Chevinedge Cres. HX3	F22	98
Cheyne Wk. BD21	B 4	7
Oakworth Rd.		
Chichester St. LS12	Y11	54
Chippendale Ri. BD8	J11	47
Chirton Gro. LS8	DD 8	39
Chiselhurst Pl. BD5	M13	66
Chiswick St. LS6	Z10	55
Burley Lodge Rd.		
Chiswick Ter. LS6	Z10	55
Burley Lodge Rd.		
Chrisharben Pk. BD14	J13	65
Christchurch Av. LS12	W10	53
Stanningley Rd.		
Christchurch Mt. LS12	W10	53
Stanningley Rd.		
Christchurch Par. LS12	X11	54
Moorfield Rd.		
Christchurch Rd. LS12	X11	54
Christchurch Ter. LS12	X11	54
Moorfield Rd.		
Christchurch Vw. LS12	W10	53
Stanningley Rd.		
Christiana Ter. LS12	X16	89
Christopher Rd. LS6	AA 9	37
Christopher St. BD5	M13	66
Christopher Ter. BD5	M13	66
Church Av. LS6	Z 7	37
Church Av., Gild. LS27	V15	71
Church Av., Hor. LS18	U 6	16
Church Bank BD1	N11	49
Church Bank HX2	C20	93
Church Bank, S.B. HX6	C21	93
Church Clo. HX2	C16	79
Church Clo. LS14	GG 9	40
Church Common Rd. HD2	O21	103
Church Cres. LS17	BB 5	20
Church Cres., Hor. LS18	U 6	16
Church Ct. BD7	K12	47
Church Ct. LS19	R 4	15
Church Farm Garth LS17	FF 5	22
Church Gate, Bram. LS16	V 1	2
Church Gate, Hor. LS18	U 6	16
Church Gdns. LS17	BB 5	20
Church Gdns. LS27	V15	71
Church Gro. LS6	Z 7	37
Church La.		
Church Gro., Hor. LS18	U 6	16
Church Hill BD17	M 5	12
Church Hill Gdns. LS28	T10	52
Church Hill Grn. LS28	T10	52
Church Hill Mt. LS28	T10	52
Church Hill Mt., Swi. LS13	T 9	34
Leeds & Bradford Rd.		
Church Hill Pl., Swi. LS13	T 9	34
Leeds & Bradford Rd.		
Church Hill St., Swi. LS13	T 9	34
Leeds & Bradford Rd.		
Church Hill Ter., Swi. LS13	T 9	34
Leeds & Bradford Rd.		
Church Hill, Bram. LS16	V 1	2
Church Hill, Thorner LS14	JJ 4	23
Church La. BD17	P 4	14
Church La. BD6	L15	66
St. Pauls Av.		
Church La. HD2	O21	103
Church La. HD6	L21	97
Church La. HD6	L22	101
Commercial St.		
Church La. HX2	D18	79
Church La. HX3	J21	96
Church La. HX5	J23	100
Church La. LS15	HH10	59
Church La. LS16	Y 5	18
Church La. LS19	P 4	14
Church La. LS2	BB11	56
Church La. LS28	S11	51
Church La. LS6	ZZ 7	37
Church La. LS7	BB 8	38
Church La., Hor. LS18	U 6	16
Church La., Southowram HX3	H21	95
Church Mt., Hor. LS18	U 6	16
Church Rd. BD6	L15	66
Church Rd. LS12	Y11	54
Church Rd. LS9	CC11	56
Church Row LS2	BB11	56
Kirkgate		
Church St. BD13	C 8	26
Church St. BD16	H 6	10
Church St. BD18	M 7	30
Church St. BD6	K15	65
Church St. BD8	L10	48
Church St. HX1	F20	94
Church St. HX5	K23	100
Church St. LS10	BB13	74
Church St. LS19	R 4	15
Church St. LS5	X 9	36
Church St. WF17	T18	87
Church St., Elland HX5	G23	99
Church St., Gild. LS27	UU15	70
Church St., Greet. HX3	F23	98
Church St., Mor. LS27	X16	89
Church St., Oakworth	YY 6	6
Church St., Oxenhope	ZZ10	42
Church St., Wood. LS26	HH15	77
Church Ter. HX2	C16	79
Church Vw. BD19	O19	103
Church Vw. LS5	X 9	36
Church Vw., Hor. LS18	U 6	16
Church Vw., S.B. HX6	C21	93
Church Vw., Thorner LS14	JJ 4	23
Church Wood Av. LS16	Y 8	36
Church Wood Mt. LS16	Y 7	36
Church Wood Rd. LS16	Y 8	36
Churchfield Pl. LS5	X 9	36
Church St.		
Churchfield Pl. LS6	AA 9	37
Holborn St.		

Street	Grid	Page
Churchfield St. LS6	AA 9	37
Institution St.		
Churchfield Ter. LS6	AA 9	37
Holborn St.		
Churchfields Rd. HD6	L21	97
Churchill Rd. LS2	AA10	55
Blenheim Wk.		
Churchill Rd. BD13	G12	46
Churn La. HX2	C19	93
Churn Milk La. HX3	E17	80
Churwell Bar LS11	Z13	73
Elland Rd.		
Churwell Ring Rd. LS11	Y14	72
Cinderhills La. HX3	G21	95
City La. HX3	D18	79
City Rd. BD8	M11	48
City Sq. LS1	AA11	55
Clapgate La. LS10	CC16	91
Clapham Dene Row LS15	GG10	58
Clapham St. BD13	D11	44
Clapton Av. HX1	E20	94
Clara Dr. LS28	Q 7	32
Clara Rd. BD2	N 8	31
Clare Cres. BD12	M18	83
Clare Rd. BD12	M18	83
Clare Rd. HX1	F20	94
Clare St. HX1	F20	94
Clare Vills. BD12	M18	83
Claremont Av. BD18	N 8	31
Claremont Av. LS3	AA10	55
Claremont BD7	M12	48
Claremont Cres. BD18	N 8	31
Claremont Cres. LS6	Z 8	37
Claremont Ct. LS6	Z 8	37
Claremont Dr. LS6	Z 8	37
Claremont Gdns. BD16	H 5	10
Claremont Gro. BD18	N 8	31
Claremont Pl. LS12	X11	54
Claremont Rd. HX3	F18	80
Claremont Rd. LS6	Z 8	37
Claremont St. LS12	X11	54
Claremont St., S.B. HD6	C20	93
Claremont Ter. LS12	X11	54
Claremont, Pud. LS28	T11	52
Claremount Gro. LS3	AA10	55
Claremount Av.		
Claremount Ter. HX3	F18	80
Claremount Rd.		
Claremount Vw. LS3	AA10	55
Claremount Av.		
Claremount Yd. LS10	CC13	74
Waterloo Rd.		
Clarence Dr., Hor. LS18	U 7	34
Clarence Gdns., Hor. LS18	U 7	34
Clarence Gro., Hor. LS18	U 7	34
Clarence Pl.	E20	94
Clarence Pl. HX1	E19	94
Clarence Rd. BD18	K 7	29
Clarence Rd. LS10	CC12	56
Clarence Rd., Hor. LS18	U 7	34
Clarence St. HX1	E19	94
Lister La.		
Clarence St. LS13	V10	53
Clarendon Pl. BD13	F15	63
Ladysmith Rd.		
Clarendon Pl. BD8	M11	48
Clarendon Pl. LS2	AA10	55
Clarendon Rd. BD16	H 5	10
Clarendon Rd. LS2	AA10	55
Clarendon St. BD21	B 4	7
Clarendon St. BD8	M11	48
Clarendon St., Haworth	ZZ 8	24
Clarendon Ter. BD8	M10	48
Clarendon Ter., Pud. LS28	T12	52
Clarges St. BD5	M13	66
Clark Av. LS9	CC11	56
Clark Ct. LS9	CC11	56
Clark La. LS9	CC12	56
Clark Mt. LS9	CC11	56
Pontefract La.		
Clark Rd. LS9	CC11	56
Clark Ter. LS9	CC11	56
Clark Vw. LS9	CC12	56
Clarke St. LS28	R 8	33
Clarkson Vw. LS6	AA 9	37
Clarksons Bldgs. LS6	AA 9	37
Woodhouse St.		
Claro Rd. LS6	AA 9	37
Servia Rd.		
Claro St. LS7	AA 9	37
Cambridge Rd.		
Claro Ter. LS7	AA 9	37
Cambridge Rd.		
Claro Vw. LS7	AA 9	37
Clay Brow, Haworth	ZZ 7	24
Spring Head La.		
Clay Hill Dr. BD12	M17	83
Clay La., Mor. LS27	Y17	89
Clay Pit La. LS2	BB10	56
Clay St., S.B. HX1	C20	93
Clay Ter., Mor. LS27	Y17	89
Clayfield Dr. BD5	L14	66
Clayfield Pl. LS7	BB 9	38
Clayhouse La., Greet.	D19	93
HX4		
Claypit La., Thorner LS14	JJ 4	23
Clayton Cft. LS10	CC14	74
Clayton Clo. LS10	CC14	74
Clayton Ct. LS16	W 7	35
Clayton Dr. LS10	CC14	74
Clayton Gra. LS16	W 7	35
Clayton La. BD14	H13	64
Clayton Rd. BD7	K13	65
Clayton Rd. LS10	CC14	74
Clayton St. BD1	M11	48
Clayton Way LS10	CC14	74
Clayton Wood Bank LS16	W 6	17
Clayton Wood Clo. LS16	W 6	17
Clayton Wood Rd. LS16	W 6	17
Clayton Wood Ri. LS16	W 6	17
Cleckheaton Rd. BD12	M16	83
Cleckheaton Rd. BD6	M16	83
Cleeve Hill LS19	R 5	15
Clement St. BD8	K11	47
Clement St. HX1	E19	94
Cleopatra Pl. LS13	V10	53
Cleopatra St. LS13	V10	53
Clervaux Ct. BD7	J12	47
Clevedon Pl. HX3	E18	80
Friendly Fold Rd.		
Cleveland Av. HX3	F21	94
Cleveland Rd. BD9	L 9	30
Cleveleys Av. LS11	Z13	73
Cleveleys Mt. LS11	Z13	73
Cleveleys Rd.		
Cleveleys Rd. LS11	Z13	73
Cleveleys St. LS11	Z13	73
Cleveleys Rd.		
Cleveleys Ter. LS11	Z13	73
Cleveleys Rd.		
Cliff Cotts BD3	Q11	50
Cliff Cres. HX2	D20	93
Cliff Gdns. HX2	D20	93
Cliff Hill La. HX2	B20	92
Cliff Hollins La. BD12	O17	84
Cliff Hollins La. BD4	O17	84
Cliff La. LS6	Z 9	37
Cliff Mt. LS6	AA 9	37
Cliff Mt. Ter. LS6	AA 9	37
Cliff Mount		
Cliff Pit St. LS6	AA 9	37
Cliff Pl. LS6	AA 9	37
Cliff Rd. LS6	AA 9	37
Cliff St., Haworth	ZZ 7	24
Cliff Ter. HD6	L22	101
Cliff Ter. LS6	AA 9	37
Cliff Ter., Hor. LS18	V 7	35
Cliff Vale Rd. BD18	L 8	30
Cliffdale Rd. LS7	AA 9	37
Cliffe Av. BD16	E 6	9
Cliffe Av. BD17	M 6	12
Cliffe Av. HX3	L19	97
Cliffe Dr. LS19	R 5	15
Cliffe Gdns. BD18	L 8	30
Cliffe La. BD13	G11	46
Cliffe La. BD17	M 6	12
Cliffe La. BD19	Q18	85
Cliffe La. LS19	S 6	15
Cliffe La. S. BD17	M 6	12
Cliffe La. W. BD17	M 6	12
Cliffe Mt. BD19	R18	86
Cliffe Park Chase LS12	X12	54
Cliffe Park Clo. LS12	X12	54
Cliffe Park Cres. LS12	X12	54
Cliffe Park Dr. LS12	W12	53
Cliffe Park Mt. LS12	X12	54
Cliffe Park Ri. LS12	W12	53
Cliffe Rd. BD3	N10	49
Cliffe Rd. HD6	L22	101
Bridge End St.		
Cliffe St. BD13	F11	45
Hill Top Rd.		
Cliffe Ter. BD17	M 6	12
Cliffe Ter. BD21	C 5	8
Cliffe Ter. BD8	M10	48
Cliffe Ter., S.B. HX3	B20	92
Cliffe Vw. BD15	H10	46
Cliffe Wood Av. BD18	L 8	30
Cliffe Wood Clo. BD9	K 9	29
Clifford Rd. BD17	M 6	12
Clifford St. BD5	N12	49
Clifton Av. HX1	D20	93
Clifton Av. LS9	DD10	57
Clifton Common HD6	M21	97
Clifton Dr., Pud. LS28	Y11	52
Clifton Gro. LS9	DD10	57
Clifton Hill, Pud. LS28	T11	52
Clifton Mt. LS9	DD10	57
Clifton Pl. BD18	L 8	30
Clifton Rd. HD6	L22	101
Clifton Rd. HX3	F21	94
Clifton Rd., Pud. LS28	T11	52
Clifton St. BD13	G14	64
Albert Rd.		
Clifton St. BD21	B 4	7
Clifton St. BD8	M10	48
Clifton St. HX3	E18	80
Wheatley La.		
Clifton St., S.B. HX6	C21	93
Clifton Ter. LS9	DD10	57
Clifton Vills. BD8	M10	48
Cliftonside HD2	N24	102
Clipston Av. LS6	Z 8	37
Clipston St. LS6	Z 8	37
Clipstone St. BD5	N14	67
Clive Pl. BD7	L12	48
Clive St. LS11	AA12	55
Clive Ter. BD7	L12	48
Cloberry St. LS2	AA10	55
Clock La. BD13	C10	44
Clogsole Rd. HD6	K21	96
Close Head Dr. BD13	E12	45
Close Lea	L22	101
Close Lea Av. HD6	K22	100
Close Lea Way HD6	K22	100
Close, The LS17	AA 4	19
Close, The LS9	CC11	56
Cloth Hall St. LS2	BB11	56
Call La.		
Clothier St. LS10	CC13	74
Waterloo Rd.		
Clough Bank	YY 4	6
Clough Bank HX2	B16	78
Clough Dr. WF17	U18	87
Clough Gate, Oakworth	ZZ 5	6
Clough La. HD6	K24	100
Clough La. HD6	M20	97
Clough La. HX2	B16	78
Clough La. HX3	J20	96
Clough La., Oakworth	ZZ 5	6
Clough Pl. HX2	B16	78
Clough St. BD5	N13	67
Clovelly Gro. LS11	AA13	73
Rowland Rd.		
Clovelly Pl. LS11	AA13	73
Rowland Rd.		
Clovelly Row LS11	AA13	73
Rowland Rd.		
Clovelly Ter. LS11	AA13	73
Clover Cres. LS28	R 7	33
Clover Ct. LS28	R 7	33
Clover Hill Clo.	E20	94
Clover Hill Rd. HX1	E20	94
Clover St. BD5	L13	66
Cloverhill Wk.	E20	94
Cloverville App. BD6	M15	66
Club La. HX2	D17	79
Club La., Rod. LS13	T 8	34
Club Row BD15	F 8	27
Club Row, Pud. LS28	T10	52
Richardshaw La.		
Club St. BD7	K12	47
Club Ter. LS5	X 9	36
Clyde App. LS12	Z12	55
Clyde Chase LS12	Z12	55
Clyde App.		
Clyde Gdns. LS12	Z12	55
Clyde St. BD16	G 5	10
Clyde St. HX3	B21	92
Boggart La.		
Clyde Vw. LS12	Z12	55
Clyde App.		
Clyde Wk. LS12	Z11	55
Co-op St., Mor. LS27	Y15	72
William St.		
Co-operative Bldgs. HX3	L19	97
Bradford Rd.		
Co-Operative Bldgs. LS27	V17	88
Coach La. BD13	G12	46
Coach Rd. BD17	L 6	12
Coach Rd. HD6	K19	96
Coach Rd. HX3	K20	96
Coal Hill Dr. LS13	T 9	34
Coal Hill Gdns. LS13	T 9	34
Coal Hill Grn. LS13	T 9	34
Coal Hill La., Rod. LS13	T 9	34
Coal Pit La. HD6	N22	102
Coal Rd. LS14	GG 7	40
Coal Rd., Sha. LS14	GG 5	22
Coal Staith Rd. LS10	BB12	56
Hunslet La.		
Coalpit La. HX3	G21	95
Coates Ter. BD5	M13	66

Name	Ref	Page
Cudworths Ct. LS1	BB11	56
Briggate		
Cullingworth Rd. BD13	C 8	26
Cullingworth Rd. BD15	C 8	26
Culver St. HX1	F19	94
Cumberland Av. HD2	L24	101
Cumberland Clo. HX2	D17	79
Cumberland Rd. BD7	L12	48
Cumberland Rd. LS6	Z 9	37
Cuncliffe Rd. BD8	M10	48
Cunliffe La. BD17	O 4	13
Cunliffe Ter. BD8	M10	48
Cunliffe Vills. BD8	M 9	30
Cure Hill, Oakworth	YY 5	6
Curlew St. BD5	M13	66
Currer Av. BD4	O14	67
Currer St. BD1	N11	49
Curzon Rd. BD3	O11	49
Curzon St. HD2	O24	102
Cutler Heights La. BD4	P13	68
Cutler Pl. BD4	P13	68
Cyprus Av. BD10	N 6	13
Cyprus Dr. BD10	O 6	13
Cyprus Mt. LS6	AA 9	37
Cyprus Pl. LS6	AA 9	37
Speedwell Mt.		
Czar St. LS11	AA12	55
Dacre St. BD3	N11	49
Daffil Av. LS27	X15	89
Daffil Gro. LS27	X15	89
Daffil Rd., Chur. LS27	X15	72
Daffil Row, Chur. LS27	X15	72
Dagenham Rd. BD4	P13	68
Dairy St. LS6	AA 9	37
Daisy Bank HX1	E20	94
Daisy Clo. WF17	T18	87
Daisy Cres. LS9	CC10	56
Lincoln Rd.		
Daisy Hill Back La. BD9	K10	47
Daisy Hill BD12	M17	83
Temperance Field		
Daisy Hill Gro. BD9	K10	47
Daisy Hill La. BD9	K10	47
Daisy Hill, Mor. LS27	Y16	89
Daisy Mt. LS9	CC10	56
Daisy Mt., S.B.	B20	92
Daisy Pl. BD18	K 7	29
Saltaire Rd.		
Daisy Rd. HD6	L22	101
Daisy St. BD7	L13	66
Daisy St. HD6	L22	101
Bridge Rd.		
Daisy St. HX1	E20	94
Hopwood La.		
Daisy St., Haworth	A 7	25
Daisy Vw. LS9	CC10	56
Lincoln Rd.		
Daisyfield LS13	V10	53
Daisyhill Av. LS27	Y16	89
Daisyhill Clo. LS27	X16	89
Dalby Av. BD3	P10	50
Dalby St. BD3	P11	50
Dalcross Gro. BD5	N13	67
Dalcross St. BD5	N13	67
Dale Croft Ri. BD15	G10	46
Dale Garth BD17	L 5	12
Summerfield Dr.		
Dale Gro. BD10	N 7	31
Dale Park Av. LS16	V 5	17
Dale Park Clo. LS16	V 5	17
Dale Park Gate LS16	V 5	17
Dale Park Ri. LS16	V 5	17
Dale Park Vw. LS16	V 5	17
Dale Park Wk. LS16	V 5	17
Dale Rd. Dr. BD4	U14	70
Dale St. BD1	N11	49
Dale St. BD18	L 7	30
Dale St., S.B. HX6	B21	92
Dale View Clo. BD21	D 4	8
Dale View Gro. BD21	D 4	8
Dale View Rd. BD21	D 4	8
Daleside Av. LS28	Q11	50
Daleside Clo. LS28	Q10	50
Daleside Gro. BD12	N17	84
Daleside Gro. LS28	P11	50
Daleside HX4	E23	98
Daleside Rd. BD18	N 7	31
Daleside Rd. LS28	Q11	50
Daleside Wk. BD5	N14	67
Daleson Clo. HX3	H17	81
Dallam Av. BD18	K 7	29
Dallam Gro. BD18	K 7	29
Dallam Rd. BD18	K 7	29
Dallam St. BD2	O10	49
Dallam Wk. BD18	K 7	29
Dalmeny Pl. LS4	Y10	54
Kirkstall Rd.		

Name	Ref	Page
Dalmeny St. LS4	Y10	54
Kirkstall Rd.		
Dalton Av. LS11	AA14	73
Dalton Gro. LS11	AA14	73
Dalton Rd. LS11	AA14	73
Dalton St., S.B. HX6	B20	92
Dalton Ter. BD8	L11	48
Dam Head Rd. HX3	C20	93
Dam Head Rd., S.B.	C20	93
Damask St. HX1	E19	94
Damems La.	A 6	7
Damems La. BD21	B 6	7
Damems La. BD22	B 6	7
Damems Rd. BD21	B 6	7
Damon Av. BD10	Q 9	32
Damside BD21	B 4	7
Dan La. BD13	J14	65
Danby Av. BD4	O15	67
Danby Wk. LS9	CC11	56
Dane Hill Dr. BD4	Q13	68
Danebury Rd. HD6	M22	101
Danecourt Rd. BD4	Q13	68
Daniel St. BD3	P11	50
Killinghall Rd.		
Danube Gro. LS12	Z12	55
Gelderd Rd.		
Danube Rd. LS12	Z12	55
Gelderd Rd.		
Danube St. LS12	Z12	55
Danum Dr. BD17	M 6	12
Darcey Hey La. HX1	D20	94
Darcy Ct. LS15	HH11	59
Darfield Av. LS8	DD 9	39
Darfield Cres. LS8	DD 9	39
Darfield Gro. LS8	CC 9	38
Harehills Pl.		
Darfield Pl. LS8	DD 9	39
Darfield Rd. LS8	DD 9	39
Darfield St. BD1	M11	48
Darfield St. LS8	DD 9	39
Dargai St. LS7	BB 9	38
Dark Clo. BD11	T16	87
Dark La. HX3	H19	95
Dark La. WF17	T17	87
Dark La., Oxenhope	ZZ 9	24
Dark La., Southowram HX3	H21	95
Dark La., Warley HX6	B20	92
Darkwood Clo. LS17	DD 5	21
Darkwood Way LS17	DD 5	21
Darley Av. LS10	BB15	91
Darley St. BD1	N11	49
Darley St. HX1	F19	94
Darnay La. BD5	N13	67
Mumford St.		
Darnes Av. HX2	D20	93
Darnley La. LS15	HH11	59
Darnley Rd. LS16	X 7	36
Darren St. BD4	Q12	50
Dartmouth St. LS11	BB13	74
Dartmouth Ter. BD8	M10	48
Darwin St. BD5	M13	66
Dastler Rd. LS28	R 8	33
David St. LS11	AA12	55
Davies Av. LS8	CC 7	38
Dawlish Av. LS9	DD11	57
Dawlish Cres. LS9	DD11	57
Dawlish Gro. LS9	DD11	57
Dawlish Mt. LS9	DD11	57
Dawlish Pl. LS9	DD11	57
Dawlish Row LS9	DD11	57
Dawlish St. LS9	DD11	57
Dawlish Ter. LS9	DD11	57
Dawnay Rd. BD7	L13	66
Dawson Av. BD6	M15	66
Dawson Hill, Mor. LS27	X16	89
Dawson La. BD4	P14	68
Dawson La., Tong. BD4	T14	70
Dawson Mt. BD4	P14	68
Dawson Pl. BD21	C 4	8
Dawson Rd. BD4	P14	68
Dawson La.		
Dawson Rd. BD21	C 4	8
Dawson Rd. LS11	AA13	73
Dawson St. BD10	O 6	13
Dawson St. BD4	P14	68
Dawson St., Pud. LS28	T10	52
Sunfield		
Dawson Ter. BD4	P14	68
Dawson Way BD21	C 4	8
Dawsons Corner LS28	S10	51
Dawsons Meadow LS28	S10	51
De Gray St. LS2	AA 9	37
Woodhouse La.		
De Lacey Ms. BD4	P14	68
De Lacy Av. BD4	O15	67
De Lacy Mt. LS5	X 9	36
Deal St. HX1	F20	94

Name	Ref	Page
Dealburn Rd. BD12	M16	83
Dean Av. LS8	DD 8	39
Dean Beck Av. BD6	N14	67
Dean Beck Ct. BD6	N14	67
Dean Clo. BD8	J10	47
Dean Clo., Elland HX5	G24	99
Dean Cres. BD13	G15	64
Dean Ct. HX3	E22	98
St. Stephens St.		
Dean Ct. LS8	DD 8	39
Dean End, Greet.	F23	98
Dean Hall Clo., Mor. LS27	W17	88
Dean Head, Yea. LS18	U 3	1
Dean Holme La. HX2	A17	78
Dean La.	YY 4	6
Dean La. BD13	F10	45
Dean La., S.B.	A21	92
Dean La., Yea. LS18	U 2	1
Dean Ms., Yea. LS18	U 3	1
Dean Park Avenue Dr. BD4	T15	70
Dean Park Dr. BD4	T15	70
Dean Park Est. BD11	S15	69
Dean Rd. BD6	M15	66
Dean St. HX1	E19	94
Dean St. LS3	Y10	54
Kirkstall Rd.		
Dean St., Greet. HX4	F23	98
Dean St., Haworth	ZZ 8	24
Deanary Gdns. BD2	P 8	32
Deane, The LS15	EE12	57
Deanfield Av., Mor. LS27	W16	88
Deanhurst Gdns., Mor. LS27	V16	88
Deans Ter. HX3	F17	80
Deans Way, Mor. LS27	W16	88
Deanstones La. BD13	F15	63
Deanswood Clo. LS17	AA 5	19
Deanswood Dr. LS17	Z 5	19
Deanswood Garth LS17	AA 5	19
Deanswood Gdns. LS17	Z 5	19
Deanswood Grn. LS17	Z 5	19
Deanswood Hill LS17	Z 5	19
Deanswood Pl. LS17	AA 5	19
Deanswood Ri. LS17	Z 5	19
Deanswood Vw. LS17	AA 5	19
Deanwood Av. BD15	H 9	28
Deanwood Cres. BD15	H 9	28
Deanwood Wk. BD15	H 9	28
Dearden St., S.B. HX6	B20	92
Deep La. BD13	E13	63
Deep La. BD14	J12	47
Deepdale Clo. BD17	L 6	12
Delamere St. BD5	M14	66
Delf Hill HD6	K23	100
Delius Av. BD10	Q 8	32
Delph Cres. BD14	H13	64
Delph Dr. BD14	H13	64
Delph End LS28	R11	51
Gibraltar Rd.		
Delph Gro. BD14	H13	64
Delph Hill BD17	M 5	12
Delph Hill, Pud. LS28	T11	52
Delph La. LS6	AA 9	37
Delph Mt. LS6	AA 9	37
Delph St. HX1	E20	94
Delph St. LS12	AA 9	37
Woodhouse St.		
Delph Ter. BD14	H13	64
Delph Ter. LS6	AA 9	37
Woodhouse Cliff		
Delph Vw. LS6	AA 9	37
Delph La.		
Delphi St. LS3	Z11	55
Delverne Gro. BD2	P 9	32
Denbigh App. LS9	EE10	57
Denbrook Av. BD10	Q15	68
Denbrook Clo. BD4	Q14	68
Denbrook Cres. BD4	Q15	68
Denbrook Way BD4	Q14	68
Denbrook Wk. BD4	Q14	68
Denbury Mt. BD4	Q14	68
Denby Clo. WF17	S18	86
Denby Ct., Oakworth	YY 6	6
Tim La.		
Denby Dr. BD17	L 6	12
Denby La. BD15	H10	46
Denby Mt., Oxenhope	ZZ10	42
Denby Rd. BD21	C 4	8
Denby St. BD8	M11	48
Dence Grn. BD4	Q12	50
Dence Cres. BD7	K13	65
Dene Hill BD17	K 5	11
Dene Mt. BD15	J10	47

Street	Ref	Page
Dene Pl. HX1	E19	94
Dene Rd. BD6	J14	65
Dene Way LS28	S10	51
Denehill BD9	J10	47
Deneside BD5	M14	66
Deneside Ter. BD5	M14	66
Denfield Av. HX3	D18	79
Denfield Cres. HX3	D18	79
Denfield Edge HX3	D18	79
Denfield Gdns. HX3	D18	79
Denfield La. HX3	D18	79
Denfield Sq. HX3	D18	79
Denholme Rd., Oxenhope	A10	43
Denison Rd. LS3	AA11	55
Dennil Cres. LS15	HH 9	41
Dennil Rd. LS15	HH 9	41
Dennis Ct. HX1	E19	94
Dennison Fold BD4	Q12	50
Dennison St. BD3	N10	49
Dennistead Cres. LS6	Y 8	36
Denshaw Dr., Mor. LS27	Y17	89
Denshaw Gro., Mor. LS27	Y17	89
Dent St. LS9	CC11	56
Denton Av. LS8	CC 7	38
Denton Gro. LS8	CC 7	38
Denton Row LS12	X11	54
Derby Rd. BD3	Q11	50
Derby Rd. LS19	P 5	14
Derby St. BD13	F14	63
Derby St. BD14	H13	64
Derby St. BD16	G 5	10
Hillside Rd.		
Derby St. BD7	L13	66
Derby St. HX3	E18	80
Rawson St. N.		
Derby Ter. BD10	Q 7	32
Derry St. BD10	O 7	31
Derwent Av. BD15	F 9	27
Derwent Av. BD17	K 6	11
Derwent Av. LS11	AA12	55
Derwent Dr. LS16	Y 5	18
Derwent Gro. LS11	AA12	55
Bath Rd.		
Derwent Pl. BD13	F1 4	63
Mill La.		
Derwent Rd. BD2	O 9	31
Derwent St. LS11	AA12	55
Derwent Ter. LS11	AA12	55
Derwent Pl.		
Derwent Vw. LS11	AA12	55
Marshall St.		
Derwentwater Gro. LS6	Y 9	36
Derwentwater Ter. LS6	Y 8	36
Detroit Av. LS15	HH11	59
Detroit Dr. LS15	HH11	59
Devon Mt. LS2	AA 9	37
Servia Hill		
Devon Rd. LS2	AA10	55
Devon St. HX1	D20	93
Devon Way HD6	L20	97
Devonshire Av. LS8	DD 6	21
Devonshire Cres. LS8	DD 6	21
Devonshire La. LS8	DD 6	21
Devonshire Ter. BD9	M10	48
St. Marys Rd.		
Devonshires, The LS8	DD 6	21
Dewhirst Pl. BD4	P12	50
Dewhirst Rd. BD17	N 6	13
Dewhirst St. BD15	F 8	27
Main St.		
Dewhirsts Bldgs., Elland HX5	G23	99
Dewhurst Clo. BD17	M 6	12
Dewhurst Rd. HD6	L21	97
Dewsbury Pl. LS11	Z15	73
Dewsbury Rd.		
Dewsbury Rd. BD19	R17	86
Dewsbury Rd. LS11	Z15	73
Dewsbury Rd. LS11	BB12	56
Dewsbury Rd., Elland HX5	H24	99
Dewsbury Ter. LS11	Z15	73
Dewsbury Rd.		
Diadem Dr. LS14	FF10	58
Dial Lawn LS6	AA 9	37
Rampart Rd.		
Dial Row LS6	AA 9	37
Dial St. LS9	CC11	56
Diamond St. BD1	N12	49
Diamond St. BD21	B 5	7
Diamond St. HX1	E19	94
Dib Clo. LS8	EE 8	39
Dib La. LS8	EE 8	39
Dick La. BD3	Q11	50
Dick La. BD4	Q11	50
Dickens St. BD5	N13	67
Dickens St. HX2	D19	93
Dickinsons Ct. LS1	AA11	55
Boar La.		
Dimples La., Haworth	YY 7	24
Dinsdale Ter. LS11	AA13	73
South Ridge St.		
Dirkhill Rd. BD7	M12	48
Dispensary Wk. HX1	F19	94
Disraeli Gdns. LS11	AA13	73
Disraeli Ter. LS11	AA13	73
Ditchfield Pl. BD10	O 7	31
Bradford Rd.		
Dixon Av. BD7	K12	47
Dixon La. LS12	Y12	54
Dixon Lane Rd. LS12	Y12	54
Dobson Av. LS11	BB13	74
Dobson Gro. LS11	BB13	74
Dobson Pl. LS11	BB13	74
Dobson St. BD16	H 5	10
Staveley Rd.		
Dobson Ter. LS11	BB13	74
Dobson Vw. LS11	BB13	74
Dock La. BD17	M 7	30
Dock La. BD18	M 7	30
Dock St. LS10	BB11	56
Dockfield Pl. BD10	M 7	30
Dockfield Rd. BD17	M 7	30
Dockfield Ter. BD17	M 7	30
Doctor Hill BD10	O 8	31
Doctor Hill HX2	D18	79
Doctor La. BD10	O 6	13
Dodge Holme Ct. HX2	C17	79
Dodge Holme Dr. HX2	C17	79
Dodge Holme Gdns. HX2	C17	79
Dodge Holme Rd. HX2	C17	79
Dodgson Av. LS7	CC 9	38
Hamilton Ter.		
Dodgson St., Elland HX5	G24	99
Dodsworth Ct. LS1	BB11	56
Briggate		
Dogkennel La. HX3	G20	95
Dole St. BD13	G12	46
Doles La. HD2	N21	103
Dolfin Pl. HD2	N24	102
Doll La. BD13	D 8	26
Dolly La. LS9	CC10	56
Dolphin La. BD3	D 7	26
Dolphin Rd. LS10	CC16	91
Dolphin Ter. BD13	F15	63
Dombey St. HX1	E19	94
Francis St.		
Domestic Gro. LS11	Z12	55
Domestic Rd.		
Domestic Pl. LS11	Z12	55
Domestic Rd.		
Domestic Rd. LS12	Z12	55
Domestic St. LS11	Z12	55
Domestic Ter. LS11	Z12	55
Domestic St.		
Domestic Vw. LS11	Z12	55
Domestic St.		
Dominion Av. LS7	BB 8	38
Donald Av. BD6	M15	66
Donald St. LS28	S10	51
Doncaster St. HX3	F21	94
Donisthorpe St. BD5	M13	66
Donisthorpe St. LS10	CC12	56
Dorchester Cres. BD17	N 5	13
Dorchester Cres. BD4	Q14	68
Dorchester Dr. HX2	D20	93
Dorchester Ter. LS19	S 4	15
Dorchester Rd. HD2	L24	101
Dorian Clo. BD10	P 8	32
Doris Clo. BD13	F15	63
Dorothy St. BD21	B 5	7
Dorset Av. LS8	DD 9	39
Dorset Clo. BD5	M13	66
Dorset Gro., Pud. LS28	T11	52
Dorset Mt. LS8	DD 9	39
Dorset Rd. LS8	DD 9	39
Dorset St. BD5	M13	66
Dorset Ter. LS8	DD 9	39
Dortmund Sq. LS1	BB11	56
The Headrow		
Douglas Cres. BD18	M 8	30
Douglas Dr. BD4	P13	68
Douglas Rd. BD4	P13	68
Douglas St. BD3	P11	50
Leeds Old Rd.		
Douglas St. HX3	E18	80
Crown Rd.		
Douglas St. LS11	BB12	56
Dove St. BD18	K 7	29
Dove St., Haworth	ZZ 7	24
Dovedale Clo. HX3	H16	82
Dovedale Garth LS15	JJ 9	41
Dovedale Gdns. LS15	JJ 9	41
Dover St. BD3	N10	49
Dover St. HX3	F19	94
Dovesdale BD5	M14	66
Dovesdale Gro. BD5	M14	66
Dovesdale Rd. BD5	M14	66
Dow St. LS11	BB12	56
Dowker St. HX1	D20	93
Fenton Rd.		
Dowley Cap La. BD16	H 6	10
Downham St. BD3	O12	49
Downside Cres. BD15	H10	46
Dracup Av. BD7	K12	47
Dracup Rd. BD7	K13	65
Dragon Cres. LS12	Y12	54
Dragon Dr. LS12	Y12	54
Dragon Rd. LS12	Y12	54
Drake La. BD11	T16	87
Drake St. BD1	N12	49
Drake St. HX3	E18	80
Rawson St. N.		
Draughton Gro. BD5	M14	66
Draycott Wk. BD4	Q14	68
Dresser St. LS10	BB12	56
Drewton St. BD1	M11	48
Driffield Pl. LS1	AA10	55
Willow Ter.		
Driftholme Road Dr. BD4	T15	70
Drill Par. BD8	M10	48
Drive, The BD10	P 8	32
Drive, The BD16	G 4	10
Drive, The HX3	J19	96
Drive, The LS15	HH10	59
Drive, The LS16	X 5	18
Drive, The LS17	Z 4	19
Drive, The LS9	CC11	56
Driver Pl. LS12	Z12	55
Wellington Rd.		
Driver St. LS12	Z12	55
Wellington Rd.		
Driver Ter. LS12	Z12	55
Wellington Rd.		
Drub La. BD19	Q18	85
Druids St. BD14	H13	64
Drummond Av. LS16	Y 8	36
Drummond Ct. LS16	Y 8	36
Drummond Rd. BD8	M10	48
Drummond Rd. LS16	Y 7	36
Drury Av., Hor. LS18	U 7	34
Drury Clo., Hor. LS18	U 7	34
Drury La., Hor. LS18	U 7	34
Drury Pl. LS12	Y11	54
Parliament Ter.		
Drury St. LS12	Y11	54
Parliament Ter.		
Drury Ter. LS12	Y11	54
Parliament Ter.		
Dry Clough La. HX3	F21	94
Dryclough Clo. HX3	F21	94
Dryden St. BD1	N12	49
Dryden St. BD16	G 5	10
Dubb La. BD16	H 5	10
Duce Row LS12	Z12	55
Spence La.		
Duchy Av. BD9	K 9	29
Duchy Cres. BD9	K 9	29
Duchy Dr. BD9	K 9	29
Duchy Gro. BD9	K 9	29
Duchy Villas BD9	K 9	29
Ducie St. BD10	O 6	13
Ducketts Gro. LS28	Q11	50
Duckworth Gro. BD9	K10	47
Duckworth La. BD9	K10	47
Duckworth Ter. BD9	K10	47
Dudley Av. WF17	U18	87
Dudley Gro. BD4	Q12	50
Dudley Hill Rd. BD2	O 9	31
Dudley St., Dudley Hill BD4	P14	68
Dudley St., East Bowling BD4	O13	67
Dudley St., Tyersal BD4	Q12	50
Dudley Ter. LS11	AA13	73
Lady Pit St.		
Dudwell Av. HX3	F22	98
Dudwell Gro. HX3	F22	98
Dudwell La. HX3	F22	98
Dufton App. LS14	GG 9	40
Duinen St. BD5	N12	49
Duke St. BD1	N11	49
Duke St. LS9	BB11	56
Duke St., Elland HX5	G24	99
Dulverton Clo. LS11	Y14	72
Dulverton Cres. LS11	Y14	72
Dulverton Gate LS11	Y14	72
Dulverton Gdns. LS11	Y14	72
Dulverton Grn. LS11	Y14	72
Dulverton Gro. BD4	P13	68
Dulverton Gro. LS11	Y14	72
Dulverton Pl. LS11	Y14	72
Dulverton Rd. LS11	Y14	72
Dulverton Sq. LS11	Y14	72

Name	Grid	Page
Dulverton Wk. LS11	Y14	72
Duncan St. BD5	N12	49
Duncan St. LS1	BB11	56
Dunce Park Clo., Elland HX5	G24	99
Duncombe St. BD8	K11	47
Duncombe St. BD8	L11	48
Duncombe St. LS1	AA11	55
Duncombe Way BD8	L11	48
Dundas St. BD21	C 4	8
Park Wood St.		
Dundas St. HX1	D20	93
Dunderdales Yd. LS12	Z12	55
Spence La.		
Dunhill Cres. LS9	FF11	58
Dunhill Ri. LS15	AA11	55
Selby Rd.		
Dunhill Ri. LS9	FF11	58
Dunkirk Cres. HX1	D20	93
Dunkirk Gdns. HX1	D20	93
Dunkirk La. HX1	D20	93
Dunkirk St. HX1	D20	93
Dunkirk Ter. HX1	D20	93
Dunningley La., Mor. LS27	Z17	90
Dunnington Wk. BD6	L16	83
Dunsford Av. BD4	O15	67
Dunstarn Dr. LS16	Z 5	19
Dunstarn Gdns. LS16	Y 5	18
Dunstarn La. LS16	Y 6	18
Dunsworth St. BD4	O13	67
Durban Av. LS11	Z14	73
Durban Cres. LS11	Z14	73
Durham Rd. BD8	L10	48
Durham St. HX2	D19	93
Albert Rd.		
Durham Ter. BD8	L10	48
Durkheim Ct. BD3	P12	50
Amberley St.		
Durleston Gro. BD12	M17	83
Durleston Ter. BD12	M17	83
Durley Av. BD9	L 9	30
Durrance St., Keighley	A 4	7
Dutton Grn. LS14	GG 7	40
Duxbury Ri. LS7	AA10	55
Dyehouse Fold BD12	N16	84
Dyehouse La., Brig.	M22	101
Dyehouse La., Pud. LS28	S13	69
Dyehouse Rd. BD12	N16	84
Dyer La. HX3	D18	79
Dyer St. LS2	BB11	56
Dyson Rd. HX1	D19	93
Dyson St. BD1	M11	48
Dyson St. BD9	L 9	30
Dyson St. HD6	L21	97
Eagle St., Haworth	A 7	25
Eaglesfield Dr. BD6	K16	82
Earl St. HX3	F19	94
Earl St., Haworth	ZZ 8	24
Ivy Bank La.		
Earl Ter. HX3	E18	80
Friendly Fold Rd.		
Earlswood Av. LS8	CC 6	20
Easby Rd. BD7	M12	48
Easdale Clo. LS14	FF 9	40
Easdale Cres. LS14	GG 8	40
Easdale Mt. LS14	FF 9	40
Easdale Rd. LS14	FF 9	40
East Causeway Cres. LS16	Z 5	19
East Causeway LS16	Y 4	18
East Causeway Vale LS16	Z 5	19
East End LS12	V13	71
Forge Row		
East Fountains HX2	C15	62
East Grange Clo. LS10	CC14	74
East Grange Dr. LS10	CC14	74
East Grange Garth LS10	CC14	74
East Grange Rd. LS10	CC14	74
East Grange Ri. LS10	CC14	74
East Grange Sq. LS10	CC14	74
East Grange Vw. LS10	CC14	74
East La. LS2	BB11	56
East Moor Av. LS8	CC 6	20
East Moor Cres. LS8	CC 6	20
East Moor Dr. LS8	DD 6	21
East Moor Rd. LS8	CC 6	20
East Par. BD1	N11	49
East Par. BD17	M 5	12
East Par. LS1	AA11	55
East Par., S.B. HX6	C20	93
East Park Dr. LS9	CC11	56
East Park Gro. LS9	DD11	57
East Park Mt. LS9	DD11	57
East Park Par. LS9	DD11	57
East Park Pl. LS9	DD11	57
East Park Rd. HX3	E18	80
East Park Rd. LS9	CC11	56
East Park St. LS9	DD11	57
East Park St., Mor. LS27	W17	88
East Park Ter. LS9	DD11	57
East Park Rd.		
East Park Vw. LS9	DD11	57
East Rd. BD12	N16	84
East Row LS12	W10	53
Armley Grange Av.		
East Royd HX3	J18	82
East Royd, Oakworth	ZZ 6	6
East Side Ct. LS28	U12	52
East Squire La. BD8	M10	48
East St. HD6	L22	101
East St. HX3	L19	97
East St. LS28	S 9	33
East St. LS9	BB11	56
East Ter., Haworth	A 7	25
East View Rd. LS19	S 4	15
East View St. HX3	L19	97
East View Ter. BD12	M17	83
East Vw. BD13	J14	65
East Vw. LS19	S 4	15
East Vw., Mor. LS27	Y15	72
Elland Rd.		
East Vw., Pud. LS28	T11	52
East Vw., Queens. BD13	F14	63
East Water La. LS9	BB11	56
East Wood Av. HX6	A21	92
East Wood St. HD6	L21	97
Eastbourne Rd. BD9	L 8	30
Eastbrook La. BD1	N12	49
Eastbury Av. BD6	J14	65
Eastdean Bank LS14	GG 8	40
Eastdean Dr. LS14	GG 8	40
Eastdean Gate LS14	GG 8	40
Eastdean Gdns. LS14	GG 8	40
Eastdean Gro. LS14	GG 8	40
Eastdean Rd. LS14	GG 8	40
Eastdean Ri. LS14	GG 8	40
Easterly Av. LS8	DD 9	39
Easterly Clo. LS8	DD 9	39
Easterly Cres. LS8	DD 9	39
Easterly Cross LS8	DD 9	39
Easterly Garth LS8	DD 9	39
Easterly Gro. LS8	DD 9	39
Easterly Mt. LS8	DD 9	39
Easterly Rd. LS8	FF 8	40
Easterly Sq. LS8	DD 9	39
Easterly Vw. LS8	DD 9	39
Eastfield Gdns. BD4	Q13	68
Eastfield St. LS9	CC11	56
Eastgate LS16	V 1	2
Breary La.		
Eastgate LS2	BB11	56
Eastgate, Bram. LS16	V 1	2
Eastgate, Elland HX5	G23	99
Easthorpe Ct. BD2	P 9	32
Eastleigh Gro. BD5	M13	66
Eastwood Av. HX2	D15	62
Eastwood Clo. HX2	D15	62
Eastwood Cres. BD16	H 7	28
Eastwood Cres. LS14	HH 9	41
Eastwood Dr. LS14	HH 8	41
Eastwood Garth LS14	HH 9	41
Eastwood Gdns. LS14	HH 9	41
Eastwood Gro. HX2	D15	62
Eastwood La. LS14	HH 9	41
Eastwood Nook LS14	HH 9	41
Eastwood St. BD4	N12	49
Eastwood St. HX3	E18	80
Turney St.		
Eastwood St. LS7	BB10	56
Cross Stamford St.		
Easy Rd. LS9	CC12	56
Eaton Hill LS16	W 5	17
Eaton St. BD21	B 5	7
Queens Rd.		
Ebberston Gro. LS6	Z 9	37
Ebberston Pl. LS6	Z 9	37
Ebenezer Pl. BD7	L13	66
Ebenezer Pl. LS12	Y11	54
Amberley Rd.		
Ebenezer Pl. LS13	V10	53
Lower Town St.		
Ebenezer St. BD1	N12	49
Ebenezer St. BD4	P12	50
Ebenezer St. LS2	BB11	56
Harewood St.		
Ebenezer St. LS28	S 9	33
Well St.		
Ebor La., Haworth	ZZ 7	24
Ebor Mt. LS6	Z10	55
Ebor Pl. LS6	Z10	55
Ebor Ter. LS10	CC14	74
Eboracum St. BD21	B 4	7
Aireworth St.		
Eccles Ct. BD2	O 9	31
Ecclesburn Av. LS9	DD11	57
Ecclesburn Rd. LS9	DD11	57
Ecclesburn St. LS9	DD11	57
Ecclesburn Ter. LS9	DD11	57
Ecclesburn St.		
Eccup La., Eccup LS16	AA 1	4
Eccup La., Eccup LS16	Z 2	4
Eccup La., Eccup LS16	Y 4	18
Eccup Moor Rd. LS16	Z 3	4
Ed. St., Brig.	L21	97
Edale Way LS16	W 5	17
Edderthorpe St. BD3	O12	49
Eddison Clo. LS16	Y 4	18
Eddison St. LS28	S10	51
Eddison Wk. LS16	Y 4	18
Eden Clo. BD12	M17	83
Eden Cres. LS4	X 9	36
Eden Dr. LS4	X 9	36
Eden Gdns. LS4	Y 9	36
Eden Gro. LS4	X 9	36
Eden Mt. LS4	X 9	36
Eden Rd. LS4	X 9	36
Eden Way LS4	X 9	36
Eden Wk. LS4	X 9	36
Ederoyd Av. LS28	R10	51
Ederoyd Cres. LS28	P10	50
Ederoyd Dr. LS28	R10	51
Ederoyd Gro. LS28	R10	51
Ederoyd Mt. LS28	R10	51
Ederoyd Ri. LS28	R10	51
Edgar St. BD14	J13	65
Edgbaston Clo. LS17	AA 4	19
Edgbaston Wk. LS17	AA 4	19
Edge Bottom BD13	C10	44
Edge End Gdns. BD6	K15	65
Edge End Rd. BD6	K15	65
Edgebank Av. BD6	K16	82
Edgehill Clo. BD13	G14	64
Edgeholme La. HX2	B19	92
Edgemoor Clo. HX3	E21	94
Edgerton Rd. LS16	X 7	36
Edgware Av. LS8	CC 9	38
Bayswater Rd.		
Edgware Gro. LS8	CC 9	38
Bayswater Rd.		
Edgware Mt. LS8	CC 9	38
Bayswater Rd.		
Edgware Pl. LS8	CC10	56
Edgware Row LS8	CC10	56
Edgware St. LS8	CC10	56
Edgware Ter. LS8	CC 9	38
Bayswater Rd.		
Edgware Vw. LS8	CC10	56
Edinburgh Av. LS12	X11	54
Edinburgh Gro. LS12	X11	54
Edinburgh Pl. LS12	X11	54
Edinburgh Rd. LS12	X11	54
Edinburgh St. BD7	M11	48
Edinburgh Ter. LS12	X11	54
Edith Ter. LS12	Y12	54
Ayrton St.		
Edith Ter. LS7	BB10	56
Bristol St.		
Edlington Clo. BD4	Q13	68
Edmonson St. BD6	M14	66
Prospect St.		
Edmonton Pl. LS7	BB 8	38
Montreal Av.		
Edmund St. BD6	M12	48
Education Rd. LS7	BB 9	38
Edward Rd. BD16	H 5	10
Edward St. BD18	K 7	29
Edward St. BD4	N12	49
Edward St. BD4	P14	68
Edward St. HD6	M21	97
Albert St.		
Edward St. LS2	BB11	56
Edward St., Hal. HD6	E20	94
Edward St., S.B. HX6	B21	92
Edward Turner Clo. BD12	M16	83
Edwards Rd. HX2	D20	93
Edwin Rd. LS6	Z10	55
Effingham Rd. BD16	E 6	9
Egbert St. BD1	N12	49
Egerton Gro. BD15	H10	46
Egerton St. HX6	B21	92
Wallis St.		
Eggleston St., Rod. LS13	T 8	34
Egglestone Dr. BD4	Q14	68
Egremont Cres. BD6	K16	82
Egremont St., S.B. HX6	B21	92
Egypt BD19	Q18	85
Egypt Rd. BD13	F11	45
Eighth Av. LS12	Z12	55
Eighth Av., Roth. LS26	GG15	76
Eightlands Av. LS13	V10	53
Eightlands La. LS13	V10	53

Elan St., Pud. LS28 T10 52
Cavendish Pl.
Elbow La. BD2 O10 49
Northcote Rd.
Elbow La. HX2 A18 78
Elder Bank BD13 C 8 26
Station Rd.
Elder Cft. LS13 V10 53
Elder Mt. LS13 V10 53
Cleopatra Pl.
Elder Pl. LS12 W10 53
Stanningley Rd.
Elder Rd. HD2 O24 102
Elder Rd. LS13 V10 53
Elder St. BD10 Q 7 32
Elder St. LS13 V10 53
Cleopatra Pl.
Elder Ter. LS13 V10 53
Eldon Pl. BD1 M11 48
Eldon Pl. BD4 P13 68
Eldon St. BD16 H 5 10
Ferrand St.
Eldon St. HX3 F19 94
Eldon Ter. BD1 M11 48
Eldon Ter. LS2 AA10 55
Blenheim Wk.
Eldroth Mt. HX1 E20 94
Eldroth Rd.
Eldroth Rd. HX1 E20 94
Eleanor Dr. LS28 Q 7 32
Eleventh Av. LS12 Z12 55
Eighth Av.
Elford Gro. LS8 CC 9 38
Elford Pl. LS8 CC 9 38
Elford Rd. LS8 CC 9 38
Elgin St. HX3 F18 80
Eli St. BD5 N13 67
Elizabeth Av. BD12 M17 83
Elizabeth Clo. BD12 M17 83
Elizabeth Cres. BD12 M17 83
Elizabeth Dr. BD12 M17 83
Elizabeth Gro., Mor. LS27 Y16 89
Elizabeth St. BD12 M17 83
Elizabeth St. BD16 H 5 10
Fernbank Dr.
Elizabeth St. BD5 N12 49
Elizabeth St., Elland G24 99
HX5
Elizabeth St., Greet. F23 98
Saddleworth Rd.
Elizabeth St., Oakworth ZZ 5 6
Elland Bri., Elland HX5 G23 99
Elland Hall, Elland HX5 G23 99
Elland La., Elland HX5 H23 99
Elland Pl. LS11 AA12 55
Elland Rd.
Elland Rd. HD6 J22 100
Elland Rd. HD6 L22 101
Elland Rd. HX5 H22 99
Elland Rd. LS11 AA12 55
Elland Rd. Pl., Mor. LS27 Y15 72
Elland Rd.
Elland Rd., Chur. LS27 X15 72
Elland St. LS28 S10 51
Varley St.
Elland Ter. LS11 AA12 55
Elland Wood Bottom HX3 F22 98
Ellar Carr Rd. BD10 P 6 14
Ellar Carr Rd. BD13 C 7 26
Ellen Royd St. HX3 F19 94
Range La.
Ellen St. BD16 H 5 10
Crow Nest Rd.
Ellen St. BD18 M 7 30
Church St.
Ellenthorpe Rd. K 6 11
BD17
Ellerby Av. LS9 CC12 56
Dial St.
Ellerby La. LS9 CC12 56
Ellerby Rd. LS9 CC11 56
Ellerby St. LS9 CC11 56
Ellerby Ter. LS9 CC12 56
Dial St.
Ellercroft Av. BD7 L12 48
Ellercroft Rd. BD7 L12 48
Ellercroft Ter. BD7 L12 48
Ellers Gro. LS8 CC 9 38
Ellers Rd. LS8 CC 9 38
Ellerton St. BD3 P11 50
Ellinthorpe St. BD4 O12 49
Wakefield Rd.
Elliot St. BD20 L 7 30
Wycliffe Gdns.
Ellis Fold LS12 X11 54
Ellis Pl. LS11 AA13 73
Lodge La.
Ellis St. BD5 M13 66

Ellison St. HX3 E18 80
Buxton St.
Ellistones Gdns. HX4 E23 98
Ellistones La., Greet. E24 98
HX4
Ellwands Yd. LS12 X11 54
Elm Av. LS13 V10 53
Elm Av., S.B. HX6 B20 92
Elm Cft. LS15 HH 7 41
Elm Ct. BD11 R17 86
Elm Gro. BD18 N 7 31
Elm Gro. BD21 B 5 7
Elm Gro. HX3 J16 82
Elm Pl., S.B. HX6 B20 92
Elm Rd. BD18 M 7 30
Elm St. ZZ10 42
Elm St. LS6 AA 9 37
Elm Ter., Brig. L20 97
Elm Tree Av. BD6 M15 66
Elm Tree Clo. BD21 C 4 8
Elm Tree Clo. BD6 M15 66
Elm Tree Gdns. BD6 M15 66
Elm Way WF17 U18 87
Elm Wk., The LS15 GG12 58
Elmet Towers LS14 HH 9 41
Elmete Av. LS8 EE 7 39
Elmete Av., Scholes LS15 JJ 8 41
Elmete Clo. LS8 EE 8 39
Elmete Ct. LS8 EE 8 39
Elmete Dr. LS8 EE 7 39
Elmete Gro. LS8 EE 7 39
Elmete Hill LS8 EE 8 39
Elmete La. LS8 EE 7 39
Elmete Mt. LS8 EE 8 39
Elmete Way LS8 EE 8 39
Elmete Wk. LS8 EE 8 39
Elmfield Av. LS12 Y12 54
Elmfield BD17 N 5 13
Elmfield Ct., Mor. LS27 X17 89
Elmfield Dr. BD6 M15 66
Elmfield Gro. LS12 Y12 54
Colmore Gro.
Elmfield Pl. LS12 Y12 54
Colmore Gro.
Elmfield Rd. LS12 Y12 54
Colmore Gro.
Elmfield St. LS12 Y12 54
Elmfield Ter. HX1 E20 94
Elmfield Ter. LS12 Y12 54
Elmfield Rd.
Elmfield Way LS13 V10 53
Elmhurst Clo. LS17 DD 5 21
Elmhurst Gdns. LS17 DD 5 21
Elmsall St. BD1 M11 48
Elmtree Chase LS10 BB13 74
Elmwood Dr. BD22 B 5 7
Elmwood La. LS7 BB10 56
Elmwood Pl. BD2 P10 50
Moor Ter.
Elmwood Pl. LS7 BB10 56
Camp Rd.
Elmwood Rd. A 5 7
Elmwood Rd. LS2 BB10 56
Elmwood St. HX1 E20 94
Free School La.
Elmwood Ter. A 5 7
Elmwood Ter. LS7 BB10 56
Camp Rd.
Elsdon Clo. BD6 N12 49
Elsham Ter. LS4 Y10 54
Elsie Cres. LS9 CC11 56
Elsie Vw. LS9 CC11 56
Elsinore Av., Elland HX5 G24 99
Elsworth Av. BD3 P10 50
Elsworth Pl. LS12 Y11 54
Elsworth St. BD4 O12 49
Wakefield Rd.
Elsworth St. LS12 Y11 54
Parliament Pl.
Elsworth Ter. LS12 Y11 54
Eltham Av. LS6 AA 9 37
Eltham St.
Eltham Clo. LS6 AA 9 37
Eltham St.
Eltham Dr. LS6 AA 9 37
Eltham Gdns. LS6 AA 9 37
Eltham Gro. LS6 L15 66
Eltham Gro. LS6 AA 9 37
Eltham St.
Eltham Pl. LS6 AA 9 37
Eltham Ri. LS6 AA 9 37
Eltham Ter. LS6 AA 9 37
Eltham Vw. LS6 AA 9 37
Eltham St.
Elton St. BD6 L14 66
Elvaston Rd., Mor. LS27 X17 89
Elvey Clo. BD2 P 9 32

Elwyn Gro. BD5 N13 67
Elwyn Rd. BD5 N13 67
Ely St. LS12 Y11 54
Chichester St.
Emerald St. BD21 B 5 7
Ingrow La.
Emerald St. LS11 AA12 55
Dame St.
Emerson Av. BD9 J 9 29
Emm La. BD9 K 9 29
Emmanual Row BD13 C12 44
Black Edge La.
Emmetts Bldgs. LS13 V 9 35
Emmfield Dr. BD9 L 9 30
Emmott Dr. LS19 S 5 15
Empire Arcade St. LS1 BB11 56
Emscote Av. HX1 E20 94
Emscote Gdns. HX1 E20 94
Emscote Gro. HX1 E20 94
Emscote Pl. HX1 E20 94
Emscote St. HX3 E18 80
Rawson St. N.
Emscote St. S. HX1 E20 94
Emsley Clo. BD4 O15 67
Emsley Pl. LS10 CC12 56
Goodman St.
Emville Av. LS17 EE 4 21
Enderley Rd. BD13 F12 45
Endon Cft. LS10 BB13 74
Endor Gro. BD7 K14 65
Enfield Av. LS7 CC10 56
Enfield Dr. BD6 L14 66
Enfield LS19 R 4 15
Enfield Par. BD6 L14 66
Enfield Rd. BD17 M 5 12
Enfield St. LS7 BB10 56
Enfield Ter. LS7 CC10 56
Enfield Wk. BD6 L14 66
Englefield Cres. BD4 Q14 68
Ennerdale Dr. BD2 O 9 31
Ennerdale Rd. BD2 O 9 31
Ennerdale Rd. LS12 V14 71
Ennerdale Way LS12 V13 71
Envoy St. LS11 Z15 73
Dewsbury Rd.
Epworth Pl. LS10 CC13 74
Ernest St. HX6 D19 93
Alabama St.
Erskine Par. BD6 K16 82
Escroft Clo. BD12 M18 83
Esholt La. BD17 N 5 13
Esholt Pl. LS12 Y11 54
Armley Rd.
Esholt St. LS12 Y11 54
Armley Rd.
Esholt Ter. LS12 Y11 54
Armley Rd.
Eshton Av. BD12 N16 84
Eskdale Av. HX3 H16 82
Eskdale Ri. BD15 J11 47
Esmond St. BD7 K13 65
Esmond St. LS12 Y11 54
Hall Rd.
Esmond Ter. LS12 Y11 54
Hall Rd.
Essex St. BD4 O12 49
Essex St. HX1 D20 93
Estcourt Av. LS6 Y 8 36
Estcourt Gro. BD7 L12 48
Estcourt Rd. BD7 L12 48
Estcourt Ter. LS6 Y 8 36
Esthwaite Gdns. LS15 FF12 58
Ethel Ter. BD7 M12 48
Etna St. BD7 K13 65
Eton St. HX1 D19 93
Eunice St. LS11 BB12 55
Euston Gro. LS11 Z12 55
Ingram St.
Euston Mt. LS11 Z12 55
Ingram St.
Euston St. LS11 Z13 73
Tilbury Vw.
Euston Ter. LS11 Z12 55
Ingram St.
Evanston Av. LS12 Y10 54
Evelyn Av. BD3 Q11 50
Evelyn Pl. LS12 Y12 54
Evens Ter. BD5 N14 67
Everest Av. BD18 N 7 31
Evergreen Wk. BD16 G 4 10
Canal Rd.
Everleigh St. LS9 DD11 57
Eversley Dr. BD4 Q13 68
Eversley Mt. HX2 D20 93
Eversley Pl. HX2 D20 93
Evesham Gro. BD10 O 7 31
Evesham Ter. LS7 Z 8 27
Meanwood Rd.

128

Street	Grid	Page
Fern Bank Vills. LS13	T 9	34
Fern Hill BD16	H 4	10
Lady La.		
Fern Hill Rd. BD18	K 7	29
Fern Pl. BD18	K 7	29
Saltaire Rd.		
Fern Pl., Pud. LS28	T10	52
Arthur St.		
Fern St. BD4	P13	68
Fern St. HX3	E18	80
Fern Ter., Pud. LS28	T10	52
Fernbank Av. BD16	H 5	10
Fernbank Dr.		
Fernbank Av. BD22	A 5	7
Fernbank Av. LS13	T 9	34
Fernbank Clo. LS13	T 9	34
Fernbank Dr. BD16	H 5	10
Fernbank Dr. BD17	L 6	12
Fernbank Dr. LS13	T 9	34
Fernbank Gdns. LS13	T 9	34
Fernbank Pl. LS13	T 9	34
Fernbank Rd. BD3	O10	49
Fernbank Rd. LS13	T 9	34
Fernbank St. BD16	H 5	10
Crow Nest La.		
Fernbank Ter. BD16	H 5	10
Fernbank Wk. LS13	T 9	34
Ferncliffe Dr. BD17	L 5	12
Ferncliffe Rd. BD16	G 5	10
Ferncliffe Rd. BD18	K 7	29
Bingley Rd.		
Ferncliffe Rd. LS13	V10	53
Ferncliffe Ter. LS13	V10	53
Ferncliffe Rd.		
Ferndale Av. BD14	H13	64
Ferndale Av. WF17	T17	87
Rochester St.		
Ferndale BD14	H13	64
Ferndale Gro. BD9	M 9	30
Ferndale Wk. WF17	T17	87
Ferndene Av. WF17	T17	87
Ferndene BD16	H 5	10
Ferndown Grn. BD5	M13	66
Fernfield Ter. HX3	E18	80
Beecher St.		
Fernhill Av. BD18	K 7	29
Fernhill Gro. BD18	K 7	29
Fernhill Mt. BD18	K 7	29
Fernlea BD13	G14	64
Highgate Rd.		
Fernlea Gdns. BD12	M17	83
Crown St.		
Fernside BD16	E 6	9
Fernwood LS8	DD 6	21
Ferrand Av. BD4	P15	68
Ferrand La. BD16	H 5	10
Main St.		
Ferrand La. BD19	R18	86
Ferrand St. BD16	H 5	10
Ferrands Clo. BD16	E 6	9
Ferrands Park Way BD16	E 6	9
Ferriby Clo. BD2	P 9	32
Ferriby Towers LS9	CC10	56
Festival Av. BD18	M 8	30
Feversham St. BD3	O12	49
Fewston Av. LS9	CC12	56
Fewston Gro. LS9	CC12	56
Fewston Rd.		
Fewston Pl. LS9	CC12	56
Fewston Rd.		
Fewston Rd. LS9	CC12	56
Fewston Ter. LS9	CC12	56
Cross Green La.		
Fewston Vw. LS9	CC12	56
Fewston Rd.		
Field Ct. BD13	F12	45
Market St.		
Field End Clo. LS15	GG11	58
Field End Cres. LS15	GG11	58
Field End Ct. LS15	GG11	58
Field End Garth LS15	GG11	58
Field End Gdns. LS15	GG11	58
Field End Grn. LS15	GG11	58
Field End Gro. LS15	GG11	58
Field End LS15	GG11	58
Field End Mt. LS15	GG11	58
Field End Rd. LS15	GG11	58
Field Head Cres. WF17	T17	87
Field Head La.	YY 8	24
Field Head La. HX2	C15	62
Field Head La. WF17	T18	87
Field La., Brig.	K23	100
Field Side HX1	D19	93
Field St. BD1	N11	49
Field St. BD18	L 7	30
Windsor Rd.		
Field Ter. LS15	GG11	58
Fieldgate Rd. BD10	P 7	32
Fieldhead St. BD7	L12	48
Fieldhouse Clo. LS17	BB 6	20
Fieldhouse Dr. LS17	BB 6	20
Fieldhouse Gro. LS28	S10	51
Fieldhouse Lawn LS17	BB 6	20
Fieldhouse Dr.		
Fieldhouse Wk. LS17	BB 6	20
Fielding Gate LS12	Y11	54
Fields Rd. BD12	N16	84
Fieldway Av. LS18	U 9	34
Fieldway BD14	H12	46
Fieldway Clo. LS18	U 9	34
Fieldway Ri. LS18	U 9	34
Fife St.	ZZ 7	24
Fifth Av. BD3	P10	50
Fifth Av. LS12	Y11	54
Fifth Av., Roth. LS26	GG15	76
Fifth St. BD12	M16	83
Filey St. BD1	N12	49
Filey St. HX3	F19	94
Fillingfir Dr. LS16	W 7	35
Fillingfir Rd. LS16	W 7	35
Fillingfir Wk. LS16	W 7	35
Finch St. BD5	M13	66
Finch Wk., Mor. LS27	X17	89
Finchley St. BD5	M13	66
Findon Ter. BD10	Q 9	32
Fink Hill, Hor. LS18	U 7	34
Finkil St. HD6	K20	96
Finkle La., Mor. LS27	V16	88
Finsbury Dr. BD2	N 8	31
Finsbury Rd. LS1	AA10	55
Willow Ter. Rd.		
Fir St. BD21	B 5	7
Hainworth Wood Rd.		
Fir Tree App. LS17	BB 5	20
Fir Tree Clo. LS17	BB 5	20
Fir Tree Gdns. BD10	P 7	32
Fir Tree Gdns. LS17	AA 5	19
Fir Tree Grn. LS17	BB 5	20
Fir Tree Gro. LS17	BB 5	20
Fir Tree La. LS17	BB 5	20
Fir Tree Ri. LS17	BB 5	21
Fir Tree Vale LS17	BB 5	20
Firbank Grn. BD2	P 9	32
Firbank Gro. LS15	FF12	58
Firbeck BD15	E 7	27
Firethorn Clo. BD8	L11	48
Back Girlington Rd.		
First Av. BD21	B 4	7
Lister St.		
First Av. BD3	P11	50
First Av. HX3	E21	94
Manor Dr.		
First Av. LS12	Y11	54
First Av. LS19	S 4	15
First Av., Roth. LS26	FF15	76
First St. BD12	N16	84
Firth Av. HD6	L21	97
Thornhill Bridge La.		
Firth Av. LS11	AA14	73
Firth Gro. LS11	AA14	73
Firth House La. HD6	L23	101
Firth La. BD15	F 8	27
Firth Mt. LS11	AA14	73
Firth Pl. LS9	BB10	56
Firth Rd. BD9	L 9	30
Firth Rd. LS11	AA14	73
Firth Row BD4	O15	67
Firth St. BD13	F12	45
Firth St. LS9	CC10	56
Firth Ter. LS9	CC10	56
Firth Vw. LS11	AA14	73
Firthorn Clo. BD8	L11	48
Back Girlington		
Fish St. LS1	BB11	56
Kirkgate		
Fishers Yd. LS11	BB11	56
Meadow La.		
Fitzgerald St. BD5	M12	48
Fitzroy Dr. LS8	DD 8	39
Fitzroy Rd. BD3	O11	49
Fitzwilliam St. BD4	N12	49
Five Oaks BD17	L 6	12
Fixby Av. HX2	D20	93
Fixby Rd. HD6	K24	100
Flat Pl. LS9	CC11	56
Flawith Dr. BD2	P10	50
Flax Mill Rd. LS10	CC13	74
Flaxton Clo. LS11	AA13	73
Flaxton St.		
Flaxton Gdns. LS11	AA13	73
Flaxton St.		
Flaxton Grn. BD2	P10	50
Flaxton Pl. BD7	L12	48
Flaxton St. LS11	AA13	73
Flaxton Vw. LS11	AA13	73
Greenmount Ter.		
Fleece Sq. LS11	AA12	55
Fleece La.		
Fleece St. BD6	K15	65
Fleet La. BD13	F14	63
Fletcher Cres. HD6	K24	100
Fletcher La. BD2	M 9	30
Fletcher Rd. BD6	L14	66
Briggs Av.		
Fletton Ter. BD2	O10	49
Flexbury Av., Mor. LS27	X17	89
Flinton Gro. BD2	P 9	32
Flockton Av. BD4	O13	67
Flockton Clo. BD4	O13	67
Flockton Cres. BD4	O13	67
Flockton Dr. BD4	O13	67
Flockton Gro. BD4	O13	67
Flockton Rd. BD4	O13	67
Flockton Ter. BD4	O13	67
Bowling Hall Rd.		
Floral Av. LS7	BB 8	38
Florence Av. BD15	E 8	27
Florence Av. LS9	CC10	56
Ashley Rd.		
Florence Gro. LS9	CC10	56
Ashley Rd.		
Florence Mt. LS9	CC10	56
Ashley Rd.		
Florence Pl. LS9	CC10	56
Ashley Rd.		
Florence Rd. LS12	Y12	54
Florence St. BD3	P12	50
Florence St. HX1	E19	94
Francis St.		
Florence St. LS12	Y11	54
Amberley Rd.		
Florence St. LS9	DD10	57
Florida Rd. BD15	H 9	28
Flower Acre Rd., Elland HX5	G24	99
Elizabeth St.		
Flower Bank BD2	N 9	31
Flower Cft.	A 4	7
Flower Garth BD10	P 8	32
Flower Haven BD9	J 9	29
Flower Hill BD9	K 9	29
Flower Mt. BD17	M 5	12
Floyd St. BD5	L13	66
Fold, The LS15	JJ 9	41
Foldings Av. BD19	N19	103
Foldings Clo. BD19	N19	103
Foldings Ct. BD19	N19	103
Foldings Gro. BD19	N19	103
Foldings Par. BD19	N19	103
Foldings Rd. BD19	N19	103
Folkestone St. BD3	P11	50
Folkton Holme BD2	P10	50
Folly Hall Av. BD6	L15	66
Folly Hall Clo. BD6	L15	66
Folly Hall Av.		
Folly Hall Gdns., The BD6	L15	66
Crofthouse Rd.		
Folly Hall Rd. BD6	L15	66
Folly Hall Wk. BD6	L15	66
Folly Hall Av.		
Folly Hall, The BD6	L15	66
Folly La. LS11	AA13	73
Folly Vw.	ZZ 8	24
Fontmell Clo. BD4	Q14	68
Football LS19	S 4	15
Forber Gro. BD4	Q12	50
Forber Pl. LS15	FF11	58
Ford Hill BD13	F15	63
Fore La. HX6	B21	92
Fore Lane Av. HX6	B21	92
Foreside Bottom La. BD13	C13	62
Foreside La. BD13	B12	43
Forest Av. HX2	D17	79
Forest Bank, Gild. LS27	V15	71
Forest Cres. HX2	D17	79
Forest Grn. HX2	D17	79
Forest Vw. HX2	D17	79
Cousin La.		
Forester St. BD13	C11	44
Longhouse La.		
Forge La. LS12	Y11	54
Forge Row LS12	V13	71
Forres St. LS7	Z 8	37
Meanwood Rd.		
Forster St. BD1	N11	49
Forster Pl. BD7	M12	48
Lady La.		
Forster Pl. LS12	X13	72
Forster Sq. BD1	N11	49
Forster Square Sta. BD1	N11	49
Forster St. BD18	M 8	30
Valley Rd.		

Street	Grid	Page
Forster St. BD7	M12	48
Lady La.		
Forster St. LS10	CC12	56
Forsters Bldgs. LS13	V 9	35
Foster Allotments Rd. BD13	D10	44
Foster Av. BD13	G12	46
Foster Clo., Mor. LS27	X16	89
Foster Cres., Mor. LS27	X16	89
Cobden St.		
Foster Park Gro. BD13	D10	44
Foster Park Vw. BD13	D10	44
Foster Pk. BD13	D10	44
Foster Rd. BD21	B 4	7
Foster St. BD13	G14	64
Foston Clo. BD2	Q10	50
Foston La. BD2	P10	50
Foulds Ter. BD16	H 5	10
Foundry App. LS9	DD10	57
Foundry Av. LS8	DD 9	39
Foundry Dr. LS9	DD 9	39
Foundry La. BD4	O13	67
Wakefield Rd.		
Foundry La. LS14	GG10	58
Foundry La. LS28	T10	52
Foundry La. LS9	EE 9	39
Foundry Mill Cres. LS14	FF 9	40
Foundry Mill Dr. LS14	FF 9	40
Foundry Mill Gdns. LS14	FF 8	40
Foundry Mill Mt. LS14	FF 9	40
Foundry Mill St. LS14	FF 9	40
Foundry Mill Ter. LS14	FF 9	40
Foundry Mill Vw. LS14	FF 9	40
Foundry Mill Wk. LS14	FF 9	40
Foundry Pl. LS8	DD 9	39
Foundry St. HD6	M22	101
Foundry St. HX1	F19	94
Foundry St. LS11	AA12	55
Foundry St. N. HX3	D17	79
Foundry St., S.B. HX1	B21	92
West St.		
Foundry Wk. LS8	DD 9	39
Fountain St. BD1	N11	49
Fountain St. BD12	M16	83
Park Rd.		
Fountain St. HX1	F20	94
Fountain St., Mor. LS27	W17	88
Fountain St., Mor. LS27	Y15	72
Co-op St.		
Fountain St., Queens. BD13	G14	64
Albert St.		
Fountain St., Thornton BD13	F12	45
Market St.		
Fountain Ter. BD12	M18	83
Fountain Way BD18	M 7	30
Fountain Wk. LS14	GG 8	40
Seacroft Cres.		
Fountains Zone HX2	C15	62
Fourlands Cres. BD10	P 7	32
Fourlands Ct. BD10	P 7	32
Fourlands Dr. BD10	P 7	32
Fourlands Gdns. BD10	P 7	32
Fourlands Gro. BD10	P 7	32
Fourlands Rd. BD10	P 7	32
Fourteenth Av. LS12	Y12	54
Eighth Av.		
Fourth Av. BD21	B 4	7
Lister Av.		
Fourth Av. BD3	P10	50
Fourth Av., Roth. LS26	GG15	76
Fourth St. BD12	N16	84
Fowler St. BD4	O12	49
Fowlers Pl. LS28	T10	52
Fox and Grapes Yd. LS2	BB11	56
Kirkgate		
Fox St. BD16	H 5	10
Foxcroft Clo. LS6	X 8	36
Foxcroft Dr., Brig.	K22	100
Foxcroft Grn. LS6	Y 8	36
Foxcroft Mt. LS6	X 8	36
Foxcroft Rd. LS6	X 8	36
Foxcroft Way LS6	X 8	36
Foxcroft Wk. LS6	X 8	36
Foxglove Av. LS8	EE 8	39
Foxglove Rd. WF17	T18	87
Foxhill Av. BD13	F14	63
Foxhill Av. LS16	Y 6	18
Foxhill BD17	L 5	12
Foxhill Clo. BD13	F14	63
Foxhill Cres. LS16	Y 6	18
Foxhill Ct. LS16	Y 6	18
Foxhill Dr. BD13	F14	63
Foxhill Dr. LS16	Y 6	18
Foxhill Garth LS16	Y 6	18
Foxhill Grn. LS16	Y 6	18
Foxhill Gro. BD13	F14	63
Foxhill Gro. LS16	Y 6	18
Foxhill Pl. LS16	Y 6	18
Foxholes Cres. LS28	R 8	33
Foxholes La. LS28	R 8	33
Foxwood Av. LS8	FF 8	40
Foxwood Clo. LS8	FF 8	40
Foxwood Gro. LS8	FF 8	40
Foxwood Ri. LS8	FF 8	40
Foxwood Wk. LS8	FF 8	40
Fraisthorpe Mead BD2	P10	50
Francis Clo. HX1	E19	94
Francis St.		
Francis Gro. LS11	AA13	73
Lodge La.		
Francis Sq. BD13	C 8	26
Church St.		
Francis St. BD4	O12	49
Heaton St.		
Francis St. HX1	E19	94
Francis St. LS28	S10	51
Francis St. LS7	BB 9	38
Frank St. BD7	L13	66
Frank St. HX1	E20	94
Frankland Gro. LS7	CC 9	38
Frankland Pl. LS7	CC 9	38
Frankland Ter. LS7	CC 9	38
Franklin St. HX1	D19	93
Fraser Av., Hor. LS18	T 7	34
Fraser Rd. LS28	Q 8	32
Fraser St. BD8	M11	48
Fraser St. LS9	CC10	56
Freak Field La. HD2	O22	102
Fred St. BD21	B 4	7
Fanny St.		
Frederick Av. LS9	DD12	57
Frederick Cl. BD10	N 6	13
Frederick St. BD1	N12	49
Frederick St. BD11	P16	85
Allen Cft.		
Frederick St. BD4	P14	68
Vulcan St.		
Freds Pl. BD4	P13	68
Free School La. HX1	E20	94
Freeman Rd. HX3	H20	95
Freemantle Pl. LS15	FF11	58
Freemont St. LS13	U10	52
Fremantle Gro. BD4	Q12	50
Frensham Av. LS27	W17	88
Frensham Dr. BD7	J13	65
Frensham Gro. BD7	J13	65
Frensham Way BD7	J13	65
Freshfield Gdns. BD15	H10	46
Friar Ct. BD10	P 8	32
Friar Pl. HD2	O24	102
Friendly Av. HX1	B20	92
Friendly Fold Rd. HX3	E18	80
Friendly St. BD13	F12	45
Friendly St. BD18	M 7	30
Leeds Rd.		
Friendly St. HX3	E18	80
Friendly Fold Rd.		
Frimley Dr. BD5	M14	66
Frith St. HD6	L22	101
Frizinghall Rd. BD9	M 9	30
Frizley Gdns. BD9	M 9	30
Frodingham Vills. BD2	P10	50
Frogmore Av. BD12	N16	84
Frogmore Ter. BD12	N16	84
Front Row LS11	AA12	55
Front St. LS11	AA12	55
Fulford Wk. BD2	P10	50
Fulham Pl. LS11	AA13	73
Fulham Sq. LS11	AA13	73
Fulham St.		
Fulham St. LS11	AA13	73
Fullerton St. BD3	O12	49
Fulneck Rd., Pud. LS28	T12	52
Fulton St. BD1	M11	48
Fur St. HX3	E18	80
Mill La.		
Furnace Gro. BD12	N16	84
Furnace Inn St. BD4	P12	50
Furnace La. BD11	R16	86
Furnace Rd. BD12	N16	84
Furness Av. HX2	C16	79
Furness Cres. HX2	C16	79
Furness Dr. HX2	C16	79
Furness Gdns. HX2	C17	79
Furness Gro. HX2	C17	79
Furness Pl. HX2	D17	79
Fyfe Cres. BD17	N 6	13
Fyfe Gro. BD17	N 6	13
Fyfe La. BD17	N 6	13
Gadd St. HX3	G18	81
Horley Green Rd.		
Gain La. BD3	P10	50
Gaine St. HX6	D20	93
Gainsborough Av. LS16	X 4	18
Gainsborough Dr. LS16	X 4	18
Gainsborough Pl. LS12	W13	71
Gaisby La. BD18	M 8	30
Gaisby Mt. BD18	M 8	30
Gaisby Pl. BD18	M 8	30
Gaisby Ri. BD18	M 8	30
Gaitskell Wk. LS11	AA12	55
Galefield Gdns. BD6	K16	82
Galloway La. LS28	R10	51
Galloway Rd. BD10	P 7	32
New Line		
Galsworthy Av. BD9	J 9	29
Gamble Hill Chase LS13	V11	53
Gamble Hill Clo. LS13	V11	53
Gamble Hill Cross LS13	V11	53
Gamble Hill Dr. LS13	V11	53
Gamble Hill Fold LS13	V11	53
Gamble Hill Lawn		
Gamble Hill Grn. LS13	V11	53
Gamble Hill Lawn LS13	V11	53
Gamble Hill LS13	V11	53
Gamble Hill Pl. LS13	V11	53
Gamble Hill Rd. LS13	V11	53
Gamble Hill Ri. LS13	V11	53
Gamble Hill Vale LS13	V11	53
Gamble Hill Vw. LS13	V11	53
Gamble La. LS12	V12	53
Ganners Clo. LS13	V 9	35
Ganners Garth LS13	V 9	35
Ganners Grn. LS13	V 9	35
Ganners Hill LS13	V 9	35
Ganners La. LS13	V 9	35
Ganners Mt. LS13	V 9	35
Ganners Rd. LS13	V 9	35
Ganners Ri. LS13	V 9	35
Ganners Way LS13	V 9	35
Ganners Wk. LS13	V 9	35
Ganney Rd. HD6	L22	101
Ganton Mt. LS6	AA 9	37
Ganton Pl. LS6	AA 9	37
Ganton Vw. LS6	AA 9	37
Gaol La. HX1	F19	94
Garden Clo. BD12	L17	83
Garden Field BD12	M17	83
Garden La. BD9	K 9	29
Garden Rd. HD6	K21	96
Garden St. BD9	K 9	29
Garden St. LS9	BB11	56
Garden St. N. HX3	F19	94
Garden Ter. BD9	L 9	30
Garden Vw. BD16	J 5	11
Gardens, The HX1	F20	94
Gardens, The LS28	S 9	33
Gardiner Row BD4	O14	47
Garfield Av. BD8	L10	48
Garfield Gro. LS12	Y11	54
Armley Rd.		
Garfield Pl. LS13	KK11	52
Harley Rd.		
Garfield St. BD15	H10	46
Garfield St. HX3	E18	80
East Park Rd.		
Garfield St. LS13	U11	52
Harley Rd.		
Garfield Ter. LS13	T11	52
Swinnow Rd.		
Garforth St. BD15	H10	46
Garforth St. LS11	Z12	55
Domestic St.		
Gargrave App. LS9	CC11	56
Gargrave Ct. LS9	CC10	56
Gargrave Pl. LS9	CC10	56
Garibaldi St. BD3	Q11	50
Garland Dr. LS15	HH11	59
Garland Fold LS9	BB11	56
Marsh La.		
Garlick St. HD6	K24	100
Garlicks St. LS11	Z15	73
Dewsbury Rd.		
Garmont Rd. LS7	BB 8	38
Garnet Av. LS11	BB13	74
Garnet Pl.		
Garnet Cres. LS11	BB13	74
Burton Rd.		
Garnet Gro. LS11	BB13	74
Garnet Pl. LS11	BB13	74
Garnet Rd. LS11	BB14	74
Garnet Ter. LS11	BB13	74
Garnet Vw. LS11	BB13	74
Garnett St. BD3	O11	49
Garrs Ter. LS11	BB12	55
Derby Cres.		
Garsdale Av. BD10	P 7	32
Garsdale Cres. BD17	N 5	13
Garth Av. LS17	AA 6	19
Garth Dr. LS17	AA 6	19

Garth Fold BD10	O 7	31
High St.		
Garth Rd. LS17	AA 6	19
Garth Wk. LS17	BB 6	20
Garth, The LS9	CC11	56
Garthwaite Mt. BD15	H10	46
Garton Av. LS9	DD11	57
Garton Dr. BD10	P 8	32
Garton Gro. LS9	DD11	57
Garton Rd. LS9	DD11	57
Garton Ter. LS9	DD11	57
Garton Vw. LS9	DD11	57
Gas St. HD6	M22	101
Gasworks Rd., S.B. HX6	C21	93
Gate Head, S.B. HX6	B20	92
Gateland Dr. LS17	FF 5	22
Gateland La. LS17	FF 5	22
Gateside Vw. LS15	FF12	58
Gathorne Av. LS8	CC 9	38
Gathorne Ter.		
Gathorne Clo. LS8	CC 9	38
Thorne Ter.		
Gathorne St. BD7	L13	66
Gathorne St. LS8	CC 9	38
Gathorne Ter. LS8	CC 9	38
Gatwick Ter., Greet.	F23	98
Saddleworth Rd.		
Gaunt St. BD3	N11	49
North Wing		
Gawcliffe Rd. BD18	M 8	30
Valley Rd.		
Gawthorne Dr. BD16	H 4	10
Gawthorpe Av. BD16	H 4	10
Gawthorpe La. BD16	H 5	10
Gawthorpe St. BD15	E 8	27
Main St.		
Gay La. BD4	P12	50
Gayles Pl. LS11	AA13	73
Greenmount St.		
Gaythorn Ter. HX3	J18	82
Gaythorne Rd. BD5	N13	67
Gaythorne Ter. BD14	J13	65
Gaythorne Wk. BD10	P 8	32
Geelong Clo. BD2	N 9	31
Gelder Rd. LS12	X11	54
Gelderd Clo. LS12	Y13	72
Gelderd La. LS12	Y13	72
Gelderd Pl. LS12	Z12	55
Gelderd Rd. LS12	Z12	55
Gelderd Rd., Mor. LS27	V16	88
George Sq. HX1	F19	94
Commercial St.		
George St. BD1	N12	49
George St. BD13	F12	45
George St. BD17	M 6	12
George St. BD18	K 7	29
George St. BD18	M 7	30
Church St.		
George St. BD21	C 4	8
Greengate		
George St. HD6	M22	101
George St. HX1	F19	94
George St. HX3	J19	96
George St. HX4	B21	92
George St. LS19	R 5	15
George St. LS2	BB11	56
George St., Elland HX5	G24	99
George St., Greet.	F23	98
Victoria St.		
Georges Sq. BD13	C 8	26
Station St.		
Georges Sq. BD21	B 4	7
Aireworth St.		
Georges St. HX3	D17	79
Geraldton Av. BD2	N 9	31
Geranium Pl. LS11	AA13	73
Cambrian St.		
Geranium St. LS11	AA13	73
Cambrian St.		
Geranium Ter. LS11	AA13	73
Cambrian St.		
Gerard Av., Mor. LS27	W17	88
Gernhill Av. HD6	K24	100
Gerrard St. HX1	E19	94
Gertrude St. BD4	P13	68
Ghyll Beck Dr., Raw. LS19	T 5	16
Ghyll Rd. LS6	X 8	36
Ghyll Royd LS19	R 4	15
Ghyll Wood Dr. BD16	H 7	28
Ghyll, The, BD16	H 7	28
Ghyllroyd Av. BD11	R17	86
Ghyllroyd Dr. BD11	R16	86
Gibb La. HX2	B17	78
Gibbet St. HX1	C19	93
Gibraltar Av. HX1	D20	93
Gibraltar Rd. HX1	D19	93
Gibraltar Rd. LS28	R11	51
Gibson Dr. LS15	HH11	59

Gibson St. BD3	O12	49
Gilbert Chase LS5	X 9	36
Sandford Rd.		
Gilbert Clo. LS5	X 9	36
Gilbert Mt. LS5	X 9	36
Gildersome La., Gild.	U15	70
LS27		
Gildersome Spur, Mor.	V16	88
LS27		
Giles St. BD5	M12	48
Giles St. BD6	L14	66
Giles's Hill La. HX3	H15	64
Gill Beck Clo. BD17	N 5	13
Gill La.	YY 5	6
Gill La. BD13	F12	45
Gill La. BD17	Q 5	14
Gill La. LS9	Q 5	14
Gillingham Grn. BD4	P13	68
Gillroyd Par., Mor. LS27	X17	89
Gills Ct. HX1	F19	94
Waterhouse St.		
Gills Sq., LS12	Z11	55
Prince St.		
Gilmour St. HX3	E18	80
Gilpin Pl. LS12	Y12	54
St. Marys Clo.		
Gilpin St. BD3	O11	49
Gilpin St. LS12	Y12	54
St. Marys Clo.		
Gilpin Ter. LS12	Y12	54
Gilpin Vw. LS12	Y12	54
St. Marys Clo.		
Gilstead Dr. BD16	J 5	11
Gilstead La. BD16	H 5	10
Gilstone Dr.	ZZ 8	24
Gipsy St. BD3	Q11	50
Gilynda Clo. BD8	K11	47
Gipsy La. LS11	AA15	73
Gipsy Wood Clo. LS15	HH11	59
Gipsy Wood Crest LS15	HH11	59
Gipton App. LS9	EE10	57
Gipton Av. LS8	CC 9	38
Gipton Sq. LS9	EE10	57
Gipton St. LS8	CC 9	38
Gipton Wood Av. LS8	DD 8	39
Gipton Wood Cres. LS8	DD 8	39
Gipton Wood Gro. LS8	DD 8	39
Gipton Wood Pl. LS8	DD 8	39
Gipton Wood Rd. LS8	DD 8	39
Gipton Wood Rd. S. LS8	DD 9	39
Girlington Rd. BD8	K10	47
Gisburn St. LS10	BB13	74
Church St.		
Gladdings, The HX3	E21	94
Gladstone Cres. LS19	R 4	15
Gladstone Pl. BD21	B 4	7
Gladstone Rd. HX1	E19	94
West Hill St.		
Gladstone Rd. LS19	R 5	15
Gladstone St. BD13	G14	64
Highgate Rd.		
Gladstone St. BD15	H10	46
Gladstone St. BD16	G 6	10
Ash Ter.		
Gladstone St. BD21	B 4	7
Gladstone St. BD3	P12	50
Gladstone St. LS11	AA13	73
Malvern St.		
Gladstone St. LS28	S 9	33
Gladstone Ter., Mor. LS27	W17	88
Gladstone Ter., Stan.	T10	52
LS28		
Gladstone Vills. LS17	FF 5	22
Gladstone Vw. HX3	G21	95
Gladstone Vw. LS11	AA13	73
Malvern St.		
Glaisdale Gro. HX3	J19	96
Glasshouse St. LS10	BB12	56
Glasshouse Vw. LS10	AA17	90
Glazier Row BD13	F14	63
Gleanings Av. HX2	C19	93
Gleanings Dr. HX2	C19	93
Glebe Av. LS5	X 9	36
Glebe Mt., Pud. LS28	T12	52
Glebe Pl. LS5	X 9	36
Glebe St., Pud. LS28	T12	52
Glebe Ter. LS16	Y 7	36
Glebelands Dr. LS8	Y 8	36
Glederd Rd. WF17	T18	87
Gledhill Rd. BD3	O12	49
Gledhow La. LS8	CC 7	38
Gledhow Dr.	ZZ 9	24
Gledhow Grange Vw. LS8	CC 7	38
Gledhow La. LS7	BB 7	38
Gledhow La. LS8	DD 8	39
Gledhow Lane End LS7	BB 7	38
Gledhow Mt. LS8	CC10	56

Gledhow Park Av. LS7	CC 8	38
Gledhow Park Cres. LS7	CC 8	38
Gledhow Park Dr. LS7	BB 8	38
Gledhow Park Gro. LS7	CC 8	38
Gledhow Park Rd. LS7	CC 8	38
Gledhow Park Vw. LS7	CC 8	38
Gledhow Pl. LS8	CC10	56
Gledhow Rd. LS8	CC10	56
Gledhow Ri. LS8	DD 8	39
Gledhow Ter. LS8	CC10	56
Gledhow Towers LS8	CC 7	38
Gledhow Valley Rd. LS7	BB 7	38
Gledhow Valley Rd. LS8	BB 7	38
Gledhow Wood Av. LS8	CC 7	38
Gledhow Wood Ct. LS8	DD 8	39
Gledhow Wood Gro. LS8	CC 7	38
Gledhow Wood Rd. LS8	CC 8	38
Glen Dale BD16	G 7	28
Glen Dene BD16	G 7	28
Glen Dower Pk. LS16	Y 6	18
Glen Gro., Mor. LS27	X17	89
Glen Lee La. BD21	C 5	8
Glen Mount BD16	G 7	28
Glen Mt., Mor. LS27	X17	89
Glen Rd. BD16	J 4	11
Glen Rd. BD17	J 5	11
Glen Rd. LS16	Y 7	36
Glen Rd., Mor. LS27	X17	89
Glen Ri. BD17	L 6	12
Glen Ter. HX1	E20	94
Glen Ter. HX3	J19	96
Glen View Gro. BD18	J 7	29
Glen Vw. BD16	E 7	27
Glenaire BD18	N 6	13
Glenaire Dr. BD17	L 6	12
Glenbrook Dr. BD7	K11	47
Glencoe Av. LS9	CC12	56
Glencoe Rd.		
Glencoe Gro. LS9	CC12	56
Glencoe Rd.		
Glencoe St. LS9	CC12	56
Glencoe Rd.		
Glencoe Ter. LS9	CC12	56
Glencoe Rd.		
Glencoe Vw. LS9	CC12	56
Glendale Clo. BD6	L15	66
Glendale Dr. BD6	L15	66
Glendare Av. BD7	K12	47
Glendare Rd. BD7	K12	47
Glendare Ter. BD7	K12	47
Gleneagles Rd. LS17	AA 5	19
Glenfield Av. BD6	M15	66
Cleckheaton Rd.		
Glenfield BD18	N 6	13
Glenfield Mt. BD6	M15	66
Cleckheaton Rd.		
Glenholm Rd. BD17	M 6	12
Glenholm Rd. W. BD17	M 6	12
Glenholm Rd.		
Glenholme BD18	N 6	13
Glenholme Rd. BD8	L10	48
Glenholme Rd. LS28	S10	51
Glenhurst Av. BD21	C 4	8
Glenhurst BD4	P14	68
Shetcliffe La.		
Glenhurst Dr. BD21	C 4	8
Glenhurst Gro. BD21	C 4	8
Glenhurst Rd. BD18	K 7	29
Glenlea Clo. LS13	U 9	34
Glenlea Gdns. LS13	U 9	34
Glenlee Rd. BD7	K12	47
Glenmore Clo. BD2	P10	50
Higher Intake Rd.		
Glenmount Clo. HX3	D18	79
Glenrose Dr. BD7	K12	47
Glenroyd Av. BD6	M15	66
Glenroyd BD18	N 6	13
Glenroyd Ct. LS28	S11	51
Glensdale Gro. LS9	CC11	56
Glensdale Mt. LS9	CC11	56
Glensdale Rd. LS9	CC11	56
Glensdale St. LS9	CC11	56
Glensdale Ter. LS9	CC11	56
Glenside Av. BD18	N 6	13
Glenside Rd. BD18	N 6	13
Glenstone Gro. BD7	K11	47
Glenthorpe Av. LS9	DD11	57
Glenthorpe Cres. LS9	DD11	57
Glenthorpe Rd. BD17	K 6	11
Lucy Hall Dr.		
Glenthorpe Ter. LS9	DD11	57
Glenton Sq. BD9	L10	48
Glenview Av. BD9	K 9	29
Glenview Clo. BD18	J 8	29
Glenview Rd.		
Glenview Dr. BD18	J 8	29
Glenview Rd. BD16	J 4	11

Name	Ref	Page
Glenview Rd. BD18	J 7	29
Glenview Ter. BD18	K 7	29
Glenwood Av. BD17	K 6	11
Globe Fold BD8	M11	48
White Abbey Rd.		
Globe Rd. LS11	AA11	55
Glossop Gro. LS6	AA 9	37
Glossop Vw.		
Glossop Mt. LS6	AA 9	37
Glossop Vw.		
Glossop St. LS6	AA 9	37
Glossop Ter. LS6	AA 9	37
Glossop Vw. LS6	AA 9	37
Gloucester Av. BD3	P10	50
Gloucester Av. LS12	Y11	54
Gloucester Cres. LS12	Z11	55
Gloucester Gro. LS12	Y11	54
Gloucester Rd.		
Gloucester Pl. LS12	Y11	54
Armley Rd.		
Gloucester Rd. BD16	H 6	10
Gloucester Rd. LS12	Y11	54
Gloucester St. LS10	BB12	56
Gloucester Ter. LS12	Z11	55
Gloucester Vw. LS12	Y11	54
Gloucester Rd.		
Glover Ct. BD5	N13	67
Bowling Old La.		
Glovershaw La. BD17	K 4	11
Glydegate BD5	N12	49
Morley St.		
Glynn Ter. BD8	L11	48
Thornton Rd.		
Glynoon Ct. HD6	L23	101
Goal La.	F19	94
Godfrey Rd. HX3	F21	94
Godfrey St. BD8	J11	47
Godley Gdns.	G18	81
Godley La. HX3	G19	95
Godley Rd. HX3	F19	94
Godwin Pl. HD6	O24	102
Godwin St. BD1	N11	49
Goff Well La. BD21	C 5	8
Goit Side BD1	M11	48
Goit Side HX2	A17	78
Goitstock Ter. BD16	E 7	27
Golcar Pl. LS6	AA 9	37
Rider Pl.		
Golcar St. LS6	AA 9	37
Gold St. HX3	E18	80
Mill La.		
Golden Ter. LS12	X12	54
Golden View Dr. BD21	D 4	8
Golf Av. HX2	C19	93
Golf Cres. HX2	C19	93
Gooder La. HD6	L22	101
Gooder St. HD6	L22	101
Goodley Colne Rd.	ZZ 6	6
Goodman St. LS10	CC12	56
Goodrick La. LS17	AA 3	4
Goose Cote La.	A 5	7
Goose Cote Way	A 5	7
Goose Eye Brow	YY 4	6
Gordale Clo. BD4	Q13	68
Gordon Dr. LS6	Z 8	37
Gordon Pl. LS6	Z 8	37
Gordon Ter.		
Gordon St. BD5	N12	49
Gordon St. HX2	B21	92
New Rd.		
Gordon St. HX3	E16	80
Beechwood Rd.		
Gordon St. HX3	E18	80
Booth Town Rd.		
Gordon St., Elland HX5	G24	99
Gordon Ter. BD10	O 6	13
Sherborne Rd.		
Gordon Ter. LS6	Z 8	37
Gordon Vw. LS6	Z 8	37
Meanwood Rd.		
Gorse Av. BD17	K 6	11
Gothic St. BD13	G14	64
High St.		
Gotts Park Av. LS12	W10	53
Gotts Park Cres. LS12	W10	53
Gotts Park Vw. LS12	W10	53
Goulbourne St. BD21	B 4	7
Government St. LS1	AA11	55
Grace St.		
Gower St. BD5	N12	49
Gower St. LS2	BB11	56
Grace Pl. LS12	X12	54
Thornhill Rd.		
Grace St. LS1	AA11	55
Gracechurch St. BD8	M11	48
Gracey La. BD6	K14	65
Grafton Clo. BD17	M 5	12
Braham Dr.		
Grafton Pl. HX3	E17	80
Athol Rd.		
Grafton Rd. BD21	B 4	7
Grafton St. BD21	B 4	7
Grafton St. BD5	N12	49
Grafton St. LS7	BB10	56
Grafton Vills. LS15	HH 9	41
Graggwood Clo. LS5	V 7	35
Graham Av. LS4	Y 9	36
Graham Gro. LS4	Y 9	36
Graham St. BD9	L10	48
Graham St. LS4	Y 9	36
Graham Ter. LS4	Y 9	36
Graham Vw. LS4	Y 9	36
Graham Wk. LS27	V15	71
Grain St. BD5	L14	66
Grammar School St. BD1	N11	49
Granby Av. LS6	Y 8	36
Granby Ter.		
Granby Gro. LS6	Y 9	36
Granby Mt. LS6	Y 8	36
Granby Ter.		
Granby Pl. LS6	Y 8	36
Granby Rd. LS6	Y 9	36
Granby St. BD13	G14	64
Granby St. BD4	N12	49
Granby St. LS6	Y 8	36
Granby Ter.		
Granby Ter. LS6	Y 8	36
Granby Vw. LS6	Y 9	36
Grand Arc. LS1	BB11	56
Vicar La.		
Grandage Ter. BD8	L11	48
Grandsmere Pl. HX3	E21	94
Manor Dr.		
Grange Av. BD15	J11	47
Grange Av. BD18	K 7	29
Grange Av. BD3	Q11	50
Grange Av. BD4	Q15	68
Grange Av. HX2	D16	79
Grange Av. LS19	S 4	15
Grange Av. LS7	BB 9	38
Grange Av., Chur. LS27	Y15	72
William St.		
Grange Clo. LS18	T 6	16
Grange Cres. LS19	S 4	15
Grange Cres. LS7	CC 9	38
Grange Ct. LS6	Z 8	37
Grange Ct., Scholes LS15	JJ 8	41
Grange Dr. BD15	J11	47
Grange Dr., Hor. LS18	T 7	34
Grange Gdns. LS16	X 6	18
Grange Gro. BD3	Q11	50
Grange La. HD6	N22	102
Grange Mt. LS19	S 4	15
Grange Park Av. LS8	EE 8	39
Grange Park Clo. LS8	FF 8	40
Grange Park Cres. LS8	EE 8	39
Grange Park Dr. BD16	H 7	28
Grange Park Gro. LS8	EE 8	39
Grange Park Pl. LS8	EE 8	39
Grange Park Rd. BD16	H 7	28
Grange Park Ri. LS8	EE 8	39
Grange Park Ter. LS8	EE 8	39
Grange Park Wk. LS8	EE 8	39
Grange Pk.	E21	94
Grange Rd. BD15	J11	47
Grange Rd. BD16	H 5	10
Grange Rd. LS19	S 4	15
Grange Rd., The LS16	X 6	18
Grange St. HX3	E18	80
Grange St. LS12	Y15	72
Grange Ter. BD15	J11	47
Grange Rd.		
Grange Ter. BD18	L 8	30
Grange Ter. LS7	BB 9	38
Grange Ter., Pud. LS28	T11	52
Grange View Gdns. LS17	FF 6	22
Grange Vills., The LS16	X 6	18
Otley Rd.		
Grange Vw. BD3	Q11	50
Grange Vw. LS7	BB 9	38
Grange Vw., Pud. LS28	T11	52
Grange Way BD15	J11	47
Grange, The LS19	R 4	15
Grangefield Ho., Pud. LS28	T10	52
Grangefield Rd., Stan. LS28	T10	52
Grangefields Mt. LS26	CC16	91
Grangefields Rd. LS26	CC16	91
Grangefields Way LS26	CC16	91
Granhamthorpe LS13	V10	53
Granite St. LS12	Y11	54
Armley Rd.		
Granny Av., Chur. LS27	Y15	72
Granny Hall Gro. HD6	K21	96
Granny Hall La. HD6	K21	96
Granny Hall Pk. HD6	K21	96
Granny La. LS12	X12	54
Grant Av. LS7	CC10	56
Grant St. BD3	O11	49
Grantham Pl. BD7	M12	48
Grantham Pl. HX3	E18	80
Crown Rd.		
Grantham Rd. BD7	M12	48
Grantham Rd. HX3	E18	80
Grantham Ter. BD7	M12	48
Grantham Towers LS9	CC10	56
Granton Rd. LS7	BB 8	38
Granton St. BD3	P11	50
Granville Pl. BD15	J10	47
Granville Rd. BD18	L 8	30
Granville Rd. LS9	CC10	56
Granville St. BD10	O 7	31
Granville St. BD14	J12	47
Granville St. LS28	S11	51
Granville St. LS28	T10	52
Granville Ter. BD16	H 5	10
Grape St. HX1	E19	94
Grape St. LS10	BB12	56
Grapes St. BD15	J10	47
Grasleigh Av. BD15	H10	46
Grasleigh Way BD15	H10	46
Grasmere Av. LS12	Y11	54
Grasmere Dr. HX5	H23	99
Grasmere Mt. LS12	Y12	54
Grasmere Rd.		
Grasmere Pl. LS12	Y11	54
Grasmere Rd. BD2	O 9	31
Grasmere Rd. LS12	Y12	54
Grass Mount St. BD11	R16	86
Allen Cft.		
Grass Rd., Scholes LS15	JJ 8	41
Grassfield Ter., Hor. LS18	U 7	34
Grassmere Rd. BD12	N18	84
Gratrix La., S.B. HX6	C20	93
Grattan Rd. BD1	M11	48
Graveley Ct. LS6	AA 9	37
Woodhouse La.		
Graveley Sq. LS15	GG11	58
Chapel St.		
Graveleythorpe Rd. LS15	GG10	58
Graveleythorpe Ri. LS15	GG10	58
Gray Ct. LS15	HH11	59
Grayrigg Clo. LS15	FF11	58
Grayrigg Ct. LS15	EE11	57
Grayrigg Fold LS16	EE11	57
Grayrigg Lawn LS15	EE11	57
Grayson Cres. LS4	X 9	36
Grayson Heights LS4	X 9	36
Grayswood Cres. BD4	P13	68
Grayswood Dr. BD4	P13	68
Great Albion St. HX1	F19	94
Great Cross St. BD1	N12	49
Great George St. LS2	AA11	55
Great Horton Rd. BD7	J14	65
Great Northern St., Mor. LS27	X17	89
Great Russell St. BD7	M11	48
Great St. BD13	F14	63
Albert Rd.		
Great Wilson St. LS11	AA12	55
Greaves Pl. LS10	CC12	56
Orchard St.		
Greaves St. BD5	M13	66
Greek St. LS1	AA11	55
Green Bank Ct. BD17	L 6	12
Green Rd.		
Green Bank LS11	BB13	74
Vicar St.		
Green Chase LS6	Z 7	37
Green Clo. BD8	K11	47
Green Clo. LS6	Z 7	37
Green Cres. LS6	Z 7	37
Green Ct. BD7	K12	47
Green Ct. LS15	JJ 7	41
Green End BD14	H12	64
Green Fold BD17	L 6	12
Green Rd.		
Green Gdns. LS17	AA 5	19
Green Hill Av. LS13	W10	53
Green Hill BD16	G 4	10
Green Hill Cft. LS12	X12	54
Green Hill Chase LS12	X12	54
Green Hill Clo. LS12	W10	53
Green Hill Dr. LS13	W10	53
Green Hill Holt LS12	X12	54
Green Hill La. LS12	X12	54
Green Hill Pl. LS13	W10	53
Green Hill Mt.		
Green Hill Rd. LS13	W10	53

Name	Ref	Page
Grove Farm Cres. LS16	W 5	17
Grove Farm Dr. LS16	W 5	17
Grove Gdns. HX3	E17	80
Grove Gdns. LS6	Z 8	37
Grove House Cres. BD2	O 9	31
Grove House Dr. BD2	O 9	31
Grove House Rd. BD2	O 9	31
Grove La. BD19	R18	86
Grove La. LS6	Y 8	36
Grove Mill La. HX3	E18	80
Grove Mt. LS28	S11	51
West Park		
Grove Pk. HX3	D17	79
Grove Pl. LS2	BB10	56
Claypit La.		
Grove Pl., Elland HX5	H23	99
Grove Rd. BD16	G 6	10
Sycamore Av.		
Grove Rd. BD18	L 8	30
Grove Rd. LS10	CC13	74
Grove Rd. LS15	GG11	58
Grove Rd. LS28	S11	51
Grove Rd. LS6	Z 8	37
Grove Rd., Elland HX5	H23	99
Grove Rd., Hor. LS18	U 7	34
Grove Rd., Pud. LS28	T11	52
Grove Ri. LS17	Z 4	19
Grove Row HX2	B17	78
Grove Royd HX3	E18	80
Grove Sq. BD19	R18	86
Oxford Rd.		
Grove Sq. HX3	E18	80
Grove St. HD6	M22	101
Grove St. HX2	D17	79
Grove St. LS28	T10	52
Grove St. S. HX1	D19	93
Gibbet St.		
Grove St., Chapeltown LS28	S11	51
Grove Rd.		
Grove St., S.B. HD6	C21	93
Grove Ter.	K22	100
Grove Ter. BD11	R17	86
Grove Ter. BD7	M12	48
Grove Ter. LS2	BB10	56
Camp Rd.		
Grove Ter. LS28	S11	51
Grove Rd.		
Grove Ville HX3	J18	82
Grove Way BD2	O 9	31
Grove, The BD16	G 4	10
Grove, The BD17	M 5	12
Grove, The BD18	K 7	29
Grove, The HX2	D17	79
Grove, The HX3	J19	96
Grove, The LS17	Z 4	19
Grove, The LS19	R 5	15
Grove, The LS28	S11	51
Grove, The Dunkhill BD10	O 7	31
Grove, The, Greengates BD10	P 7	32
Grove, The, Hor. LS18	U 7	34
Grovehall Av. LS11	Z14	73
Grovehall Dr. LS11	Z14	73
Grovehall Par. LS11	Z14	73
Grovehall Rd. LS11	Z14	73
Grovelands BD2	O 9	31
Grunberg Gro. LS6	Y 8	36
Bennett Rd.		
Grunberg Pl. LS6	Y 9	36
North La.		
Grunberg Rd. LS6	Y 8	36
Bennett Rd.		
Grunberg St. LS6	Y 9	36
North La.		
Guild Way HX2	B19	92
Guildford St. BD4	O12	49
Bowling Back La.		
Gurney Clo. BD5	M13	66
Guy St. BD4	N12	49
Gwynne Av. BD3	Q10	50
Haddon Av. HX3	F21	94
Haddon Pl. LS4	Y10	54
Haddon Rd. LS4	Y10	54
Hadleigh Ct. LS17	BB 6	20
Shadwell La.		
Hag La. HX3	F17	80
Haigh Av., Roth. LS26	EE15	75
Haigh Corner BD10	P 7	32
Haigh Fold BD2	P 9	32
Haigh Gdns., Roth. LS26	EE15	75
Haigh Hall BD10	P 7	32
Haigh Hall Rd. BD10	P 7	32
Haigh La. HX3	F21	94
Haigh Park Rd. LS10	DD14	75
Haigh Park Vw. LS10	DD14	75
Haigh Park Rd.		
Haigh Row BD2	O10	49
Haigh St. BD4	O13	67
Haigh St. HX4	L21	97
Haigh Ter., Roth. LS26	EE15	75
Haigh Vw., Roth. LS26	EE15	75
Haigh Wood Grn. LS16	V 5	17
Haigh Wood LS16	V 5	17
Haigh Wood Rd. LS16	V 5	17
Haighback Vw. BD10	P 7	32
Haincliffe Rd. BD21	B 5	7
Hainsworth Moor BD13	F15	63
Hainsworth Moor Cres. BD13	F15	63
Hainsworth Moor Garth BD13	F15	63
Hainsworth Moor Gro. BD13	F15	63
Hainsworth Moor Vw. BD13	F15	63
Hainworth Crag Rd. BD21	B 6	7
Hainworth La. BD21	B 5	7
Hainworth Rd. BD21	B 5	7
Hainworth Shaw La. BD21	C 6	8
Hainworth Wood Rd. BD21	B 5	8
Hainworth Wood Rd. N. BD21	C 4	8
Halcyon Way BD5	M13	66
Hales Rd. LS12	Y12	54
Halesworth Cres. BD4	Q14	68
Haley Bank HX1	F19	94
Haley Hill HX3	F18	80
Haleys Yd. LS13	V 9	35
Warrels Rd.		
Half Acre Rd. BD13	E11	45
Half House La. HD6	K20	96
Half Mile Clo., Stan. LS28	T10	52
Half Mile Gdns. LS13	T 9	34
Half Mile Grn. LS13	T10	52
Half Mile La. LS13	T 9	34
Half Mile LS13	T10	52
Halifax & Keighley Rd. BD13	C 9	26
Halifax La. HX2	A18	78
Halifax Old Rd. HX3	H19	95
Halifax Rd.	A 7	25
Halifax Rd. BD21	B 6	7
Halifax Rd. BD6	K15	65
Halifax Rd. HX3	O20	103
Halifax Rd., Cullingworth BD13	C 8	26
Halifax Rd., Denholme BD13	D11	44
Halifax Rd., Elland HX5	F22	98
Halifax Rd., Queens. BD13	F16	80
Halifax Row BD12	M18	83
Hall Av. BD2	P 8	32
Hall Bank Clo. BD5	M14	66
Hall Bank Dr. BD16	H 5	10
Hall Bank Dr. BD5	M14	66
Hall Cliffe BD17	M 5	12
Hall Clo. LS16	W 1	2
Hall Dr., Bram. LS16	V 1	2
Hall Gro. LS6	Z10	55
Hall Ings BD1	N11	49
Hall La. BD18	M 7	30
Hall La. BD4	N12	49
Hall La. HX3	G17	81
Hall La. LS7	BB 9	38
Hall La., Armley LS12	Y11	54
Hall La., Farnley LS12	Y12	53
Hall La., Hor. LS18	Y 7	34
Hall Park Av., Hor. LS18	T 6	16
Hall Park Clo., Hor. LS18	U 6	16
Hall Park Garth, Hor. LS18	U 6	16
Hall Park Mt., Hor. LS18	U 6	16
Hall Park Ri., Hor. LS18	U 6	16
Hall Pl. LS9	UC11	56
Hall Rd. LS12	Y11	54
Hall Ri. LS16	W 1	2
Hall Rise Cft. LS16	W 1	2
Hall Rise Clo. LS16	W 1	2
Hall St. HD6	L22	101
Bethel St.		
Hall St. HX1	E19	94
Hallas La. BD13	D 8	26
Halley Rd. BD8	J11	47
Hallfield Dr. BD17	M 5	12
Hallfield Pl. BD1	N11	49
Hallfield Rd. BD1	M11	48
Hallfield St. BD1	N11	49
Manor Row		
Hallgate BD1	N11	49
Salem St.		
Halliday Av. LS12	X11	54
Halliday Dr. LS12	X11	54
Halliday Gro. LS12	X11	54
Halliday Mt. LS12	X11	54
Halliday Pl. LS12	X11	54
Halliday Rd. LS28	S11	51
Halliday St., Pud. LS28	T11	52
Hallowes Gro. BD13	C 8	26
Hallowes Park Rd. BD13	C 8	26
Halls North HX3	E18	80
Hallwood Grn. LS28	Q 8	32
Halstead Pl. BD7	L13	66
Halt Lane Ct. LS16	X 5	18
Halton Dr. LS15	GG11	58
Halton Hill LS15	FF11	58
Halton Moor Av. LS9	EE12	57
Halton Moor Rd. LS15	FF12	58
Halton Moor Rd. LS9	DD12	57
Halton Pl. BD5	L13	66
Halycon Hill LS7	BB 7	38
Hambledon Av. BD4	O14	67
Hambleton Bk. HX2	B16	78
Hambleton Dr.		
Hambleton Cres. HX2	B16	78
Hambleton Dr. HX2	B16	78
Hambleton La.	A11	43
Hamilton Av. LS7	CC 9	38
Hamilton Gdns. LS7	BB 9	38
Hamilton Pl. LS7	CC 9	38
Hamilton St. BD8	M11	48
Hamilton Ter. LS7	CC 9	38
Hamilton Vw. LS7	CC 9	38
Hammerstone Leach La., Elland HX5	F24	98
Hammerstones Rd., Elland HX5	F24	98
Hammerton Gro. LS28	T11	52
Crimbles Rd.		
Hammerton St. BD3	O12	49
Hammerton St. BD4	O12	49
Hammerton St., Pud. LS28	T11	52
Hammond Cres. BD11	S15	69
Hammond Crescent Dr. BD4	T15	70
Hammond Pl. BD9	L 9	30
Hammond St. LS3	CC12	56
Hampden Pl. BD5	M13	66
Hampden Pl. HX1	E19	94
Hampden St. BD5	M13	66
Hampshire Ter. LS7	BB10	56
Claypit La.		
Hampton Pl. BD10	O 7	31
Bradford Rd.		
Hampton St. HX1	D20	93
Fenton Rd.		
Handel St. BD7	M11	48
Hanging Gate La.	YY 8	24
Hanley Rd., Mor. LS27	X17	89
Hanover Av. LS3	Z10	55
Hanover Clo. BD8	L10	48
Hanover La. LS3	AA11	55
Hanover Mt. LS3	AA10	55
Hanover Sq.		
Hanover Sq. BD1	M11	48
Hanover Sq. LS3	AA10	55
Hanover St. LS13	V 9	35
Upper Town St.		
Hanover St., S.B. HX6	C20	93
Hanover Vw. LS3	Z10	55
Hanover Av.		
Hanover Way LS3	AA11	55
Hanover Wk. LS1	AA11	55
Denison Rd.		
Hansby Av. LS14	GG 8	40
Hansby Bank LS14	GG 8	40
Hansby Clo. LS14	GG 9	40
Hansby Dr. LS14	GG 8	40
Hansby Garth LS14	GG 8	40
Hansby Gdns. LS14	GG 9	40
Hansby Pl. LS14	GG 8	40
Hanson Ct. BD12	L18	83
Hanson Fold BD12	M17	83
Town Gate		
Hanson La. HX1	D19	93
Hanson Mt. BD12	M18	83
Hanson Rd. HD6	K23	100
Hanson St. BD12	M16	83
Common Rd.		
Hanworth BD12	M16	83
Hanworth Pl.	ZZ 6	6
Harbeck Dr. BD16	E 6	9
Harbour Cres. BD6	L15	66
Harbour Pk. BD6	K15	65
Harbour Rd. BD6	L15	66
Harcourt Av. BD13	F11	63
Harcourt Pl. LS1	AA11	55
Harcourt St. BD4	O13	67
Harcourt St. LS1	AA11	55
Grace St.		
Hard Nese La.	YY10	42

Street	Grid	Page
Hardaker La. BD17	L 6	12
Hardaker St. BD8	M11	48
Harden Brow La. BD16	E 6	9
Moor Edge Low Side		
Harden Gr. BD21	D 4	8
Harden Gro. BD10	Q 9	32
Harden La. BD16	E 7	27
Harden Rd. BD16	E 6	9
Harden Rd. BD21	D 4	8
Hardgate La.	A 7	25
Hardistys Yd. LS10	CC13	74
Waterloo Rd.		
Hardknot Clo. BD7	K13	65
Hardrow Gro. LS12	Y12	54
Highfield Gro.		
Hardrow Rd. LS12	Y12	54
Hardrow Ter. LS12	Y12	54
Highfield Gro.		
Hardwick St. LS10	CC14	74
Hardwicks Yd. LS1	BB11	56
Briggate		
Hardy Av. BD6	M15	66
Hardy Av., Chur. LS27	Y15	72
Hardy Ct. LS27	X17	89
Hardy Fold BD12	M15	66
Hardy Gro. LS11	AA13	73
Wickham St.		
Hardy Pl. HD6	K20	96
Green La.		
Hardy St. BD19	N18	84
Hardy St. BD4	N12	49
Hardy St. BD6	M14	66
Hardy St. HX3	F18	80
Heap St.		
Hardy St. HX3	L21	97
Hardy St. LS11	AA13	73
Hardy St. LS27	X17	89
Hardy Ter. BD6	M14	66
Horsley St.		
Hardy Ter. LS11	AA13	73
Lodge La.		
Hare Av. LS12	V11	53
Hare Farm Av. LS12	V11	53
Hare Farm Clo. LS12	V11	53
Hare La., Pud. LS28	T12	52
Hare Park Mt. LS12	V11	53
Hare St. HX1	D19	93
Harefield Dr. WF17	U18	87
Harefield E. LS15	FF11	58
Harefield W. LS15	FF11	58
Harehill Clo. BD10	O 6	13
Harehill Rd.		
Harehill Rd. BD10	O 6	13
Harehills Av. LS7	CC 9	38
Harehills Av. LS8	CC 9	38
Harehills La. LS7	CC 8	38
Harehills La. LS8	CC 8	38
Harehills La. LS9	EE10	57
Harehills Park Av. LS9	DD10	57
Harehills Park Rd. LS9	DD10	57
Harehills Park Ter. LS9	DD10	57
Harehills Park Vw. LS9	DD10	57
Harehills Pl. LS8	CC 9	38
Harehills Rd. LS8	CC 9	38
Hares Av. LS8	CC 9	38
Hares Mt. LS8	CC 9	38
Hares Rd. LS8	CC 9	38
Hares Ter. LS8	CC 9	38
Hares Vw. LS8	CC 9	38
Harewood Av. HX2	C19	93
Harewood Cres.	A 5	7
Harewood Pl. HX2	D20	93
Harewood Rd.	A 6	7
Harewood Ri.	A 5	7
Harewood St. BD3	O11	47
Harewood St. LS2	BB11	56
Hargreaves St. BD18	M 7	30
Phoenix St.		
Harker Rd. BD12	M15	66
Harker Ter. LS28	S10	51
Harland Clo. BD2	N10	49
Queens Rd.		
Harland Sq. LS2	AA 9	37
Raglan St.		
Harlech Av. LS11	AA14	73
Harlech Cres. LS11	AA14	73
Harlech Gro. LS11	AA14	73
Harlech Mt. LS11	AA14	73
Harlech Rd.		
Harlech Rd. LS11	AA14	73
Harlech St. LS11	AA14	73
Harlech Ter. LS11	AA14	73
Harley Clo. BD8	K11	47
Harley Clo. LS13	U11	52
Harley Ct. LS13	U11	52
Harley Dr. LS13	U11	52
Harley Gdns., Pud. LS28	U11	52
Harley Grn. LS13	U11	52
Harley Rd. LS13	U11	52
Harley Ri. LS13	U11	52
Harley Ter. LS13	U11	52
Harley Vw. LS13	U11	52
Harley Wk. LS13	U11	52
Harlow Rd. BD7	L12	48
Harold Av. LS6	Z10	55
Harold Gro. LS6	Z10	55
Harold Mt. LS6	Z10	55
Harold Pl. BD18	K 7	29
Saltaire Rd.		
Harold Pl. LS6	Z10	55
Harold Rd. LS6	Z10	55
Harold St. BD16	G 5	10
Harold St. LS6	Z10	55
Harold Ter. LS6	Z10	55
Harold Vw. LS6	Z10	55
Harold Wk. LS6	Z10	55
Harp La. BD13	F14	63
Harper Av. BD10	O 6	13
Harper Cres. BD10	P 6	14
Harper Gro. BD10	O 6	13
Harper La. LS19	R 4	15
Harper Pl. LS2	BB11	56
Harper St.		
Harper St. LS2	BB11	56
Harriet St. BD8	L11	48
Harriet St. HD6	L21	97
Lee St.		
Harriet St. LS7	BB 9	38
Harrington St. BD7	M11	48
Handel St.		
Harris Ct. BD7	L13	66
Harris St. BD1	N11	49
Harris St. BD16	H 6	10
Harrison Av., Stan. LS28	T10	52
Harrison Cres. LS9	EE10	57
Harrison Pl. WF17	T18	87
Blackburn Rd.		
Harrison Rd. HX1	F20	94
Harrison St. BD16	H 6	10
Church St.		
Harrison St. LS1	BB11	56
Harrogate Av. BD3	O10	49
Harrogate Pl. BD3	O10	49
Harrogate Rd. BD10	O10	49
Harrogate Rd. BD2	O10	49
Harrogate Rd. LS19	R 5	15
Harrogate Rd. LS7	BB 8	38
Harrogate Rd.,	Q 7	32
Greengates BD10		
Harrogate Rd., Yea. LS19	T 3	1
Harrogate St. BD3	O10	49
Harrogate Ter. BD3	O10	49
Harrop La. BD15	E 9	27
Harrow St. HX1	D19	93
Harrowby Cres. LS16	X 7	36
Harrowby Rd. LS16	X 7	36
Harry La. BD14	H13	64
Harry St. BD4	P14	68
Hart St. BD7	L13	66
Harthill Av., Gild. LS27	V15	71
Harthill Clo., Gild. LS27	V15	71
Harthill La., Gild. LS27	V15	71
Harthill LS27	V15	71
Harthill Ri., Gild. LS27	V15	71
Hartington Ter. BD7	L12	48
Hartland Rd. BD4	Q13	68
Hartley Av. LS6	AA 9	37
Hartley Bank La. HX3	J17	82
Hartley Bldgs., Mor. LS27	X17	89
Hartley Cres. LS6	AA 9	37
Hartley Gro. LS6	AA 9	37
Hartley St. BD4	O12	49
Hartley St., Chur. LS27	X15	72
Hartley St., Mor. LS27	X17	89
Hartlington Ct. BD17	N 5	13
Kirklands La.		
Hartman Pl. BD9	K10	47
Harton Ter. LS11	AA13	73
Cemetery Rd.		
Hartwell Rd. LS6	Z10	55
Harwill App., Chur. LS27	Y15	72
Harwill Av., Chur. LS27	Y15	72
Harwill Gro., Chur. LS27	Y15	72
Harwill Ri., Chur. LS27	Y15	72
Haslam Clo. BD3	O11	49
Haslam Gro. BD18	N 8	31
Haslewood Clo. LS9	CC11	56
Haslewood Ct. LS9	CC11	56
Haslewood Dene LS9	CC11	56
Haslewood Dr. LS9	CC11	56
Haslewood Gdns. LS9	CC11	56
Haslewood Grn. LS9	CC11	56
Haslewood Lawn LS9	CC11	56
Haslewood Mt. LS9	CC11	56
Haslewood Pl. LS9	CC11	56
Haslewood Sq. LS9	CC11	56
Haslingden Dr. BD9	K10	47
Hastings Av. BD5	M14	66
Hastings Pl. BD5	M14	66
Hastings St. BD5	M14	66
Hastings Ter. BD5	M14	66
Hatchet La. BD12	O17	84
Hatfield Rd. BD2	O10	49
Hatfield St. LS9	CC11	56
Shannon St. 9		
Hathaway Av. BD9	J 9	29
Hathaway Dr. LS14	GG 6	22
Hathaway La. LS14	GG 7	40
Hathaway Ms. LS14	GG 6	22
Hathaway Wk. LS14	GG 6	22
Hatters Fell HX1	F19	94
Thomas St.		
Hatton Clo. BD6	M15	66
Haugh End La. HX6	B21	92
Haugh Shaw Rd. HX1	E20	94
Hauxwell Dr. LS19	R 4	15
Havelock Sq. BD13	G12	46
Havelock St. BD13	G12	46
Havelock St. BD7	K13	65
Haven Cft. LS16	W 5	17
Haven Chase LS16	W 5	17
Haven Clo. LS16	W 5	17
Haven Ct. LS16	W 5	17
Haven Garth LS16	W 5	17
Haven Gdns. LS16	W 5	17
Haven Grn. LS16	W 5	17
Haven Ri. LS16	W 5	17
Haven Vw. LS16	W 5	17
Haven, The BD10	P 8	32
Haven, The LS15	HH11	59
Havercroft LS12	X11	54
Cross La.		
Hawes Av. BD5	M14	66
Hawes Cres. BD5	M14	66
Hawes Dr. BD5	M14	66
Hawes Gro. BD5	M14	66
Hawes Mt. BD5	M14	66
Hawes Mt. LS6	AA 9	37
Hawes Pl. LS6	AA 9	37
Hawes Rd. BD5	L14	66
Hawes Ter. BD5	M14	66
Hawes Ter. LS6	AA 9	37
Hawkesbridge La.	YY 9	24
Hawkhill Av. LS15	GG 9	40
Hawkhill Dr. LS15	GG 9	40
Hawkhill Gdns. LS15	GG 9	40
Hawkhills LS7	CC 7	38
Hawkhurst Rd. LS12	Y12	54
Hawkins Dr. LS7	BB10	56
Hawks Nest Gdns. E. LS17	BB 5	20
Hawks Nest Gdns. S. LS17	BB 5	20
Hawks Nest Gdns. W. LS17	BB 5	20
Hawks Nest Ri. LS17	BB 5	20
Hawkshead Clo. BD5	N12	49
Hawkshead Cres. LS14	FF 9	40
Hawkshead Dr. BD5	N12	49
Hawkshead Wk. BD5	N13	67
Hawkshead Dr.		
Hawkstone Av. LS20	P 4	14
Hawkswood Av. BD9	K 9	29
Hawkswood Av. LS5	W 7	35
Hawkswood Clo. BD17	N 5	13
Hawkswood Cres. LS5	W 7	35
Hawkswood Gro. LS5	W 8	35
Hawkswood Mt. LS5	W 7	35
Hawkswood Pl. LS5	W 8	35
Hawkswood St. LS5	W 8	35
Hawkswood Ter. LS5	W 8	35
Hawkswood Vw. LS5	W 7	35
Hawksworth Gro. LS5	W 8	35
Hawksworth Rd. BD17	M 4	12
Hawksworth Rd., Hor. LS18	V 7	35
Hawkyards Bldgs., Elland HX5	H24	99
Hawley Ter. BD10	Q 9	32
Haworth Gro. BD9	K 9	29
Haworth Rd. BD13	B 8	25
Haworth Rd. BD15	H 9	28
Haworth Rd. BD9	H 9	28
Hawthorn Av. BD18	M 8	30
Hawthorn Av. BD3	Q11	50
Hawthorn Dr. BD10	P 7	32
Hawthorn Dr. LS13	S 8	33
Hawthorn Gro. BD17	N 5	13
Hawthorn Gro. LS13	S 8	33
Hawthorn Mt. LS7	BB 7	38
Hawthorn Pl. LS12	Y11	54
Hall La.		
Hawthorn Rd. LS7	BB 7	38
Hawthorn St. HX1	E20	94
Hyde Park Rd.		

135

136

Street	Ref	Page
Henshaw La. LS19	R 4	15
Henshaw Oval LS19	R 4	15
Henworth Rd. BD12	M16	83
Hepworth Av., Chur. LS27	X15	72
Hepworth Clo., Chur. LS27	X15	72
Hepworth Av.		
Hepworth Cres. LS27	X15	72
Herbalist St. LS12	X11	54
Tong Rd.		
Herbert Gro. LS7	BB10	56
Oatland Rd.		
Herbert Pl. BD3	Q11	50
Herbert St. BD14	J13	65
Herbert St. BD16	H 8	28
Main St.		
Herbert St. BD18	K 7	29
Herbert St. BD5	M13	66
Herbert St. HX1	D20	93
Herbert St.,	H 5	10
Bingley BD16		
Hereford Way BD4	O13	67
New Hey Rd.		
Herman St. BD4	P14	68
Hermit St. BD21	B 6	7
Hermon Av. HX1	E20	94
Hermon Gro. HX1	E20	94
Hermon Rd. LS15	GG10	58
Hermon St. LS15	GG10	58
Heron Clo. LS17	CC 5	20
Heron Gro. LS17	CC 5	20
Herschel Rd. BD8	J11	47
Hertford Cft. LS15	HH12	59
Hertford Chase LS15	HH12	59
Hertford Clo. LS15	HH12	59
Darnley La.		
Hertford Fold LS15	HH12	59
Hertford Lawn LS15	HH12	59
Darnley La.		
Hertford St. LS10	CC13	74
Waterloo Rd.		
Heshbon St. BD4	P13	68
Hesketh Av. LS5	X 9	36
Hesketh Mt. LS5	X 8	36
Hesketh Pl. HX3	L19	97
East View St.		
Hesketh Pl. LS5	X 8	36
Hesketh Rd. LS5	X 8	36
Hesketh Ter. LS5	X 9	36
Hessle Av. LS6	Z 9	37
Hessle Mt. LS6	Z 9	37
Hessle Pl. LS6	Z 9	37
Hessle St. LS6	Z 9	37
Walmsley Rd.		
Hessle Ter. LS6	Z 9	37
Hessle Vw. LS6	Z 9	37
Hessle Wk. LS6	Z 9	37
Hetton Rd. LS8	DD 8	39
Hey St. BD7	M11	48
Hey St. HD6	L21	97
Rayner Rd.		
Hey St., Brig.	L21	97
Heybeck Wk. BD4	Q14	68
Heygate Clo. BD17	M 5	12
Heygate La. BD17	M 5	12
Heys Av. BD13	G12	46
Heys Cres. BD13	H12	46
Heysham Dr. BD4	Q14	68
Heywood Clo. HX3	H18	81
Heywood Lawn LS10	BB13	74
Heywood Pl. LS10	BB13	74
Hulland St.		
Heywood St. HX1	E19	94
West Hill St.		
Heywood St. LS10	BB13	74
Hulland St.		
Hick St. BD1	N11	49
Higgin La. HX3	G20	95
High Ash Av. LS17	CC 4	20
High Ash BD18	N 7	31
High Ash Cres. LS17	CC 4	20
High Ash Dr. LS17	CC 4	20
High Ash Mt. LS17	CC 4	20
High Ash Pk. BD15	G10	46
High Bank App. LS15	HH11	59
High Bank Clo. LS15	HH11	59
High Bank Cotts. BD18	K 7	29
Moorhead La.		
High Bank Gate LS15	HH11	59
High Bank Gdns. LS15	JJ11	59
High Bank La. BD18	J 8	29
High Bank LS28	S 9	33
Water La.		
High Bank Pl. LS15	HH11	59
High Bank Vw. LS15	HH11	59
High Bank Way LS15	JJ11	59
High Binns	ZZ10	42
High Busy La. BD10	N 7	31
High Busy La. BD18	N 7	31
High Cliffe LS4	Y 9	36
St. Michaels La.		
High Clo. LS19	R 5	15
High Court La. LS2	BB11	56
High Cross La. BD13	G15	64
High Cross La. HX3	G15	64
High Dale Ter. BD10	O 7	31
High Fernley Ct. BD12	M17	83
High Fernley Rd. BD12	L17	83
High Fold	A 4	7
High Fold LS19	R 5	15
High Garth BD17	L 6	12
High Gro. LS28	S11	51
High Grove La. HX3	G20	95
High Grove Ter. HX3	G20	95
High House Av. BD2	O 9	31
High House Rd. BD2	O 9	31
High La. HX2	B19	92
High Level Way HX1	D19	93
High Markland St. LS9	CC11	56
Ellerby Rd.		
High Meadows HX4	F23	98
High Moor Av. LS17	CC 6	20
High Moor Clo. LS17	CC 5	20
High Moor Cres. LS17	CC 5	20
High Moor Ct. LS17	CC 6	20
High Moor Dr. LS17	CC 5	20
High Moor Gro. LS17	CC 5	20
High Moor Rd. HD6	N20	103
High Park Cres. BD9	K 9	29
High Park Dr. BD9	K 9	29
High Park Gro. BD9	K 9	29
High Ridge Av., Roth.	EE15	75
LS26		
High Ridge Pk., Roth.	EE15	75
LS26		
High Ridge Way, LS16	W 2	2
High Ridge, Roth. LS26	FF15	76
High Spring Rd. BD21	D 4	8
High St. BD10	O 7	31
High St. BD6	L14	66
High St. HD6	L21	97
High St. HX1	E20	94
Kent St.		
High St. LS19	S 4	15
High St. LS28	S 9	33
High St. Pl. BD10	O 7	31
High St.		
High St. WF17	T18	87
High St., Greet.	F23	98
High St., Luddenden HX2	A18	78
High St., Mor. LS27	X17	89
High St., Queens. BD13	G14	64
High St., Rod. LS13	T 9	34
High St., Thornton BD13	F12	45
High Sunderland La. HX3	F18	80
Highbridge Ter. BD5	N14	67
Highbury Clo. LS6	Z 8	37
Highbury Gro. LS13	U11	52
Harley Rd.		
Highbury La. LS6	Z 8	37
Monks Bridge Rd.		
Highbury Mt. LS6	Z 8	37
Highbury Pl. LS13	U11	52
Highbury Pl. LS6	Z 8	37
Highbury Rd. BD4	P12	50
Highbury Rd. LS6	Z 8	37
Highbury St. LS13	U11	52
Harley Rd.		
Highbury St. LS6	Z 8	37
Highbury Ter. LS13	U11	52
Harley Rd.		
Highbury Ter. LS6	Z 8	37
Highcliffe Dr. HX2	C19	93
Highcliffe Rd., Mor. LS27	W17	88
Highcroft Clo. LS28	S11	51
Higher Brockwell HX6	A21	92
Higher Downs BD8	J11	47
Higher Grange Rd., Pud.	T11	52
LS28		
Surrey Rd.		
Higher Intake Rd. BD2	P10	50
Higher School BD18	K 7	29
Victoria Rd.		
Highfield Av. BD10	O 7	31
Highfield Av. HD6	L19	97
Highfield Av. HX3	J15	65
Highfield Av. LS12	Y12	54
Highfield Av., Elland	H23	99
HX5		
Highfield Av., Greet.	E23	98
HX4		
Highfield Clo. LS12	Y12	54
Highfield Clo., Gild.	W15	71
LS27		
Highfield Cres. BD17	M 5	12
Highfield Cres. BD9	J 9	29
Highfield Cres. LS28	S11	51
Highfield Cres., Wood.	HH15	77
LS26		
Highfield Ct.	ZZ 6	6
Highfield Dr. BD9	J 9	29
Highfield Dr. HX2	A19	92
Highfield Dr. LS19	S 5	15
Highfield Dr. WF17	T18	87
Highfield Dr., Gild. LS27	V15	71
Highfield Garth LS12	Y12	54
Highfield Gdns. BD9	J 9	29
Highfield Gdns. LS12	Y12	54
Highfield Gdns., Gild.	V15	71
LS27		
Highfield Gro. BD10	O 8	31
Highfield HX3	H16	82
Highfield La.	ZZ 5	6
Highfield La., Wood.	HH15	77
LS26		
Highfield Pl. HX1	D20	93
Highfield Pl. LS12	Z11	55
Bruce St.		
Highfield Pl., Mor. LS27	X17	89
Highfield Rd. BD10	O 8	31
Highfield Rd. BD9	M 8	30
Highfield Rd. HD6	K23	100
Highfield Rd. HX2	A19	92
Highfield Rd. LS13	V10	53
Highfield Rd. LS28	S11	51
Highfield Rd., Elland HX5	G23	99
Highfield St. LS13	V10	53
Lower Town St.		
Highfield St. LS28	S11	51
Highfield St., Elland	G24	99
HX5		
Highfield Ter. BD12	M17	83
Highfield Ter. BD13	F15	63
Highfield Ter. BD18	K 7	29
Highfield Ter. LS13	V10	53
Lower Town St.		
Highfield Ter. LS28	S11	51
Highfield Vw., Gild. LS27	W15	71
Highgate BD9	K 9	29
Highgate Clo. BD13	J14	65
Highgate Gro. BD13	J14	65
Highgate Rd. BD13	G14	64
Highgate Rd. LS10	CC13	74
Highland Pl. HX2	D16	79
Highlands Clo. BD7	K13	65
Highlands Clo. LS26	CC15	91
Highlands Dr. LS26	CC15	91
Highlands Gro. BD7	K13	65
Highlands La. HX2	D16	79
Highlands Pk. HX2	D16	79
Highlands Wk. LS26	CC15	91
Highlandville HX3	J19	96
Highlea Clo. LS19	Q 4	14
Highlees Rd. HX2	B16	78
Highley Pk., Brig.	N21	103
Highmoor Cres. HD6	M21	97
Highroad Well Ct. HX2	C19	93
Highroad Well La. HX2	C19	93
Highthorne Av. BD3	P10	50
Highthorne Dr. LS17	CC 5	20
Highthorne Gro. LS12	X11	54
Highthorne St.		
Highthorne Mt. LS17	CC 5	20
Highthorne St. LS12	X11	54
Highthorne Vw. LS12	X11	54
Highthorne St.		
Highways LS14	FF10	58
Highwood Av. LS17	BB 5	20
Highwood Cres. LS17	BB 5	20
Highwood Gro. LS17	BB 5	20
Hilda St. BD9	L 9	30
Highgate		
Hill Cft. BD17	G11	46
Hill Clo. BD17	L 6	12
Hill Cres. HX3	G20	95
Hill Cres. LS19	S 4	15
Hill Crest Clo. LS26	JJ14	77
Hill Crest Rd. BD13	F11	45
Hill End Clo. LS12	W11	53
Hill End Cres. LS12	W11	53
Hill End Gro. BD7	K13	65
Hill End La.,	D 7	26
Cullingworth BD23		
Hill End La.,	F15	63
Queens. BD13		
Hill End LS12	W11	53
Hill End Rd. LS12	W11	53
Hill Foot BD18	K 7	29
Hill House Edge La.	YY10	42
Hill House La.	ZZ10	42
Hill Lands BD12	L16	83
Hill Park Av. HX3	D18	79
Hill Rise Av. LS13	V 9	35
Hill Rise Gro. LS13	V 9	35
Hill Side Mt. LS28	T10	51

Name	Grid	Page
Hill Side Rd. BD3	O11	49
Hill Side Ter. BD3	O11	49
Nuttall Rd.		
Hill Side Vw., Stan. LS28	T10	52
Hill Side WF17	T18	87
Upper Batley La.		
Hill St. BD21	B 4	7
Hill St. BD4	O12	49
Hill St. BD6	L14	66
Hill St. LS11	AA13	73
Hill St. LS9	CC10	56
Hill St., Haworth	ZZ 8	24
Hill Top Av. LS8	CC 9	38
Hill Top Clo. LS11	W12	53
Hill Top Gro. BD15	H10	46
Hill Top La. BD15	H10	46
Hill Top LS12	W10	53
Stanningley Rd.		
Hill Top Mt. LS8	CC 9	38
Hill Top Rd. BD13	E11	45
Hill Top Rd. BD21	B 5	7
Hill Top Rd. LS12	W11	53
Hill Top Rd. LS6	Z10	55
Hill Top Rd., S.B. HD6	B20	92
Hill View Av. LS7	BB 7	38
Norfolk Gdns.		
Hill View Gdns. HX3	H18	81
Hill View Mt. LS7	BB 7	38
Pasture La.		
Hill View Pl. LS7	BB 7	38
Pasture La.		
Hill View Ter. LS7	BB 7	38
Pasture La.		
Hill Vw. HX2	D15	62
Hillam Rd. BD2	M 9	30
Hillam Rd. BD8	M10	48
Hillam St. BD5	L13	66
Hillam St. LS11	Z12	55
Domestic St.		
Hillary Pl. LS2	AA10	55
Hillary Rd. BD18	N 7	31
Hillcourt Av. LS13	V 9	35
Hillcourt Dr. LS13	V 9	35
Hillcourt Gro. LS13	V 9	35
Hillcrest Av. LS7	CC 9	38
Hillcrest Av.,	C10	44
Denholme BD13		
Hillcrest Av.,	G15	64
Queens. BD13		
Hillcrest Dr. BD13	C10	44
Hillcrest Mt. BD13	C10	44
Hillcrest Mt. BD19	N19	103
Hillcrest Mt. LS16	W 5	17
Hillcrest Pl. LS7	CC 9	38
Hillcrest Rd.,	C10	44
Denholme BD13		
Hillcrest Rd., Queens.	G15	64
BD13		
Hillcrest Ri. LS16	W 5	17
Hillcrest Vw. BD13	C10	44
Hillcrest Vw. LS7	CC 9	38
Hillcroft Ct. BD5	N13	67
Ripley St.		
Hillfoot Av. LS28	R11	51
Hillfoot Cres. LS28	R11	51
Hillfoot Dr. LS28	R11	51
Hillfoot Ri. LS28	R11	51
Hillhead Dr. WF17	U18	87
Hillidge Rd. LS10	BB13	74
Hillidge Sq. LS10	BB13	74
Hillingdon Way LS17	AA 4	19
Hillside Av.	YY 6	6
Hillside Ct. LS7	CC 7	38
Hillside Grn.	YY 6	6
Hillside Gro., Pud. LS28	T11	52
Hillside Mt., Pud. LS28	U11	52
Hillside Rd. BD16	G 5	10
Hillside Rd. BD18	M 8	30
Hillside Rd. LS7	BB 7	38
Hillside St. LS9	CC10	56
Hill St.		
Hillside Ter. BD17	M 5	12
Brow Gate		
Hillside Vw., Pud. LS28	T11	52
Hillsman Park Clo. LS27	Y15	72
Hillsman Park La. LS27	Y15	72
Hillthorpe Rd., Pud. LS28	T12	52
Hillthorpe Sq. LS28	T12	52
Hillthorpe St. LS28	T12	52
Hillthorpe Ter. LS28	T12	52
Hillview Ri. BD4	Q13	68
Hilton Av. BD18	L 8	30
Hilton Cres. BD17	M 6	12
Hilton Dr. BD18	L 8	30
Hilton Gro. BD18	L 8	30
Hilton Gro. BD7	L12	48
Hilton Gro. LS8	CC 9	38
Hilton Pl. LS8	CC 9	38
Hilton Rd. BD18	L 8	30
Hilton Rd. BD7	L12	48
Hilton Rd. LS8	CC 9	38
Hinchcliffe Av. BD17	M 6	12
Hinchcliffe St. BD3	O11	49
Hind St. BD12	M18	83
Hind St. BD8	M11	48
Hindley Wk BD7	J14	65
Hird Av. BD6	M15	66
Hird Rd. BD12	M16	83
Hird St. BD17	L 7	30
Hird St. BD21	B 4	7
Lister St.		
Hird St. LS11	AA13	73
Tempest Rd.		
Hirst La. BD18	K 7	29
Hirst Lodge Ct. BD2	N 8	31
Wood La.		
Hirst Mill La. BD16	K 6	11
Hirst Wood Cres. BD18	K 7	29
Hirst Wood Rd. BD18	J 7	29
Hirsts Yd. LS1	BB11	56
Briggate		
Hive St. BD21	B 4	7
Hob Cote La.	YY 6	6
Hobberley La. LS17	FF 5	22
Hobson Fold BD12	M18	83
Craiglea Dr.		
Hockney Rd. BD8	L11	48
Hodeon Yd. BD2	P 9	32
Victoria Rd.		
Hodgson Av. BD3	P11	50
Hodgson Av. LS17	DD 5	21
Hodgson Cres. LS17	DD 5	21
Hodgson Fold BD2	N 9	31
Hodgson La. BD11	R16	86
Hodgson La. BD4	R16	86
Hodgson Sq. BD4	P12	50
Laisterdyke		
Hoglands Pass. HX1	F19	94
Pellon La.		
Holbeck La. LS11	Z12	55
Holbeck Moor Rd. LS11	AA12	55
Holborn App. LS6	AA 9	37
Holborn Ct. BD12	M16	83
Holborn Ct. LS6	AA 9	37
Shay St.		
Holborn Gdns. LS6	AA 9	37
Holborn Grn. LS6	AA 9	37
Cathcart St.		
Holborn Gro. LS6	AA 9	37
Holborn App.		
Holborn St. LS6	AA 9	37
Holborn Ter. LS6	AA 9	37
Holborn Towers LS6	AA 9	37
Shay St.		
Holborn Vw. LS6	AA 9	37
Cathcart St.		
Holden La.	YY10	42
Holden La. BD17	N 5	13
Station Rd.		
Holden Rd. BD6	L14	66
Holden St.	A 4	7
Holderness Pl. LS6	Z10	55
Holderness Ter. LS6	Z10	55
Kings Rd.		
Holdforth Chase LS12	Z11	55
Holdforth Gdns. LS12	Z11	55
Holdforth Grn. LS12	Z11	55
Holdforth Pl. LS12	Z11	55
Holdforth Sq. LS9	BB11	56
Cotton St.		
Holdsworth Bldgs. BD2	P 9	32
Holdsworth Sq.		
Holdsworth La. HX2	E16	80
Holdsworth Sq. BD2	P 9	32
Holdsworth St. BD1	N11	49
Holdsworth St. BD12	M17	83
Temperance St.		
Holdsworth St. BD18	M 8	30
Crag Rd.		
Holdsworths Fold LS9	CC11	56
Richmond St.		
Holker St. BD8	L10	48
Holland St. BD4	P12	50
Hollin Close La. BD2	N 9	31
Hollin Cres. LS16	Y 7	36
Hollin Dr. LS16	Y 7	36
Hollin Gdns. LS16	Y 7	36
Hollin Greaves La. HX3	F18	80
Hollin Hall Rd. BD18	K 8	29
Hollin Head BD17	N 5	13
Hollin Head Clo. BD18	K 7	29
Hollin Hill Av. LS8	EE 8	39
Hollin Hill Dr. LS8	EE 8	39
Hollin La. BD18	M 8	30
Hollin La. LS16	Y 7	36
Hollin Mt. LS16	Y 7	36
Hollin Park Av. LS8	EE 8	39
Hollin Park Cres. LS8	EE 8	39
Hollin Park Dr. LS28	R 8	33
Hollin Park Mt. LS8	EE 8	39
Hollin Park Pl. LS8	EE 8	39
Hollin Park Rd. LS28	R 8	33
Hollin Park Rd. LS8	EE 8	39
Hollin Park Ter. LS8	EE 8	39
Hollin Park Vw. LS8	EE 8	39
Hollin Pl. LS16	Y 6	18
Weetwood La.		
Hollin Rd. BD18	M 8	30
Hollin Rd. LS16	Y 7	36
Hollin Ri. BD18	M 8	30
Crag Rd.		
Hollin Ter. BD18	M 8	30
Crag Rd.		
Hollin Vw. LS16	Y 7	36
Hollingbourne Rd. LS15	JJ10	41
Hollings Rd. BD8	L11	48
Hollings St. BD16	H 7	28
Hollings St. BD8	L11	48
Hollings Ter. BD8	L11	48
Hollingwood Av. BD7	K13	65
Hollingwood Ct. BD7	K13	65
Hollingwood Dr. BD7	K13	65
Hollingwood La. BD7	K13	65
Hollingwood Mt. BD7	K13	65
Hollins Hill BD17	O 4	13
Hollins La. HX2	C16	79
Hollins La., S.B. HX6	B20	92
Hollis Pl. LS3	Z10	55
Holly Av. LS8	V 5	17
Holly Bank Dr. HX3	J19	96
Holly Dr. LS16	V 5	17
Holly Hall La. BD12	M17	83
Holly Park Dr. BD7	K13	65
Holly Park Gro. BD7	K13	65
Holly St. BD6	J14	65
Hollybank Gdns. BD7	K13	65
Hollybank Gro. BD7	K13	65
Hollybank Rd. BD7	K13	65
Hollybank Rd. HD6	K23	100
Hollycroft Ct. LS16	X 5	18
Hollyshaw Cres. LS15	HH11	59
Hollyshaw Gro. LS15	HH11	59
Hollyshaw La. LS15	HH10	59
Hollyshaw St. LS15	HH11	59
Hollyshaw Ter. LS15	HH11	59
Hollyshaw St.		
Hollyshaw Wk. LS15	HH10	59
Hollywell Ash La. BD8	M10	48
Manningham La.		
Hollywell La. LS12	X11	54
Holm La. HX2	A16	78
Holm Ter. HD6	L19	97
Holme Dr. HX2	B20	92
Holme House La.	YY 4	6
Holme House La.	ZZ 4	6
Holme House La. HX2	A17	78
Holme House La. BD4	Q13	68
Holme Mill La.	A 4	7
Holme Rd. HX2	B20	92
Holme St.	ZZ10	42
Holme St. BD5	M13	66
Holme Top La. BD5	M13	66
Holme Top St. BD5	M13	66
Newstead Wk.		
Holme Wood Rd. BD4	P13	68
Holmes La. BD2	M 9	30
Holmes Rd., S.B. HX6	C21	93
Holmes St. BD8	M11	48
White Abbey Rd.		
Holmes St. LS11	BB12	56
Holmewood Rd.	A 4	7
Holmfield Dr. LS8	CC 6	20
Holmfield Gdns. HX2	E16	80
Holmsley Crest, Wood.	GG15	76
LS26		
Holmsley Garth, Wood.	GG15	76
LS26		
Holmwood Av. LS6	Z 7	37
Holmwood Clo. LS6	Z 7	37
Holmwood Cres. LS6	Z 7	37
Holmwood Dr. LS6	Z 7	37
Holmwood Gro. LS6	Z 7	37
Holmwood Mt. LS6	Z 7	37
Holmwood Vw. LS6	Z 7	37
Holroyd Hill BD6	M14	66
Holroyd St. LS7	BB10	55
Holroyd Yd. LS11	BB12	56
Meadow La.		
Holsworthy Rd. BD4	P14	68
Holt Av. LS16	Y 4	18
Holt Clo. LS16	Y 5	18
Holt Dr. LS16	X 4	18

Street	Grid	Page
Holt Farm Ri. LS16	W 4	17
Holt Garth LS16	X 4	18
Holt Gate LS16	X 4	18
Holt Rd.		
Holt Gdns. LS16	Y 4	18
Holt Grn. LS16	X 4	18
Holt La. LS16	W 4	17
Holt Lane Ct. LS16	X 5	18
Holt Park App. LS16	X 4	18
Holt Park Av. LS16	X 4	18
Holt Park Clo. LS16	X 4	18
Holt Park Cres. LS16	X 4	18
Holt Park Dr. LS16	X 4	18
Holt Park Gate LS16	X 4	18
Holt Park Gdns. LS16	X 4	18
Holt Park Grange LS16	X 4	18
Holt Park Grn. LS16	X 4	18
Holt Park Gro. LS16	W 4	17
Holt Park La. LS16	X 4	18
Holt Park Rd. LS16	X 4	18
Holt Park Ri. LS16	X 4	18
Holt Park Vale LS16	X 4	18
Holt Park Way LS16	X 4	18
Holt Rd. LS16	X 4	18
Holt Ri. LS16	X 4	18
Holt St. HX1	E20	94
Holt Vale LS16	X 4	18
Holt Rd.		
Holt Vw. LS16	Y 4	18
Holt Way LS16	X 4	18
Holt Wk. LS16	X 4	18
Holt Rd.		
Holt, The BD18	M 7	30
Holtby Gro. HX3	L19	97
Holtdale App. LS16	W 4	17
Holtdale Av. LS16	W 4	17
Holtdale Cft. LS16	W 4	17
Holtdale Clo. LS16	W 4	17
Holtdale Dr. LS16	W 4	17
Holtdale Fold LS16	W 4	17
Holtdale Garth LS16	W 4	17
Holtdale Gdns. LS16	W 4	17
Holtdale Grn. LS16	W 4	17
Holtdale Gro. LS16	W 4	17
Holtdale Pl. LS16	W 4	17
Holtdale Rd. LS16	W 4	17
Holtdale Vw. LS16	W 4	17
Holtdale Way LS16	W 4	17
Holts La. BD14	H12	46
Holybrook Av. BD10	P 8	32
Holycroft St. BD21	B 4	7
Holyoake Av. BD16	H 6	10
Holywell Ash La. BD1	M10	48
Holywell La. LS17	EE 4	21
Holywell Vw. LS17	EE 4	21
Home Lea, Roth. LS26	EE15	75
Home Vw. Ter. BD8	L10	48
Hopbine Av. BD5	N14	67
Hope Av. BD18	M 7	30
Hope Av. BD5	M14	66
Hope Av. LS12	Y11	54
Hope Cres. LS12	W10	53
Stanningley Rd.		
Hope Gro. LS12	W10	53
Stanningley Rd.		
Hope Gro. LS12	Y11	54
Hope Hill St. HX1	F20	94
Hope Hill Vw. BD16	H 7	28
Hope La. BD17	L 5	12
Hope Mt. LS12	Y11	54
Hope Pl. BD21	B 4	7
Hope Pl. LS12	Y11	54
Hope Pl. LS2	BB10	56
Hope St. BD18	L 7	30
Ives St.		
Hope St. HX1	E19	94
Hope St. HX3	H17	81
Hope St. HX6	B21	92
Boggart La.		
Hope St., Mor. LS27	X17	89
Hope Vw. BD18	M 7	30
Hope Vw. LS12	W10	53
Stanningley Rd.		
Hopes Farm Mt. LS26	CC15	74
Hopes Farm Rd. LS26	CC15	74
Hopes Farm Vw. LS26	DD15	75
Hopewell Pl. LS6	Z10	55
Harold Rd.		
Hopewell Ter. LS10	BB13	74
Glasshouse St.		
Hopewell Vw. LS10	BB16	91
Hopkinson Av. BD4	P15	68
Hopkinson St. HX3	D17	79
Hopswell St. BD3	P11	50
Hopton Av. BD4	O14	67
Hopwood La. HX1	D20	93
Hopwood Rd., Hor. LS18	V 6	17
Horley Green La. HX3	G18	81

Street	Grid	Page
Horley Green Rd. HX3	G18	81
Horley St. HX3	G19	95
Hornbeam Way LS14	HH 7	41
Hornby St. HX1	D20	93
Fenton Rd.		
Hornby Ter. HX1	D20	93
Fenton Rd.		
Horne St. HX1	E19	94
Hornsea Dr. BD15	F 8	27
Horseman St. BD4	P14	68
Horsfall St. HX1	E20	94
Eldroth Rd.		
Horsfall St., Mor. LS27	W16	88
Horsforth New Rd., Rod.	T 8	34
LS13		
Horsham Clo.	A 4	7
Horsham Rd. BD4	Q14	68
Horsley St. BD6	M14	66
Horton Grange Rd. BD7	L12	48
Horton Hall Clo. BD6	M12	48
Horton Park Av. BD5	L12	48
Horton Park Av. BD7	L12	48
Horton Pl. HX2	D15	62
Horton St. HX1	F20	94
Hospital La. LS16	W 5	17
Hough Clo. LS13	U11	52
Hough End Av. LS13	V10	53
Hough End Clo. LS13	V10	53
Hough End Cres. LS13	V10	53
Hough End Ct. LS13	V10	53
Hough End Garth LS13	V10	53
Hough End Gdns. LS13	V10	53
Hough End Av.		
Hough End La. LS13	V10	53
Hough HX3	H18	81
Hough La. LS13	V10	53
Hough Side Clo., Pud.	U11	52
LS28		
Hough Side La., Pud. LS28	U11	52
Hough Side Rd., Pud. LS28	T11	52
Hough Top LS13	U11	52
Hough Tree Rd. LS13	V11	53
Hough Tree Ter. LS13	V11	53
Pudsey Rd.		
Houghley Av. LS12	W10	53
Houghley Clo. LS13	W10	53
Houghley Cres. LS12	W10	53
Houghley Gro. LS12	W10	53
Houghley La. LS13	W10	53
Houghley Mt. LS12	W10	53
Houghley Pl. LS12	W10	53
Houghley Rd. LS12	W10	53
Houghley Sq. LS12	W10	53
Houghley St. LS12	W10	53
Houghley Ter. LS12	W10	53
Houghley Vw. LS12	W10	53
Houghton Pl. BD1	M11	48
Hougomont BD13	H13	64
Hougomont St. LS11	Z12	55
Wortley La.		
Hoults La., Greet. HX4	E23	98
Hoults, The, Greet. HX4	F23	98
Hovingham Av. LS8	DD 9	39
Hovingham Gro. LS8	DD 9	39
Hovingham Mt. LS8	DD 9	39
Hovingham Av.		
Hovingham Ter. LS8	DD 9	39
Hovingham Av.		
Howard Av. LS15	FF11	58
Howard St. BD5	M12	48
Howard St. HX1	E19	94
Salt St.		
Howarth Av. BD2	O 8	31
Howarth Cres. BD2	O 8	31
Howarth Pl. LS7	BB10	56
Howarth St. LS7	BB10	56
Howarth Pl.		
Howarth Ter. LS7	BB10	56
Howcans La. HX3	E17	80
Howden Clo. BD4	Q14	68
Howden Clough Rd., Mor.	V17	88
LS27		
Howden Gdns. LS6	Z10	55
Howden Pl. LS6	Z10	55
Howden Way, Mor. LS27	V17	88
Howes La. HX3	G17	81
Howgate BD10	P 7	32
Howgill Grn. BD6	L16	83
Hoxton Clo. LS11	Z13	73
Hoxton Mt. LS11	Z13	73
Hoxton Pl. LS11	Z13	73
Hoxton St. BD8	L11	48
Hoxton Ter. LS11	Z13	73
Hoyle Court Av. BD17	N 5	13
Hoyle Court Dr. BD17	N 5	13
Hoyle Court Rd. BD17	N 5	13
Hoyle Ct. BD17	N 5	13
Kirklands Gdns.		

Street	Grid	Page
Hoyle Ing Rd. BD13	G12	46
Hubert St. BD3	O12	49
Hubert St. HX2	C19	93
Huddersfield Rd. BD12	L19	97
Huddersfield Rd. BD6	M15	66
Huddersfield Rd. HD6	L19	97
Huddersfield Rd. HX3	F21	94
Huddersfield Rd. HX4	F22	98
Huddersfield Rd.,	H24	99
Elland HX5		
Huddersfield Rd.,	L23	101
Rastrick HD6		
Huddersfield Rd.,	M16	83
Low Moor BD12		
Hudson Av. BD7	L13	66
Hudson Cres. BD7	L13	66
Hudson Gdns. BD7	L13	66
Cross La.		
Hudson Rd. LS9	DD10	57
Hudson Sq. LS5	X 9	36
Commercial Rd.		
Hudson St. BD3	P11	50
Killinghall Rd.		
Hudson St. LS28	S10	51
New St.		
Hudson St. LS9	DD10	57
Hudson Rd.		
Hudson Ter. LS10	BB13	74
Beza St.		
Hudswell Rd. LS10	BB13	74
Huggan Row LS28	T11	52
Hughenden Dr. BD13	H12	46
Hugill St. BD13	F12	45
Hulbert St. BD16	H 6	10
Hull St., Mor. LS27	X17	89
Hullen Edge, Greet. HX4	F24	98
Hullen Rd., Elland HX5	F24	98
Hullenedge Gdns.,	F24	98
Elland HX5		
Hullenedge La., Greet.	F24	98
HX5		
Hulme St. HX6	B21	92
West St.		
Humane Pl. LS10	CC13	74
Low Rd.		
Humble Pl. LS11	AA12	55
Beeston Rd.		
Humboldt St. BD1	O11	49
Harris St.		
Hume St. HX1	E19	94
Hunger Hill HX1	F20	94
Hunger Hill, Mor. LS27	X17	89
Hunger Hills Av., Hor.	U 6	16
LS18		
Hunger Hills Dr., Hor.	U 6	16
LS18		
Hunslet Hall Rd. LS11	AA13	73
Hunslet La. LS10	BB12	56
Hunslet Rd. LS10	BB11	56
Hunsworth La. BD19	P18	85
Hunt Yd. BD7	L13	66
Great Horton Rd.		
Hunter Hill Rd. HX2	B16	78
Hunters Park Av. BD7	J12	47
Huntingdon Rd. HD6	M22	101
Huntley Pl. LS11	AA13	73
Chester Pl.		
Huntley St. BD18	L 8	30
Valley Rd.		
Huntsman Clo. BD16	J 4	11
Hurst Sq. BD4	Q13	68
Hurstville Av. BD4	Q16	85
Husler Gro. LS7	BB 9	38
Husler Pl. LS7	BB 9	38
Savile Mt.		
Husler Vw. LS7	BB 9	38
Savile Mt.		
Hustler St. BD3	O10	49
Hustlergate BD1	N11	49
Hustlers Row LS6	Y 7	36
Hutchinson La. HD6	L22	101
Commercial St.		
Hutchinson St. HX3	E18	80
Wheatley La.		
Hutchinsons Sq. LS11	Z15	73
Dewsbury Rd.		
Hutson St. BD5	M13	66
Hutton Rd. BD5	M14	66
Hutton Ter. BD2	P 8	32
Hutton Ter., Pud. LS28	T11	52
Huttons Row LS28	Z 7	37
Green Rd.		
Hydale Clo. BD21	D 4	8
Long Lee La.		
Hydale Ct. BD12	M16	83
Hyde Av. BD4	O14	67
Hyde Park Corner LS6	Z 9	37
Hyde Park Rd. HX1	E20	94

139

Street	Ref	Pg
Hyde Park Rd. LS6	Z10	55
Hyde Park St. HX1	E20	94
Hyde Park Ter. LS6	Z 9	37
Hyde Pk. HX1	E20	94
Hyde Pl. LS2	AA10	55
Hyde Ter.		
Hyde St. BD10	O 6	13
Hyde St. LS2	AA10	55
Hyde Ter. LS2	AA10	55
Ida Cres. LS10	DD14	75
Ida Gro. LS10	DD14	75
Ida Mt. LS10	DD14	75
Ida St. BD5	M13	66
Ida St. LS10	DD14	75
Ida Ter. LS10	DD14	75
Ida Vw. LS10	DD14	75
Iddesleigh St. BD4	P12	50
Idle Rd. BD2	O 8	31
Idlecroft Rd. BD10	O 7	31
Idlethorpe Way BD10	P 7	32
Ilbert Av. BD4	O14	67
Ilford St., Mor. LS27	X17	89
Illingworth Av. HX2	D15	62
Illingworth Clo. HX2	D15	62
Illingworth Cres. HX2	D15	62
Illingworth Gdns. HX2	D16	79
Illingworth Gro. HX2	D15	62
Illingworth Rd. BD12	N17	84
Illingworth Rd. HX2	D16	79
Independent St. BD5	M13	66
Industrial Av. WF17	S18	86
Industrial Rd., S.B. HX6	B21	92
Industrial St. BD16	G 5	10
Industrial St. BD19	N19	103
Scholes La.		
Industrial St. BD21	B 4	7
Industrial Ter. HX1	E20	94
Infirmary St. BD1	M11	48
Infirmary St. LS1	AA11	55
Ing St. BD3	P12	50
Ingham La. HX2	D14	62
Ingham St. LS10	BB11	56
Hunslet Rd.		
Ingham St. LS28	S10	51
Varley St.		
Inghams Av. LS28	R11	51
Inghams Ct. HX3	E18	80
East Park Rd.		
Inghams Ter. LS28	R11	51
Inghams Vw. LS28	R11	51
Inghead Gdns. HX3	H17	81
Ingle Av., Mor. LS28	W16	88
Ingle Cres., Mor. LS27	X16	89
Ingle Gro., Mor. LS27	W16	88
Ingleborough Dr., Mor. LS27	Y17	89
Ingleby Pl. BD7	L12	48
Ingleby Rd. BD7	L11	48
Ingleby Rd. BD8	L11	48
Ingleby St. BD8	L11	48
Ingleby Way LS10	CC15	91
Ingledew Cres. LS8	DD 6	21
Ingledew Ct. LS17	BB 5	20
Ingledew Dr. LS8	DD 6	21
Ingleton Dr. LS15	FF11	58
Ingleton Gro. LS11	AA13	73
Rowland		
Ingleton Pl. LS11	AA13	73
Rowland		
Ingleton St. LS11	AA13	73
Rowland		
Inglewood App. LS14	GG 9	40
Inglewood Dr. LS14	GG 9	40
Inglewood Pl. LS14	GG 9	40
Inglewood Ter. LS6	AA 9	37
Delph La.		
Ingram Av. LS15	FF11	58
Ingram Clo. LS11	Z12	55
Cross Ingram Rd.		
Ingram Cres. LS11	Z12	55
Ingram Rd.		
Ingram Gdns. LS11	Z12	55
Ingram Row LS11	AA12	55
Ingram St. HX1	E20	94
Ingram St. LS11	AA12	55
Ingram Vw. LS11	Z12	55
Ingrow La. BD22	B 5	7
Ings Cres. LS9	DD11	57
Ings Rd. LS9	DD11	57
Ings Way BD8	K11	47
Ings, The HX3	L20	97
Inkerman St. BD2	P 9	32
Inkerman St. BD4	P13	68
Institute Rd. BD2	P 8	32
Institution Row LS6	AA 9	37
Raglan Rd.		
Institution St. LS6	AA 9	37
Intake Gro. BD2	P10	50
Intake La.	YY10	42
Intake La. LS10	BB17	91
Intake La. LS19	S 5	15
Intake La., Thorner LS14	HH 5	23
Intake Mt. LS10	BB17	91
Intake Rd. BD2	P10	50
Intake Rd., Pud. LS28	T11	52
Intake Sq. LS10	BB17	91
Intake Ter. BD2	P10	50
Intake Vw. LS10	BB17	91
Intake Vw. LS13	U 9	34
Intercity Ct. LS28	V10	52
Intercity Way LS13	U10	52
Invertrees Av. LS19	S 5	15
Iona St. HX3	F18	80
Ireland Cres. LS16	W 5	17
Ireland St. BD16	G 5	10
Ireland Ter. BD16	G 5	10
Ireton St. BD7	L12	48
Irish La.	YY 6	6
Ironwood App. LS14	GG 9	40
Ironwood Cres. LS14	GG 9	40
Ironwood Vw. LS14	GG 9	40
Irvin App. LS15	FF11	58
Irving St. HX1	D20	93
Irving Ter. BD14	J13	65
Irwell St. BD4	O12	49
Irwin St. LS28	S10	51
Isaac St. BD8	L11	48
Island Ter. LS11	Z12	55
Isle La. LS11	Z12	55
Balm Wk.		
Isles St. BD8	K11	47
Ivanhoe Rd. BD7	L12	48
Ive House La. HX2	A19	92
Ivegate BD1	N11	49
Iveridge Mt. LS10	CC13	74
Iveridge St.		
Ives St. BD17	L 7	30
Iveson App. LS16	W 6	17
Iveson Clo. LS16	W 6	17
Iveson Cres. LS16	W 6	17
Iveson Dr. LS16	W 6	17
Iveson Garth LS16	X 6	18
Iveson Gdns. LS16	W 6	17
Iveson Grn. LS16	W 6	17
Iveson Gro. LS16	W 6	17
Iveson Rd.		
Iveson Lawn LS16	X 6	18
Iveson Rd. LS16	W 6	17
Iveson Ri. LS16	X 6	18
Iveson Wk. LS16	X 6	18
Ivory St. LS10	BB12	56
Ivy Av. LS9	DD11	57
Ivy Bank La.	ZZ 8	24
Ivy Cres. LS9	DD11	57
Ivy Gro. BD18	K 7	29
Ivy Gro. LS9	DD11	57
Ivy La. BD15	H10	46
Ivy Mt. LS9	DD11	57
Ivy Pl. LS13	V 9	35
Ivy Rd. BD18	K 7	29
Ivy Rd. BD21	D 4	8
Ivy Rd. LS9	DD11	57
Ivy St. HX1	E20	94
Ivy St. HX3	K21	96
Ivy St. LS9	DD11	57
Ivy St. S. BD21	B 5	7
Hainsworth Wood Rd.		
Ivy Ter. BD21	D 4	8
Ivy Ter. BD6	L15	66
Ivy Ter. HX3	K19	96
Ivy Vw. LS9	DD11	57
Jack La. LS11	AA12	55
Jackman Dr., Hor. LS18	V 7	35
Jackman Sq. LS6	AA 9	37
Institution St.		
Jackson Av. LS8	CC 7	38
Jackson Hill La. BD13	G15	64
Jackson Ho. LS9	CC11	56
Jackson Rd. LS7	BB 9	38
Jackson St. BD3	O12	49
Jackson St. WF17	T18	87
High St.		
Jacky La.	ZZ 8	24
Cold St.		
Jacob St. BD5	M13	66
Hutson St.		
Jacob St. LS2	BB10	56
Camp Rd.		
James Av. LS8	CC 7	38
James Gate BD1	N11	49
James St.		
James St. BD1	N11	49
James St. BD11	R16	86
Town St.		
James St. BD13	F11	45
James St. BD15	J10	47
James St. BD18	M 8	30
Valley Rd.		
James St. E. BD21	C 4	8
Park La.		
James St. HX4	L21	97
James St. LS19	R 5	15
James St., Elland HX5	G24	99
James St., Oakworth	ZZ 6	6
Jamiecourt BD10	P 8	32
Jane St. BD13	C10	44
Jane St. BD18	K 7	29
Janet St.	A 7	25
Jardine Rd. BD16	H 5	10
Herbert St.		
Jarrat St. BD8	L11	48
Jarrom Clo. BD4	P13	68
Jason Ter. WF17	U18	87
Jasper St. BD10	O 7	31
Jasper St. HX1	D19	93
Queens Rd.		
Jay St.	ZZ 8	24
Jayhouse La. HD6	M20	97
Jean Av. LS15	GG11	58
Jenkinson Clo. LS11	AA12	55
Jenkinson La. LS11	AA12	55
Jenkinson Lawn LS11	AA12	55
Jenkinson Wk. LS11	AA12	55
Jenning St. BD18	M 7	30
Leeds Rd.		
Jennings Pl. BD7	L13	66
Jennings St. BD7	L13	66
Cross La.		
Jenny La. BD17	M 5	12
Jepson La., Elland HX5	G24	99
Jer Gro. BD7	K14	65
Jer La. BD7	K14	65
Jericho St. LS10	CC13	74
Low Rd.		
Jermyn St. BD1	N11	49
Jerry La. HX6	B21	92
Jervaulx Cres. BD8	M11	48
Jerwood Hill Clo. HX3	F18	80
Jerwood Hill Rd. HX3	F18	80
Jesmond Av. BD9	K10	47
Jesmond Gro. BD9	K10	47
Jessamine Av. LS11	Z14	73
Jesse St. BD5	N12	49
Jesse St. BD8	J11	47
Jesse St. LS12	X11	54
Privilege St.		
Jessop St. BD4	Q14	68
Holme La.		
Jester Pl. BD13	F14	63
Jew La.	ZZ10	42
Jinny Nook La., Swil. LS26	JJ15	77
Joggers La. BD22	ZZ 8	24
John Edward St. LS12	Z12	55
Wellington Rd.		
John Escrit Rd. BD16	H 6	10
John Nelson Clo. WF17	T18	87
Brookroyd La.		
John St. BD1	N11	49
John St. BD13	C10	44
John St. BD13	F12	45
John St. BD14	J13	65
John St. BD17	M 6	12
John St. BD18	L 7	30
John St. BD4	Q14	68
John St. HX1	F19	94
Broad St.		
John St. HX4	L21	97
Piggott St.		
John St. LS19	R 5	15
John St. LS28	S 9	33
Water La.		
John St. LS6	Z 9	37
John St. W., S.B. HX6	B21	92
John St. WF17	T18	87
John St., Elland HX5	G24	99
John St., Greet.	F23	94
John St., Oakworth	ZZ 5	6
John St., S.B. HX6	C21	93
Johnson St. BD16	G 5	10
Johnson St. BD3	P11	50
Killinghall Rd.		
Johnson Ter., Mor. LS27	X17	89
Johnston St. LS6	AA 9	37
Johnston Ter. LS6	AA 9	37
Joseph Av. HX3	H18	81
Joseph St. BD3	O11	49
Joseph St. BD4	Q14	68
Joseph St. LS10	BB13	74

Street	Ref	Page
Joshua St. BD5	N13	67
Spring Mill St.		
Jowett Park Cres. BD10	O 6	13
Jowett St. BD1	M11	48
Joys Fold LS9	CC11	56
York Rd.		
Jubilee Dr. BD21	B 4	7
Jubilee Mt. LS6	AA 9	37
Jubilee Pl. LS6	AA 9	37
Jubilee Ter.		
Jubilee Pl., Mor. LS27	X17	89
Jubilee Rd. HX3	F22	98
Jubilee Rd. LS6	AA 9	37
Jubilee St. BD1	M10	48
Jubilee St. BD4	P13	68
Jubilee St. BD8	M10	48
Jubilee St. HX3	F20	94
Jubilee St. LS6	AA 9	37
Jubilee St. N. HX3	E17	80
Jubilee St., Mor. LS27	X17	89
Jubilee Ter. LS6	AA 9	37
Jubilee Ter., Mor. LS27	X17	89
Julian Dr. BD13	J14	65
Jumble Dyke, Brig.	K23	100
Jumbles Ter. LS28	S12	51
Smalewell Rd.		
Jumples Ct. HX2	C17	79
Junction St. LS10	BB12	56
Junction Ter. BD2	O 9	31
Idle Rd.		
Juniper Pl. LS9	DD10	57
Juno St. BD4	P12	50
Karnac Rd. LS8	CC 9	38
Katherine St. BD18	K 7	29
Saltaire Rd.		
Kay St. BD18	M 8	30
Kaycell St. BD4	O14	67
Kaye Hill BD13	C 8	26
Church St.		
Kaye St. LS11	AA12	55
Water La.		
Kearsley Pl. LS10	CC14	74
Nursery Mount Rd.		
Kedleston Rd. LS8	CC 5	20
Keelham Pl. BD13	D12	44
Keeper La. BD4	S13	69
Keeper La., Pud. LS28	T14	70
Keeton St. LS9	CC11	56
Keighley and Hebden	ZZ10	31
Bridge Rd.		
Keighley Clo. HX2	C16	79
Keighley Dr. HX2	D16	79
Keighley Rd.	A 5	7
Keighley Rd.	ZZ 5	6
Keighley Rd. BD13	C 7	26
Keighley Rd. BD16	D 5	8
Keighley Rd. BD16	F 4	9
Keighley Rd. BD9	L 9	30
Keighley Rd. LS28	T10	52
Keighley Rd., Moor Side HX2	D17	79
Keighley Rd., Ogden HX2	C14	62
Keldholme Clo. LS13	T 8	34
Keldholme Rd., Rod. LS13	T 8	34
Keldregate HD6	N24	102
Kell La. HX3	G17	81
Kell St. BD16	H 5	10
Kellee St. BD19	P18	85
Hunsworth La.		
Kellett Av. LS12	Y13	72
Kellett Cres. LS12	Y13	72
Kellett Dr. LS12	Y13	72
Kellett Gro. LS12	Y13	72
Kellett La. LS12	X12	54
Kellett Mt. LS12	Y13	72
Kellett Pl. LS12	Y13	72
Kellett Rd. LS12	X12	54
Kellett Ter. LS12	Y13	72
Kellett Wk. LS12	Y13	72
Kelmore Gro BD6	K16	82
Kelmscott Av. LS15	XH 9	41
Kelmscott Cres. LS15	YH 9	41
Kelmscott Gdns. LS15	YH 9	41
Kelmscott Grn. LS15	XH 9	41
Kelmscott Gro. LS15	YH 9	41
Kelmscott La. LS15	YH 9	41
Kelsall Av. LS6	Z10	55
Kelsall Gro. LS6	Z10	55
Kelsall Pl. LS6	Z10	55
Kelsall Rd. LS6	Z10	55
Kelsall Ter. LS6	Z10	55
Kelso Gdns. LS2	Z10	55
Kelso Pl. LS2	Z10	55
Kelso Rd. LS2	Z10	55
Kelso St. LS2	Z10	55
Kelvin Av. HX2	C20	93
Kelvin Cres. HX2	C20	93
Kelvin Pl. BD4	O12	49
Bowling Back La.		
Kelvin Rd., Elland HX5	G24	99
Kelvin St. BD4	O12	49
Bowling Back La.		
Kelvin Way BD2	P10	50
Kemsing Wk. LS15	JJ 9	41
Kendal Bank LS1	Z10	55
Belle Vue Rd.		
Kendal Clo. LS3	Z10	55
Kendal Dr. LS15	FF11	58
Kendal Gro. LS3	Z10	55
Kendal La.		
Kendal La. LS3	Z10	55
Kendal St. BD21	C 4	8
Kendall Av. BD18	K 7	29
Kendell St. LS10	BB11	56
Kenilworth Av., Gild. LS27	V15	71
Kenilworth Av., Mor. LS27	V16	88
Kenilworth Dr. HD6	L20	97
Kenilworth Gdns. LS27	V15	71
Town St.		
Kenilworth Rd. LS12	Y12	54
Kenilworth St. BD4	O13	67
Kenley Av. BD6	L14	66
Kenley Mt. BD6	L14	66
Kenley Par. BD6	K14	65
Kenmore Cres. BD6	L14	66
Kenmore Dr. BD6	L14	66
Kenmore Gro. BD6	L14	66
Kenmore Rd.		
Kenmore Rd. BD6	L14	66
Kenmore Wk. BD6	L14	66
Kennedy Av. HD6	L24	101
Kennerleigh Av. LS15	HH10	59
Kennerleigh Cres. LS15	HH10	59
Kennerleigh Dr. LS15	HH10	59
Kennerleigh Garth LS15	HH10	59
Kennerleigh Glen LS15	HH10	59
Kennerleigh Gro. LS15	HH10	59
Kennerleigh Ri. LS15	HH10	59
Kennerleigh Wk. BD4	Q14	68
Kennerleigh Wk. LS15	HH10	59
Kenneth St. LS11	Z12	55
Kennion St. BD5	M12	48
Kensington Clo. HX3	E21	94
Kensington Pl. BD10	O 7	31
Bradford Rd.		
Kensington Rd. HX3	E21	94
Kensington St. BD21	B 4	7
Kensington St. BD8	L10	48
Kensington Ter. LS6	Z 9	37
Kent Av., Pud. LS28	U11	52
Kent Clo. LS28	U11	52
Kent Cres., Pud. LS28	T11	52
Kent Dr., Pud. LS28	U11	52
Kent Rd. BD16	H 5	10
Kent Rd., Pud. LS28	T11	52
Kent St. HX1	E20	94
Kentmere App. LS14	FF 8	40
Kentmere Av. LS14	FF 7	40
Kentmere Clo. LS14	FF 8	40
Kentmere Cres. LS14	FF 8	40
Kentmere Gate LS14	FF 7	40
Kentmere Gdns. LS14	FF 8	40
Kentmere Grn. LS14	FF 8	40
Kentmere Ri. LS14	GG 8	40
Kenton Dr. BD4	P13	68
Kenton Way BD4	P13	68
Kenworthy Clo. LS16	X 4	18
Kenworthy Garth LS16	X 4	18
Kenworthy Gdns. LS16	X 4	18
Kenworthy Ri. LS16	X 4	18
Kenworthy Vale LS16	X 4	18
Kenyon La. HX2	C19	93
Kepler Gro. LS8	CC10	56
Kepler Mt. LS8	CC10	56
Kepler Ter. LS8	CC10	56
Kepstorn Clo. LS6	X 8	36
Kepstorn Ri. LS16	X 7	36
Kepstorn Ri. LS6	X 8	36
Kerry Hill, Hor. LS18	U 6	16
Kerry St., Hor. LS18	U 6	16
Kershaw St. BD3	P11	50
Kesteven Clo. BD4	Q14	68
Kesteven Rd. BD4	Q14	68
Kestrel Clo. LS17	CC 5	20
Kestrel Dr. BD2	O 9	31
Kestrel Gro. LS17	CC 5	20
Kestrel Mt. BD2	O 9	31
Keswick Clo. HX3	G21	95
Keswick St. BD4	P12	50
Kettlewell Dr. BD5	L13	66
Kewton Way BD17	M 5	12
Keys St. BD4	O14	67
Khandalla Ter. LS11	AA13	73
Lady Pit St.		
Kildare Cres. BD15	H10	46
Kildare Ter. LS12	Z12	55
Killinghall Av. BD2	O10	49
Killinghall Dr. BD2	O10	49
Killinghall Gro. BD2	O10	49
Killinghall Rd. BD2	O10	49
Kiln Fold HD6	M21	97
Kilner Rd. BD6	L14	66
Kilnsea Mt. BD4	Q13	68
Kilnsey Rd. BD3	O12	49
Leeds Rd.		
Kilroyd Av. BD19	P18	85
Kilroyd Dr. BD19	Q18	85
Kimberley Pl. HX3	E17	80
Kimberley St.		
Kimberley Pl. HX3	E17	81
Kimberley Pl. LS9	DD10	57
Kimberley Rd. LS9	DD10	57
Kimberley St. BD4	P12	50
Kimberley St. HD6	L21	97
Kimberley St. HX3	E17	80
King Alfreds Dr. LS6	AA 6	19
King Alfreds Grn. LS6	AA 6	19
King Alfreds Way LS6	AA 6	19
King Alfreds Wk. LS6	AA 6	19
King Charles Cft. LS1	BB11	56
King Charles St.		
King Charles St. LS1	BB11	56
King Clo. LS17	AA 5	19
King Cross Rd. HX1	D20	93
King Cross St. HX1	E20	94
King Dr. LS17	Z 4	19
King Edward Av., Hor. LS18	U 7	34
King Edward Cres., Hor. LS18	V 6	17
King Edward St. HX1	F19	94
King Edward St. LS1	BB11	56
King Edward Ter. BD13	F12	45
King Edwins Ct. LS8	DD 8	39
King George Av. LS7	BB 7	38
King George Av., Hor. LS18	V 6	17
King George Av., Mor. LS27	X16	89
King George Cft., Mor. LS27	X16	89
King George Gdns. LS7	BB 7	38
King George Rd., Hor. LS18	V 6	17
King Gro. BD17	K 6	11
King La. LS16	Y 3	3
King La. LS17	BB 6	20
King St. BD11	T16	87
King St. BD15	F 8	27
King St. BD2	P 8	32
King St. BD21	B 4	7
King St. HD6	L22	101
King St. HX1	E20	94
King St. HX6	A21	92
Queen St.		
King St. LS1	AA11	55
King St. LS19	R 5	15
King St. LS28	S10	51
King St., Mor. LS27	X17	89
Kingfisher Clo. LS17	CC 5	20
Kingfisher Way LS17	CC 5	20
Kings Av. LS7	Z10	55
Kings Croft Gdns. LS17	BB 6	20
Kings Ct. BD16	G 5	10
Main St.		
Kings Clo. LS6	AA 9	37
Kings Dr. BD2	N 8	31
Kings Dr. LS16	W 2	2
Kings Dr. WF17	T18	87
Kings Lea HX3	E22	98
Kings Mt. LS17	BB 7	38
Kings Rd. BD1	N 9	31
Kings Rd. BD16	G 4	10
Kings Rd. BD2	N 9	31
Kings Rd. LS6	Z10	55
Kings Rd., Bram. LS16	X 2	3
Kings Vw. HX3	H21	95
Kingsbury Pl. HX1	D19	93
Queens Rd.		
Kingsdale Av. BD11	T16	87
Kingsdale Av. BD2	O 9	31
Kingsdale BD11	T16	87
Kingsdale Cres. BD2	O 9	31
Kingsdale Ct. BD2	O 9	31
Kingsdale Dr. BD2	O 9	31
Kingsdale Est. BD11	T16	87
Kingsdale Gdns. BD11	T16	87
Kingsdale Gro. BD2	N 9	31
Kingsley Av. BD11	R17	86
Kingsley Av. BD2	N 9	31

Name	Ref	Page
Kingsley Av. HX6	A21	92
Kingsley Av. LS16	X 4	18
Kingsley Clo. BD11	R17	86
Kingsley Cres. BD11	R17	86
Kingsley Cres. BD17	M 6	12
Kingsley Dr. BD11	R17	86
Kingsley Dr. LS16	X 4	18
Kingsley Pl. HX1	D20	93
Kingsley Rd. LS16	X 4	18
Kingsmead Dr. LS14	FF 6	22
Kingsmead LS14	GG 7	40
Kingston Clo. BD15	F 8	27
Kingston Clo. HX1	D20	93
Kingston Dr. HX1	D20	93
Kingston Gdns. LS15	GG 9	40
Kingston Gro. BD10	O 6	13
Kingston Gro. LS2	AA10	55
Bagby St.		
Kingston Pl. LS2	Z10	55
Woodhouse La.		
Kingston Rd. BD10	O 6	13
Kingston Rd. LS2	AA10	55
Kingston St. HX1	D20	93
Kingston Ter. LS2	AA10	55
Kingsway BD16	H 5	10
Kingsway BD2	N 7	31
Kingsway LS15	HH11	59
Kingsway WF17	T18	87
Kingswear Clo. LS15	HH10	59
Kingswear Cres. LS15	HH10	59
Kingswear Garth LS15	HH10	59
Kingswear Glen LS15	HH10	59
Kingswear Gro. LS15	HH10	59
Kingswear Par. LS15	HH10	59
Kingswear Ri. LS15	HH10	59
Kingswear Vw. LS15	HH10	59
Kingswood Av. LS8	DD 5	21
Kingswood Cres. LS8	CC 5	20
Kingswood Dr. LS8	CC 5	20
Kingswood Gdns. LS8	CC 5	20
Kingswood Grn. HX3	G18	81
Kingswood Gro. LS8	DD 5	21
Kingswood Pl. BD7	L13	66
Kingswood St.		
Kingswood Rd. LS12	Y12	54
Kingswood St. BD7	L13	66
Kingswood Ter. BD7	L13	66
Kinnaird Clo.	G23	99
Kipling Ct. BD10	P 7	32
Kippax Clo. LS9	CC11	56
Kippax Mt. LS9	CC11	56
Kippax Pl. LS9	CC11	56
Kippax Ter. LS9	CC11	56
Kippax Vw. LS9	CC11	56
Kipping La. BD13	F12	45
Kipping Pl. BD13	F12	45
Lower Kipping La.		
Kirby Hill Pl. LS11	AA13	73
Greenmount St.		
Kirk Dr. BD17	M 5	12
Kirk Hills, Thorner LS14	JJ 4	23
Kirk La. HX3	J19	96
Kirkbourne Av. BD10	N 6	13
Kirkburn Pl. BD7	L12	48
Kirkdale Av. LS12	X13	72
Kirkdale Cres. LS12	X13	72
Kirkdale Dr. LS12	X13	72
Kirkdale Gdns. LS12	X13	72
Kirkdale Gro. LS12	X13	72
Kirkdale Mt. LS12	X13	72
Kirkdale Ter. LS12	X13	72
Kirkdale Vw. LS12	X13	72
Kirkfield BD17	HH11	59
Kirkfield Gdns. LS15	HH11	59
Darnley La.		
Kirkfield La., Thorner LS14	KK 4	
Kirkfield Vw. LS15	HH11	59
Kirkfields BD17	N 5	13
Kirkgate BD1	N11	49
Kirkgate BD18	L 7	30
Kirkgate LS1	BB11	56
Kirkgate LS2	BB11	56
Kirkgate Market BD1	N11	49
Kirkgate Ter. BD11	R16	86
Kirkgate WF17	S18	86
Kirkgate WF17	T18	87
Kirkham Rd. BD7	L12	48
Kirkham St., Rod. LS13	T 8	34
Kirklands Av. BD13	G12	46
Kirklands Av. BD17	N 5	13
Kirklands Clo. BD17	N 6	13
Kirklands Gdns. BD17	N 5	13
Kirklands La. BD17	N 5	13
Kirklands Rd. BD17	N 5	13
Kirklees Cft. LS28	S 9	33
Kirklees Clo., Rod. LS13	T 9	34
Kirklees Dr. LS28	S 9	33
Kirklees Garth LS28	S 9	33
Kirklees Rd. BD15	H11	46
Kirklees Ri. LS28	S 9	33
Kirkley Av. BD12	M18	83
Kirkstall Av. LS5	W 9	35
Kirkstall Gro. BD8	J11	46
Kirkstall Hill LS4	X 9	36
Kirkstall La. LS5	X 9	36
Kirkstall La. LS6	X 9	36
Kirkstall Mt. LS5	W 9	35
Kirkstall Rd. LS3	Z11	55
Kirkstall Rd. LS4	X 9	36
Kirkstall Zone HX3	C15	62
Kirkstone Dr. HX2	B19	92
Kirkstone St. BD7	M12	48
Cobden St.		
Kirkwall Av. LS9	DD11	57
Victoria Av.		
Kirkwall Dr. BD4	Q13	68
Kirkwood Av. LS16	V 5	17
Kirkwood Clo. LS16	V 4	17
Kirkwood Cres. LS16	V 4	17
Kirkwood Dr. LS16	V 4	17
Kirkwood Gdns. LS16	W 4	17
Kirkwood Gro. LS16	V 4	17
Kirkwood La. LS16	V 4	17
Kirkwood Ri. LS16	W 4	17
Kirkwood Vw. LS16	W 4	17
Kirkwood Way LS16	W 4	17
Kitchener Av. LS9	DD10	57
Kitchener Gro. LS9	DD10	57
Kitchener St. BD12	O16	84
Kitchener St. LS9	DD10	57
Kitson Clo. LS12	Y12	54
Kitson Gdns. LS12	Y12	54
Kitson Rd. LS10	BB12	56
Kitson St. BD18	M 7	30
Kitson St. LS9	CC11	56
Kliffen Pl. HX3	F21	94
Knight St. HX1	D20	93
Knights Clo. LS15	HH11	59
Knights Fold BD7	L13	66
Knights Hill LS15	HH11	59
Knightsway LS15	HH10	59
Knoll Gdns. BD17	L 5	12
Denby Dr.		
Knoll Park Dr. BD17	L 6	12
Knoll Wood Pk., Hor. LS18	V 7	35
Knostrop La. LS9	CC12	56
Cross Green La.		
Knott La., Raw. LS19	T 7	34
Knowle Av. LS4	Y 9	36
Knowle Gro. LS4	Y10	54
Knowle La. BD12	M18	83
Knowle Mt. LS4	Y 9	36
Knowle Pl. LS4	Y10	54
Knowle Ter.		
Knowle Rd. LS4	Y 9	36
Knowle St. BD21	B 4	7
South St.		
Knowle Ter. LS4	Y10	54
Knowle Top Dr. HX3	K19	96
Knowle Top Rd. HX3	K19	96
Knowles Av. BD4	P14	68
Knowles La. BD19	R17	86
Knowles La. BD4	P14	68
Knowles Rd. HD6	L23	101
Knowles St. BD13	C11	44
Old Rd.		
Knowles St. BD4	P14	68
Knowles Vw. BD4	P14	68
Knowsley St. BD3	O12	49
Knowsthorpe Cres. LS9	CC12	56
Knowsthorpe Gate LS9	DD13	75
Knowsthorpe La. LS9	DD13	75
Knowsthorpe LS9	DD12	56
Knowsthorpe Rd. LS9	DD12	57
Knowsthorpe Way LS9	DD13	75
Knox St. LS13	S 8	33
Knutsford Gro. BD4	Q14	68
Kyffin Av. LS15	FF11	58
Kyffin Pl. BD4	Q12	50
Laburnham Gro.	A 7	25
Laburnum Dr. BD17	M 5	12
Laburnum Gro. BD19	R18	86
Laburnum Gro. HX3	L19	97
Smith House La.		
Laburnum Pl. BD10	Q 7	32
Laburnum Pl. BD8	M10	48
Laburnum Rd. BD18	M 8	30
Laburnum St. BD21	B 4	7
Apsley St.		
Laburnum St. BD8	M10	48
Laburnum St. LS11	AA13	73
Cambrian St.		
Laburnum St. LS28	S11	51
Ladbroke Gro. BD4	Q14	68
Ladderbanks La. BD17	M 5	12
Lady Field BD13	F12	45
Lady La. BD16	H 4	10
Lady La. BD7	M11	48
Lady La. LS2	BB11	56
Lady Pit Cres. LS11	AA13	73
Lady Pit La.		
Lady Pit La. LS11	AA13	73
Lady Wood Mead LS8	EE 8	39
Lady Wood Rd. LS8	DD 8	39
Ladyfield BD13	F12	45
Chapel Ter.		
Ladyroyd Dr. BD4	Q16	85
Ladysmith Rd. BD13	F15	63
Ladywell Clo. BD5	N13	67
Mark St.		
Ladywood Grange LS8	EE 8	39
Laisterdyke BD4	P12	50
Laisteridge BD5	M12	48
Laisteridge BD7	M12	48
Laith Clo. LS16	W 5	17
Laith Garth LS16	W 5	17
Laith Gdns. LS16	X 5	18
Laith Grn. LS16	W 5	17
Laith Rd. LS16	W 5	17
Laithe Gro. BD6	L14	66
Laithe Rd. BD6	L14	66
Lake Gro. LS10	BB14	74
Arthington Rd.		
Lake St. BD4	O12	49
Lake St. LS10	BB14	74
Arthington Rd.		
Lake Ter. LS10	BB14	74
Lake Vw. HX3	E19	94
Lake Vw. LS10	BB13	74
Moor Rd.		
Lakeland Cres. LS17	Z 4	19
Lakeland Dr. LS17	AA 4	19
Lakeside Ter. LS19	S 5	15
Lambcote Rd. HD2	M24	101
Lambert Av. LS8	CC 8	38
Lambert Clo. HD6	F23	98
Green La.		
Lambert Dr. LS8	CC 8	38
Lambert St., Greet.	F23	98
Lambert Ter., Hor. LS18	U 7	34
Lamberts Yd. LS1	BB11	56
Briggate		
Lambeth St. LS8	CC 9	38
Lambeth Ter. LS8	CC 9	38
Lambourne Av. BD10	Q 8	32
Lambrigg Cres. LS14	GG 9	40
Lambton Gro. LS8	BB 9	38
Roundhay Rd.		
Lambton Pl. LS8	BB 9	38
Roundhay Rd.		
Lambton Vw. LS8	BB 9	38
Roundhay Rd.		
Lampards Clo. BD15	H10	46
Lanark Dr., Troy LS18	U 5	16
Lancaster Av. LS5	W 9	35
Lancaster Gro. LS5	W 9	35
Lancaster St. BD4	O12	49
Wakefield Rd.		
Land Ct. LS11	AA12	55
Water La.		
Land St. BD8	M10	48
Land St. LS28	S 9	33
Landemere Syke HX3	H17	81
Lands End BD10	P 8	32
Norman La.		
Lands Head La. HX3	G17	81
Lands La. LS1	BB11	56
Landscove Av. BD4	Q14	68
Landseer Av. LS13	W 9	35
Landseer Clo. LS13	V 9	35
Landseer Cres. LS13	W 9	35
Landseer Dr. LS13	V 9	35
Landseer Gdns. LS13	V 9	35
Landseer Dr.		
Landseer Grn. LS13	V 9	35
Landseer Gro. LS13	W 9	35
Landseer Mt. LS13	W 9	35
Landseer Rd. LS13	V 9	35
Landseer Ri. LS13	V 9	35
Landseer Ter. LS13	W 9	35
Landseer Vw. LS13	W 9	35
Landseer Way LS13	V 9	35
Landseer Wk. LS13	V 9	35
Landside Clo. BD12	L17	83
Landsmoor Gro. BD16	J 4	11
Landsowne Pl. BD5	M12	48
Lane End Cft. LS17	Z 4	19
Lane End Ct. LS17	Z 4	19
Lane End LS11	AA12	55
Lane End Mt., Pud. LS28	T11	52
Lane End Pl. LS11	AA12	55
Lane End, Pud. LS28	T11	52

143

Lee Ct. BD21	D 4	8	Leshmore Gro. BD7	K14	65	Lily St. BD8	L10	48
Thwaites Brow Rd.			Leslie Ter. LS6	AA 9	37	Lilycroft Rd. BD9	L10	48
Lee La.	YY 9	24	*Woodhouse St.*			Lilycroft Wk. BD9	L10	48
Lee La. BD16	F 7	27	Levens Bank. LS15	EE12	57	Lilythorne Av. BD10	P 7	32
Lee La. E., Hor. LS18	U 6	16	Levens Clo. LS15	FF12	58	Lime Gro. LS19	R 5	15
Lee La. HX3	F17	80	Levens Garth LS15	FF12	58	Lime St.	ZZ 8	24
Lee La. W., Hor. LS18	T 6	16	Levens Pl. LS15	FF12	58	Lime St. HX3	E18	80
Lee La., Hor. LS18	U 6	16	Lever St. BD6	L14	66	Lime Tree Av. LS17	CC 6	20
Lee Mount Gdns. HX3	E18	80	*Beacon Rd.*			Limes Av. HX3	F21	94
Lee Mt. HX3	E19	94	Levisham Clo. BD10	P 8	32	Limetree Av. BD19	R15	69
Lee St. BD1	N12	49	Levita Gro. BD4	P13	68	Limetree Av., Elland	H24	99
Lee St. BD13	F15	63	*Levita Pl.*			Limetree Cres. BD19	R15	69
Lee St. HD6	L21	97	Levita Pl. BD4	P13	68	Limetree Gro. BD19	R15	69
Leech La. BD16	D 7	26	Levita Pl. LS15	FF11	58	Limewood App. LS14	GG 7	40
Leeds and Bradford Rd.,	T10	52	Lewis St. HX1	E19	94	Limewood Rd. LS14	GG 8	40
LS28			*Richmond St.*			Lincoln Av. LS9	CC10	56
Leeds and Bradford Rd.,	W 9	35	Lewisham Gro., Mor. LS27	X17	89	Lincoln Green Rd. LS9	CC10	56
Stan. LS13			Lewisham St., Mor. LS27	W17	88	Lincoln Gro. LS9	CC10	56
Leeds Old Rd. BD3	P11	50	Ley Fleaks Rd. BD10	O 7	31	*Lincoln Rd.*		
Leeds Rd. BD1	N11	49	Ley La. LS12	Y11	54	Lincoln Mt. LS9	CC10	56
Leeds Rd. BD1	Q11	50	Ley Top La. BD15	J11	47	Lincoln Rd. BD8	M11	48
Leeds Rd. BD10	M 7	30	Leybourne St. BD8	L10	48	Lincoln Rd. LS9	CC10	56
Leeds Rd. BD18	M 7	30	Leyburn Av. HX3	K19	96	Lincoln St. BD15	J11	47
Leeds Rd. BD2	O 9	31	Leyburn Gro. BD16	H 5	10	Lincoln St. BD19	R16	86
Leeds Rd. BD3	N11	49	Leyburn Gro. BD18	L 7	30	*Grange Rd.*		
Leeds Rd. BD3	Q11	50	Leyburn Pl. LS11	AA13	73	*Allen Cft.*		
Leeds Rd. HD2	O24	102	*Cemetery Rd.*			Lincoln Ter. BD8	M11	48
Leeds Rd. HX3	G18	81	Leyburn St. LS11	AA13	73	Lincoln Ter. LS9	CC10	56
Leeds Rd. LS15	JJ 9	41	*Cemetery Rd.*			*Lincoln Rd.*		
Leeds Rd. LS16	W 1	2	Leyfield BD17	L 5	12	Lincoln Towers LS9	CC10	56
Leeds Rd. LS19	S 5	15	*Alder Carr*			Lincoln Vw. LS9	CC10	56
Leeds Rd. WF17	T18	87	Leyland Rd. WF17	S18	86	Lincombe Bank LS8	CC 7	38
Leeds Rd., Thackley BD10	O 6	13	Leyland St. HX3	E18	80	Lincombe Dr. LS8	CC 7	38
Leeds Ter. LS7	BB10	56	*Mill La.*			Lincombe Mt. LS8	CC 7	38
Leek Chase LS10	CC13	74	Leylands Av. BD9	K 9	29	Lincombe Ri. LS8	CC 7	38
Leeming Sq. LS1	AA10	55	Leylands Gro. BD9	K 9	29	Lincroft Cres. LS13	V 9	35
Cankerwell La.			Leylands La. BD21	C 4	8	Lind St.	ZZ 8	24
Leeming St. BD1	N11	49	Leylands La. BD9	K 9	29	Lind St. BD16	G 5	10
Lees Bank Av.	A 7	25	Leylands Rd. LS2	BB10	56	Lindale Clo. LS10	BB15	91
Lees Bank Dr.	A 7	25	Leylands Ter. BD9	K 9	29	Linden Av. BD3	Q11	50
Lees Bank Hill	A 7	25	Leysholme Cres. LS12	X12	54	Linden Ct. LS16	Y 7	36
Lees Bank Rd.	A 7	25	Leysholme Ter. LS12	X12	54	*Hollin La.*		
Lees Bldgs. HX3	J19	96	Leysholme Vw. LS12	X12	54	Linden Gro. LS11	BB13	74
Lees Clo. BD13	C 8	26	Leyside Dr. BD15	H10	46	Linden Mt. LS11	AA13	73
Lees La. HX3	K18	82	Leyton Cres. BD10	O 7	31	*Linden Rd.*		
Lees La. LS28	S 9	33	Leyton Dr. BD10	O 7	31	Linden Pl. LS11	AA13	73
Lees Moor Rd. BD13	C 8	26	Leyton Ter. BD10	O 7	31	*Linden Rd.*		
Lees Yd. LS11	BB12	56	Lichen Clo. BD7	L13	66	Linden Rd. HX3	F21	94
Legrams Av. BD7	K12	47	*Southfield La.*			Linden Rd. LS11	AA13	73
Legrams La. BD7	L12	48	Lichfield Mt. BD2	N 9	31	Linden Rd., Elland HX5	G24	99
Legrams La. BD7	L12	48	Lickless Av., Hor. LS18	V 6	17	Linden Ri. BD21	D 4	8
Legrams Mill La. BD7	L12	48	Lickless Dr., Hor. LS18	V 6	17	Linden St. LS11	AA13	73
Legrams St. BD7	L11	48	Lickless Gdns., Hor. LS18	V 6	17	*Linden Rd.*		
Legrams Ter. BD7	L11	48	Lickless Ter., Hor. LS18	V 6	17	Linden Ter. LS11	BB13	74
Leicester Av. LS2	AA10	55	Lidget Av. BD7	K12	47	Lindholm Gdns. BD15	H11	46
Devon Rd.			Lidget Hill, Pud. LS28	T11	52	Lindisfarne Rd. BD18	K 7	29
Leicester Gro. LS7	AA10	55	Lidget Pl. BD7	K12	47	Lindley Dr. BD7	K14	65
Leicester Mt. LS2	AA10	55	Lidget Ter. BD14	J13	65	Lindley Rd. BD5	M13	66
Devon Rd.			Lidget Ter. BD7	K12	47	Lindrick Gro. HX2	D15	62
Leicester Pl. LS2	AA10	55	Lidgett Av. LS8	CC 7	38	Lindrick Way HX2	D15	62
Leicester St. BD4	O13	67	Lidgett Cres. LS8	CC 7	38	Lindrick Wk. HX2	D15	62
Leicester Ter. HX3	E21	94	Lidgett Ct. LS8	CC 7	38	Lindsey Ct. LS9	CC10	56
Manor Dr.			Lidgett Gro. LS8	CC 7	38	Lindsey Gdns. LS9	CC10	56
Leicester Ter. LS2	AA 9	37	Lidgett Hill LS8	CC 7	38	Lindsey Mt. LS9	CC10	56
Devon Rd.			Lidgett La. LS17	BB 6	20	Lindsey Rd. LS9	CC10	56
Leigh St., S.B. HD6	C20	93	Lidgett La. LS8	BB 6	20	Lindwell Av., Greet.	F23	98
Leighton La. LS1	AA11	55	Lidgett Mt. LS8	CC 6	20	Lindwell Gro., Greet.	F23	98
Lemington Av. HX1	E20	94	Lidgett Park Av. LS8	CC 6	20	Ling Bob Cft. HX2	C18	79
Lemon St. BD5	M13	66	Lidgett Park Ct. LS8	CC 6	20	Ling Bob Clo. HX2	C19	93
Lemon St. HX1	D19	93	Lidgett Park Gdns. LS8	CC 7	38	Ling Park App. BD15	F 9	27
Queens Rd.			Lidgett Park Gro. LS8	CC 7	38	Ling Park Av. BD15	F 9	27
Lenhurst Av. LS12	W 9	35	Lidgett Park Ms. LS8	DD 6	21	Ling Royd Av. HX2	C19	93
Lennie St. BD21	B 4	7	Lidgett Park Rd. LS8	CC 6	20	Ling St. BD21	B 4	7
Kensington St.			Lidgett Pl. LS8	CC 7	38	*Oakworth Rd.*		
Lennon Dr. BD8	L10	48	Lidgett Row LS8	CC 6	20	Lingcroft Grn. BD5	N14	67
Lennox Rd. LS4	Y10	54	Lidgett Vw. LS8	CC 6	20	Lingdale Rd. BD6	L16	83
Lens Dr. BD17	M 5	12	Lidgett Wk. LS8	CC 7	38	Lingfield App. LS17	AA 5	19
Lentilfield Gro. HX3	E18	80	Lifton Pl. LS2	AA10	55	Lingfield Bank LS17	AA 5	19
Friendly Fold Rd.			Light Clo. HX1	E19	94	Lingfield Clo. LS17	BB 5	20
Lentilfield HX3	E18	80	Lightcliffe Rd. HD6	L21	97	Lingfield Cres. BD13	J14	65
Lentilfield Pl. HX3	E18	80	Lightowler Rd. HX1	E19	94	Lingfield Cres. LS17	AA 5	19
Friendly Fold Rd.			Lightridge Rd. HD2	K24	100	Lingfield Dr. BD21	B 6	7
Lentilfield Ter. HX3	E18	80	Lilac Gro. BD18	M 8	30	Lingfield Dr. LS17	BB 5	20
Lenton Dr. LS11	BB14	74	Lilac Gro. BD19	R18	86	Lingfield Gate LS17	AA 5	19
Lenton Vills. BD10	O 6	13	Lilac Gro. BD4	P12	50	Lingfield Gdns. LS17	AA 5	19
Leonard Pl. LS7	CC 9	38	Lilac Gro. LS7	BB10	56	Lingfield Grn. LS17	AA 5	19
Rayner St.			*Skinner La.*			Lingfield Gro. BD15	F 8	27
Leonard St. BD12	M17	83	Lilac Pl. LS10	BB14	74	Lingfield Gro. LS17	BB 5	20
Leonard St. BD16	H 6	10	*Arthington Av.*			Lingfield Hill LS17	AA 5	19
Leonards Pl. BD16	H 6	10	Lilac St. HD3	E18	80	Lingfield Mt. LS17	BB 5	20
Leopold Gdns. LS7	CC 9	38	Lilac St. LS2	BB10	56	Lingfield Par. LS17	BB 5	20
Leopold St.			Lilian St. LS4	Y10	54	Lingfield Rd. BD15	F 8	27
Leopold Gro. LS7	BB 9	38	Lilian St. BD4	P13	68	Lingfield Rd. LS17	AA 5	19
Leopold Rd. LS7	CC 9	38	Lilian St. LS4	Y10	54	Lingfield Ter. BD13	J14	65
Leopold Sq. LS7	BB 9	38	Lillands La. HD6	K22	100	Lingfield Vw. LS17	AA 5	19
Leopold St.			Lilly St. HX6	B21	92	Lingfield Wk. LS17	AA 5	19
Leopold St. LS7	BB 9	38	*West St.*			Lingwell Av. LS10	BB16	91
Leopold Ter. LS7	BB 9	38	Lily Cft. BD8	L10	48	Lingwell Cres. LS10	BB16	91
Lepton Pl., Gild. LS27	V15	71						

144

Name	Ref	Page
Lingwell Gro. LS10	BB17	91
Lingwell Sq. LS10	BB16	91
Lingwell St. LS10	BB16	91
Lingwood Av. BD8	K10	47
Lingwood Rd. BD8	K11	47
Lingwood Ter. BD8	K11	47
Link, The, Swil. LS26	JJ14	77
Links Av. BD19	P18	85
Linkway BD16	H 7	28
Grange Park Rd.		
Linnhe Av. BD6	K16	82
Linton Av. LS17	CC 5	20
Linton Clo. LS17	CC 5	20
Linton Cres. LS17	CC 5	20
Linton Dr. LS17	CC 5	20
Linton Gro. HD6	K23	100
Linton Gro. LS17	CC 5	20
Linton Rd. LS17	CC 5	20
Linton Ri. LS17	CC 5	20
Linton St. BD4	N13	67
Linton St., Keighley	A 4	7
Lisbon St. LS1	AA11	55
Lister Av. BD4	O13	67
Lister Hill, Hor. LS18	V 6	17
Lister Hills Rd. BD7	M12	48
Lister La. BD2	N10	49
Lister La. HX1	E19	94
Lister St. BD21	B 4	7
Lister St. BD4	P14	68
Lister St. HD6	L21	97
Lister St. HX1	F19	94
Lister St. LS28	S 9	33
Wade St.		
Lister Ville BD15	F 8	27
Lister Vw. BD8	M10	48
Listers Ct. HX1	E19	94
Crossley Gdns.		
Listers Rd. HX3	G19	95
Lithgow Way BD2	N 9	31
Little Baines St. HX1	E19	94
Oak La.		
Little Beck Dr. BD16	J 5	11
Little Bradley HX4	F24	98
Little Cross St. BD5	N14	67
Little Ct. BD16	H 7	28
Little Fountain St., Mor.	X17	89
LS27		
Little Horton Grn. BD5	M12	48
Little Horton La. BD5	M13	66
Little La. BD9	K10	47
Little La. HX3	H19	95
Little La., Chur. LS27	Y15	72
Little Moor BD13	H14	64
Highgate Rd.		
Little Moor Gdns. HX2	D16	79
Little Moor Pl. LS12	X11	54
Little Neville St. LS1	AA11	55
Little Pk. BD10	Q 6	14
Little Providence St. LS9	BB11	56
Little Queen St. LS1	AA11	55
Little Russell St. LS12	Y12	54
Whitehall Rd.		
Little Templar La. LS2	BB11	56
Edward St.		
Little Town La. LS11	Z13	73
Little Way LS17	BB 6	20
Falkland Mt.		
Little Woodhouse St. LS1	AA10	55
Clarendon Rd.		
Littlefield Wk. BD6	L15	66
Littlelands BD16	H 7	28
Littlemoor BD13	H14	64
Littlemoor Bottom, Pud.	T12	52
LS28		
Littlemoor Cres. S. LS28	T12	52
Littlemoor Cres.		
Littlemoor Cres., Pud.	T12	52
LS28		
Littlemoor Gdns., Pud.	T12	52
LS28		
Littlemoor La., Thorner	JJ 4	23
LS14		
Littlemoor Rd. HX2	D16	79
Littlemoor Rd., Pud. LS28	T12	52
Littlemoor Vw., Pud. LS28	T12	52
Littlewood Ho. HD6	L22	101
Litton Rd. BD21	B 4	7
Litton Way LS14	GG 7	40
Littondale Clo. BD17	N 5	13
Livingstone Clo. BD2	N 8	31
Livingstone Rd. BD18	M 7	30
Livingstone Rd. BD2	N 8	31
Livingstone St. HX3	E18	80
Livingstone St. N. HX2	E16	80
Watkinson Rd.		
Locarno Av. BD9	K10	47
Lochy Rd. BD6	K16	82
Lock St. HX3	F20	94

Name	Ref	Page
Lockerbie Grn. BD15	H10	46
Locksley Rd. HD6	M22	101
Lockwood Clo. LS11	AA14	73
Lockwood Ms. BD18	K 7	29
Exhibition Rd.		
Lockwood Pk. LS11	BB14	74
Lockwood St. BD12	N16	84
Lockwood St. BD18	K 7	29
Victoria Rd.		
Lockwood St. BD6	L13	66
Acre La.		
Lockwood Way LS11	BB14	74
Lode Pit La. BD16	J 5	11
Lodge Av., Brig.	J23	100
Lodge Dr., Brig.	J23	100
Lodge Gate BD13	D10	44
Main Rd.		
Lodge Hill BD17	K 5	11
Lodge La. LS11	AA13	73
Lodge Pl., Brig.	J23	100
Lodge Rd. LS28	S11	51
Lodge St. BD13	C 8	26
Lodge St. LS1	AA10	55
Lodore Av. BD2	O 9	31
Lodore Pl. BD2	O 9	31
Lodore Rd. BD2	O 9	31
Loft St. BD8	L11	47
Lofthouse Pl. LS2	AA10	55
Lofthouse Ter. LS2	BB10	56
Lombard St. HX1	D20	93
Lombard St. LS15	FF11	58
Lombard St. LS19	R 5	15
Lomond Av., Troy LS18	U 5	16
Lomond Pl. LS7	BB10	56
Grosvenor Av.		
Lomond St. LS7	BB10	56
Grosvenor Av.		
Lomond Ter. LS7	BB10	56
Grosvenor Av.		
Londesboro Gro. LS9	DD11	57
Londesboro Ter. LS9	DD11	57
London La. LS19	P 5	14
London Sq. LS19	R 5	15
London La.		
London St. LS19	R 5	15
Long Causeway BD13	B10	43
Long Causeway LS16	Y 6	18
Long Causeway LS9	CC12	56
Long Cft. BD21	C 4	8
Long Clo. BD12	L17	83
Long Close La. LS9	CC11	56
Long Heys, Elland HX5	F24	98
Long La. BD13	F15	63
Long La. BD15	F10	45
Long La. BD16	E 6	9
Long La. BD9	J 8	29
Long La. HX2	D18	79
Long La. HX3	G19	95
Long Lee La. BD21	C13	62
Long Lover La. HX2	D19	93
Long Meadows, Bram.	W 2	2
LS16		
Long Row BD12	M16	83
Long Row BD13	F11	45
Hill Top Rd.		
Long Row LS28	S11	51
Long Row, Hor. LS18	V 6	17
Long St. BD4	O12	49
Long Wall, Elland HX5	G24	99
Longbottom Av. HX6	A21	92
Longbottom Ter. HX3	F21	94
Longcroft Pl. BD1	M11	48
Longfallas Cres. HD6	L23	101
Longfield Av. HX3	H18	81
Longfield Av., Pud. LS28	T11	52
Longfield Dr., Rod. LS13	T 8	34
Longfield Garth, Rod.	T 8	34
LS13		
Longfield Gro., Pud. LS28	T11	52
Longfield Mt., Pud. LS28	T11	52
Longfield Rd., Pud. LS28	T11	52
Longfield Ter. BD7	K12	47
Longfield Ter. HX3	H17	81
Bradford Rd.		
Longfield Ter., Pud. LS28	T11	52
Longhouse Dr. BD13	C11	44
Longhouse La. BD13	C10	44
Longhouse La. HX2	C16	79
Longland St. BD1	K11	47
West Gate		
Longlands Av. BD13	C10	44
Longridge HD6	L23	101
Longroyd Av. LS11	BB13	74
Longroyd Cres. LS11	BB13	74
Longroyd Gro. LS11	BB13	74
Longroyd Pl. LS11	BB13	74
Longroyd St. LS11	BB13	74
Longroyd St. N. LS11	BB13	74

Name	Ref	Page
Longroyd Ter. LS11	BB13	74
Longroyd Vw. LS11	BB13	74
Longroyde Castle HD6	K23	100
Longroyde Clo. HD6	K22	100
Longroyde Rd. HD6	L22	101
Longside La. BD7	M12	48
Longwood Av. BD16	G 4	10
Longwood Clo. LS17	DD 4	21
Longwood Cres. LS17	DD 4	21
Longwood Pk. BD16	F 4	9
Longwood Vw. BD16	G 4	10
Longwood Way LS17	DD 4	21
Plantation Gdns.		
Lonsdale St. BD3	O11	49
Lord La.	YY 7	24
Lord St. BD11	T16	87
Lord St. BD4	O12	49
Rutland St.		
Lord St. HX1	F19	94
Lord St. LS12	Z12	55
Lord St., Haworth	ZZ 7	24
Prince St.		
Lord St., S.B. HX6	C20	93
Lord Ter. LS12	Z12	55
Coleman St.		
Lords La. HD6	L22	101
Lordsfield Pl. BD4	P14	68
Loris St. BD4	P14	68
Lorne Pl. LS6	AA 9	37
Woodhouse St.		
Lorne St. BD18	L 8	30
Valley Rd.		
Lorne St. BD4	O13	67
Lorraine Pl. LS7	BB 9	38
Lorry Bank LS7	BB 9	38
Loughrigg St. BD5	N13	67
Louis Av. BD5	M13	66
Louis Gro. LS7	CC 9	38
Louis St.		
Louis St. BD5	M13	66
Louis St. LS7	BB 9	38
Louisa St. BD10	O 7	31
Love La. HX1	E20	94
Lovell Gro. LS7	BB10	56
Lovell Rd.		
Lovell Park Gate LS7	BB10	56
Lovell Park Hill LS7	BB10	56
Lovell Park Rd. LS7	BB10	56
Lovell Park Vw. LS7	BB10	56
Lovell Pl. LS7	BB10	56
Lovell Rd.		
Low Ash Av. BD18	M 7	30
Low Ash Cres. BD18	N 8	31
Low Ash Dr. BD18	M 7	30
Low Ash Gro. BD18	M 7	30
Low Ash Rd. BD18	N 7	31
Low Bank Dr. BD22	YY 5	6
Low Bank La.		
Low Bank La. BD22	YY 5	6
Low Bank St. LS28	S 9	33
Low Clo. BD16	H 6	10
Low Close St. LS2	AA 9	37
St. Marks Rd.		
Low Field BD13	G14	64
Low Fields Rd. LS11	Z13	73
Low Fields Rd. LS12	Z13	73
Low Fold BD11	R16	86
Low Fold BD19	N19	103
Town Gate		
Low Fold LS9	CC12	56
Low Fold, Hor. LS18	U 7	34
Low Gipton Cres. LS9	EE 9	39
Low Grange Cres. LS10	CC14	74
Low Grange Vw. LS10	CC15	74
Low Green Ter. BD7	L13	66
Low Hall Pl. LS11	Z12	55
Low Hall Rd., Hor. LS18	T 7	34
Low Hills La. LS12	X13	72
Lower Wortley Rd.		
Low La. BD13	F13	63
Low La. BD14	H12	46
Low La. HX2	M20	97
Low La. WF17	T18	87
Low La., Hor. LS18	V 6	17
Low Mill La. LS12	X13	72
Low Mills Rd. LS12	X13	72
Low Moor Side La. LS12	V14	71
Low Moor Side LS11	AA12	55
Towngate		
Low Moor St. BD12	M16	83
Low Moorside Clo. LS12	V13	71
School Clo.		
Low Moorside Rd. LS12	V13	71
Low Rd. LS10	CC13	74
Low Row BD5	N13	67
Low Shops La. LS26	EE15	75
Low Side BD16	E 6	9
Harden Rd.		

145

Street	Grid	Page
Low Spring Rd. BD21	D 4	8
Low Well Rd. BD5	M13	66
Lowell Av. BD7	K12	47
Lowell Gro. LS13	U11	52
Lowell Pl. LS13	U11	52
Lowell Ter. LS13	U11	52
Lowell Rd.		
Lower Alfred St. LS7	BB10	56
Alfred Pl.		
Lower Ashgrove BD5	M12	48
Lower Bright St. BD7	M12	48
Richmond Rd.		
Lower Brunswick St.	BB10	56
LS2		
Lower Claypits HX1	D19	93
Lower Clipster Hall HX3	G21	95
Lower Clyde St. HX6	B21	92
Boggart La.		
Lower Cobden St. BD7	M12	48
Lower Crow Nest Dr. HX3	L19	97
Lower Edge Rd. HX5	J23	100
Lower Edge Rd., Elland	H23	99
HX5		
Lower Fleet BD13	F14	63
Lower George St. BD6	K14	65
Upper George St.		
Lower Globe St. BD8	M11	48
Lower Grange Clo. BD8	J11	47
Lower Grattan Rd. BD1	M11	48
Grattan Rd.		
Lower Green Av. BD19	N19	103
Scholes La.		
Lower Grn. BD17	L 6	12
Green Rd.		
Lower Grn. BD19	N19	103
Oddfellows St.		
Lower Heights Rd. BD13	F11	45
Lower Holme BD17	M 6	12
Lower Holme Dock La.	M 6	12
BD17		
Lower Horley Grn. HX3	G18	81
Horley Green La.		
Lower Hunsworth La. BD19	P18	85
Hunsworth La.		
Lower Ings La. HX2	B14	61
Lower Kipping La. BD13	F12	45
Lower Kirkgate HX1	F19	94
Lower La. BD4	P16	85
Lower La., East Bowling	O13	67
BD4		
Lower Newlands HD6	L22	101
Lower Quarry Rd. HD5	O24	102
Lower Rushton Rd. BD3	Q11	50
Lower School BD18	K 7	29
Victoria Rd.		
Lower School St. BD12	M16	83
Lower Skircoat Grn. HX3	E22	98
Lower Town St. LS13	V10	53
Lower Westfield Rd. BD9	L10	48
Lower Wortley Rd. LS12	X12	54
Lower Wyke Gro. BD12	L19	97
Lower Wyke La. BD12	L19	97
Loweswater Dr. BD6	K16	82
Lowfield Clo. BD12	N16	84
Lowmoorside Clo. LS12	W13	71
Lawns La.		
Lowmoorside Ct. LS12	W13	71
Lawns La.		
Lowood La. WF17	T17	87
Lowry Vw. BD21	C 4	8
Lowther Dr., Swil. LS26	JJ14	77
Lowther St. BD2	O10	49
Lowther St. LS8	CC 9	38
Lowtown, Pud. LS28	T11	52
Lucas Pl. LS6	AA 9	37
Lucas St. LS6	AA 9	37
Lucas Ter. LS6	AA 9	37
Institution St.		
Lucy Av. LS15	FF11	58
Lucy Hall Dr. BD17	K 6	11
Lucy St. HX3	F19	94
Luddenden La. HX2	A19	92
Luddendon Pl. BD13	F14	63
Ludgate Hill LS2	BB11	56
Vicar La.		
Ludlam St. BD5	N12	49
Ludolf Dr. LS17	FF 5	22
Luke Rd. BD5	M13	66
Lulworth Av. LS15	HH11	59
Lulworth Clo. LS15	HH10	59
Lulworth Cres. LS15	HH10	59
Lulworth Dr. LS15	HH11	59
Lulworth Garth LS15	HH10	59
Lulworth Gro. BD4	P14	68
Lulworth Vw. LS15	HH10	59
Lulworth Wk. LS15	HH10	59
Lumb Bottom Dr. BD4	T15	70
Lumb La. BD8	M10	48
Lumb La. HX3	A16	78
Wainstalls		
Lumb Sq. LS9	BB11	56
York St.		
Lumb Ter. HX2	A16	78
Lumby Clo., Pud. LS28	T12	52
Lumby La., Pud. LS28	T12	52
Lumby St. BD10	O 7	31
New St.		
Lumley Av. LS4	Y 9	36
Lumley Gro. LS4	Y 9	36
Lumley Rd		
Lumley Mt. LS4	Y 9	36
Lumley Rd.		
Lumley Pl. LS4	Y 9	36
Lumley Rd.		
Lumley Rd. LS4	Y 9	36
Lumley St. LS4	Y 9	36
Lumley Rd.		
Lumley Ter. LS4	Y 9	36
Lumley Rd.		
Lumley Vw. LS4	Y 9	36
Lumley Rd.		
Lumley Wk. LS4	Y 9	36
Lumley Rd.		
Lunan Pl. LS8	CC 9	38
Lunan Ter. LS8	CC 9	38
Lund La.	YY 4	6
Lund St. BD16	G 5	10
Lund St. BD8	K11	47
Lupton Av. LS9	DD11	57
Lupton St. BD18	M 7	30
Phoenix St.		
Lupton St. BD8	N10	49
Lupton St. LS10	CC13	74
Luth St. LS13	S 8	33
Luther St. HX3	E18	80
Luther St., Rod. LS13	T 8	34
Luther Way BD2	N 9	31
Luton St. HX1	D19	93
Queens Rd.		
Luttrell Clo. LS16	X 6	18
Luttrell Cres. LS16	X 6	18
Luttrell Gdns. LS16	X 6	18
Luttrell Pl. LS16	X 6	18
Luttrell Rd. LS16	X 6	18
Luxor Av. LS8	CC 9	38
Luxor Rd. LS8	CC 9	38
Luxor St. LS8	CC 9	38
Luxor Vw. LS8	CC 9	38
Lydbrook Pk. HX3	E22	98
Lyddon Ter. LS2	AA10	55
Lyden Ri. BD15	H11	46
Lydgate HX3	H17	81
Lydgate LS9	CC10	56
Lydgate Pk. HX2	J19	96
Lydgate Pl. LS28	R 7	33
Lydia St. LS2	BB11	56
Lyefield Av. BD18	N 7	31
Lyme Chase LS14	FF10	58
Lymington Dr. BD4	Q13	68
Lyncroft BD2	N 9	31
Lyndale Dr. BD18	N 7	31
Lyndale Rd. BD16	J 4	11
Lyndhurst Av. HD6	L23	101
Lyndhurst Clo. LS15	JJ 7	41
Lyndhurst Cres. LS15	JJ 8	41
Lyndhurst Gro. BD15	J10	47
Lyndhurst Rd. HD6	L23	101
Lyndhurst Rd.,	JJ 8	41
Scholes LS15		
Lyndhurst Vw.,	JJ 8	41
Scholes LS15		
Lyndon St. BD16	H 5	10
Clyde St.		
Lyndon Ter. BD16	H 5	10
Mornington Rd.		
Lynfield Dr. BD9	J 9	29
Lynfield Mt. BD18	N 7	31
Lynnfield Gdns.,	JJ 8	41
Scholes LS15		
Lynthorne Rd. BD9	L 9	30
Lynton Av. BD9	K10	47
Lynton Dr. BD18	L 7	30
Lynton Dr. BD9	K 9	29
Lynton Gro. BD9	K10	47
Lynton Av.		
Lynton Gro. HX2	D14	62
Lynton Vills. BD8	K10	47
Lynwood Av. BD18	N 7	31
Lynwood Clo. BD11	R17	86
Lynwood Cres. HX1	D20	93
Lynwood Cres. LS12	Y12	54
Lynwood Ct.	A 4	7
Lynwood Garth LS12	Y12	54
Lynwood Gdns. LS28	S11	51
Lynwood Gro. LS12	Y13	72
Lynwood Mt. LS12	Y12	54
Lynwood Rd. LS12	Y12	54
Lynwood Ri. LS12	Y12	54
Lynwood Vw. LS12	Y12	54
Lyon St. BD13	F11	45
Lyon St., Queens. BD13	G14	64
Sandbeds		
Lytham Dr. BD13	H14	64
Lytham Gro. LS12	X13	72
Cow Close Rd.		
Lytham Pl. LS12	X13	72
Cow Close Rd.		
Lytham St. HX1	D19	93
Lytton Rd. BD8	K11	47
Lytton St. HX3	F18	80
Range St.		
Lytton Ter. LS10	BB13	74
Cariss St.		
Mabel Rd. BD7	K12	47
Mabgate LS9	BB11	56
Macaulay St. LS9	CC11	56
MacKingstone Dr.	YY 5	6
Wide La.		
MacKingstone La.	YY 5	6
Mackintosh St. HX3	D20	93
MacTurk St. BD8	L10	48
Jarratt St.		
Maddocks St. BD18	L 7	30
Madison Av. BD4	Q14	68
Madni Clo.	E19	94
Mafeking Av. LS11	Z15	73
Dewsbury Rd.		
Mafeking Gro. LS11	Z15	73
Dewsbury Rd.		
Mafeking Mt. LS11	Z15	73
Dewsbury Rd.		
Magdalene Clo. LS16	X 5	18
Maidstone Cres. LS28	T12	52
Maidstone St. BD3	P11	50
Mail Clo. LS15	JJ 9	41
Main Pl. LS10	BB11	56
Hunslet Rd.		
Main Rd. BD13	D10	44
Main St. BD15	F 8	27
Main St. BD17	P 4	14
Main St. LS17	FF 5	22
Main St., Bingley BD16	G 5	10
Main St., Cottingley	H 8	28
BD16		
Main St., Low Moor BD12	N16	84
Main St., Scholes LS15	JJ 8	41
Main St., Thorner LS14	JJ 4	23
Main St., Wyke BD12	M17	83
Mainspring Rd. BD15	F 8	27
Maitland Clo. BD15	H11	46
Maitland Pl. LS11	AA13	73
St. Lukes Rd.		
Maitland St. LS11	AA13	73
Colville Ter.		
Maize St. BD21	B 5	7
Malham Av. BD9	J 9	29
Malham Av. HD6	K23	100
Malham Clo. LS14	GG 9	40
Malham Rd. HD6	K23	100
Mallard Clo. BD10	P 8	32
Mallard Clo. LS26	CC15	91
Bewick Gro.		
Mallington La. BD11	R16	86
Mallory Clo. BD7	K12	47
Malmesbury Clo. BD4	Q14	68
Malmesbury Gro. LS12	Y11	54
Amberley Rd.		
Malmesbury Pl. LS12	Y12	54
Malmesbury St. LS12	Y11	54
Amberley Rd.		
Malmesbury Ter. LS12	Y12	54
Malmesby Clo. LS12	Y12	54
Malsis Cres. BD21	B 4	7
Oakworth Rd.		
Malsis Ct. BD21	B 4	7
Oakworth Rd.		
Malsis Rd. BD21	B 4	7
Malt Kiln La. BD13	E12	45
Malt St. BD22	B 5	7
Wheat St.		
Maltby Ct. LS15	HH11	59
Maltby Pl. LS10	BB13	74
Church St.		
Maltby St. BD4	P12	50
Maltings Rd. HX2	C18	79
Malton St. HX3	F18	80
Malvern Brow BD15	J10	47
Malvern Gro. BD9	J10	47
Malvern Gro. LS11	AA13	73
Malvern Rd.		
Malvern Pl. LS11	AA13	73
Malvern Rd.		
Malvern Rd. BD9	J10	47
Malvern Rd. LS11	AA13	73

147

Mayfield Av. HX4	E20	94
Mayfield Dr. HX1	E20	94
Mayfield Gdns. HX1	E20	94
Mayfield Gro. BD15	E 8	27
Mayfield Gro. BD17	N 5	13
Mayfield Gro. HD6	L19	97
Mayfield Gro. HX1	E20	94
Mayfield Pl. BD12	M17	83
Mayfield Rd. LS15	GG11	58
Mayfield St. HX1	E20	94
Mayfield Ter. BD12	M17	83
Mayfield Ter. BD14	J13	65
Mayfield Ter. HX1	D19	93
Queens Rd.		
Mayfield Vw. BD12	M17	83
Mayflower St. LS10	DD14	75
Mayo Av. BD5	M14	66
Mayo Clo. LS8	EE 8	39
Mayo Cres. BD5	N14	67
Mayo Dr. BD5	N14	67
Mayo Grn. BD5	N14	67
Mayo Rd. BD5	N14	67
Mayster Gro., Brig.	K23	100
Maythorne Cres. BD14	J13	65
Maythorne Dr. BD14	J13	65
Mayville Av. LS6	Z 9	37
Mayville Pl. LS6	Z 9	37
Mayville Rd. LS6	Z 9	37
Mayville St. LS6	Z 9	37
Mayville Ter. LS6	Z 9	37
Mazebrook Av. BD19	Q18	85
Mazebrook Cres. BD19	Q18	85
McBurney Clo. HX3	E18	80
Mill La.		
McBurney St. HX3	E18	80
Mead Vw. BD4	P13	68
Meadow Av. HX3	D18	79
Meadow Cft. HD2	N24	102
Meadow Clo. BD16	E 6	9
Meadow Clo. HX3	J16	82
Meadow Clo. WF17	U18	87
Meadow Cres. HX3	D18	79
Meadow Ct. LS11	AA12	55
Jack La.		
Meadow Dr. HX3	D18	79
Meadow End, Bram. LS16	W 2	2
Meadow Garth, Bram. LS16	W 2	2
Meadow Hurst Gdns. LS28	S11	51
Meadow La. HX3	D18	79
Meadow La. LS11	BB12	56
Meadow Lands BD19	N18	84
Meadow Park Cres. LS28	R10	51
Meadow Park Dr. LS28	R10	51
Meadow Rd. BD10	Q 7	32
Meadow Rd. LS11	AA12	55
Meadow Valley LS17	AA 4	19
Meadow Vw.	ZZ 6	6
Meadow Vw. BD12	M18	83
Meadow Vw. LS6	Z 9	37
Meadow Way LS17	AA 4	19
Meadow Wk. HX3	D18	79
Meadowbank Av. BD15	H10	46
Meadows, The LS16	Y 5	18
Meadowside Rd. BD17	N 5	13
Meadway BD6	K16	82
Meanwood Clo. LS7	AA 9	37
Meanwood Gro. LS6	Z 6	37
Meanwood Rd. LS6	Z 8	37
Meanwood Rd. LS7	BB10	56
Meanwood Ter. LS7	BB 9	38
Servia Ter.		
Mearclough Av., S.B. HX6	C21	93
Medeway LS28	S10	51
Medley La. HX3	G17	81
Medway Rd. BD13	G15	64
Meeke Ter. LS12	Y12	54
Hartington Rd.		
Meggison Gro. BD5	M13	66
Melba Rd. BD5	L13	66
Melbourne Gro. BD3	Q11	50
Melbourne Gro. LS13	V10	53
Melbourne Pl. BD5	M12	48
Melbourne St. BD18	L 7	30
Melbourne St. HX3	E18	80
East Park Rd.		
Melbourne St. LS2	BB10	56
Melbourne St. LS28	S10	51
Melbourne St., Mor. LS27	X17	89
Melbourne Ter. BD12	M12	48
Melcombe Wk. BD4	Q13	68
Melford St. BD4	P14	68
Mellor St. HD6	L22	101
Phoenix Rd.		
Mellor Ter. HX1	E20	94
Moorfield St.		
Melrose Ct., Elland HX5	G24	99
Melrose Gro., Hor. LS18	V 7	35
Melrose Pl. LS28	S12	51
Melrose Pl., Hor. LS18	V 7	35
Melrose St. BD7	L13	66
Melrose St. HX3	E18	80
Melrose Ter., Hor. LS18	V 7	35
Melton Av. LS26	CC17	91
Melton Clo. LS26	CC16	91
Melton Garth LS26	CC17	91
Melton Ter. BD10	Q 9	32
Melville Av. LS6	AA 9	37
Melville Rd.		
Melville Clo. LS6	AA 9	37
Melville Rd.		
Melville Gdns. LS6	AA 9	37
Melville Gro. LS6	AA 9	37
Melville Pl.		
Melville Mt. LS6	AA 9	37
Melville Pl. LS6	AA 9	37
Melville Rd. LS6	AA 9	37
Melville Row LS6	AA 9	37
Melville Rd.		
Melville St. BD7	M11	48
Melville St. LS6	AA 9	37
Melville Ter. LS6	AA 9	37
Memorial Dr. LS6	Z 7	37
Menin Dr. BD17	M 4	12
Menstone St. BD8	M11	48
City Rd.		
Mentone Gro. LS2	AA10	35
Little Woodhouse St.		
Mercia Way LS15	JJ 9	41
Merlin Gro. BD8	J11	47
Merrion Cres. HX3	G20	95
Merrion Pl. LS2	BB11	56
Merrion St. HX3	G20	95
Merrion Cres.		
Merrion St. LS2	BB11	56
Merrivale Rd. BD15	H11	46
Merrydale Rd. BD4	O16	84
Merton Av. LS28	S10	51
Merton Dr. LS28	S10	51
Merton Gdns. LS28	S10	51
Merton Hold BD5	N13	67
Spring Mill St.		
Merton Rd. BD7	M12	48
Merville Av. BD17	M 4	12
Mesham Ct. LS6	Z 8	37
Shaw La.		
Methley Dr. LS7	BB 8	38
Methley Gro. LS7	BB 8	38
Methley La. LS7	BB 8	38
Methley Mt. LS7	BB 8	38
Methley Pl. LS7	BB 8	38
Methley Ter. LS7	BB 8	38
Methley Vw. LS7	BB 8	38
Methuen Oval BD12	M18	83
Mexborough Av. LS7	BB 9	38
Mexborough Dr. LS7	BB 9	38
Mexborough Gro. LS7	BB 9	38
Mexborough Pl. LS7	BB 9	38
Mexborough Rd. BD2	M 8	30
Mexborough Rd. LS7	BB 9	38
Mexborough St. LS7	BB 9	38
Meynell App. LS11	AA12	55
Meynell Clo. LS11	AA12	55
Meynell App.		
Meynell Heights LS11	AA12	55
Meynell App.		
Meynell Rd. LS15	HH12	59
Meynell Sq. LS11	AA12	55
Meynell Clo.		
Miall St. HX1	E19	94
Micklefield Clo. BD7	K13	65
Mickledore Ridge BD7	K13	65
Micklefield Ct. LS19	R 5	15
Micklefield La.		
Micklefield La. LS19	R 5	15
Micklefield Rd. LS19	R 5	15
Micklethwaite La. BD16	G 4	10
Mickley Pl. LS12	Y11	54
Mickley St.		
Mickley St. LS12	Y11	54
Mickley Ter. LS12	Y11	54
Mickley St.		
Middle Cross St. LS12	Y11	54
Middle Dean St., Greet. HX4	F24	98
Middle Fold LS9	BB11	56
Middle La. BD14	J12	47
Middle St. BD1	N11	49
Broad St.		
Middle Wk. LS8	EE 6	21
Middlebrook Clo. BD8	K11	47
Middlebrook Cres. BD8	J12	47
Middlebrook Dr. BD8	J11	47
Middlebrook Hill BD8	J11	47
Middlebrook Ri. BD8	J11	47
Middlebrook Vw. BD8	K11	47
Middlebrook Way BD8	J12	47
Middlebrook Wk. BD8	K11	47
Middlecroft Clo. LS26	CC15	91
Middlecroft Rd. LS26	CC15	91
Middlegate WF17	T18	87
Middlemoor LS14	GG 7	40
Litton Way		
Middleton Av. LS9	CC10	56
Middleton Clo., Mor. LS27	X17	89
Middleton Cres. LS11	AA14	73
Middleton Gro. LS11	AA14	73
Middleton La. LS10	BB17	90
Middleton Park Grn. LS10	AA17	90
Middleton Park Gro.		
Middleton Pk. Av. LS10	AA17	90
Middleton Pk. Circ. LS10	AA16	90
Middleton Pk. Cres. LS10	BB17	91
Middleton Pk. Gro. LS10	AA16	90
Middleton Pk. LS10	BB17	91
Middleton Pk. Mt. LS10	AA17	90
Middleton Pk. Pl. LS10	BB17	91
Middleton Pk. Rd. LS10	AA16	90
Middleton Pk. Sq. LS10	BB17	91
Middleton Pk. Sq. N. LS10	AA16	90
Middleton Park Gro.		
Middleton Pk. Sq. S LS10	AA16	90
Middleton Park Gro.		
Middleton Rd. LS10	CC15	74
Middleton Rd., Mor. LS27	X17	89
Middleton Ring Rd. LS10	CC16	91
Middleton Ring Road LS26	CC14	74
Middleton St. BD8	L10	48
Middleton Ter. LS10	BB17	91
Middleton Ter., Mor. LS27	Y17	89
Midgeham Gro. BD16	E 6	9
Midgeley Bldgs. HX2	D17	79
Keighley Rd.		
Midgeley Rd. BD17	L 6	12
Midgley Gdns. LS6	AA 9	37
Holborn App.		
Midgley Pl. LS6	AA 9	37
Holborn App.		
Midgley Row BD4	O14	67
Midgley St. LS6	AA 9	37
Institution St.		
Midgley Ter. LS6	AA 9	37
Holborn App.		
Midgley Vw. LS6	AA 9	37
Midgley Ter.		
Midland Av. LS10	CC14	74
Leasowe Rd.		
Midland Clo. LS10	CC13	74
Midland Rd.		
Midland Cres. LS10	CC14	74
Leasowe Rd.		
Midland Garth LS10	CC13	74
Midland Gro. LS10	CC14	74
Leasowe Rd.		
Midland Hill BD16	G 5	10
Waterloo Rd.		
Midland Mt. LS10	CC14	74
Leasowe Rd.		
Midland Pass. LS6	Z 9	37
Midland Rd. BD1	M10	48
Midland Rd. BD17	M 6	12
Midland Rd. BD8	M10	48
Midland Rd. BD9	M 8	30
Midland Rd. LS10	CC13	74
Midland Rd. LS6	Z 9	37
Midland Ter. BD9	M 8	30
Midland Vw. LS10	CC14	74
Leasowe Rd.		
Midway Av. BD16	H 7	28
Milan Rd. LS8	CC 9	38
Milan St. LS8	DD 9	39
Mildred St. BD3	D10	49
West End Rd.		
Mile Cross Gdns. HX1	D20	93
Mile Cross Pl. HX1	D20	93
Mile Cross Rd. HX1	D20	93
Mile Cross Ter. HX1	D20	93
Mile Thorn St.	D19	93
Miles Hill Av. LS7	AA 8	37
Miles Hill Cres. BD4	P14	68
Miles Hill Cres. LS7	AA 8	37
Miles Hill Dr. BD4	P14	68
Miles Hill Gdns. LS7	AA 8	37
Miles Hill Gro. LS7	AA 8	37
Miles Hill Mt. LS7	AA 7	37
Miles Hill Rd. LS7	AA 8	37
Miles Hill Sq. LS7	AA 8	37
Miles Hill Rd.		
Miles Hill St. LS7	AA 8	37
Miles Hill Ter. LS7	AA 8	37
Miles Hill Vw. LS7	AA 8	37

Milethorn St. HX1	D19	93

Gibbet St.

Milford Gro. BD19	R17	86
Milford Pl. BD9	L 9	30
Milford Pl. LS4	Y10	54
Mill Carr Hill Rd. BD12	O17	84
Mill Carr Hill Rd. BD4	O17	84
Mill Field BD10	O 7	31

Railway Rd.

Mill Green Clo. LS14	HH 9	41
Mill Green Garth LS14	HH 9	41
Mill Green Gdns. LS14	HH 8	41
Mill Green Pl. LS14	HH 8	41
Mill Green Rd. LS14	HH 8	41
Mill Green Vw. LS14	GG 8	40
Mill Grn. LS12	Z12	55
Mill Hey	ZZ 7	24
Mill Hill HX2	N22	102
Mill Hill La. HD6	K21	96
Mill Hill LS1	BB11	56
Mill Hill Top BD16	E 7	27
Mill Hill, Pud. LS28	T12	52
Mill La. BD11	R16	86
Mill La. BD13	F14	63
Mill La. BD16	J 4	11
Mill La. BD19	P17	85
Mill La. BD4	N12	49
Mill La. BD5	N12	49
Mill La. BD6	K16	82
Mill La. HD6	L22	101
Mill La. HX2	C15	62
Mill La. HX3	E18	80
Mill La. LS13	U 9	34
Mill La., Gild. LS27	V15	71
Mill La., Oakworth	YY 6	6
Mill La., Oxenhope	ZZ 9	24
Mill La., Tong BD4	T13	70
Mill Pit La., Roth. LS26	EE15	75
Mill St. BD1	N11	49
Mill St. BD13	C 8	26
Mill St. BD6	L14	66
Mill St. HX3	E22	98
Mill St. LS9	BB11	56
Mill St., Mor. LS27	X17	89
Millersdale Clo. BD4	O15	67
Millgate BD16	G 5	10
Milligan Av. BD2	N 8	31
Millroyd St. HD6	L22	101
Mills St. HX3	F19	94
Millshaw LS11	Y15	72
Millshaw LS11	Z14	73
Millshaw Mt. LS11	Z15	73
Millshaw Park Av. LS27	Y15	89
Millshaw Park Dr. LS12	Y14	72
Millshaw Park Way LS11	Y14	72
Millshaw Pk. LS12	Y15	72
Millshaw Rd. LS11	Z15	73
Millwright St. LS2	BB10	56
Milne St. BD7	M11	48
Milner Fold LS28	S12	51
Milner Gdns. LS9	CC12	56
Milner Ing BD12	L17	83
Milner La., Greet. HX4	F23	98
Milner La., Thorner LS14	JJ 4	23
Milner Pl. HX2	E19	94

Hanson La.

Milner Royd La. HX6	D21	93
Milner St. LS10	BB13	74
Milnes St. LS12	Z12	55
Milnes Ter. LS12	Z12	55

Wellington Rd.

Milroyd Cres. WF17	U18	87
Milton Av., S.B. HX6	B20	92
Milton Dr., Scholes LS15	JJ 7	41
Milton Pl. HX1	D17	79

Nursery La.

Milton Pl., S.B. HX6	B20	92
Milton St. BD13	D11	44
Milton St. BD7	M11	48
Milton St. HX1	E19	94
Milton St., S.B. HX6	B20	92
Milton Ter. HX1	E19	94

West Hill St.

Milton Ter. LS5	X 9	36

Church St.

Minnie St. BD21	B 4	7

Ashfield St.

Minnie St. LS4	Y10	54
Minnie St., Haworth	ZZ 8	24
Minor St. LS4	Y10	54

Kirkstall Rd.

Minorca Mt. BD13	C10	44
Minstead Av. HD6	J23	100
Mint St. BD2	O10	49
Mirfield Av. BD2	O 8	31
Mirycarr La., Thorner LS14	JJ 6	23
Mission St. HD6	M22	101

Mistress La. LS12	Y11	54
Mitcham Dr. BD9	L10	48
Mitchell Clo. BD10	P 6	14
Mitchell La. BD10	P 6	14
Mitchell Sq. BD5	N13	67

Bowling Old La.

Mitchell St. BD5	N13	67

Bowling Old La.

Mitchell St. HD6	E17	80

Nursery La.

Mitchell St., S.B. HX6	C21	93
Mitchell Ter. BD16	G 6	10
Mitford Pl. LS12	Y11	54
Mitford Rd. LS12	Y11	54
Mitford Ter. LS12	Y11	54
Mitton St. BD5	M13	66
Mixenden Ct. HX2	C17	79
Mixenden Rd. HX2	C16	79
Moat End, Thorner LS14	JJ 4	23
Moat Hill WF17	T18	87
Modder Pl. LS12	X11	54
Modder Ter. LS12	X11	54
Model Av. LS12	Y11	54
Model Rd. LS12	Y11	54
Model Ter. LS12	Y11	54
Moffat Clo. BD6	K15	65
Moffat Clo. HX2	D17	79
Mond Av. BD3	P10	50
Monk Bridge Av. LS6	Z 8	37

Monk Bridge Ter.

Monk Bridge Dr. LS6	Z 8	37
Monk Bridge Gro. LS6	Z 8	37

Monk Bridge Ter.

Monk Bridge Pl. LS6	Z 8	37

Monk Bridge Ter.

Monk Bridge Rd. LS6	Z 8	37
Monk Bridge St. LS6	Z 8	37
Monk Bridge Ter. LS6	Z 8	37
Monk Ings Av. WF17	S18	86
Monk St. BD7	M11	48
Monkbarn Clo. BD16	H 5	10
Monkswood Av. LS14	FF 7	40
Monkswood Bank LS14	FF 7	40
Monkswood Clo. LS14	FF 7	40
Monkswood Dr. LS14	FF 7	40
Monkswood Gate LS14	GG 7	40
Monkswood Grn. LS14	FF 7	40
Monkswood Hill LS14	FF 7	40
Monkswood Ri. LS14	FF 7	40
Monkswood Wk. LS14	FF 7	40
Monson Av. LS28	R 8	33
Montagu Av. LS8	DD 8	39
Montagu Cres. LS8	EE 8	39
Montagu Dr. LS8	DD 8	39
Montagu Gdns. LS8	DD 8	39
Montagu Gro. LS8	DD 8	39
Montagu Pl. LS8	DD 8	39
Montagu Ri. LS8	EE 8	39
Montagu Vw. LS8	DD 8	39
Montague Gro. BD5	M13	66

Montague St.

Montague St. BD5	M13	66
Montague St., S.B. HD6	B21	92
Montcalm Cres. LS10	CC14	74
Montfort Clo., Hor. LS18	U 5	16
Montpelier LS6	AA 9	37

Cliff Rd.

Montreal Av. LS7	BB 8	38
Montreal Pl. LS7	CC 8	38

Montreal Av.

Montrose Pl. BD13	F14	63

Mill La.

Montrose St. BD18	L 8	30

Valley Rd.

Montrose St. BD18	M 9	30
Montserrat Rd. BD4	Q14	68
Moody St. BD4	N12	49
Moor Allerton Av. LS17	CC 6	20
Moor Allerton Cres. LS17	CC 6	20
Moor Allerton Dr. LS17	CC 6	20
Moor Allerton Gdns. LS17	BB 6	20
Moor Allerton Way LS17	CC 6	20
Moor Av. BD7	K14	65
Moor Av. LS15	FF11	58
Moor Bottom BD13	C 8	26
Moor Bottom La. BD16	H 5	10
Moor Bottom La. BD21	B 6	7
Moor Bottom La. HX2	D16	79
Moor Bottom La., Greet. HX4	E23	98
Moor Cft. LS16	Y 5	18

Long Causeway

Moor Clo. LS10	BB14	74
Moor Close Av. BD13	F15	63
Moor Close La. BD13	F15	63
Moor Close Par. BD13	F14	63
Moor Close Rd. BD13	F14	63

Moor Crescent Chase	BB13	74

LS11

Moor Croft Av.	A 5	7
Moor Dr. LS6	Z 8	37
Moor Dr., Oakworth	ZZ 5	6
Moor Dr., Pud. LS28	T12	52
Moor Edge High Side BD16	E 6	9
Moor Edge Low Side BD16	E 6	9
Moor End	ZZ 8	24
Moor End Av. HX2	C18	79
Moor End Gdns. HX2	C18	79
Moor End Rd. HX2	B18	78
Moor Farm Gdns. LS7	BB 7	38
Moor Flatts Av. LS10	BB16	91
Moor Flatts Rd. LS10	BB16	91
Moor Grange Clo. LS16	X 7	36
Moor Grange Ct. LS16	W 7	35
Moor Grange Dr. LS16	X 7	36
Moor Grange Ri. LS16	X 7	36
Moor Grange Vw. LS16	X 7	36
Moor Gro. HX3	J15	65
Moor Gro., Pud. LS28	T12	52
Moor Haven Ct. LS17	AA 5	19
Moor Hey La. HD6	J24	100
Moor House Clo.	ZZ 9	24
Moor La. BD11	S17	86
Moor La. BD19	R18	86
Moor La. BD19	S17	86
Moor La. HX2	D17	79
Moor La., Bram. LS16	V 2	2
Moor Lea Dr. BD17	M 5	12
Moor Park Av. LS6	Y 8	36
Moor Park Clo. BD3	P11	50

Moor Park Rd.

Moor Park Dr. BD3	P11	50
Moor Park Dr. LS6	Y 8	36
Moor Park Mt. LS6	Z 8	37
Moor Park Rd. BD3	P11	50
Moor Park Vills. LS6	Z 8	37
Moor Rd. LS11	BB13	74
Moor Rd. LS6	Y 8	36
Moor Rd., Bram. LS16	V 2	2
Moor Royd HX3	E21	94
Moor Side St. BD12	L16	83
Moor St. BD13	G14	64

Albert Rd.

Moor St., Oakworth	ZZ 5	6
Moor Top BD11	P10	50
Moor Top Gdns. HX2	D15	62
Moor Top Rd. BD12	L16	83
Moor Top Rd. HX2	B19	92
Moor View Av. BD18	L 7	30
Moor View Dr. BD18	N 7	31

Near Welwyn Av.

Moor Way	ZZ 5	6
Moorcroft Av. BD3	P10	50
Moorcroft Dr. BD4	H 4	10
Moorcroft Dr. BD4	Q15	68
Moorcroft Rd. BD4	Q15	68
Moorcroft Ter. BD4	Q15	68
Moore Av. BD5	K14	65
Moore Vw. BD7	K13	65
Moorfield Av. BD3	P10	50
Moorfield Av. LS12	X11	54
Moorfield Cft. LS12	S 4	15
Moorfield Cres. LS12	X11	54

Tower La.

Moorfield Cres. LS28	S12	51
Moorfield Dr. BD17	M 5	12
Moorfield Dr. LS19	S 4	15
Moorfield Dr., Oakworth	ZZ 5	6
Moorfield Gdns. LS28	S12	51
Moorfield Gro. LS28	X11	54
Moorfield Gro. LS28	S12	51
Moorfield Pl. BD10	O 7	31
Moorfield Rd. BD16	H 7	28
Moorfield Rd. LS12	X11	54
Moorfield St. HX1	E20	94
Moorfield St. LS12	X11	54
Moorfield St. LS2	AA 9	37

Raglan Rd.

Moorfield Ter. BD13	C 8	26
Moorfield, Gild. LS27	V15	71
Moorfields LS13	V 9	35
Moorgarth Av. BD3	P10	50
Moorgate Av. BD3	P10	50
Moorgate St. HX1	D20	93

Lombard St.

Moorhead Cres. BD18	K 7	29
Moorhead La. BD18	K 7	29
Moorhead Ter. BD18	K 7	29
Moorhouse Av. BD2	O 8	31
Moorhouse Dr. BD4	Q15	68
Moorhouse La. BD11	Q15	68
Moorhouse La., Oxenhope	ZZ 9	24
Moorland Av. BD16	J 4	11
Moorland Av. BD17	M 5	12

149

Name	Grid	Page
Moorland Av. HX2	D17	79
Moorland Av. LS6	Z10	55
Moorland Av., Gild. LS27	U15	70
Moorland Clo. HX2	D17	79
Moorland Clo. LS27	U15	70
Moorland Av.		
Moorland Cres. BD17	M 5	12
Moorland Cres. HX2	D17	79
Moorland Cres. LS17	BB 6	20
Moorland Cres. LS28	R11	51
Moorland Cres., Gild LS27	U15	70
Moorland Dr. BD11	R16	86
Moorland Dr. HX3	D18	79
Moorland Dr. LS17	BB 6	20
Moorland Dr. LS28	R11	51
Moorland Garth LS17	BB 6	20
Moorland Gdns. LS17	BB 6	20
Moorland Gro. LS17	BB 6	20
Moorland Gro. LS28	R10	51
Moorland Ings LS17	BB 6	20
Moorland Mt. LS6	Z10	55
Hyde Park Rd.		
Moorland Pl. BD12	N16	84
Cleckheaton Rd.		
Moorland Pl. LS6	Z10	55
Hyde Park Rd.		
Moorland Rd. BD11	T16	87
Moorland Rd. LS28	R10	51
Moorland Rd. LS6	Z10	55
Moorland Rd., Bram. LS16	V 2	2
Moorland Ri. LS17	BB 6	20
Moorland Ter. BD11	T16	87
Moorland Ter. BD21	D 4	8
Moorland Vw. BD12	N16	84
Moorland Vw. BD15	F 9	27
Moorland Vw. LS17	BB 7	38
Moorland Wk. LS17	BB 6	20
Moorlands Av. BD3	P10	50
Moorlands Av. LS19	S 4	15
Moorlands Dr. LS19	S 4	15
Moorlands Leys LS17	AA 6	19
Moorlands Rd. BD11	R15	69
Moorlands Rd., Greet. HX4	E23	98
Moorlands, Oakworth	A 5	7
Moorlands, The LS17	CC 5	20
Moorside App. BD11	T16	87
Moorside Av. BD11	R15	69
Moorside Av. BD2	P10	50
Moorside Av., Moorside BD11	T16	87
Moorside BD9	K10	47
Moorside Cft. BD2	P10	50
Moorside Clo. BD11	T16	87
Moorside Clo. BD2	P 9	32
Moorside Cres. BD11	T16	87
Moorside Dr. BD11	T16	87
Moorside Dr. LS13	V 9	35
Moorside Gdns. BD2	P 9	32
Moorside Gdns. HX3	D17	79
Moorside Grn. BD11	T16	87
Moorside Wk.		
Moorside Gro. LS13	V 9	35
Moorside St.		
Moorside HX2	O20	103
Moorside La.	YY 9	24
Moorside La. BD3	P11	50
Moorside Maltings LS11	BB13	74
Moorside Ms. BD2	P10	50
Moorside Mt. BD11	T16	87
Moorside Par. BD11	T16	87
Moorside Pl. BD11	O 8	31
Moorside Pl. BD2	P10	50
Moorside Pl. BD3	P11	50
Moorside Rd. BD11	T16	87
Moorside Rd. BD15	F 8	27
Main St.		
Moorside Rd. BD2	P 9	32
Moorside Rd. BD3	P11	50
Moorside La.		
Moorside St. LS13	V 9	35
Moorside Ter. BD11	T16	87
Moorside Ter. BD2	P10	50
Moorside Ter. LS13	V 9	35
Moorside St.		
Moorside Vale BD11	T16	87
Moorside Vw. BD11	T16	87
Moorside Wk. BD11	T16	87
Moorthorpe Av. BD3	P10	50
Moortown Ring Rd. LS17	DD 5	21
Moorview Cres. BD16	G 8	28
Moorview Gro. BD21	C 4	8
Moorville Av. BD3	P10	50
Moorville Clo. LS11	AA13	73
Moorville Rd.		
Moorville Ct. LS11	AA13	73
Colville Ter.		
Moorville Dr. BD11	R15	69
Moorville Gro. LS11	AA13	73
Moorville Pl. LS11	AA13	73
Moorville Rd. LS11	AA13	73
Moorwell Pl. BD2	P 9	32
Moravian Pl. BD5	M13	66
Holme Top La.		
Moray St. BD18	L 8	30
Valley Rd.		
Moresby Rd. BD6	K16	82
Moresdale La. LS14	FF 9	40
Morley Av. BD3	P10	50
Morley Bottoms, Mor. LS27	X16	89
Morley Carr Rd. BD12	M16	83
Morley Rd., Mor. LS27	W16	88
Morley St. BD7	M12	48
Morley Vw. HX3	G21	95
Backhold La.		
Morning St. BD21	B 5	7
Hainworth Wood Rd.		
Morningside BD8	L10	48
Mornington Rd. BD16	H 5	10
Mornington Vills. BD8	M10	48
Morpeth St. BD13	G14	64
High St.		
Morpeth St. BD7	M11	48
Morphet Gro. LS7	BB10	56
Upper Elmwood St.		
Morphet Ter. LS7	BB10	56
Howarth Pl.		
Morris Av. LS6	X 8	36
Morris Fold LS12	X12	54
Lower Wortley St.		
Morris Gro. LS5	Y 9	36
Morris La. LS6	X 8	36
Morris Mt. LS5	X 9	36
Abbey Rd.		
Morris Pl. LS27	W16	88
Morris St. LS11	Z15	73
Dewsbury Rd.		
Morris Vw. LS5	X 9	36
Morritt Av. LS15	GG10	58
Morritt Dr. LS15	FF11	58
Morritt Gro. LS15	FF11	58
Mortimer Av. BD3	P10	50
Mortimer Row BD3	P12	50
Mortimer St. BD8	K11	47
Morton La. BD16	G 4	9
Morton Rd. BD4	P12	50
Morton St. HX3	E17	80
Nursery La.		
Mortons Clo.	G21	95
Mortons Pl. HX3	G21	95
Morwick Gro. LS15	JJ 8	41
Moseley Dr. HX2	D16	79
Moseley Pl. LS6	AA 9	37
Crowther Pl.		
Moseley Wood App. LS16	V 5	17
Moseley Wood Av. LS16	V 4	17
Moseley Wood Bank LS16	V 4	17
Moseley Wood Cft. LS16	V 4	17
Moseley Wood Clo. LS16	V 5	17
Moseley Wood Cres. LS16	V 4	17
Moseley Wood Dr. LS16	V 4	17
Moseley Wood Gdns. LS16	V 4	17
Moseley Wood Grn. LS16	V 4	17
Moseley Wood La. LS16	W 4	17
Moseley Wood Ri. LS16	V 4	17
Moseley Wood Vw. LS16	W 4	17
Moseley Wood Way LS16	V 4	17
Moseley Wood Wk. LS16	V 4	17
Moser Av. BD2	O 8	31
Moser Cres. BD2	O 8	31
Moss Bridge Rd., Rod. LS13	T 8	34
Moss Carr Av. BD21	D 4	8
Moss Carr Gro. BD21	D 4	8
Moss Carr Rd. BD21	D 4	8
Moss Carr Ter. BD21	D 4	8
Calton Rd.		
Moss Dr. HX2	D16	79
Moss Gdns. LS17	AA 4	19
Moss La. HX2	D16	79
Moss Ri. LS17	AA 4	19
Moss Row BD15	E 8	27
Moss Row LS28	S11	51
Moss St. BD13	F11	45
Moss Valley LS17	AA 4	19
Mosscar St. BD3	O12	49
Mossdale Av. BD9	J 9	29
Mossy Bank BD13	G14	64
Thornton Rd.		
Mostyn Cres. BD6	L15	66
Mostyn Gro. BD6	L15	66
Mostyn Mt. HX3	E17	80
Athol Rd.		
Mount Av. BD2	O 8	31
Mount Av. HX2	C19	93
Mount Cres. HX2	C19	93
Mount Dr. LS17	AA 4	19
Mount Gdns. LS17	AA 4	19
Mount Gro. BD2	O 8	31
Mount La. HD6	K24	100
Mount Pellon Rd. HX2	D19	93
Mount Pl. LS11	Z15	73
Dewsbury Rd.		
Mount Pleasant Av. HX1	E19	94
Mount Pleasant Av. LS8	CC 8	38
Mount Pleasant BD10	O 7	31
Mount Pleasant BD13	C11	44
Mount Pleasant BD6	K15	65
Mount Pleasant LS10	BB16	91
Mount Pleasant LS13	U 9	34
Mount Pleasant Rd., Pud. LS28	T11	52
Mount Pleasant St. BD13	G14	64
High St.		
Mount Preston LS2	AA10	55
Mount Preston St. LS2	AA10	55
Mount Rd. BD2	O 8	31
Mount Rd. BD6	L14	66
Mount Ri. LS17	AA 4	19
Mount Royd BD8	M10	48
Mount St. BD2	O 8	31
Mount St. BD3	O12	49
Mount St. BD4	O12	49
Mount St., S.B. HD6	B21	92
Mount Tabor LS9	CC11	56
Burmantofts St.		
Mount Tabor Rd. HX2	A16	78
Mount Tabor St. LS28	S11	51
Waterloo Rd.		
Mount Ter. BD2	O 8	31
Mount Vw.	YY 6	6
Bridge St.		
Mount Vw. St. BD13	F14	63
Chapel La.		
Mount WF17	T18	87
Mount, The BD17	M 6	12
Mount, The LS15	GG10	58
Mount, The LS17	AA 4	19
Mountain Vw. BD18	M 8	30
Mountbatten Ct. BD5	N14	67
Newroyd St.		
Mountcliffe Vw. LS27	X15	89
Mountfields HX3	K19	96
Mountleigh Clo. BD4	O15	67
Mowbray Clo. BD13	C 8	26
Mowbray Cres. LS14	GG 9	40
Moynihan Ho. LS9	BB11	56
Mud Hill HX3	H17	81
Muirhead Dr. BD4	Q14	68
Mulberry Av. LS16	Z 5	19
Mulberry Garth LS16	Z 4	19
Mulberry Ri. LS16	Z 5	19
Mulberry St. LS10	BB12	56
Mulberry St. LS28	S10	51
Bradford Rd.		
Mulberry Vw. LS16	Z 5	19
Mulcott Rd. BD4	P13	68
Mulcture Hall Rd. HX1	F19	94
Mulgrave St. BD3	O12	49
Mullins Ct. LS9	CC11	56
Kippax Pl.		
Mumford St. BD5	N13	67
Munby St. BD8	K11	47
Munster St. BD4	O13	67
Murdstone Clo. BD5	N13	67
Humford St.		
Murgatroyd St. BD5	N14	67
New Cross St.		
Murton Clo. LS14	GG 9	40
Muschamp Ter. LS7	BB10	56
Benson St.		
Musgrave Bank LS13	W10	53
Musgrave Bldgs., Pud. LS28	T11	52
Town End Pl.		
Musgrave Dr. BD2	P10	50
Musgrave Gro. BD2	P10	50
Musgrave Mt. BD2	P10	50
Musgrave Mt. LS13	W10	53
Musgrave Rd. BD2	P10	50
Musgrave Ri. LS13	W10	53
Musgrave St. WF17	T18	87
Low La.		
Musgrave Vw. LS13	W10	53
Musgraves Fold LS9	CC11	56
Richmond St.		
Mushroom St. LS9	BB10	56
Musselburgh St. BD7	M11	48
Mutton Lane. BD15	F10	45
Myers Av. BD2	O 9	31
Myers La. BD2	N 9	31
Myrtle Av. HX2	D16	79
Myrtle Ct. BD16	G 6	10

Name	Grid	Page
Myrtle Dr. HX2	D17	79
Myrtle Dr., Haworth	A 7	25
Halifax Rd.		
Myrtle Gdns. HX2	D17	79
Myrtle Gro. BD13	F15	63
Myrtle Gro. HX2	D17	79
Myrtle Gro., Haworth	A 7	25
Halifax Rd.		
Myrtle Pl. BD16	G 5	10
Myrtle Pl. BD18	K 7	29
Saltaire Rd.		
Myrtle Pl. HX2	D17	79
Myrtle Rd., Elland HX5	G24	99
Myrtle Sq. LS6	Z 7	37
Myrtle St. BD16	H 5	10
Herbert St.		
Myrtle St. BD3	O12	49
Myrtle Ter.	A 6	7
Myrtle Vw., Haworth	A 7	25
Myrtle Vw., Oakworth	ZZ 5	6
Mytholmes La.	ZZ 7	24
Nab End BD13	J14	65
Union Ho. La.		
Nab End La., Greet. BD13	F23	98
Nab La. BD15	E 8	27
Nab La. BD18	J 7	29
Nab La. WF17	U18	87
Nab Water La.	ZZ12	42
Nab Wood Bank BD18	J 7	29
Nab Wood Clo. BD18	K 7	29
Nab Wood Cres. BD18	J 7	29
Nab Wood Dr. BD16	J 8	29
Nab Wood Dr. BD18	J 7	29
Nab Wood Gdns. BD18	K 7	29
Nab Wood Gro. BD18	J 7	29
Nab Wood Mt. BD18	J 7	29
Nab Wood Pl. BD18	J 7	29
Nab Wood Rd. BD18	J 7	29
Nab Wood Ri. BD18	J 7	29
Nab Wood Ter. BD18	J 7	29
Naburn App. LS14	GG 6	22
Naburn Chase LS14	GG 7	40
Naburn Clo. LS14	GG 7	40
Naburn Dr. LS14	GG 7	40
Naburn Fold LS14	GG 7	40
Naburn Gdns. LS14	GG 7	40
Naburn Grn. LS14	GG 7	40
Naburn Pl. LS14	GG 7	40
Naburn Rd. LS14	GG 7	40
Naburn Vw. LS14	GG 7	40
Naburn Wk. LS14	GG 7	40
Nancroft Cres. LS12	Y11	54
Brooklyn Ter.		
Nancroft Mt. LS12	Y11	54
Brooklyn Ter.		
Nansen Av. LS13	U10	52
Station Mt.		
Nansen Gro. LS13	U10	52
Station Mt.		
Nansen Mt. LS13	U10	52
Station Mt.		
Nansen Pl. LS13	U10	52
Station Mt.		
Nansen St. LS13	U10	52
Nansen Ter. LS13	U10	52
Station Mt.		
Nansen Vw. LS13	U10	52
Station Mt.		
Napier Rd. BD3	P11	50
Napier Rd., Elland HX5	G24	99
Napier St. BD21	C 4	8
Napier Ter. BD3	P11	50
Naples St. BD8	L10	48
Narrow La. BD16	E 6	9
Narrows, The BD16	F 6	9
Naseby Dr. BD13	G14	64
Naseby Garth LS9	CC10	56
Naseby Gdns. LS9	CC10	56
Naseby Grange LS9	CC10	56
Naseby Pl. LS9	CC10	56
Cromwell Mt.		
Naseby Ter. LS9	CC10	56
Naseby Vw. LS9	CC11	56
Naseby Wk. LS9	CC10	56
Nashville Rd. BD3	B 4	7
Nashville Rd. BD21	B 4	7
Nashville Ter. BD21	B 4	7
Nassau Pl. LS7	CC 9	38
Nathan St. BD1	N11	49
Natty La. HX3	D15	62
Navigation Rd. HX3	F20	94
Navigation St. LS10	BB11	56
Naylor St. HX1	D19	93
Naylor St. LS11	AA11	55
Meynell St.		
Neal St. BD5	N12	49
Near Peat La.	YY11	17
Nearcliffe Rd. BD9	L10	48
Neath Gdns. LS9	EE 9	39
Necropolis Rd. BD7	K12	47
Ned Hill Rd. HX2	D14	62
Ned La. BD4	Q13	68
Needle Row HX2	D15	62
Needles Inn La., Wood. LS26	HH15	77
Neill St. LS12	Y11	54
Armley Rd.		
Nellie Cres. LS9	CC11	56
Nellie Vw. LS9	CC11	56
Nelson Pl. BD13	G14	64
Albert Rd.		
Nelson Pl., Mor. LS27	X16	89
Nelson St. BD1	N12	49
Nelson St. BD13	G14	64
Nelson St. BD15	J10	47
Nelson St. BD17	L 6	12
Green La.		
Nelson St. BD5	N12	49
Nelson St. HX1	F19	94
Nelson St., S.B. HX6	C21	93
Nene St. BD5	M13	66
Nepshaw La., Mor. LS27	V17	88
Neptune St. LS9	BB11	56
Nesfield Clo. LS10	CC16	91
Nesfield Cres. LS10	CC16	91
Nesfield Garth LS10	CC16	91
Nesfield Gdns. LS10	CC16	91
Nesfield Rd. LS10	CC16	91
Nesfield St. BD1	M11	48
Nesfield Vw. LS10	CC16	91
Nesfield Wk. LS10	CC16	91
Nessfield Dr.	A 4	7
Nessfield Gro.	A 4	7
Nessfield Rd.	A 4	7
Nether Green Ct. LS6	AA 9	37
Woodhouse St.		
Nether St. LS28	S 9	33
Bagley La.		
Netherall Rd. BD17	M 5	12
Netherby St. BD3	O11	49
Heath Ter.		
Nethercope Ter. LS28	S 9	33
Bagley La.		
Netherlands Av. BD12	M15	66
Netherlands Av. BD6	M15	66
Netherlands Sq. BD12	M15	66
Nethermoor Vw. BD16	H 5	10
Nettle Gro. HX3	G18	81
Nettleton Clo. BD4	T14	70
Nettleton Ct. LS15	HH11	59
Nevill Gro. BD9	J 9	29
Neville App. LS9	EE12	57
Neville Av. BD4	O14	67
Neville Av. LS9	EE12	57
Neville Clo. LS9	EE12	57
Neville Cres. LS9	EE11	57
Neville Garth LS9	EE12	57
Neville Gro. LS9	EE11	57
Neville Mt. LS9	EE12	57
Neville Par. LS9	EE12	57
Neville Pl. LS9	EE11	57
Neville Rd. BD4	O13	67
Neville Rd. LS9	EE11	57
Neville Row LS9	EE12	57
Neville St. LS1	AA11	55
Neville St. LS11	AA11	55
Neville Ter. LS9	EE12	57
Neville Vw. LS9	EE11	57
Neville Wk. LS9	EE11	57
New Adel Av. LS16	X 5	18
New Adel Gdns. LS16	X 5	18
New Adel La. LS16	X 5	18
New Bank HX3	F19	94
New Bank St., Mor. LS27	X16	89
New Bond St. HX1	E19	94
New Briggate LS2	BB11	56
New Brighton BD16	J 8	29
New Brighton LS13	V10	53
New Brighton Rd. BD12	O17	84
New Brunswick St. HX1	E19	94
New Clayton Ter. BD13	C 8	26
New Cres., Hor. LS18	U 7	34
New Cross St. BD5	N14	67
New Delight Bldgs. HX3	E17	80
New England Rd. BD21	C 4	8
Woodhouse Rd.		
New Farmers Hill, Wood. LS26	HH15	77
New Fold BD6	K15	65
New Gain Wk. LS11	AA12	55
Gain Wk.		
New Grange Vw. HX2	D15	62
New Hay Rd. BD4	O13	67
New Holme Rd.	ZZ 8	24
New House La. BD13	H14	64
New Inn St. LS12	X11	54
Tong Rd.		
New John St. BD1	M11	48
New Kirkgate BD18	L 7	30
Westgate		
New La. BD19	O20	103
New La. BD4	P12	50
New La. HX3	E21	94
New La. LS10	AA16	90
New La. LS11	AA12	55
New La., Gild. LS27	U15	70
New La., Siddal HX3	F21	94
New La., Tong BD4	R14	69
New Laithe Rd. BD6	L14	66
New Line BD10	P 7	32
New Market St. LS1	BB11	56
New Occupation La. LS28	S12	51
Occupation La.		
New Otley Rd. BD3	O11	49
New Park Av., Rod. LS13	T 9	34
New Park Cft., Rod. LS13	T 9	34
New Park Clo., Rod. LS13	T 9	34
New Park Ct. LS18	T 9	34
New Park Gro. LS18	T 9	34
Springbank Clo.		
New Park Pl., Rod. LS13	T 9	34
New Park Rd. BD13	F14	63
New Park St., Mor. LS27	W17	88
New Park Vale Rd., Rod. LS13	T 9	34
New Park Vw., Rod. LS13	T 9	34
New Park Way, Rod. LS13	T 9	34
New Park Wk. LS18	T 9	34
New Pepper Rd. LS10	CC13	74
New Pl. HD6	L21	97
New Popplewell La. BD19	N19	103
New Princess St. LS11	AA12	55
New Pudsey St. LS28	S10	51
New Rd. BD19	N18	84
New Rd. E. BD19	N19	103
New Rd. HX1	F20	94
New Rd. LS19	Q 4	14
New Rd., Greet. HX4	E23	98
New Ring Rd., Sea. LS14	GG 8	40
New Road Side, Hor. LS18	U 7	34
New Row BD20	M18	83
New Row BD16	H 7	28
New Row BD8	K10	47
New St.	ZZ 8	24
Sun St.		
New St. BD10	O 7	31
New St. BD12	O16	84
New St. BD4	C10	44
New St. BD4	O15	67
New St. Clo., Pud. LS28	T12	52
New St. Gdns., Pud. LS28	T12	52
New St. Gro., Pud. LS28	T12	52
New St. HX3	L19	97
New St., Brig. HD6	M21	97
New St., Farsley LS28	S10	51
New St., Hor. LS18	U 7	34
New St., Pud. LS28	T12	52
New St., Southowram HD6	H21	95
New Station St. LS1	AA11	55
New Temple Gate LS15	GG11	58
New Toftshaw BD4	P15	68
New Town HX3	F18	80
New Victoria St. BD1	N12	49
New Wk. LS8	DD 6	21
New Woodhouse La. LS2	AA10	55
New Works St. BD12	M16	83
New Works St. BD12	M16	83
New York La. LS19	S 6	15
New York Rd. LS2	BB11	56
New York Rd. LS9	BB11	56
New York St. LS2	BB11	56
Newall St. BD5	M13	66
Newark Rd. BD16	G 4	10
Newark St. BD4	O12	49
Newburn Rd. BD7	L12	48
Newbury Rd. HD6	K23	100
Newby Sq. BD5	N13	67
Newclews St. BD7	K13	65
Newclose Rd. BD18	J 7	29
Newcombe St., Elland HX5	H24	99
Newcroft LS18	U 7	34
Kerry Hill		
Newforth Gro. BD5	M14	66
Newhall Bank LS10	BB16	91
Newhall Cft. LS10	CC15	74
Newhall Chase LS10	BB16	91
Newhall Clo. LS10	BB16	91
Newhall Cres. LS10	BB16	91
Newhall Dr. BD6	N15	67
Newhall Garth LS10	BB16	91
Newhall Gdns. LS10	BB16	91
Newhall Grn. LS10	BB16	91

Name	Grid	Page
Newhall Mt. BD6	N15	67
Newhall Mt. LS10	BB16	91
Newhall Rd. BD4	O14	67
Newhall Rd. LS10	BB16	91
Newhall Wk. LS10	CC16	91
Newhey Rd. HD6	K24	100
Newill Clo. BD5	O14	67
Newington St. BD8	M11	48
City Rd.		
Newlaithes Garth, Hor.	U 7	34
LS18		
Newlaithes Gdns., Hor.	U 7	34
LS18		
Newlaithes Rd., Hor.	U 7	34
LS18		
Newlaithes Rd., Hor.	U 8	34
LS18		
Newlands Av. BD3	P10	50
Newlands Av. HX3	A21	92
Newlands Av., Northowram	H17	81
HX3		
Newlands Cres. LS27	Y17	89
Newlands Dr. BD16	G 4	10
Newlands Dr. HX3	H17	81
Newlands Dr., Mor.	Y16	89
LS27		
Newlands Gro. HX3	H17	81
Newlands LS28	S10	51
Newlands Pl. BD3	O10	49
Undercliffe La.		
Newlands Rd. HX2	B19	92
Newlands Vw. HX3	H17	81
Newlay Clo. BD10	Q 7	32
Newlay Gro., Hor. LS18	U 8	34
Newlay La. LS13	V 9	35
Newlay La. Pl. LS13	V 9	35
Newlay La., Hor. LS18	U 7	34
Newlay Mt., Hor. LS18	U 8	34
Newlay Wood Av., Hor.	V 7	35
LS18		
Newlay Wood Clo., Hor.	V 7	35
LS18		
Newlay Wood Cres., Hor.	V 7	35
LS18		
Newlay Wood Dr., Hor.	V 7	35
LS18		
Newlay Wood Rd., Hor.	U 7	34
LS18		
Newlay Wood Ri. LS18	V 7	35
Newman St. BD4	O14	67
Newmarket App. LS9	DD12	57
Newmarket Grn. LS9	DD12	57
Newmarket La. LS9	DD12	57
Newport Cres. LS6	Y 9	36
Newport Gdns. LS6	Y 9	36
Newport Mt. LS6	Y 9	36
Newport Pl. BD8	M11	48
Newport Rd. BD8	M10	48
Newport Rd. LS6	Y 9	36
Newport St. BD2	O10	49
Newport Vw. LS6	Y 9	36
Newroyd Rd. BD5	N14	67
Newsam Ct. LS15	GG11	59
Newsam Green Rd.	HH14	77
LS15		
Newsholme New Rd.	YY 5	6
Newsome Ct. LS15	GG11	58
Newstead Av. HX1	D19	93
Newstead Gdns. HX1	D19	93
Newstead Gro. HX1	D19	93
Newstead Pl. HX1	D19	93
Newstead Ter. HX1	D19	93
Newstead Wk. BD5	M13	66
Newton Clo. LS7	BB 8	38
Newton Cres. LS7	BB 8	38
Newton Ct. LS8	EE 8	39
Newton Garth LS7	CC 8	38
Newton Gro. LS7	BB10	56
Chapeltown Rd.		
Newton Hill Rd. LS7	BB 8	38
Newton Lodge Dr. LS7	BB 8	38
Newton Pk. HD6	K20	96
Newton Pl. BD5	N13	67
Newton St.		
Newton Rd. LS7	CC 9	38
Newton Sq. LS12	V13	71
Newton St. BD5	N13	67
Newton St., S.B. HX6	B21	92
Newton Vills. LS7	BB 8	38
Newton Vw. LS7	BB 8	38
Newton Way BD17	M 5	12
West Gate		
Newton Wk. LS7	CC 9	38
Newtonpark Dr. LS7	CC 9	38
Newtonpark Vw. LS7	CC 9	38
Nice Av. LS8	CC 9	38
Harehills La.		
Nice St. LS8	CC 9	38
Nice Vw. LS8	CC 9	38
Harehills Rd.		
Nichol St. HX1	E20	94
Nicholas Clo. BD7	K11	47
Cemetery Rd.		
Nickleby Rd. LS9	DD11	57
Nidd St. BD3	O12	49
Leeds Rd.		
Nidderdale Wk. BD17	N 5	13
Nile Cres.	A 4	7
Nile St., Haworth	A 7	25
Albion St.		
Nile St., Keighley	A 4	7
Nina Rd. BD7	K13	65
Nineveh Gdns. LS11	AA12	55
Nineveh Par. LS11	AA12	55
Nineveh Rd. LS11	AA12	55
Nineveh Ter. LS11	AA12	55
Marshall St.		
Ninth Av. LS12	Y12	54
Nippet La. LS9	CC11	56
Nixon Av. LS9	DD11	57
Noble St. BD7	L12	48
Nook Gdns. LS15	JJ 7	41
Nook Rd., Scholes LS15	JJ 7	41
Nook St. LS10	BB13	74
Hillidge Rd.		
Nook, The LS17	BB 4	20
Nook, The, Gild. LS27	V15	71
Nora Pl. LS13	U 9	34
Nora Rd. LS13	U 9	34
Nora Ter. LS13	U 9	34
Norbreck Dr.	A 7	25
Norbury Rd. BD10	Q 8	32
Norcroft Brow BD7	M12	48
Norcroft St. BD7	M11	48
Norfolk Clo. LS7	BB 7	38
Norfolk Gdns. BD1	N11	49
Channing Way		
Norfolk Gdns. LS7	BB 7	38
Norfolk Grn. LS7	BB 7	38
Norfolk Mt. LS7	BB 7	38
Norfolk Pl. HX1	E20	94
Norfolk Pl. LS7	BB 7	38
Norfolk St. BD16	H 5	10
Clyde St.		
Norfolk St. LS10	BB12	56
Norfolk Ter. LS7	BB 7	38
Pasture La.		
Norfolk Vw. LS7	BB 7	38
Norham Gro. BD12	M18	83
Norland Rd. HX4	B21	92
Norland St. BD7	K13	65
Norland Vw., S.B. HX6	C21	93
Norman Av. BD2	O 8	31
Norman Av., Elland	H24	99
Norman Cres. BD2	O 8	31
Norman Gro. BD2	O 8	31
Norman Gro. LS5	X 9	36
Norman Gro., Elland	H24	99
Norman La. BD2	O 8	31
Norman Mt. BD2	O 8	31
Norman Mt. LS5	X 9	36
Norman Pl. LS8	DD 6	21
Norman Row LS5	X 9	36
Norman St. BD16	H 5	10
Norman St. BD18	M 7	30
Norman St. HX1	D20	93
Fenton Rd.		
Norman St. LS5	X 9	36
Norman St., Elland HX5	H24	99
Norman St., Haworth	ZZ 7	24
Norman Ter. BD2	O 8	31
Norman Ter. LS8	DD 6	21
Norman Ter., Elland	H24	99
Norman Towers LS16	X 7	36
Norman Vw. LS5	X 9	36
Normanton Gro. LS11	AA13	73
Normanton Pl. LS11	AA13	73
Normanton Ter. LS11	AA13	73
Cambrian Rd.		
Normanton Vw. LS11	AA13	73
Cambrian Rd.		
North Av. BD8	M 9	30
North Bank Rd. BD16	H 8	28
North Beck	A 4	7
North Bolton HX2	D15	62
North Bri. HX1	F19	94
North Broadgate La., Hor.	V 6	17
LS18		
North Brook St. BD1	N11	49
North Brook St. BD1	N11	49
North Cliffe Av. BD13	G12	46
North Cliffe Clo. BD13	G11	46
North Cliffe Dr. BD13	G11	46
North Cliffe Gro. BD13	G11	46
North Cliffe La. BD13	G11	46
North Cliffe Rd. BD18	L 8	30
Bradford Rd.		
North Clo. LS8	EE 8	39
North Cut HD6	K22	100
North Dr., Bram. LS16	W 2	2
North Farm Rd. LS8	DD 9	39
North Field Ter. BD13	H14	64
North Fold BD10	O 7	31
The Green		
North Gate BD1	N11	49
North Gate BD17	M 5	12
North Gate, Elland HX5	G23	99
North Grange Mt. LS6	Z 8	37
North Grange Rd. LS6	Z 9	37
North Grove Clo. LS8	EE 8	39
North Grove Dr. LS8	EE 8	39
North Grove Ri. LS8	EE 8	39
North Hall Av. BD10	O 6	13
North Hall St. LS3	Y10	54
Burley Rd.		
North Hall Ter. LS3	Z11	55
Newton St.		
North Hill Rd. LS6	Z 9	37
North Holme St. BD1	N11	49
North La. LS6	Y 9	36
North La. LS8	EE 7	39
North Lingwell Rd. LS10	BB16	91
North Mead, Bram. LS16	W 2	2
North Par. BD1	N11	49
North Par. BD15	H10	46
North Par. HX1	F19	94
North Par. LS16	X 7	36
North Park Av. LS8	CC 7	38
North Park Gro. LS8	DD 7	39
North Park Par. LS8	CC 6	20
North Park Rd. BD9	L 9	30
North Park Rd. LS8	DD 7	39
North Park Ter. BD9	M10	48
North Parkway LS14	FF 8	40
North Pl. LS7	BB10	56
North St.		
North Rd. BD6	L14	66
North Rd. LS15	HH10	59
North Rd., Troy LS18	U 5	16
North Selby HX2	C16	79
North St.	YY 7	24
North St. BD1	N11	49
North St. BD10	O 6	13
North St. BD12	M15	66
North St. LS19	R 5	15
North St. LS2	BB10	56
North St. LS2	BB10	56
North St., Farsley LS28	S 9	33
North St., Greet.	F23	98
Victoria St.		
North St., Oakenshaw	O17	84
BD12		
Green Side		
North St., Pud. LS28	T11	52
North Ter. LS15	HH10	59
North Ter. WF17	T18	87
North View Rd. BD3	N10	49
North View Rd. BD4	R15	69
North View St. LS28	T10	52
North View Ter. HX1	F20	94
North View Ter. LS28	T10	52
North View Ter., Haworth	ZZ 7	24
North Vw. BD12	F14	63
North Vw., Allerton BD15	H10	46
North Vw., Wilsden BD15	F 8	27
North Way LS28	EE 8	39
North West Gro. LS6	AA 9	37
North West Pl. LS6	AA 9	37
North West Rd. LS6	AA 9	37
North West St. LS6	AA 9	37
North West Ter. LS6	AA 9	37
North West Vw. LS6	AA 9	37
North Wing BD3	N11	49
Northallerton Rd. BD3	N10	49
Northampton St. BD3	N10	49
Northbrook Pl. LS7	BB 7	38
Northbrook St. LS7	BB 7	38
Northcote Cres. LS11	AA13	73
Northcote Dr. LS11	AA13	73
Northcote Grn. LS11	AA13	73
Northcote St. LS28	S10	51
Northcote Rd. BD2	O10	49
Northcroft Ri. BD8	K10	47
Northdale Av. BD5	M14	66
Northdale Mt. BD5	M14	66
Northdale Rd. BD9	L 9	30
Northedge La. HX3	J18	82
Northedge Pk. HX3	J18	82
Northern Rd. BD7	K14	65
Northern St. BD13	F14	63
Albert Rd.		
Northern St. LS1	AA11	55

Name	Grid	Page
Northfield Gdns. BD6	M14	66
Northfield Gro. BD6	M14	66
Northfield Pl. BD8	M10	48
Northfield Rd. BD6	L14	66
Northfields Cres. BD16	H 7	28
Northfold BD10	O 7	31
Bradford Rd.		
Northgate HX1	F19	94
Northlea Av. BD10	O 6	13
Northolme Av. LS16	X 7	36
Northolme Cres. LS16	X 7	36
Northope Clo. BD8	L10	48
Back Girlington Rd.		
Northowram Grn. HX3	H17	81
Northrops Yd., Pud. LS28	T11	52
Church La.		
Northside Av. BD7	L12	48
Northside Rd. BD7	K12	47
Northside Ter. BD7	K12	47
Northwood Clo., Wood.	HH15	77
LS26		
Northwood Cres. BD10	P 7	32
Northwood Falls, Wood.	HH15	77
LS26		
Northwood Mt. LS28	T12	52
Northwood Pk., Wood.	HH15	77
LS26		
Northwood Vw. LS28	T12	52
Norton Clo. HX2	B19	92
Norton Dr. HX2	B19	92
Norton Pl. HX2	D15	62
Norton Rd. LS8	DD 5	21
Norton St., Elland HX5	G24	99
Norwich Row LS10	BB14	74
Norwich Av.		
Norwich St. LS10	BB14	74
Norwich Av.		
Norwood Av. BD11	R17	86
Norwood Av. BD18	L 8	30
Norwood Cres. BD11	R17	86
Norwood Green Hill HX3	K18	82
Norwood Gro. BD11	R17	86
Norwood Gro. LS6	Z 9	37
Norwood Mt. LS6	Z 9	37
Norwood Pl. BD18	L 8	30
Norwood Pl. LS6	Z 9	37
Norwood Rd. BD18	L 8	30
Norwood St. BD18	L 8	30
Norwood St. BD5	M14	66
Norwood Ter. BD18	L 8	30
Norwood Ter. LS6	Z 9	37
Nostell Clo. BD8	M11	48
Noster Gro. LS11	Z13	73
Noster Pl. LS11	Z13	73
Noster Rd. LS11	Z13	73
Noster St. LS11	Z13	73
Noster Ter. LS11	Z13	73
Noster Vw. LS11	Z13	73
Noster Rd.		
Nottingham St. BD3	Q11	50
Nova Cotts. WF17	S18	86
Nova La.		
Nova La. WF17	S18	86
Nowell App. LS9	DD10	57
Nowell Av. LS9	DD10	57
Nowell Clo. LS9	DD10	57
Nowell Cres. LS9	DD10	57
Nowell End Row LS9	DD10	57
Nowell Gdns. LS9	DD10	57
Nowell Gro. LS9	DD10	57
Nowell La. LS9	DD10	57
Nowell Mt. LS9	DD10	57
Nowell Par. LS9	DD10	57
Nowell Pl. LS9	DD10	57
Nowell St. LS9	DD10	57
Nowell Ter. LS9	DD10	57
Nowell Vw. LS9	DD10	57
Nowell Wk. LS9	DD10	57
Nunburnholme Wk. BD10	P 8	32
Nunlea Royd HX3	L20	97
Nunnery La. HD6	J23	100
Nunnington Av. LS12	Y10	54
Armley Park Rd.		
Nunnington St. LS12	Y11	54
Nunnington Ter. LS12	Y10	54
Armley Park Rd.		
Nunroyd Av. LS17	BB 6	20
Nunroyd Gro. LS17	BB 6	20
Nunroyd Lawn LS17	BB 6	20
Nunroyd Rd. LS17	BB 6	20
Nunroyd St. LS17	BB 6	20
Nunroyd Ter. LS17	BB 6	20
Nunthorpe Rd., Pud. LS13	T 8	34
Nurser La. BD5	M13	66
Nurser Pl. BD5	M13	66
Nursery Av. HX3	D17	79
Nursery Clo. HX3	D17	79
Nursery Clo. LS17	BB 5	20
Nursery Gro. HX3	D17	79
Nursery Gro. LS17	AA 5	19
Nursery La. HX3	D17	79
Nursery La. LS17	AA 5	19
Nursery Mount Rd. LS10	CC14	74
Nursery Mt. LS10	CC14	74
Nursery Rd. BD14	H13	64
Nursery Rd. BD7	K14	65
Nussey Av. WF17	T18	87
Nuttall Rd. BD3	O11	49
Nutter La. BD19	S18	86
Nutter La. WF17	S18	86
Nutting Gro. LS12	X11	54
Cross La.		
O'Grady Sq. LS9	CC11	56
Dent St.		
Oak Av. BD16	H 6	10
Oak Av. BD8	M10	48
Oak Av., Mor. LS27	X17	89
Oak Av., S.B. HD6	B20	92
Oak Bank BD18	M 8	30
Oak Bank Ct.	A 5	7
Oak Bank La.	A 5	7
Oak Bank Mt.	A 5	7
Oak Bank Ri.	A 5	7
Oak Bank, Keighley	A 5	7
Oak Cres. LS15	FF11	58
Oak Dale BD16	H 4	10
Oak Gro. BD21	B 5	7
Oak Gro., Mor. LS27	Y17	89
Oak La. BD9	L10	48
Oak La. HX1	E19	94
Oak Mt. BD8	M10	48
Oak Pl. BD17	N 5	13
Oak Pl. HX1	E19	94
Oak Pl., S.B. HX6	B20	92
Oak Rd. HD2	O24	102
Oak Rd. LS12	Z11	55
Oak Rd. LS15	FF11	58
Oak Rd. LS7	BB 8	38
Oak Rd., Mor. LS27	W17	88
Oak St. BD14	H13	64
Oak St. BD16	G 4	10
Foster St.		
Oak St. LS28	S11	51
Oak St., Chur. LS27	X15	72
Oak St., Oxenhope	ZZ 9	24
Oak St., S.B. HX6	B20	92
Oak Ter. HX1	E19	94
Hanson La.		
Oak Tree Clo. LS9	EE 9	39
Oak Tree Cres. LS9	EE 9	39
Oak Tree Dr. LS8	EE 9	39
Oak Tree Gro. LS9	EE 9	39
Oak Tree Mt. LS9	EE 9	39
Oak Tree Pl. LS9	EE 9	39
Oak Tree Wk. LS9	EE 9	39
Oak Vills. BD8	M10	48
Oak Vills. LS17	CC 5	20
Oak Way BD11	R17	86
Oakbank Av.	A 4	7
Oakbank Dr.	A 4	7
Oakbank Gro.	A 4	7
Oakbank Av.		
Oakdale Av. BD18	N 8	31
Oakdale Av. BD6	L14	66
Oakdale Clo. BD10	Q 9	32
Oakdale Clo. HX3	E18	80
Oakdale Dr. BD10	Q 9	32
Oakdale Dr. BD18	N 8	31
Oakdale Garth LS14	GG 6	22
Oakdale Gro. BD18	N 8	31
Oakdale Meadow LS14	GG 6	22
Oakdale Rd. BD18	N 8	31
Oakdale Ter. BD6	L14	66
Oakdene Clo., Pud. LS28	T12	52
Oakdene Ct. LS17	DD 5	21
Oakdene Vale		
Oakdene Gdns. LS17	DD 4	21
Oakdene Vale LS17	DD 5	21
Oakdene Way LS17	DD 5	21
Oakenshaw La. BD12	N17	84
Oakenshaw La. BD19	N17	84
Oakfield Av. BD16	J 6	11
Oakfield Clo., Elland	G24	99
Oakfield Dr. BD17	M 6	12
Oakfield Gro. BD9	M10	48
Oakfield Rd. BD21	B 5	7
Oakfield St. LS7	AA 9	37
Cambridge Rd.		
Oakfield Ter. BD18	M 7	30
Oakfield Ter. LS6	Z 8	37
Oakham Wk. BD4	O13	67
New Hey Rd.		
Oakhampton Ct. LS8	EE 7	39
Oakhill Rd. HD6	L21	97
Oakhurst Av. LS11	AA14	73
Oakhurst Gro. LS11	Z14	73
Oakhurst Mt. LS11	Z14	73
Oakhurst Rd. LS11	Z14	73
Oakland Vw. LS27	Y15	72
Oaklands Av. HX3	H17	81
Oaklands Av., Rod. LS13	T 8	34
Oaklands BD10	O 7	31
Oaklands Clo. LS28	T 8	34
Oaklands Gro., Rod. LS13	T 8	34
Oaklands HD6	K22	100
Oaklands Rd., Rod. LS13	T 8	34
Oaklea Gdns. LS16	Y 6	18
Oaklea Hall Clo. LS16	Y 6	18
Oaklea Rd., Scholes LS15	JJ 8	41
Oakleigh Av. BD14	H13	64
Oakleigh Av. HX3	F21	94
Oakleigh Clo. BD14	H13	64
Oakleigh Rd.		
Oakleigh Gdns. BD14	H13	64
Oakleigh Gro. BD14	H13	64
Oakleigh Rd. BD14	H13	64
Oakleigh Ter. BD14	H13	64
Oakley Gro. LS11	BB13	74
Oakley St. BD13	F14	63
Albert Rd.		
Oakley Ter. LS11	BB13	74
Oakridge Ct. BD16	H 5	10
Oakroyd Av. BD6	L15	66
Oakroyd Dr. HD6	L20	97
Oakroyd Mt., Pud. LS28	T11	52
Oakroyd Rd. BD6	L14	66
Oakroyd Ter. BD17	N 6	13
Oakroyd Ter. BD8	M10	48
Oakroyd Ter. LS28	T11	52
North St.		
Oakroyd Ter., Mor. LS27	Y15	72
Elland Rd.		
Oakroyd Vill. BD8	M10	48
Oaks Dr. BD15	J11	47
Oaks Fold BD5	N13	67
Birch La.		
Oaks Green Mt. HD6	K24	100
Oaks La. BD8	J11	47
Oaks, The BD15	E 8	27
Oakwell Av. LS8	DD 8	39
Oakwell Clo. BD11	U16	87
Oakwell Cotts. WF17	S18	86
Bradford Rd.		
Oakwell Dr. LS8	DD 8	39
Oakwell Gdns. LS8	DD 8	39
Oakwell Gro. LS28	T10	52
Broad La.		
Oakwell Mt. LS8	DD 8	39
Oakwell Oval LS8	DD 8	39
Oakwell Rd. BD11	U16	87
Oakwood Av. BD11	R17	86
Oakwood Av. BD2	M 9	30
Livingstone Rd.		
Oakwood Av. LS8	DD 8	39
Oakwood Boundary Rd.	DD 8	39
LS8		
Oakwood Dr. BD16	H 4	10
Oakwood Dr. LS8	DD 8	39
Oakwood Gdns. LS8	EE 8	39
Oakwood Grange La. LS8	EE 8	39
Oakwood Grange LS8	EE 8	39
Oakwood Grn. LS8	EE 8	39
Oakwood Gro. BD8	L10	48
Oakwood Gro. LS8	DD 8	39
Oakwood La. LS8	DD 8	39
Oakwood Mt. LS8	DD 8	39
Oakwood Nook LS8	DD 8	39
Oakwood Pl. LS8	DD 8	39
Oakwood Rd. LS8	DD 8	39
Oakwood Ter., Pud. LS28	T12	52
Oakwood Vw. LS8	EE 8	39
Oakwood Wk. LS8	EE 8	39
Oakworth Rd. BD21	B13	61
Oakworth Ter.	ZZ 6	6
Oastler Ho. LS9	BB11	56
Oastler Pl. BD12	M16	83
Oastler Rd. BD18	K 7	29
Oatland Av. LS7	BB 7	38
Camp Rd.		
Oatland Clo. LS7	BB10	56
Oatland Grn. LS7	BB10	56
Oatland La. LS7	BB10	56
Oatland Pl. LS7	BB 9	38
Oatland Rd. LS7	BB10	56
Oatland St. LS7	BB10	56
Oatland Ter. LS7	BB 7	38
Camp Rd.		
Oatlands St. LS7	Z 8	37
Meanwood Rd.		
Oats St. BD22	B 5	7

155

Street	Grid	Page
Pasture St. LS7	BB 7	38
Pasture Av.		
Pasture Ter. LS7	BB 7	38
Pasture Av.		
Pasture Vw. LS12	X11	54
Pasture Wk. BD14	J13	65
Pastureside Ter. BD14	J13	65
Pastureside Ter. E. BD14	J13	65
Pasture La.		
Pastureside Ter. W. BD14	J13	65
Pasture La.		
Patent Rd. BD9	L10	48
Paternoster La. BD7	L13	66
Paved Track BD17	K 4	11
Pavement La. HX2	D15	62
Pavenham Wk. BD4	Q14	68
Paw La. BD13	G15	64
Pawson St. BD4	P12	50
Pawson St., Mor. LS27	W17	88
Peabody St. HX3	E18	80
Peace St. BD4	P12	50
Peach Wk. BD4	O13	67
Brompton Av.		
Pear St. BD21	B 5	7
Damems Rd.		
Pear St. HX1	D20	93
Pearl St. BD21	B 5	7
Ingrow La.		
Pearson Av. LS6	Z 9	37
Brudenell Rd.		
Pearson Fold BD12	N17	84
Pearson Gro. LS6	Z 9	37
Pearson La. BD9	J10	47
Pearson Rd. BD6	M15	66
Pearson Rd. W. BD6	M15	66
Scott St.		
Pearson Row BD12	M17	83
Pearson St. BD3	P12	50
Pearson St. LS10	BB12	56
Pearson St. LS28	R 7	33
Pearson Ter. LS6	Z 9	37
Peashill Clo. LS19	S 5	15
Peashill Pk. LS19	S 5	15
Peckover St. LS28	Q11	50
Peckover St. BD1	N11	49
Peel Bow BD7	L13	66
Peel Clo. BD4	Q12	50
Peel Ct. LS6	AA 9	37
Woodhouse St.		
Peel Park Dr. BD2	O10	49
Peel Park Ter. BD2	O10	49
Peel Park Vw. BD3	O10	49
Peel Sq. BD1	M11	48
Peel St. BD1	N12	49
Peel St. BD13	F12	45
Peel St. BD13	G14	64
Highgate Rd.		
Peel St. BD15	F 8	27
Peel St. BD16	H 5	10
Peel St. HX6	B21	92
Wallis St.		
Peel St. LS28	S12	51
Peel St., Mor. LS27	X17	89
Peel St., Shipley	M 8	30
Valley Rd.		
Pelham Rd. BD2	O 9	31
Pellon La. HX1	D19	93
Pellon New Rd. HX1	D19	93
Pellon Ter. BD10	O 6	13
Pellon Wk. BD10	O 6	13
Pemberton Dr. BD7	M12	48
Pembroke Dr., Pud. LS28	T11	52
Pembroke La.		
Pembroke Grange LS9	EE10	57
Pembroke Rd., Pud. LS28	T11	52
Pembroke St. BD5	N13	67
Pembroke Towers LS9	EE10	57
Pembury Mt. LS15	JJ 9	41
Chelsfield Way		
Pen-y-ffynnon Rd. LS6	Z 6	19
Parkside La.		
Pendas Dr. LS15	HH10	59
Pendas Gro. LS15	HH 9	41
Pendas Way LS15	HH10	59
Pendas Wk. LS15	HH10	59
Pendil Clo. LS15	HH11	59
Pendle Rd. BD16	H 5	10
Pendleton St. BD4	O12	49
Wakefield Rd.		
Pendragon BD2	O 9	31
Pendragon La. BD2	O 9	31
Penfield Gro. BD14	J13	65
Penfield Rd. BD11	T16	87
Pengarth BD16	J 4	11
Penlands Cres. LS15	HH11	59
Penlands Lawn LS15	HH11	59
Penlands Wk. LS15	HH11	59
Penn St. HX1	E19	94
Salt St.		
Pennine Clo. BD13	F15	63
Pennington Ct. LS6	AA 9	37
Woodhouse St.		
Pennington Pl. LS6	AA 9	37
Pennington St. LS6	AA 9	37
Pennington Ter. BD5	M13	66
Pennington Ter. LS6	AA 9	37
Pennithorne Av. BD17	M 5	12
Pennwell Dean LS14	HH 8	41
Pennwell Fold LS14	HH 8	41
Pennwell Garth LS14	HH 8	41
Pennwell Gate LS14	HH 8	41
Pennwell Grn. LS14	HH 8	41
Pennwell Lawn, LS14	HH 8	41
Penny St. BD3	O12	49
Joseph St.		
Pennygate BD16	J 4	11
Penraevon Av. LS7	BB 9	38
Penraevon Gro. LS7	BB 9	38
Penraevon Av.		
Penraevon Pl. LS7	Z 8	37
Meanwood Rd.		
Penraevon Ter. LS7	Z 8	37
Meanwood Rd.		
Penrith Gro. LS12	Y12	54
Penrose Pl. HX3	H18	81
Penrose Pl. HX3	H18	81
Upper La.		
Pentland Av. BD14	J13	65
Pentland Gro. BD14	J13	65
Pentland Way LS27	X17	89
Penwel Pl. HX3	G21	95
Jubilee Rd.		
Pepper La. LS10	CC13	74
Pepper La. LS13	V 9	35
Pepper Pl. LS10	CC13	74
Pepper Rd. LS10	CC14	74
Pepper Vw. LS10	CC13	74
Pepper La.		
Per La. HX2	C15	62
Percival St. BD3	O11	49
Percival St. LS2	AA11	55
Cookridge St.		
Percy St. BD13	F14	63
Old Guy Rd.		
Percy St. BD16	H 5	10
Percy St. BD21	B 5	7
Hainworth Wood Rd.		
Percy St. LS12	Y12	54
Perkin La. BD10	N 6	13
Perseverance La. BD7	L13	66
Perseverance Rd. BD13	E13	63
Perseverance Rd. HX2	E13	63
Perseverance St. BD11	R16	86
Allen Cft.		
Perseverance St. BD12	M17 '	83
Perseverance St. BD17	M 5	12
Hall Cliffe		
Perseverance St. LS10	DD14	75
Perseverance St. LS11	Z12	55
Sydenham St.		
Perseverance St. LS28	S11	51
Perseverance Ter. HX1	E20	94
Perseverance St. BD17	M 4	12
Hall Cliffe		
Perth Av. BD2	N 9	31
Perth Mt., Troy LS18	U 5	16
Peter La. HX2	B19	92
Peter La., Mor. LS27	Z16	90
Peterborough Pl. BD2	O 9	31
Peterborough Rd. BD2	O10	49
Peterborough Ter. BD2	O 9	31
Petergate BD1	N11	49
Petersfield Av. LS10	CC15	91
Petrie Cres. LS13	S 8	33
Petrie Gro. BD3	Q11	50
Petrie Rd. BD3	Q11	50
Petrie St. LS28	S 8	33
Petrie St., Rod. LS13	T 8	34
Peverell Clo. BD4	Q13 '	68
Peveril Mt. BD2	P 9	32
Phoebe La. HX3	F21	94
Phoenix St. HD6	L22	101
Piccadilly BD1	N11	49
Piccadilly BD18	L 7	30
Briggate		
Pickard Ct. LS15	HH11	59
Pickard St. LS12	G11	29
Campbell St.		
Pickard St. BD4	P12	50
Wellington St.		
Pickering Mt. LS12	Y11	54
Pickering St.		
Pickering Pl. LS12	Y11	54
Pickering St.		
Pickering St. LS12	Y11	54
Pickering Ter. LS12	Y11	54
Pickering St.		
Pickles La. BD7	K14	65
Pickles St. BD21	B 4	7
Victoria Rd.		
Pickpocket La., Wood. LS26	GG15	76
Picton Pl. LS12	Y11	54
Piece Hall Yd. BD1	N11	49
Kirkgate		
Piecewood Rd. LS16	V 5	17
Pierce Clo.	A 6	7
Pigeon Cote Clo. LS14	GG 8	40
Pigeon Cote Rd. LS14	FF 8	40
Piggott St. HD6	L21	97
Pigman La. HX6	B20	92
Pilot St. LS9	CC10	56
Pinder Av. LS12	W13	71
Pinder Gro. LS12	W13	71
Pinder St. LS12	W13	71
Pinder Vw. LS12	W13	71
Pine Dale BD16	H 4	10
Pine St. BD1	N11	49
Pine St. HX1	F20	94
Pinfold Ct. LS15	GG11	58
Pinfold Gro. LS15	GG11	58
Pinfold Hill LS15	GG11	58
Pinfold La. HD2	J24	100
Pinfold La. LS12	X11	54
Town St.		
Pinfold La. LS15	GG11	58
Pinfold La. LS16	W 4	17
Pinfold Mt. LS15	GG11	58
Pinfold Rd. LS15	GG11	58
Pink St.	ZZ 8	24
Pinnar La. HX3	G20	95
Pipe & Nook La. LS12	W11	53
Pirie Clo. BD2	N 9	31
Pit La. BD19	R18	86
Pit La. BD3	O11	49
Pit La. BD6	K15	65
Pit La., Denholme BD13	C10	44
Pit La., Queens. BD13	F13	63
Pitfall St. LS2	BB11	56
Call La.		
Pits la. BD19	N20	103
Pitts St. BD4	P13	68
Places Rd. LS9	CC11	56
Plaid Row LS9	CC11	56
Plains La., Elland HX5	G23	99
Plane Tree Av. LS17	CC 5	20
Plane Tree Cft. LS17	CC 5	20
Plane Tree Clo. LS17	CC 5	20
Plane Tree Av.		
Plane Tree Gdns. LS17	CC 5	20
Plane Tree Gro. LS19	S 4	15
Plane Tree Nest HX2	D20	93
Plane Tree Nest La. HX2	D20	93
Plane Tree Rd., S.B. HX6	B20	92
Plane Tree Ri. LS17	CC 5	20
Plane Tree Vw. LS17	CC 5	20
Plane Tree Av.		
Plane Trees Clo. BD19	P17	85
Plane Trees St. BD15	H10	46
Planetrees Rd. BD4	P12	50
Plantation Av. LS15	FF11	58
Plantation Av. LS17	DD 4	21
Plantation Gdns. LS17	DD 4	21
Plantation Pl. BD4	P13	68
Plantation Way BD17	M 5	12
Playfair Av. LS10	BB14	74
Royal Rd.		
Playfair Cres. LS10	BB14	74
Royal Rd.		
Playfair Rd. LS10	BB14	74
Playfair Vw. LS10	BB13	74
Playground LS12	V13	71
Pleasant Av. LS11	Z12	55
Pleasant St.		
Pleasant Ct. LS6	AA 9	37
Woodhouse St.		
Pleasant Grn. LS6	AA 9	37
Rampart Rd.		
Pleasant Gro. LS11	Z12	55
Pleasant St.		
Pleasant Mt. LS11	Z12	55
Domestic St.		
Pleasant Pl. BD15	H10	46
Pleasant Pl. LS11	AA12	55
Pleasant Rd. LS11	Z12	55
Pleasant St.		
Pleasant Row BD13	F15	63
Pleasant St. BD7	L13	66
Pleasant St. LS11	Z12	55
Pleasant St., S.B. HX6	C21	93

Pleasant Ter. LS11	Z12	55
Domestic St.		
Pleasant Vw. HX2	D14	62
Syke La.		
Pleasant Vw. LS11	AA12	55
Plevna St. LS10	DD14	75
Plevna Ter. BD16	G 5	10
Plevna Ter. LS10	CC13	74
Grove Rd.		
Plimsoll St. BD4	O13	67
Plough Croft La. HX3	E18	80
Plover St. BD5	M13	66
Plum St. BD21	B 5	7
Damems Rd.		
Plum St. HX1	D20	93
Plum St. LS2	BB11	56
Gower St.		
Plumpton Av. BD2	N 8	31
Plumpton Clo. BD2	O 8	31
Plumpton Dr. BD2	N 8	31
Plumpton End BD2	O 8	31
Plumpton Gdns. BD2	N 8	31
Plumpton Lea BD2	N 8	31
Plumpton Mead BD2	N 8	31
Plumpton St. BD8	L11	48
Plumpton Wk. BD2	N 8	31
Plymouth Gro. HX1	E19	94
Pellon La.		
Poets Pl., Hor. LS18	V 6	17
Pohlman St. HX1	D20	93
Fenton Rd.		
Pollard Av. BD16	H 4	10
Pollard Av. BD19	R18	86
Pollard La. BD2	O10	49
Pollard La. LS13	V 8	35
Pollard La., Swi. LS13	T 9	34
Leeds & Bradford Rd.		
Pollard Pl. LS12	Z12	55
Lord St.		
Pollard St. BD4	N12	49
Pollard St. N. HX3	F19	94
Spring Ter.		
Pollard Way BD19	R18	86
Pond Ter. HD6	K20	96
Pontefract Av. LS9	CC11	56
Pontefract Gro. LS9	CC11	56
Pontefract St.		
Pontefract La. LS26	JJ14	77
Pontefract La., Swil. LS9	CC11	56
Pontefract Lane Clo. LS9	CC11	56
Pontefract Rd., Roth. & Wood. LS10	DD14	75
Pontefract St. LS9	CC11	56
Pool Bank Rd. LS16	U 1	1
Poole Cres. LS15	GG10	58
Poole Mt. LS15	GG10	58
Poole Rd. LS15	GG10	58
Poole Sq. LS15	GG10	58
Poplar Av. BD18	M 8	30
Poplar Av. BD7	K14	65
Poplar Av. LS15	HH10	59
Poplar Av., S.B. HX6	C20	93
Poplar Cft. LS13	W11	53
Poplar Cres. BD18	M 8	30
Poplar Cres. HX2	D15	62
Poplar Ct. LS13	W11	53
Poplar Dr. BD18	M 8	30
Poplar Dr., Hor. LS18	T 6	16
Poplar Garth LS13	W11	53
Poplar Gdns. LS13	W11	53
Poplar Grn. LS13	W11	53
Poplar Gdns.		
Poplar Gro. BD16	E 6	9
Poplar Gro. BD18	M 8	30
Poplar Gro. BD7	K14	65
Poplar Gro. LS4	Z10	55
Poplar St.		
Poplar Mt. LS13	W11	53
Poplar Pl. LS28	R11	51
Gibraltar Rd.		
Poplar Rd. BD18	M 8	30
Poplar Rd. BD7	L14	66
Poplar Rise LS13	W10	53
Poplar St. HX3	F19	94
Haley Hill		
Poplar Vw. BD7	K14	65
Poplar Vw. HX3	L20	97
Poplar Vw. LS13	W10	53
Poplar Way LS13	W11	53
Poplars Park Rd. BD2	N 9	31
Poplars, The LS6	Z 8	37
Poplars, The, Bram. LS16	W 2	2
Popples Dr. HX2	D15	62
Popular Sq. LS28	S10	51
Old Rd.		
Portage Av. LS15	FF11	58
Portage Cres. LS15	FF11	58
Porthill Ct. LS12	V11	53
Portland Cres. LS1	AA11	55
Portland Ct. BD21	B 4	7
Portland Gate LS1	AA11	55
Portland Pl. BD16	H 6	10
York St.		
Portland Pl. HX1	F20	94
Portland Rd. HX3	F19	94
Portland Rd. LS12	Y12	54
Portland St. BD16	H 5	10
Ferrand St.		
Portland St. BD5	N12	49
Portland St. HX1	F19	94
Northgate		
Portland St. LS1	AA11	55
Portland St., Haworth	ZZ 7	24
Portland Way LS1	AA10	55
Portman St. LS28	R 8	33
Portsmouth Av. BD3	N10	49
Portwood St. BD9	J10	47
Post Office Rd. BD2	P 8	32
Pothouse Rd. BD6	L15	66
Potter St. BD3	O12	49
Mulgrave St.		
Potternewton Av. LS7	AA 8	37
Potternewton Cres. LS7	AA 8	37
Potternewton Ct. LS7	AA 8	37
Potternewton Gro. LS7	AA 8	37
Potternewton Heights LS7	BB 8	38
Potternewton La. LS7	AA 8	37
Potternewton Mt. LS7	AA 8	37
Potternewton Vw. LS7	AA 8	37
Pottery La., Wood. LS26	HH15	77
Pottery Rd. LS10	BB13	74
Poulton Pl. LS11	BB13	74
Powell Av. BD5	M13	66
Powell Rd. BD16	H 5	10
Powell St. HX1	F19	94
Pratt La. BD18	M 8	30
Pratt St. HX1	F19	94
Prescott St. HX1	F20	94
Prestcott Ter. BD15	H10	46
Preston La. HX2	C18	79
Preston Par. LS11	AA14	73
Preston Pl. HX1	E19	94
Francis St.		
Preston St. BD7	M11	48
Preston Ter. BD16	G 4	10
Slenningford Rd.		
Priesthorpe Av. LS28	R10	51
Priesthorpe Ct. LS28	S 9	33
Priesthorpe La. LS28	R 9	33
Priesthorpe Rd. LS28	R 9	33
Priestley Av. BD6	L15	66
Priestley Clo. LS28	T11	52
Priestley Dr. LS28	T10	52
Priestley Gdns. HX3	K18	82
Priestley Gdns., Pud. LS28	T11	52
Priestley Rd. BD13	F12	45
Priestley Sq. WF17	T18	87
Priestley St. BD1	N11	49
Priestley St. BD13	F12	45
Thornton Rd.		
Priestley Vw. LS28	T11	52
Priestley Wk. LS28	T10	52
Priestman St. BD8	M10	48
Primley Gdns. LS17	BB 5	20
Primley Park Av. LS17	BB 5	20
Primley Park Clo. LS17	BB 5	20
Primley Park Cres. E. LS17	BB 5	20
Primley Park Cres. LS17	BB 5	20
Primley Park Cres. W. LS17	BB 5	20
Primley Park Ct. LS17	BB 5	20
Primley Park Dr. LS17	BB 5	20
Primley Park Garth LS17	BB 5	20
Primley Park Grn. LS17	BB 5	20
Primley Park Gro. LS17	BB 5	20
Primley Park La. LS17	BB 5	20
Primley Park Mt. LS17	BB 5	20
Primley Park Rd. LS17	BB 5	20
Primley Park Ri. LS17	BB 5	20
Primley Park Vw. LS17	BB 5	20
Primley Park Way LS17	BB 4	20
Primley Park Wk. LS17	BB 4	20
Primrose Av. LS15	GG11	58
Primrose Bank BD16	H 6	10
Primrose Clo. LS15	GG11	58
Primrose Cres. LS15	GG10	58
Primrose Dr. BD16	J 6	11
Primrose Dr. LS15	GG11	58
Primrose Garth LS15	FF11	58
Primrose Gdns. LS15	GG10	58
Primrose Gro. LS15	GG10	58
Primrose Hill BD16	J 6	11
Primrose La.		
Primrose Hill LS12	X12	54
Primrose Hill LS15	GG11	58
Primrose Hill LS28	S11	51
Primrose Hill, Stan. LS28	T10	52
Richardshaw La.		
Primrose La. BD16	H 6	10
Primrose La. BD2	M 9	30
Livingstone Rd.		
Primrose La. LS11	BB13	74
Primrose La. LS15	FF11	58
Primrose Rd. LS15	GG11	58
Primrose Row BD17	N 5	13
Primrose St. BD8	M11	48
South Wood St.		
Primrose St. HX3	G19	95
Horley Green Rd.		
Primrose Wk., Chur. LS27	Y15	72
Prince Albert Sq. BD13	H14	64
Highgate Rd.		
Prince Edward Gro. LS12	X13	72
Prince Edward Rd. LS12	X13	72
Prince Royd Way BD7	L12	48
Prince St. BD18	M 7	30
Leeds Rd.		
Prince St. BD4	P14	68
Prince St., Haworth	ZZ 8	24
Princes Av. LS8	DD 7	39
Princes Gate HX3	E21	94
Princes St. BD6	K15	65
Princes Vw. BD5	N12	49
Princes Way BD5	N12	49
Princess Ct. LS17	BB 5	20
Princess Field Pl. LS11	AA12	55
Princess St. BD16	H 5	10
Clyde St.		
Princess St. BD21	B 4	7
Starkie St.		
Princess St. HX1	F19	94
Princess St. HX4	L22	101
Princess St. LS19	R 5	15
Princess St., Greet.	F23	98
Victoria St.		
Princeville Rd. BD7	L11	48
Princeville St. BD7	L11	48
Prior Pl. HD3	N24	102
Priory Clo. BD16	H 5	10
Priory Ct. BD8	M11	48
Gracechurch		
Priory Gro. BD16	H 5	10
Privilege St. LS12	X11	54
Proctor Sq. BD4	P14	68
Tong St.		
Proctor St. BD4	P14	68
Proctor Ter. BD4	P14	68
Tong St.		
Prod La. BD17	K 6	11
Progress Av. BD16	E 6	9
Prospect Av. BD18	M 7	30
Prospect Av. HX2	D21	93
Prospect Av. LS13	V 9	35
Prospect Vw.		
Prospect Av. LS28	S11	51
Prospect Av. LS9	BB13	74
Prospect St.		
Prospect Clo. BD18	M 7	30
Prospect Clo. HX2	D21	93
Prospect Cres.	A 4	7
Prospect Ct. HX2	B19	92
Prospect Dr. LS28	S11	51
Prospect Dr., Keighley	A 4	7
Prospect Gro. BD18	M 7	30
Prospect La. BD11	R16	86
Prospect Mt. BD18	M 7	30
Prospect Mt., Keighley	A 4	7
Prospect Pl. BD13	G14	64
Chapel La.		
Prospect Pl. BD2	P10	50
Prospect Pl. BD9	K10	47
Prospect Pl. HD3	L22	101
Prospect Pl. HX2	D17	79
Prospect Pl. LS13	V 9	35
Prospect Vw.		
Prospect Pl., Hor. LS18	U 7	34
Prospect Pl., Mor. LS27	Y15	72
Little La.		
Prospect Rd. BD16	J 4	11
Prospect Rd. BD10	N10	49
Prospect Row HX2	C15	62
Prospect St. BD10	P 8	32
Prospect St. BD13	G12	46
Prospect St. BD18	M 7	30
Prospect St. BD4	N12	49
Prospect St. BD6	K15	65
Prospect St. LS10	DD14	75
Prospect St. LS13	V 9	35

Name	Ref	Page
Prospect St. LS19	S 5	15
Prospect St., Beck Hill BD6	M14	66
Prospect St., Chapeltown LS28	S11	51
Prospect St., Farsley LS28	S 9	33
Prospect St., Haworth	ZZ 8	24
Prospect St., Keighley	A 4	7
Prospect Ter. BD15	J10	47
Prospect Ter. HX2	E14	63
Prospect Ter. LS10	BB13	74
Prospect Ter. LS13	V 9	35
Prospect Vw.		
Prospect Ter. LS28	S10	51
Prospect Terrace Dr. BD4	T15	70
Prospect Vw. LS13	V 9	35
Prospect Wk. BD18	M 7	30
Prosper Ter. LS10	BB13	74
Joseph St.		
Providence Av. BD17	M 5	12
Providence Av. LS6	AA 9	37
Providence Cres.	ZZ 6	6
Providence Ct.	ZZ 6	6
Providence La.	ZZ 6	6
Providence Mt., Mor. LS27	X16	89
Providence Rd. LS6	AA 9	37
Providence Row BD17	M 5	12
Providence Row BD2	O 9	31
Providence Row HX1	D17	79
Club La.		
Providence Row HX2	C15	62
Providence St. BD1	M11	48
Providence St. BD19	N18	84
Providence St. LS28	S10	51
Providence St. LS9	BB11	56
Providence St., Elland	G23	99
Providence Ter. BD13	F12	45
Thornton Rd.		
Providence Ter. LS2	AA 9	37
Raglan Rd.		
Provost St. LS11	AA12	55
Prune Park La. BD15	G 9	28
Pudsey Rd. LS28	U11	52
Pudsey Rd., Pud. LS12	W11	53
Pule Green La. HX3	E17	80
Pullan Av. BD2	O 9	31
Pullan Dr. BD2	P 9	32
Pullan Gro. BD2	P 9	32
Pullan La. BD17	P 4	14
Pullan St. BD5	M12	48
Pump La. HX3	H19	95
Purcey Wk. BD6	L15	66
Bourbon Clo.		
Purley Wk. BD6	L15	66
Bourbon Clo.		
Pye Nest Av. HX2	D20	93
Pye Nest Dr. HX2	D21	93
Pye Nest Gdns. HX2	D20	93
Pye Nest Grn. HX2	D20	93
Pye Nest Rd. HX2	D21	93
Pye Nest Ri. HX2	D21	93
Pyrah Rd. BD12	M16	83
Pyrah St. BD12	M17	83
Pyrah St. HX3	J19	96
Whitehall St.		
Quaker La. BD5	L13	66
Quakers La. LS19	R 4	15
Quarry Bank Ct. LS5	W 8	35
Quarry Gap Row BD4	Q12	50
Quarry Gdns. LS17	AA 4	19
Quarry Hill HX6	B21	92
Quarry La. WF17	T18	87
Brookroyd La.		
Quarry Mount Pl. LS6	AA 9	37
Lucas St.		
Quarry Mount St. LS6	AA 9	37
Delph La.		
Quarry Mount Ter. LS7	AA 9	37
Lucas St.		
Quarry Mt. LS6	AA 9	37
Delph La.		
Quarry Pl. BD2	O10	49
Quarry Pl. LS6	AA 9	37
Quarry Rd. HX3	L23	101
Quarry St. BD9	L 9	30
Quarry St. LS6	AA 9	37
Quarry Ter., Hor. LS18	U 6	16
Quarry View Ter. LS13	V10	53
Hough End La.		
Quarry, The LS17	AA 4	19
Quebec St. BD1	N12	49
Quebec St. LS1	AA11	55
Quebec St., Elland HX5	H23	99
Queen Sq. LS2	Z 9	37
Woodhouse La.		
Queen Sq. LS2	BB10	56
Queen St. BD10	P 7	32
Queen St. BD13	C 8	26
Queen St. BD15	F 9	27
Queen St. BD16	G 5	10
Queen St. BD17	M 6	12
Queen St. BD19	R18	86
Queen St. BD6	K15	65
Queen St. HD6	L21	97
Clifton Rd.		
Queen St. HX6	A21	92
Queen St. LS1	AA11	55
Queen St. LS10	DD14	75
Queen St. LS19	R 5	15
Queen St. LS28	S 9	33
Town St.		
Queen St., Greet. HX4	F24	98
Queen St., Mor. LS27	X17	89
Queen Victoria Cres. HX3	H17	81
Queen Victoria St. LS1	BB11	56
Queens Arc. LS1	BB11	56
Briggate		
Queens Av. BD2	N10	49
Queens Clo. BD16	H 6	10
Queens Clo. LS7	BB 7	38
Queens Ct. BD18	K 7	29
Queens Ct. LS1	BB11	56
Briggate		
Queens Ct. LS14	GG 8	40
Seacroft Cres.		
Queens Gate HX3	E21	94
Queens Gro. BD21	B 4	7
Queens Gro., Mor. LS27	W17	88
Queens Par. LS14	GG 8	40
Seacroft Cres.		
Queens Pl. BD18	K 7	29
Queens Pl. LS27	X17	89
Queens Prom., Mor. LS27	X16	89
Queens Rd. BD16	G 4	10
Queens Rd. BD18	K 7	29
Queens Rd. BD21	B 5	7
Queens Rd. BD8	M10	48
Queens Rd. HX1	D19	93
Queens Rd. HX3	K18	82
Queens Rd. LS6	Z10	55
Queens Rd., Mor. LS27	W17	88
Queens Vw. HX3	H21	95
Queens Vw. LS14	GG 8	40
Queens Way BD16	H 6	10
Queensbury Rd. HX3	E17	80
Queensbury Sq. BD13	G14	64
Albert Rd.		
Queensgate BD1	N11	49
Queenshill App. LS17	BB 6	20
Queenshill Av. LS17	BB 6	20
Queenshill Clo. LS17	BB 6	20
Queenshill Av.		
Queenshill Cres. LS17	BB 5	20
Queenshill Ct. LS17	BB 6	20
Queenshill Way		
Queenshill Dr. LS17	AA 6	19
Queenshill Garth LS17	BB 6	20
Queenshill Gdns. LS17	AA 6	19
Queenshill Rd. LS17	BB 6	20
Queenshill Vw. LS17	BB 6	20
Queenshill Way LS17	BB 6	20
Queenshill Wk. LS17	BB 6	20
Queensthorpe Av. LS13	V11	53
Queensthorpe Clo. LS13	W11	53
Queensthorpe Ri. LS13	V11	53
Queensway HX1	D19	93
Queensway LS15	GG11	58
Queensway, Mor. LS27	X17	89
Queenswood Clo. LS6	X 8	36
Queenswood Dr. LS6	X 7	36
Queenswood Gdns. LS6	Y 9	36
Queenswood Grn. LS6	X 7	36
Queenswood Mt. LS6	X 8	36
Queenswood Rd. LS6	X 8	36
Queenswood Ri. LS6	X 9	36
Raby Av. LS7	BB 9	38
Buslingthorpe La.		
Raby Mt. LS7	BB 9	38
Raby Av.		
Raby St. LS7	BB 9	38
Raby Ter. LS7	BB 9	38
Raby Av.		
Race Moor La.	YY 5	6
Radcliffe Av. BD2	O 8	31
Radcliffe Gdns., Pud. LS28	T12	52
Radcliffe La., Pud. LS28	T11	52
Radcliffe Ter., Pud. LS28	T12	52
Radfield Dr. BD6	N14	67
Radfield Rd. BD6	N14	67
Radnor St. BD3	P11	50
Radwell Dr. BD5	N12	49
Raeburn Dr. BD6	L15	66
Raglan Av.	A 4	7
Raglan Clo. HX1	E19	94
Crossley Gdns.		
Raglan Ct. HX1	E19	94
Crossley Gdns.		
Raglan Dr. BD3	P11	50
Raglan Pl. LS6	AA 9	37
Woodhouse St.		
Raglan Rd. LS6	AA 9	37
Holborn App.		
Raglan St. BD13	G14	64
Sandbeds		
Raglan St. BD16	H 6	10
Church St.		
Raglan St. BD3	Q11	50
Raglan St. HX1	E19	94
Raglan St., Keighley	A 4	7
Raglan St., Queens. HX1	Q16	64
Raglan Ter. BD3	P11	50
Raglan Ter. LS2	AA 9	37
Raglan Rd.		
Raikes La. BD4	Q15	68
Raikes La. BD4	R14	69
Raikes La. WF17	T18	87
Raikes Wood Dr. BD4	Q15	68
Railsford Mt. LS13	V10	53
Railsford Ri. LS13	V10	53
Railsford Way LS13	V10	53
Railsthorpe Way BD10	Q 8	32
Reighton Cft.		
Railway Rd. BD10	O 7	31
Railway Rd. LS15	HH10	59
Railway St. BD13	F14	63
Albert Rd.		
Railway St. LS9	CC11	56
Railway St., Dudley Hill BD4	P14	68
Railway St., Tyersal BD4	Q12	50
Railway Ter. BD12	N16	84
Railway Ter. BD4	Q14	68
Railway Ter. HX3	E22	98
Raincliffe Gro. LS9	DD11	57
Raincliffe Rd. LS9	DD11	57
Raincliffe St. LS9	DD11	57
Raincliffe Ter. LS9	DD11	57
Raincliffe Rd.		
Rainville Av. LS13	W 9	35
Rainville Clo. LS13	W 9	35
Rainville Av.		
Rainville Gro. LS13	W 9	35
Rainville Mt. LS13	W 9	35
Rainville Ter. LS13	W 9	35
Raistrick Way BD18	M 7	30
Rakehill Rd., Scholes LS15	JJ 7	41
Raleigh St. HX1	D20	93
Fenton Rd.		
Rampart Rd. LS6	AA 9	37
Ramsden Av. BD7	K12	47
Ramsden Ct. BD7	L13	66
Great Horton Rd.		
Ramsden Pl. BD14	H12	46
Ramsden St. HX3	D18	79
Ramsden Ter. LS7	BB10	56
Ramsey St. BD5	M13	66
Ramsey St. LS12	Y11	54
Parliament Rd.		
Ramsgate St. HX1	D19	93
Ramshead App. LS14	GG 8	40
Ramshead Clo. LS14	FF 7	40
Ramshead Cres. LS14	FF 7	40
Ramshead Dr. LS14	FF 7	40
Ramshead Gdns. LS14	FF 7	40
Ramshead Gro. LS14	GG 8	40
Ramshead Hill LS14	FF 8	40
Ramshead Pl. LS14	GG 8	40
Ramshead Vw. LS14	GG 8	40
Rand Pl. BD7	M12	48
Rand St. BD7	M12	48
Randall Pl. BD9	L 9	30
Randall Well St. BD7	M12	48
Randolph St. HX3	F19	94
Randolph St. LS13	U10	52
Random Clo. BD22	A 4	7
Ranelagh Av. BD10	Q 8	32
Range Bank HX3	F18	80
Range Gdns. HX3	F18	80
Range La. HX3	F19	94
Range St. HX3	F18	80
Ransdale Dr. BD5	M13	66
Ransdale Gro. BD5	M13	66
Ransdale Rd. BD5	M13	66
Raskelf Down BD10	Q 8	32
Roans Brae		
Rastrick Common HD6	L23	101
Rathmell Rd. LS15	FF11	58

Name	Grid	Page
Rosemont St. LS13	V10	53
Rosemont St. LS13	U10	52
Station Mt.		
Rosemont Vw. LS13	V10	53
Rosemont Av.		
Rosemont Wk. LS13	V10	53
Rosemount Av., Elland	H24	99
HX5		
Rosemount Av., Pud. LS28	T11	52
Rosemount Dr., Pud. LS28	T11	52
Rosemount Ter., Pud. LS28	T11	52
Roseneath Pl. LS12	Y12	54
Roseneath St. LS12	Y12	54
Roseneath Ter. LS12	Y12	54
Rosetta Dr. BD8	K11	47
Roseville Av. LS8	CC10	56
Roseville Rd.		
Roseville Rd. LS8	CC10	56
Roseville St. LS8	CC10	56
Roseville Ter. LS15	HH 9	41
Roseville Ter. LS8	CC10	56
Roseville Way LS8	CC10	56
Rosewood Ct. LS26	FF15	76
Rosewood Gro. BD4	P12	50
Rosgill Dr. LS14	FF 8	40
Rosgill Wk. LS14	FF 8	40
Rosley Mt. BD6	K16	82
Roslyn Pl. BD7	L12	48
Ross Gro. LS13	U 9	34
Rossall Rd. LS8	CC 9	38
Rosse St. BD18	L 7	30
Rosse St. BD8	L11	48
Rossefield App. LS13	V10	53
Rossefield Av. LS13	V10	53
Rossefield Chase LS13	V10	53
Rossefield Clo. LS13	V10	53
Rossefield Dr. LS13	V10	53
Rossefield Grn. LS13	V10	53
Rossefield Gro. LS13	V10	53
Rossefield Lawn LS13	V10	53
Rossefield Pl. LS13	V10	53
Rossefield Rd. BD9	L 9	30
Rossefield Ter. LS13	V10	53
Rossefield Way LS13	V10	53
Rossefield Wk. LS13	V10	53
Rossfield Garth LS13	V10	53
Rossington Gro. LS8	CC 9	38
Rossington Pl. LS8	CC 9	38
Gathorne Ter.		
Rossington Rd. LS8	DD 8	39
Rossington St. LS2	AA10	55
Rosslyn Gro.	ZZ 8	24
Rosslyn St. BD18	L 8	30
Valley Rd.		
Rossmore Dr. BD15	J10	47
Rosy St.	A 7	25
Rothbury Gdns. LS16	X 5	18
Rothesay Ter. BD7	M12	48
Rothsay Mt. LS11	Z13	73
Little Town La.		
Rothsay Pl. LS11	Z13	73
Elland Rd.		
Rothsay St. LS11	Z13	73
Elland Rd.		
Rothsay Ter. LS11	Z13	73
Little Town La.		
Rothsay Vw. LS11	Z13	73
Little Town La.		
Rothwell Dr. HX1	E20	94
Rothwell Mt. HX1	E20	94
Rothwell Rd. HX1	E20	94
Rough Hall La. HX2	A16	78
Round Hill Clo. HX2	D16	79
Round Hill HX2	E16	80
Round St. BD5	N13	67
Roundell Av. BD4	O15	67
Roundhay Av. LS8	CC 8	38
Roundhay Cres. LS8	CC 8	38
Roundhay Gdns. LS8	CC 8	38
Roundhay Gro. LS8	CC 8	38
Roundhay Mt. LS8	CC 8	38
Roundhay Pk. La. LS17	DD 5	21
Roundhay Pl. LS8	CC 8	38
Roundhay Rd. LS7	BB10	56
Roundhay Rd. LS8	DD 8	39
Roundhay Ter. LS7	BB10	56
Roundhay Rd.		
Roundhay Vw. LS8	CC 8	38
Roundhay, The, Mor. LS27	W17	88
Roundhill Av. BD16	H 7	28
Roundhill Clo. BD13	H14	64
Roundhill Pl. BD1	M11	48
Roundhill Pl. BD13	H14	64
Roundhill St. BD5	M13	66
Roundthorn Pl. BD8	L11	48
Thornton Rd.		
Roundwood Av. BD10	Q 8	32
Roundwood Av. BD17	N 5	13
Roundwood BD18	K 7	29
Roundwood Glen BD10	Q 8	32
Roundwood Rd. BD17	N 5	13
Roundwood Vw. BD10	Q 8	32
Roundwood Glen		
Rouse Fold BD4	N12	49
Routh Copse BD10	Q 8	32
Reighton Cft.		
Rowan Av. BD3	Q11	50
Rowan Clo. WF17	U18	87
Rowan Tree Av. BD17	L 5	12
Rowanberry Clo. BD2	O 9	31
Stone Hall Rd.		
Rowans, The BD17	K 5	11
Rowans, The, Bram. LS16	W 2	2
Rowantree Av. BD17	L 5	12
Rowantree Dr. BD10	O 8	31
Rowland Pl. LS11	AA13	73
Rowland Rd. LS11	AA13	73
Rowland Ter. LS11	Z15	73
Dewsbury Rd.		
Rowlestone Ri. BD10	Q 8	32
Rowley Lea BD10	Q 8	32
Rowton Thorpe BD10	Q 8	32
Roxburgh Gro. BD15	H11	46
Roxby Clo. LS9	CC10	56
Roxby St. BD5	M13	66
Roxby Thorne BD10	Q 8	32
Roundwood Glen		
Roxholme Av. LS7	CC 8	38
Roxholme Gro. LS7	CC 8	38
Roxholme Pl. LS7	CC 8	38
Roxholme Rd. LS7	CC 8	38
Roxholme Ter. LS7	CC 8	38
Roy Rd. BD6	J14	65
Royal Clo. LS10	BB14	74
Royal Ct. LS10	BB14	74
Royal Dr. LS10	BB14	74
Royal Gdns. LS10	BB14	74
Royal Gro. LS10	BB14	74
Royal Park Av. LS6	Z10	55
Royal Park Gro. LS6	Z10	55
Royal Park Rd. LS6	Z10	55
Royal Park Ter. LS6	Z10	55
Royal Park Vw. LS6	Z10	55
Royal Park Gro.		
Royal Pl. LS10	BB14	74
Royal St. LS10	BB14	74
Norwich Pl.		
Royal Ter. LS10	BB14	74
Royal Rd.		
Royd Av. BD16	J 5	11
Royd Cres. HX1	D19	93
Royd Gro. BD18	M 7	30
Royd House Dr. BD21	D 4	8
Royd House Gro. BD21	D 4	8
Royd House Rd.		
Royd House Rd. BD21	D 4	8
Royd House Way BD21	D 4	8
Royd House Wk. BD21	D 4	8
Royd House Rd.		
Royd La. HX3	E17	80
Royd Pl. HX3	F18	80
Royd Rd. BD13	F12	45
Royd St. BD15	F 8	27
Royd St. BD20	M17	83
Main St.		
Royd Ter. HX3	E21	94
Royden Gro. BD9	L10	48
Royds Av. BD11	R16	86
Royds Clo. LS12	Y13	72
Royds Cres. HD6	L19	97
Wyke Old La.		
Royds Farm Rd. LS12	Y14	72
Royds Hall Av. BD6	M15	66
Royds Hall La. BD12	L16	83
Royds Hall La. BD6	L16	83
Royds Hall Rd. LS12	Y13	72
Royds La. LS12	Y13	72
Roydscliffe Dr. BD9	K 9	29
Roydscliffe Rd. BD9	K 9	29
Roydsdale Way BD4	O16	84
Roydstone Rd. BD3	P11	50
Roydstone Ter. BD3	P11	50
Roydwood Ter. BD13	C 8	26
Royland St. HX3	J19	96
Royston Pl. LS6	AA 9	37
Woodhouse St.		
Ruby St. BD21	B 5	7
Ingrow La.		
Ruby St. HX1	E19	94
Ruby St. LS9	BB10	56
Rudby Haven BD10	Q 8	32
Rudd St. BD7	L13	66
Rudding Av. BD15	H10	46
Rudding Cres. BD15	H10	46
Rudstone Gro. BD10	Q 8	32
Reighton Cft.		
Ruffield Side BD12	M16	83
Rufford Av. LS19	R 4	15
Rufford Bank LS19	S 4	15
Rufford Clo. LS19	S 4	15
Rufford Cres. LS19	S 4	15
Rufford Dr. LS19	S 4	15
Rufford Pl. HX3	E21	94
Rufford Rd. HX3	E21	94
Rufford Rd., Elland	G24	99
HX5		
Rufford Ridge LS19	S 4	15
Rufford St. BD3	P11	50
Rufford Vills. HX3	E21	94
Rufus St. BD5	L13	66
Rufus St. LS10	CC12	56
Orchard St.		
Rugby Av. HX3	D17	79
Rugby Dr. HX3	D17	79
Rugby Gdns. HX3	D17	79
Rugby Mt. HX3	D17	79
Rugby Pl. BD7	L12	48
Rugby Ter. HX3	D17	79
Runswick Av. LS11	Z12	55
Runswick Pl. LS11	AA12	55
Runswick St. BD5	M14	66
Runswick St. LS11	Z12	55
Runswick Ter. BD5	M14	66
Runswick Ter. LS11	AA12	55
Rushcroft Ter. BD7	M 5	12
Rushmoor Rd. BD4	P14	68
Rusholme Dr. LS28	S 9	33
Rushton Av. BD3	Q11	50
Rushton Hill Clo. HX2	C18	79
Rushton Rd. BD3	P11	50
Rushton St. LS28	R 8	33
Rushton Ter. BD3	Q11	50
Rushworth St. HX3	E18	80
Wheatley La.		
Ruskin Av. BD9	J 9	29
Ruskin St. LS28	S10	51
Ruskin Ter. HX3	E18	80
East Park Rd.		
Russel Gro. BD11	R16	86
Russell Av. BD13	G15	64
Russell Hall La. BD13	G15	64
Russell Rd. BD13	F15	63
Russell St. BD18	M 8	30
Russell St. BD5	M12	48
Russell St. HX1	F19	94
Market St.		
Russell St. LS1	AA11	55
Russell St., Queens. BD13	G14	64
High St.		
Russell St., S.B.	B21	92
Ruswapp Cres. BD10	P 8	32
Ruth St. LS12	Y11	54
Mickley St.		
Ruth St., Haworth	A 7	25
Ruth Ter. LS12	Y11	54
Mickley St.		
Ruthven Vw. LS8	DD 9	39
Rutland Dr. BD16	H 5	10
Clyde St.		
Rutland St. BD21	B 4	7
Rutland St. BD4	O12	49
Rutland St. LS1	Z11	55
Cavendish St.		
Rutland Ter. LS1	Z11	55
Cavendish St.		
Ryan St. BD5	M13	66
Ryburn Ct. HX1	D19	93
Ryburn Ter. HX1	D19	93
Hanson La.		
Rycroft Av. LS13	U10	53
Rycroft Clo. LS13	U10	53
Rycroft Ct. LS13	U10	53
Rycroft Dr. LS13	U10	53
Rycroft Grn. LS13	U10	53
Rycroft Pl. LS13	U10	53
Rycroft Sq. LS13	U10	53
Rycroft St. BD18	M 8	30
Rycroft Towers LS13	U10	52
Rydal Av. BD9	M 9	30
Rydal Cres., Mor. LS27	Y16	89
Rydal Dr., Mor. LS27	Y16	89
Rydal Gro. BD5	N13	67
Rydal St. BD21	B 4	7
Rydale Holt LS12	Y12	54
Rydale Way BD15	H10	46
Rydall Pl. LS11	Z12	55
Rydall St. LS11	Z12	55
Rydall Ter. LS11	Z12	55
Ryder Gdns. LS8	DD 7	39

Rydings Clo. HD6   K21   96
Rydings Dr. HD6   K21   96
Rye La. HX2   C18   78
Rye Pl. LS14   FF10   58
Rye St. BD21   B5   7
Corn St.
Ryecroft Av. BD16   H7   28
Ryecroft Cres. HX2   C18   79
Ryecroft La. HD6   M23   101
Ryecroft La. HX2   C19   93
Ryecroft Rd. BD13   C6   8
Ryecroft Rd. BD16   C6   8
Ryecroft Ter. HX2   C18   79
Ryedale Av. LS12   X13   72
Ryefield Av. BD14   H12   46
Ryelands Av. BD16   J5   11
Ryelands Gro. BD9   J9   29
Rylstone Gdns. BD3   O10   49
Rylstone Lawn LS10   BB13   74
Rylstone Rd. BD17   K6   11
Ryshworth Av. BD16   F4   9
Ryton Dale BD10   Q8   32
Sackville App. LS7   BB9   38
Sackville St. BD1   N11   49
Sackville St. LS7   BB9   38
Sackville Ter. LS7   BB10   56
Saddler St. BD12   M17   83
Huddersfield Rd.
Saddleworth Rd., Greet.   E23   98
HX4
Saffron Dr. BD15   H10   46
Sagar Musgraves Pl. LS13   V9   35
Out Gang
Sagar Musgraves Row LS13 V9   35
Out Gang
Sagar Pl. LS6   Y8   36
Sage St. BD5   M13   66
St. Abbs Clo. BD6   M15   66
St. Abbs Dr. BD6   M15   66
St. Abbs Fold BD6   M15   66
St. Abbs Gate BD6   M15   66
St. Abbs Way BD6   M15   66
St. Abbs Wk. BD6   M15   66
St. Adrians Rd. BD17   M6   12
St. Alban App. LS9   EE10   57
St. Alban Clo. LS9   EE10   57
St. Alban Cres. LS9   EE10   57
St. Alban Gro. LS9   EE10   57
St. Alban Mt. LS9   EE10   57
St. Alban Rd. LS9   EE10   57
St. Alban Vw. LS9   EE10   57
St. Albans Av. HX3   F21   94
St. Albans Pl. LS2   BB11   56
Wade La.
St. Albans Rd. HX3   F21   94
St. Andrews Av., Mor.   W17   88
LS27
St. Andrews Clo. HX2   E16   80
Beechwood Rd.
St. Andrews Clo., Mor.   W17   88
LS27
St. Andrews Clo., Rod.   T8   34
LS13
St. Andrews Cres. BD12   O17   84
St. Andrews Dr. HD6   N21   103
St. Andrews Gro., Mor.   W17   88
LS27
St. Andrews Pl. BD7   M12   48
Lister Hills
St. Andrews Pl. LS3   Z11   55
Darlington St.
St. Andrews St. LS3   Z11   55
St. Andrews Vills. BD7   M11   48
St. Andrews Wk. LS17   BB5   20
St. Ann St. LS2   AA11   55
St. Annes Av. LS4   Y10   54
St. Annes Clo. LS4   Y9   36
St. Annes Dr. LS4   Y9   36
St. Annes Gdns. LS4   Y9   36
St. Annes Grn. LS4   Y9   36
St. Annes La. LS4   Y9   36
St. Annes Pl. HX1   E19   94
Pellon La.
St. Annes Rd. HX3   F22   98
St. Annes Rd. LS6   Y8   36
St. Annes Ter. BD17   M6   12
St. Anns Mt. LS4   Y9   36
St. Anns Ri. LS4   X9   36
St. Anns Sq. LS4   Y9   36
St. Anns Way LS4   Y9   36
St. Anthonys Dr. LS11   Z14   73
St. Anthonys Rd. LS11   Z14   73
St. Augustines Ter. HX1   E19   94
Hanson La.
St. Augustines Ter.BD3   O10   49
St. Barnabas Rd. LS11   AA12   55
St. Barnabas St. LS11   AA12   55
Sweet La.

St. Barnabas Ter. LS11   AA12   55
Sweet La.
St. Blaise Ct. BD6   N12   49
St. Catherines Cres.   V9   35
LS13
St. Catherines Dr.LS13   V9   35
St. Catherines Grn.   V8   35
LS13
St. Catherines Hill   V9   35
LS13
St. Catherines Wk. LS8   DD8   39
Green La.
St. Chads Av. HD6   K20   96
St. Chads Av. LS6   Y8   36
St. Chads Dr. LS6   Y8   36
St. Chads Gro. LS6   Y8   36
St. Chads Rd. BD8   L10   48
St. Chads Rd. LS16   Y8   36
St. Chads Ri. LS6   Y8   36
St. Chads Vw. LS6   Y8   36
St. Clares Av. BD2   P10   50
St. Columba St. LS2   Z10   55
Woodhouse La.
St. Cyprians Gdns. LS9   DD10   57
St. Elmo Gro. LS9   DD11   57
St. Eloi Av. BD17   M5   12
St. Enochs Rd. BD5   L14   66
St. Enochs Rd. BD6   L14   66
St. Francis Pl. LS11   AA12   55
Back Row
St. George Pl. BD4   O13   67
St. Georges Av. LS26   EE15   75
St. Georges Cres.   EE15   75
LS26
St. Georges Pl. BD5   N12   49
Fitzgerald St.
St. Georges Rd. HX1   E18   80
St. Georges Rd. LS2   AA10   55
St. Georges St. BD3   O12   49
St. Giles Clo., Brig.   K20   96
St. Giles Rd. HD6   K20   96
St. Giles Rd. HX3   K19   96
St. Helena Rd. BD6   L14   66
St. Helens Av. LS16   Y5   18
St. Helens Clo. LS16   Y5   18
St. Helens La. LS16   X5   18
St. Helens St. LS10   BB12   56
St. Helens Way LS16   Y5   18
St. Helier Gro. BD17   N5   13
St. Hildas Av. LS9   CC12   56
St. Hildas Cl. LS9   CC12   56
St. Hildas Gro. LS9   CC12   56
St. Hildas Mt. LS9   CC12   56
St. Hildas Pl. LS9   CC12   56
St. Hildas Rd. LS9   CC12   56
St. Hildas Ter. BD3   Q11   50
St. Ives Gdns. HX3   F21   94
St. Ives Gro. BD16   F6   9
St. Ives Gro. LS12   X11   54
St. Ives Mt. LS12   X11   54
St. Ives Pl. BD16   F6   9
St. Ives Rd. BD16   F6   9
St. Ives Rd. HX3   F21   94
St. James App. LS14   GG9   40
St. James Av., Hor.   V6   17
LS18
St. James Cres. LS18   R11   51
St. James Ct. LS9   CC10   56
St. James Dr., Hor.   V6   17
LS18
St. James Pl. BD17   N5   13
St. James Rd. BD17   N5   13
St. James St. BD5   N12   49
St. James Ter., Hor.   V6   17
LS18
St. James Wk., Hor.   V6   17
LS18
St. Jamess Rd. HX1   F19   94
St. Jamess St. HX1   F19   94
St. Johns Av. LS28   S10   51
St. Johns Av. LS6   Z10   55
St. Johns Av., Thorner   JJ4   23
LS14
St. Johns Cres. BD8   K11   47
St. Johns Ct. BD17   N6   13
Otley Rd.
St. Johns Ct. LS19   R4   15
St. Johns Dr. LS19   R4   15
St. Johns La. HX1   F20   94
St. Johns Pl. BD11   R16   86
Town St.
St. Johns Pl. HX1   F20   94
St. Johns Rd. LS19   R4   15
St. Johns Rd. LS3   Z10   55
St. Johns St. BD16   H5   10
Hill St.
St. Johns St. HD6   L22   101
St. Johns Way LS19   R4   15

St. Judes St. BD1   M11   48
St. Judes St. HX1   E20   94
St. Lawrence Clo. LS28   S11   51
St. Lawrence Ter., Pud.   T11   52
LS28
St. Lawrences Clo.BD18   M8   30
St. Leonards Gro. BD8   K10   47
St. Leonards Rd. BD8   K10   47
St. Lukes Av. LS11   AA13   73
Normanton St.
St. Lukes Cres. LS11   AA13   73
Yarm St.
St. Lukes Grn. LS11   AA13   73
St. Lukes Gro. LS11   AA13   73
Normanton St.
St. Lukes Mt. LS11   AA13   73
Normanton St.
St. Lukes Pl. LS11   AA13   73
Normanton St.
St. Lukes Rd. LS11   AA13   73
St. Lukes St. LS11   AA13   73
St. Margarets Av. BD4   P14   68
St. Margarets Av. LS8   CC8   38
St. Margarets Av., Troy   U6   16
LS18
St. Margarets Clo.,   U6   16
Troy LS18
St. Margarets Dr. LS8   DD8   39
St. Margarets Dr., Troy   U6   16
LS18
St. Margarets Gro. LS8   DD8   39
St. Margarets Pl. BD7   L12   48
St. Margarets Rd. BD7   L12   48
St. Margarets Rd., Troy   U6   16
LS18
St. Margarets Ter. BD7   L12   48
St. Margarets Vw. LS8   DD8   39
St. Mark St. HX3   E18   80
St. Marks Av. BD12   M16   83
St. Marks Pl. BD12   M16   83
St. Marks Rd. LS2   AA10   55
St. Marks Rd. LS6   AA9   37
St. Marks St. LS2   AA10   55
St. Marks Ter. BD12   M16   83
St. Marks Ter. Pl. BD12   M16   83
St. Martins Av. LS7   BB8   38
St. Martins Cres. LS7   BB8   38
St. Martins Dr. LS7   BB8   38
St. Martins Gdns. LS7   BB8   38
St. Martins Gro. LS7   BB8   38
St. Martins Rd. LS7   BB8   38
St. Martins Vw. HD6   L21   97
St. Martins Vw. LS7   BB8   38
St. Marys Av. BD12   M18   83
St. Marys Clo. BD12   L18   83
St. Marys Clo. LS12   Y12   54
St. Marys Clo. LS7   BB8   38
Newton Cres.
St. Marys Cres. BD12   L18   83
St. Marys Ct. LS7   BB8   38
Newton Cres.
St. Marys Dr. BD12   M18   83
St. Marys Gate, Elland   G23   99
HX5
Crown St.
St. Marys Gdns. BD12   M18   83
St. Marys Mt. BD12   L18   83
St. Marys Rd. BD4   P12   50
St. Marys Rd. BD9   M10   48
St. Marys Rd. LS7   BB8   38
St. Marys Sq. BD12   M18   83
St. Marys St. HX1   E20   94
St. Marys St. LS9   BB11   56
St. Matthews Dr. HX3   H18   81
St. Matthews Rd. BD5   M14   66
St. Matthews Sq. LS7   BB8   38
Town St.
St. Matthews Wk. LS7   BB7   38
St. Matthias Ct. LS4   Y10   54
St. Matthias Gro. LS4   Y10   54
St. Matthias Pl. LS4   Y10   54
St. Matthias St. LS4   Y10   54
St. Michaels Clo. BD16   H8   28
Cottingley Cliffe Rd.
St. Michaels Cres. LS6   Y9   36
St. Michaels Gro. LS6   Y9   36
St. Michaels La. LS6   Y9   36
St. Michaels Rd. BD8   M11   48
St. Michaels Rd. LS6   Y9   36
St. Michaels Ter. LS6   Y9   36
St. Pauls Av. BD11   R16   86
St. Pauls Av. BD6   L15   66
St. Pauls Clo. BD8   M10   48
Conduit St.
St. Pauls Gro. BD6   L15   66
St. Pauls Rd. BD11   R16   86
St. Pauls Rd. BD18   L7   30

School St. LS10	DD14	75	Second Av. HX3	E21	94	Shakespeare Ct. LS9	CC10	56
Stourton St.			*Manor Dr.*			Shakespeare Gdns. LS9	CC10	56
School St. WF17	T18	87	Second Av. LS12	Z11	55	Shakespeare Grange LS9	CC10	56
School St., Bierley BD4	O15	67	Second Av. LS19	S 4	15	Shakespeare Lawn LS9	CC10	56
School St., Chur. LS27	Y15	72	Second Av., Roth. LS26	FF15	76	Shakespeare St. HX1	F20	94
School St., Cullingworth	C 8	26	Second St. BD12	N16	84	*Wards End*		
BD13			Sedan Pl. LS7	BB10	56	Shakespeare St. LS9	CC10	56
School St., Denholme	D10	44	*Camp Rd.*			Shakespeare Towers LS9	CC10	56
BD13			Sedbergh Clo. LS15	EE11	57	Shann Ter. BD2	M 9	30
School St., East Bowling	P13	68	Sedburgh Rd. HX3	F20	94	Shannon Clo. HD6	K23	100
BD4			Sedge Gro.	ZZ 7	24	Shannon Rd. HD6	K23	100
School St., Farsley LS28	S 9	33	Sedgefield Ter. BD1	M11	48	Shannon Rd. LS9	CC11	56
School St., Greet. HX4	E23	98	Sedgwick Clo. BD8	M11	48	Shannon St. LS9	CC11	56
School St., Mor. LS27	X17	89	*Lumb La.*			Sharp Av. BD6	M15	66
School St., Oakenshaw	O17	84	Sedgwick St. WF17	T18	87	Sharp House Rd. LS10	CC17	91
BD12			Seed Hill Ter. HX2	C16	79	Sharp La. LS10	BB16	91
Wyke La.			Seed Row BD4	O15	67	Sharp St. BD6	M14	66
School St., Pudsey LS28	S12	51	Seed St. BD12	M16	83	Sharpe St. BD5	N12	49
School Ter. BD19	N19	103	Seed St. BD21	B 4	7	Shaw Booth La. HX7	A17	78
New Rd. E.			*Oakworth Rd.*			Shaw Hill HX1	F20	94
School Vw. LS6	Z 9	37	Seedling Mount St. HX1	F19	94	Shaw Hill La. HX3	F20	94
School Vw., Stan. LS28	T10	52	*Dean Clough*			Shaw La.	YY10	42
Score Hill HX3	H17	81	Sefton Av. HD6	K20	96	Shaw La. HD6	J23	100
Scoresby St. BD1	N11	49	Sefton Av. LS11	AA13	73	Shaw La. HX3	G16	81
Scotchman Rd. BD9	K10	47	*Wickham St.*			Shaw La. LS6	Y 8	36
Scotland Clo., Hor. LS18	U 5	16	Sefton Cres. HD6	K20	96	Shaw La., Shaw Hill HX3	F21	94
Scotland La., Troy LS18	U 5	16	Sefton Dr. HD6	K20	96	Shaw St. BD12	L16	83
Scotland La., Yea. &	U 3	1	Sefton Gro. BD2	O 9	31	Shaw St. HX4	D20	93
Troy LS18			Sefton Pl. BD2	O 9	31	Shay Clo. BD9	K 9	29
Scotland Mill La. LS6	Z 6	19	Sefton St. HX1	E19	94	Shay Cres. BD9	K 9	29
Scotland St. BD19	S18	86	Sefton Ter. HX1	E19	94	Shay Dr. BD9	K 9	29
Scotland Way, Hor. LS18	U 5	16	Sefton Ter. LS11	AA13	73	Shay Fold BD9	K 9	29
Scotland Wood Clo. LS17	Z 6	19	Selborne Gro. BD21	B 4	7	Shay Gro. BD9	K 9	29
Scotland Wood Garth LS17	Z 6	19	Selborne Gro. BD9	L10	48	Shay La. BD15	F 8	27
Scotland Wood Lawn LS17	Z 6	19	Selborne Mt. BD9	M10	48	Shay La. BD3	E17	81
Scotland Wood Rd. LS17	Z 6	19	Selborne Ter. BD18	L 8	30	Shay La. BD4	Q13	68
Scott Green Cres., Gild.	U15	70	Selborne Ter. BD9	L10	48	Shay La. BD9	K 9	29
LS27			Selborne Vills. BD14	J13	65	Shay La. HX2	E17	80
Scott Green Dr., Gild.	U15	70	Selbourne Vills. BD9	L 9	30	Shay St. LS6	AA 9	37
LS27			Selby Av. LS9	FF11	58	Shay Syke HX1	F20	94
Scott Green Gro., Gild.	V15	71	Selby Rd. LS15	GG11	58	Sheaf St. LS10	BB12	56
LS27			Selby Rd. LS9	FF11	58	Shearbridge Rd. BD7	M12	48
Scott Green Mt., Gild.	U15	70	Selby Zone HX2	C15	62	Shearbridge Ter. BD7	M12	48
LS27			Seldon St. BD5	L13	66	Sheep Hill La. BD13	H14	64
Scott Green Vw., Gild.	U15	70	Selene Clo. BD19	S18	86	Sheepscar Av. LS7	BB 9	38
LS27			Selkirk St. BD2	O 9	31	*Sheepscar St.*		
Scott Grn., Gild. LS27	U15	70	Selkirk St. LS12	AA13	73	Sheepscar Gro. LS7	BB10	56
Scott Hall Cres. LS7	AA 8	37	*Berwick St.*			Sheepscar Link Rd. LS7	BB11	56
Scott Hall Dr. LS7	BB 9	38	Sellars Fold BD7	L13	66	Sheepscar Pl. LS7	BB10	56
Scott Hall Grn. LS7	BB 8	38	*Great Horton Rd.*			*Skinner La.*		
Scott Hall Gro. LS7	BB 8	38	Sellerdale Av. BD12	M18	83	Sheepscar St. N. LS7	BB 9	38
Scott Hall Pl. LS7	BB 8	38	Sellerdale Dr. BD12	M18	83	Sheepscar St. S. LS7	BB10	56
Scott Hall Rd. LS17	BB 6	20	Sellerdale Ri. BD12	M18	83	Sheepscar Way LS7	BB 9	38
Scott Hall Rd. LS7	BB 9	38	Sellerdale Way BD12	M18	83	Shelf Hall La. HX3	H16	81
Scott Hall Row LS7	BB 9	38	Seminary St. LS2	AA10	55	Shelf Moor HX3	J15	65
Scott Hall Sq. LS7	BB 8	38	Semon Av. BD2	N 8	31	Shelf Moor Rd. HX3	J16	82
Scott Hall St. LS7	BB 9	38	Servia Gdns. LS7	BB 9	38	Shell La. LS28	R 8	33
Scott Hall Ter. LS7	BB 8	38	Servia Hill LS6	AA 9	37	Shelley Gro. BD8	K11	47
Scott Hall Way LS7	BB 8	38	Servia Hill LS7	AA 9	37	*Bull Royd La.*		
Scott Hall Wk. LS7	BB 9	38	Servia Rd. LS7	BB 9	38	Shepcote Clo. LS16	W 5	17
Scott Hill BD1	N11	49	Service Rd. LS14	GG 7	40	Shepcote Cres. LS16	W 5	17
Scott La. Bar.	GG 4	22	Sevenoaks	E22	98	Shepherd St. BD7	L13	66
Scott La. BD19	R18	86	Sevenoaks Mead BD15	H10	46	*Great Horton Rd.*		
Oxford Rd.			Seventh Av. LS12	Y11	54	Shepherds Fold LS11	BB12	56
Scott La. LS12	W11	53	Seventh Av., Roth. LS26	GG15	76	*Meadow La.*		
Scott La. LS27	W17	88	Severn Rd. BD2	O10	49	Shepherds La. LS7	CC 9	38
Scott St. BD6	M15	66	Severn Rd. LS10	CC13	74	Shepherds La. LS8	CC 9	38
Scott St. HX3	E18	80	Severn Way LS10	CC13	74	Shepherds Pl. LS8	CC 9	38
Wheatley La.			Sewage Works Rd. LS9	EE13	75	Shepherds Thorn La. HD6	L23	101
Scott St., Pud. LS28	T12	52	Sewage Works Rd., Elland	H23	99	Shepherds Thorn La. HD6	M24	101
Scott Ter. BD2	P 9	32	Sewell Rd. BD3	O12	49	Sherborne Dr.	A 4	7
Scott Wood La. LS7	AA 8	37	Seymour St. BD3	O12	49	Sherborne Rd. BD10	O 6	13
Scotts Hill Clo.,	JJ 4	23	Shackleton St. LS1	BB11	56	Sherborne Rd. BD7	M12	48
Thorner LS14			*Sovereign St.*			Sherbrooke Av. LS15	FF11	58
Main St.			Shackleton Ter. BD16	E 6	9	Sherburn App. LS14	HH 8	41
Scotty Bank HD6	L22	101	Shadwell Av. LS8	DD 6	21	Sherburn Clo. BD11	R16	86
Sea Croftgate LS14	GG 8	40	Shadwell La. LS17	BB 6	20	Sherburn Clo. LS14	HH 8	41
Seacroft Arc. LS14	GG 8	40	Shadwell La. LS17	EE 4	21	Sherburn Gro. BD11	R16	86
Seacroft Cres.			Shadwell LS17	FF 6	22	Sherburn Pl. LS14	HH 8	41
Seacroft Av. LS14	GG 8	40	Shadwell Park Av. LS17	EE 4	21	Sherburn Rd. HD6	K23	100
Seacroft Chase LS14	GG 8	40	Shadwell Park Clo. LS17	EE 4	21	Sherburn Rd. LS14	HH 8	41
Seacroft Cres.			Shadwell Park Ct. LS17	EE 5	21	Sherburn Rd. N. LS14	GG 7	40
Seacroft Clo. LS14	GG 8	40	Shadwell Park Dr. LS17	DD 5	21	Sherburn Row LS14	HH 8	41
Seacroft Cres. LS14	GG 8	40	Shadwell Park Gdns. LS17	EE 5	21	Sherburn Sq. LS14	HH 8	41
Seacroft LS14	GG 7	40	Shadwell Park Gro. LS17	EE 5	21	Sherburn Wk. LS14	HH 8	41
Seacroft LS14	GG 8	40	Shadwell Ring Rd. LS14	EE 4	21	Sherd St. BD7	L13	66
Seaforth Av. LS9	DD 9	39	Shadwell Ring Rd. LS17	FF 6	22	Sheridan St. BD4	O13	67
Seaforth Gro. LS9	DD 9	39	Shadwell Wk. LS17	CC 5	20	Sheriff La. BD16	J 5	11
Strathmore Ter.			Shaftesbury Av. BD18	M 7	30	Sheriff Rd. BD16	J 4	11
Seaforth Mt. LS9	DD 9	39	Shaftesbury Av. BD9	J10	47	Sherwell Gro. BD15	J10	47
Strathmore Ter.			Shaftesbury Av. HD6	L23	101	Sherwell Ri. BD15	J10	47
Seaforth Pl. LS9	DD 9	39	Shaftesbury Rd. LS8	DD 6	21	Sherwood Av. HD6	N24	102
Seaforth Rd. LS9	DD 9	39	Shafton La. LS11	Z12	55	Sherwood Clo. BD16	J 4	11
Seaforth Ter. LS9	DD 9	39	Shafton Pl. LS11	Z12	55	Sherwood Gro. BD18	K 7	29
Seaton St. BD3	O11	49	Shafton St. LS1	AA12	55	Sherwood Pl. BD2	O10	49
Second Av. BD21	B 4	7	Shafton Vw. LS11	Z12	55	Sherwood Rd. HD6	M22	101
Lister St.			Shakespeare App. LS9	CC10	56	Shetcliffe La. BD4	O15	67
Second Av. BD3	P10	50	Shakespeare Av. LS9	CC10	56	Shetcliffe Rd. BD4	O15	67

Shibden Grange Dr. HX3 G18 81
Shibden Hall Rd. HX3 G19 95
Shibden Head La. BD13 F15 63
Shield Clo. LS15 JJ 9 41
  Bower Rd.
Ship St. HD6 L22 101
Shipley Fields Rd. BD18 L 8 30
Shipley Sta. BD18 M 7 30
Shire Oak Rd. LS6 Z 8 37
Shire Oak St. LS6 Y 8 36
Shirley Av. BD12 M18 83
Shirley Av. WF17 S18 86
Shirley Cres. BD12 L18 83
Shirley Dr. LS13 V 9 35
Shirley Gro. HX3 L19 97
Shirley Pl. BD12 M18 83
Shirley Rd. BD4 P14 68
Shirley Rd. BD7 L12 48
Shirley St. BD18 K 7 29
Shirley St., Haworth YY 7 24
Sholebroke Av. LS7 BB 9 38
Sholebroke Mt. LS7 BB 9 38
Sholebroke Pl. LS7 BB 9 38
Sholebroke St. LS7 BB 9 38
Sholebroke Ter. LS7 BB 8 38
Sholebroke Vw. LS7 BB 9 38
Shoreham Rd. LS12 Y11 54
Short Clo. BD12 L16 83
Short La. LS7 BB 7 38
Short Row BD12 M16 83
Short Way BD13 H12 46
Shotts La. HX3 K18 82
Shroggs Rd. HX3 D18 79
Shroggs St. HX1 E19 94
Shroggs Vue Ter. HX1 E19 94
  Pellon La.
Shuttleworth La. BD8 K11 47
Siddal Gro. HX3 F21 94
Siddal La. HX3 G21 95
Siddal New Rd. HX3 F20 94
Siddal St. HX3 F21 94
Siddal Top La. HX3 G21 95
Siddall Pl. LS11 AA12 55
  Sweet St.
Siddall Sq. HX6 B21 92
  West St.
Siddall St. LS11 AA12 55
Sidings, The BD18 M 7 30
Sidney St. LS2 BB11 56
  Vicar La.
Siegen Clo., Mor. X17 89
  LS27
Silk Mill App. LS5 W 6 17
Silk Mill Av. LS16 V 5 17
Silk Mill Bank LS16 V 6 17
Silk Mill Clo. LS16 V 5 17
Silk Mill Dr. LS16 W 5 17
Silk Mill Gdns. LS16 V 6 17
Silk Mill Grn. LS16 W 5 17
Silk Mill Rd. LS16 V 6 17
Silk St. BD9 L10 48
Silkstone St. BD3 O11 49
Silson La. BD17 N 5 13
Silver Birch Av. BD12 M18 83
Silver Birch Clo. BD12 M18 83
Silver Birch Dr. BD12 M18 83
Silver Birch Gro. BD12 M18 83
Silver Cross St. LS11 Z15 73
  Dewsbury Rd.
Silver Royd Av. LS12 W12 53
Silver Royd Clo. LS12 W12 53
Silver Royd Dr. LS12 W12 53
Silver Royd Garth LS12 W12 53
Silver Royd Gro. LS12 W12 53
Silver Royd Hill LS12 W12 53
Silver Royd Pl. LS12 W12 53
Silver Royd Rd. LS12 W12 53
Silver Royd St. LS12 W12 53
Silver Royd Ter. LS12 W12 53
Silver St. BD19 N18 84
  Tabbs La.
Silver St. BD19 R18 86
  Oxford Rd.
Silver St. HX1 F19 94
Silver St. LS11 AA12 55
  Water La.
Silver St., Beeston LS11 Z14 73
  Town St.
Silverdale Av. LS17 DD 4 21
Silverdale Rd. BD5 N14 67
Silverdale Ter., Greet. E24 98
  HX4
Silverhill Av. BD3 P11 50
Silverhill Dr. BD3 P11 50
Silverhill Rd. BD3 P11 50
Silverwood Av. HX2 C18 79
Silverwood Wk. HX2 C18 79
Silwood Dr. BD2 P 9 32

Simes St. BD1 M11 48
Simm Carr La. HX3 F17 80
Simmonds La. HX1 F20 94
Simms Dene BD15 H 9 28
Simon Clo. BD4 Q14 68
Simpson Gro. BD10 P 7 32
Simpson Gro. LS12 Y11 54
Simpson St. HX3 E18 80
  Booth Town Rd.
Sinclair Rd. BD2 N 8 31
Sinden Mews BD10 O 6 13
Single Row BD2 O10 49
Singleton St. BD1 N11 49
Sion Hill HX3 G21 95
Sir George Martin Dr. Y 5 18
  LS16
Sir Karl Cohen Sq. LS12 X11 54
  Town St.
Sir Wilfred Pl. BD10 O 7 31
  New St.
Sissons Av. LS10 AA17 90
Sissons Cres. LS10 AA17 90
Sissons Dr. LS10 AA17 90
Sissons Grn. LS10 AA17 90
Sissons Gro. LS10 AA17 90
Sissons La. LS10 AA17 90
Sissons Mt. LS10 AA17 90
Sissons Pl. LS10 AA16 90
Sissons Rd. LS10 AA17 90
Sissons Row LS10 AA17 90
Sissons St. LS10 AA17 90
Sissons Ter. LS10 AA17 90
Sissons Vw. LS10 AA17 90
Sixteenth Av. LS12 Y12 54
Sixth Av. BD3 P10 50
Sizers Ct. LS19 R 4 15
Sizers Hill LS19 R 4 15
Skelton Av. LS9 DD11 57
Skelton Cres. LS9 DD11 57
Skelton Grange Rd. LS10 DD14 74
Skelton Rd. LS9 DD11 57
Skelton Ter. LS9 DD11 57
Skelton Wk. BD10 P 7 32
Skeltons La., Sha. LS14 GG 6 22
Skelwith App. LS14 GG 9 40
Skelwith Wk. LS14 GG 9 40
Skinner La. BD8 M10 48
Skinner La. LS7 BB10 56
Skircoat Green Rd. HX3 F21 94
Skircoat Grn. HX3 F22 98
Skircoat Moor Clo. HX3 E21 94
Skircoat Moor Rd. HX3 D20 93
Skircoat Rd. HX1 F20 94
Skirrow St. BD16 H 7 28
Slack Bottom Rd. BD6 L15 66
Slack La. YY 5 6
Sladden St. HX3 E18 80
  Mill La.
Slade La. HD6 K24 100
Slaid Hill Ct. LS17 DD 4 21
Slaters Rd. LS28 T10 52
Slaymaker La. ZZ 5 6
Slead Av. HD6 K20 96
Slead Cres. HD6 K20 96
Slead Gro. HD6 K21 96
Slead Royd HD6 K21 96
Sledmere Clo. LS14 HH 8 41
Sledmere Croft LS14 HH 8 41
Sledmere Garth LS14 HH 8 41
Sledmere Grn. LS14 HH 8 41
Sledmere La. LS14 HH 8 41
Sledmere Pl. LS14 HH 8 41
Sledmere Sq. LS14 HH 8 41
Slenningford Gro. BD18 K 7 29
Slenningford Rd. BD16 G 4 10
Slenningford Rd. BD18 K 7 29
Slenningford Ri. BD16 G 4 10
Slippy La. HX2 C17 79
Sloan Sq. BD8 L11 48
Sloan Sq. E. BD8 L10 48
  Sloan Sq.
Sloan Sq. W. BD8 L11 48
  Sloan Sq.
Sloe St. BD21 C 4 8
Smalewell Clo. LS28 S12 51
Smalewell Dr. LS28 S12 51
Smalewell Gdns. LS28 S12 51
  Occupation La.
Smalewell Grn. LS28 S12 51
Smalewell Rd. LS28 S12 51
Small Page Fold LS28 G14 64
  Albert Rd.
Smeaton App. LS15 JJ 9 41
Smeaton Av. BD8 J11 47
Smeaton Gro. LS10 BB12 56
  Carlisle Rd.
Smeaton Pl. LS10 BB12 56
  Carlisle Rd.

Smeaton St. LS10 BB12 56
  Carlisle Rd.
Smeaton Ter. LS10 BB12 56
  Carlisle Rd.
Smiddles La. BD5 M14 66
Smith Av. BD6 M14 66
Smith House Av. HD6 L20 97
Smith House Cres. HD6 K20 96
Smith House Grn. HD6 L20 97
Smith House La. HD6 L20 97
Smith La. BD9 K10 47
Smith Rd. BD7 L13 66
Smith Row LS13 V 9 35
Smith St. BD16 H 7 28
Smith St. BD18 M 7 30
  Phoenix St.
Smith St. BD7 M11 48
Smithchurch Gro. HD6 K23 100
Smithfield Av. HX3 J19 96
Smithfield La. BD2 D 9 26
Smithfield Vw. BD2 P 9 32
Smithy Carr La. HD6 L21 97
Smithy Fold BD13 J14 65
  Great Horton Rd.
Smithy Hill BD13 D12 44
Smithy Hill BD19 N19 103
Smithy Hill BD6 L14 66
Smithy Hill LS19 R 5 15
Smithy La. BD15 F 8 27
Smithy La. LS16 W 4 17
Smithy La. LS6 Y 6 18
  Weetwood La.
Smithy Mills La. LS16 Y 6 18
Smithy St. HX1 F19 94
Smools La., Chur. LS27 X15 72
Smythe St. HX1 F19 94
Snake Hill BD12 O16 84
Snake La. LS9 DD12 57
Snape Dr. BD7 J14 65
Snape St. BD21 C 4 8
Snelsins La. BD19 P18 85
Snelsins Rd. BD19 P18 85
Snowden Clo. LS13 V10 53
Snowden Cres. LS13 V10 53
Snowden Fold LS13 V10 53
Snowden Gro. LS13 V10 53
Snowden Lawn LS13 V10 53
Snowden Rd. BD18 M 7 30
Snowden St. BD1 N11 49
Snowden Vale LS13 V10 53
  Out Gang
Snowdon App. LS13 V 9 35
Snydal HX3 G20 95
Soaper House La. HX3 J18 82
Soaper La. BD6 J15 65
Soaper La. HX3 J15 65
Society St. LS10 CC13 74
  Low Rd.
Sod House Grn. HX3 E17 80
Soho St. HX1 D19 93
Somerdale Clo. LS13 V10 53
Somerdale Gdns. LS13 V10 53
  Somerdale Clo.
Somerdale Gro. LS13 V10 53
Somerdale Wk. LS13 V10 53
Somers St. LS1 AA11 55
Somerset Av. BD17 M 5 12
Somerset Rd., Pud. LS28 T11 52
Somerton Dr. BD4 P14 68
Somerville Av. BD6 L15 66
Somerville Dr. LS14 FF 9 40
Somerville Grn. LS14 FF10 58
Somerville Gro. LS14 FF 8 40
  Somerville Grn.
Somerville Mt. LS14 GG10 58
Somerville Pk. BD6 L15 66
Somerville Vw. LS14 FF10 58
Sonning Rd. BD15 H11 46
Sourbrook Rd. BD7 M11 48
South Accommodation BB12 56
  Rd. LS10
South Accommodation BB12 56
  Rd. LS9
South Av. LS28 D17 79
South Bank BD13 G14 64
  Highgate Rd.
South Broadgate La., Hor. V 6 17
  LS18
South Brook St. LS10 BB12 56
South Cliffe BD13 F12 45
  Thornton Rd.
South Dr. LS28 S10 51
South Edge BD18 K 7 29
South Edge Ter. HX3 J19 96
  Brighouse Rd.
South End Av. LS13 V10 53

South End Gro. LS13	V10	53
South End Mt. LS13	V10	53
South End Ter. LS13	V10	53
South Farm Cres. LS9	EE10	57
South Farm Rd. LS9	EE10	57
South Field Av. LS17	CC 6	20
South Field Dr. LS17	CC 6	20
South Fields, Bram. LS16	W 2	2
South Gate BD1	N11	49
South Gro. BD18	J 7	29
South Hill Cft. LS26	CC15	91
South Hill Clo. LS26	CC15	91
South Hill Dr. BD16	J 6	11
South Hill Gdns. LS26	CC15	74
South Hill Gro. LS26	CC15	91
South Hill Ri. LS26	CC15	91
South Hill Way LS26	CC15	91
South La. HX3	H15	64
South Lane Gdns., Elland HX5	G24	99
South Lee, Hor. LS18	U 6	16
South Mead, Bram. LS16	W 2	2
South Nelson St.	X16	89
South Par. HX1	F20	94
South Par. LS1	AA11	55
South Par. LS18	R 4	15
South Par. LS28	S12	51
South Par. LS6	Y 8	36
South Par., Elland HX5	G24	99
South Par., Mor. LS27	X17	89
South Par., Pud. LS28	T12	52
South Parade Clo. LS28	S12	51
South Par.		
South Park Ter., Pud. LS28	T13	70
South Parkway App. LS9	FF 9	40
South Parkway LS14	FF 9	40
South Pl., Mor. LS27	X17	89
South St.		
South Queen St., Mor. LS27	X17	89
South Rd. BD13	C 8	26
South Rd. BD9	M 9	30
Frizinghall Rd.		
South Row, Hor. LS18	V 6	17
South Royd Av. HX3	F21	94
South Selby HX2	C16	79
South Sq. BD13	F12	45
South St. BD13	C10	44
South St. BD18	M 8	30
Valley Rd.		
South St. BD21	B 5	7
South St. BD5	M13	66
South St. HX1	L21	97
South St. LS19	R 5	15
South St., Mor. LS27	X17	89
South Ter. LS10	BB12	56
Hunslet La.		
South View Clo. LS19	S 4	15
South View Dr. BD4	Q15	68
South View Rd. BD4	Q15	68
South View Rd. LS10	CC14	74
South View Rd. LS19	P 4	14
South View Ter. BD16	J 4	11
South View Ter. BD17	M 5	12
South View Ter. LS19	S 4	15
South Vw. BD10	P 7	32
South Vw. BD20	L 9	30
Keighley Rd.		
South Vw. HX3	G21	95
South Vw. LS15	HH10	59
Church La.		
South Vw. WF17	T18	87
Leeds Rd.		
South Vw., Haworth	ZZ 7	24
South Vw., Pud. LS28	T11	52
South Vw., Southowram HX3	H21	95
South Way BD16	J 4	11
South Way BD18	J 7	29
South Way BD4	Q15	68
South Wk. BD16	E 6	9
Southampton St. BD3	N11	49
Southbrook Ter. BD7	M12	48
Southcliffe Dr. BD17	M 6	12
Southcliffe Way BD17	M 6	12
Southcote Pl. BD10	O 7	31
Albion Rd.		
Southcroft Av. BD11	R16	86
Southcroft Dr. BD11	R16	86
Southcroft Ga. LS10	BB16	91
Southcroft Gate BD11	R16	86
Southcroft Gate LS10	BB16	91
Southcroft Gdns. LS10	BB16	91
Southcroft Grn. LS10	BB16	91
Southcroft Way LS10	BB16	91
Southdown Rd. BD17	L 6	12
Southdown Rd. BD9	K10	47

Southend St. BD3	O12	49
Southfield Av. BD6	M15	66
Southfield La. BD7	L13	66
Southfield Mt. LS10	CC14	74
Woodhouse Hill Rd.		
Southfield Mt. LS12	Y11	54
Wesley Rd.		
Southfield Rd. BD16	H 6	10
Southfield Rd. BD5	M13	66
Southfield Sq. BD8	M10	48
Southfield St. LS12	Y11	54
Wesley Rd.		
Southfield Ter. BD11	R16	86
Southfield Ter. HX3	J18	82
Southfield Way BD17	M 6	12
Southgate HX1	F19	94
Southgate, Elland HX5	G24	99
Southlands Av. BD13	J12	47
Southlands Av. BD16	H 6	10
Southlands Av. LS17	BB 7	38
Southlands Av., Raw. LS19	T 6	16
Southlands BD17	L 6	12
Southlands Cres. LS17	BB 7	38
Southlands Dr. LS17	BB 7	38
Southlands Gro. BD13	J12	47
Southlands Gro. BD16	H 6	10
Southlea Av.	A 6	7
Southlea Clo. BD12	N16	84
Southleigh Av. LS11	AA15	73
Southleigh Cft. LS11	AA15	73
Southleigh Cres. LS11	AA15	73
Southleigh Dr. LS11	AA15	73
Southleigh Garth LS11	AA15	73
Southleigh Gdns. LS11	AA15	73
Southleigh Grange LS11	AA15	73
Southleigh Gro. LS11	AA15	73
Southleigh Rd. LS11	AA15	73
Southleigh Vw. LS11	AA15	73
Southmere Av. BD7	L13	66
Southmere Cres. BD7	L13	66
Southmere Dr. BD7	K13	65
Southmere Gro. BD7	L13	66
Southmere Oval BD7	K14	65
Southmere Rd. BD7	L13	66
Southmere Ter. BD7	L13	66
Southolme Clo. LS5	W 8	35
Southroyd Par., Pud. LD28	T12	52
Southroyd Pk., Pud. LS28	T12	52
Southroyd Ri., Pud. LS28	T12	52
Southview LS18	V 7	35
Regent Av.		
Southwaite Clo. LS14	FF 9	40
Brooklands Av.		
Southwaite Garth LS14	FF 9	40
Brooklands Vw.		
Southwaite La. LS14	FF 9	40
Southwaite Pl. LS14	FF 9	40
Brooklands Dr.		
Southway BD16	H 4	10
Southway, Hor. LS18	U 5	16
Southwood Clo. LS14	HH 9	41
Southwood Cres. LS14	HH 9	41
Southwood Gate LS14	HH 9	41
Southwood Rd. LS14	HH 9	41
Sovereign St. HX1	E19	94
Stead St.		
Sovereign St. LS1	AA11	55
Sowden La. BD12	K17	82
Sowden La. HX3	K17	82
Sowden Rd. BD9	J 9	29
Sowden St. BD7	L13	66
Sowerby New Rd. HX6	A21	92
Sowerby St. HX6	B21	92
Sowood St. LS4	Y10	54
Spa La. BD16	H 4	10
Spalding Towers LS9	CC10	56
Sparable La. BD16	J 5	11
Spark St. LS3	Z11	55
Kirkstall Rd.		
Speedwell Av. LS6	AA 9	37
Speedwell St.		
Speedwell Gro. LS6	AA 9	37
Speedwell St.		
Speedwell Mt. LS6	AA 9	37
Speedwell Pl. LS6	AA 9	37
Ridge Rd.		
Speedwell Rd. LS6	AA 9	37
Ridge Rd.		
Speedwell St. LS6	AA 9	37
Speeton Av. BD7	K14	65
Speeton Gro. BD7	J14	65
Speights Pl. BD4	P14	68
Railway St.		
Spen App. LS16	W 7	35
Spen Bank LS16	X 7	36
Spen Clo. BD4	O15	67
Spen Cres. LS16	W 7	35
Spen Dr. LS16	X 7	36

Spen Gdns. LS16	X 7	36
Spen Grn. LS16	W 7	35
Spen La. LS16	X 6	18
Spen La. LS5	X 8	36
Spen Lawn LS16	W 7	35
Spen Ms. LS16	X 7	36
Spen Rd. LS16	X 7	36
Spen View La. BD4	O15	67
Spen Wk. LS16	W 7	35
Spence La. LS12	Z12	55
Spenceley St. LS2	AA 9	37
St. Marks Rd.		
Spencer Av. BD7	L12	48
Spencer Mt. LS8	CC 9	38
Spencer Pl. LS7	CC 9	38
Spencer Rd. BD7	K12	47
Spennithorne Av. LS16	X 6	18
Spennithorne Dr. LS16	X 6	18
Spibey Cres., Roth. LS26	EE15	75
Spibey La., Roth LS26	EE15	75
Spicer St. BD5	M13	66
Spindle St. HX2	E16	80
Shay La.		
Spink Pl. BD8	M11	48
Spink Rd. LS9	CC10	56
Spink St. BD8	M11	48
Spinks Gdns. LS14	GG 9	40
Stocks App.		
Spinkwell St. BD3	N10	49
Spinney, The LS17	CC 6	20
Spinney, The LS19	R 6	15
Spout Hill HD6	K24	100
Spout House La. HD6	K20	96
Spread Eagle Yd. LS11	BB12	56
Meadow La.		
Spring Av. BD4	D 4	8
Spring Av., Gild. LS27	V15	71
Spring Bank BD13	C 8	26
Spring Bank Clo., Rod. LS13	T 9	34
Spring Bank Cres. LS6	Z 9	37
Spring Bank Pl. BD8	M10	48
Spring Bank Rd. BD21	C 5	8
Spring Clo. BD16	H 6	10
Spring Clo. BD21	D 4	8
Spring Av.		
Spring Clo. LS9	CC12	56
Spring Close Av. LS9	CC12	56
Spring Close Gdns. LS9	CC12	56
Spring Close Wk. LS9	CC12	56
Spring Close Av.		
Spring Dr. BD21	D 4	8
Spring Dr. BD21	D 4	8
Spring Av.		
Spring Edge N. HX1	E20	94
Spring Edge S. HX1	E20	94
Spring Edge W. HX1	D20	93
Spring Farm La. BD16	E 6	9
Spring Farm Ms. BD15	F 8	27
Spring Gardens Rd. BD9	L 9	30
Spring Gardens St. BD13	G14	64
High St.		
Spring Gdns. BD1	N11	49
Spring Gro. BD10	O 7	31
Spring Gro. LS6	Z10	55
Hyde Park Rd.		
Spring Grove Av. LS6	Z10	55
Hyde Park Rd.		
Spring Grove Ter. LS6	Z10	55
Spring Grove Wk. LS6	Z10	55
Alexandra Rd.		
Spring Hall Clo. HX3	H16	81
Spring Hall Dr. HX2	D20	93
Spring Hall Gdns. HX2	D19	93
Spring Hall Gro. HX2	D19	93
Spring Hall La. HX1	D20	93
Spring Hall La., BD13	F21	94
Skircoat HX1		
Spring Head La.	ZZ 7	24
Spring Head Mt. BD13	G12	46
Spring Head Rd. BD13	G12	46
Spring Hill BD18	N 7	31
Spring Hill LS16	Z 5	19
Spring Hill LS7	BB 9	38
Spring Holes La. BD13	F11	45
Spring La. BD16	J 4	11
Spring La., Greet. HX4	E23	98
Spring Lodge Pl. BD8	M10	48
Spring Mill St. BD5	N12	49
Spring Mt. BD21	D 4	8
Spring Av.		
Spring Park Rd. BD15	F 8	27
Spring Pl. BD21	D 4	8
Spring Av.		
Spring Pl. BD7	M12	48
Spring Rd. BD16	E 6	9
Harden Rd.		
Spring Rd. BD21	B 4	7

Street	Ref	Page
Spring Rd. LS6	Y 9	36
Spring Ri. BD21	D 4	8
Spring Av.		
Spring Row BD16	E 6	9
Harden Rd.		
Spring Row HX2	C15	62
Spring Row, Cullingworth BD13	D 8	26
Spring Row, Haworth	ZZ 7	24
Spring Row, Oakworth	ZZ 6	6
Spring Row, Oxenhope	A10	43
Spring Row, Queens. BD13	G14	64
Prospect Pl.		
Spring St. BD10	O 7	31
Spring St. BD15	H 9	28
Spring St. HD6	L22	101
Owlerings Rd.		
Spring St. HX1	D20	93
Spring Ter. BD15	F 8	27
Spring Ter. BD21	D 4	8
Spring Av.		
Spring Ter. HX3	F19	94
Spring Valley Av. LS13	V10	53
Spring Valley Clo. LS13	V10	53
Spring Valley Cres. LS13	V10	53
Spring Valley Croft LS13	V10	53
Spring Valley Ct. LS13	V10	53
Spring Valley Dr. LS13	V10	53
Spring Valley Vw. LS13	V10	53
Spring Valley Wk. LS13	V10	53
Spring Valley, Pud. LS28	S10	51
Spring Vw. LS27	V15	71
Spring Way BD21	D 4	8
Springbank Av., Gild. LS27	V15	71
Springbank Av., Rod. LS13	T 9	34
Springbank Cres., Gild. LS27	V15	71
Springbank Gro., Rod. LS13	T 9	34
Springbank Rd., Gild. LS27	V15	71
Springbank Rd., Rod. LS13	T 9	34
Springbank Ri., Rod. LS13	T 9	34
Springcliffe BD8	L10	48
Springcliffe St. BD8	L10	48
Springdale Cres. BD10	P 7	32
Springfield Av. BD7	K12	47
Springfield Av., Mor. LS27	W16	88
Springfield BD13	G12	46
Springfield Clo., Hor. LS18	W 6	17
Springfield Cres. LS10	CC14	74
Woodhouse Hill Rd.		
Springfield Cres., Mor. LS27	W16	88
Springfield Gdns., Hor. LS18	V 6	17
Springfield Gdns., Pud. LS28	T12	52
Springfield Grn. LS10	CC14	74
Springfield Pl.		
Springfield Gro. BD16	G 5	10
Springfield Gro. HD6	L20	97
Springfield La., Mor. LS27	X16	89
Springfield La., Tong BD4	T14	70
Springfield Mt. LS12	X11	54
Springfield Mt. LS2	AA10	55
Springfield Mt., Hor. LS18	V 6	17
Springfield Pl. BD1	M11	48
Springfield Pl. BD1	O 8	31
Bradford Rd.		
Springfield Pl. BD2	P10	50
Springfield Pl. LS10	DD14	75
Springfield Pl. LS5	X 9	36
Kirkstall La.		
Springfield Rd. BD17	M 5	12
Springfield Rd., Mor. LS27	X16	89
Springfield Ri., Hor. LS18	V 6	17
Springfield St. BD13	F14	63
Springfield St. BD8	M11	48
Springfield Ter. BD19	N18	84
Tabbs La.		
Springfield Ter. HX3	J19	96
Springfield Ter. LS28	S10	51
Sun Field Pl.		
Springfield Ter. LS28	T11	52
Springfield Ter. LS5	X 9	36
Kirkstall La.		
Springfield Ter. LS9	CC14	74
Springfield Av.		
Springfield Vw. LS5	X 9	36
Kirkstall La.		
Springfield Wk., Hor. LS18	V 6	17
Springfield, S.B.	B21	92
Springhill BD17	K 5	11
Springhurst Rd. BD18	L 7	30
Springroyd Ter. BD8	K11	47
Springs Rd. BD17	Q 4	14
Springs Rd. LS20	Q 4	14
Springswood Av. BD18	L 7	30
Springswood Rd. BD18	L 7	30
Springville Ter. BD10	O 7	31
Springwell Clo. LS19	S 4	15
Springwell Mt. LS6	AA 9	37
Craven Rd.		
Springwell Pl. LS12	Z12	55
Springwell Rd. LS12	Z12	55
Springwell St. LS12	Z12	55
Springwell Vw. LS11	Z12	55
Holbeck La.		
Springwell Vw. WF17	T18	87
Leeds Rd.		
Springwood Av. BD5	N13	67
Springwood Av. HX3	E22	98
Springwood Gdns.	E22	98
Wakefield Rd.		
Springwood Gdns. BD5	N14	67
Springwood Gdns. LS8	DD 8	39
Springwood Gro. LS8	EE 8	39
Springwood Pl. BD18	L 8	30
Springwood Rd. LS19	R 5	15
Springwood Rd. LS8	DD 8	39
Spur Dr. LS15	JJ 9	41
Spurgeon St. BD15	G 9	28
Square Rd. HX1	F19	94
Square St. BD4	O12	49
Square, The BD8	J11	47
Squire Grn. BD8	K10	47
Squire La. BD8	K10	47
Squirrel La. BD13	E12	45
Stable La. HX3	E18	80
Stacey St. BD21	B 4	7
Catherine St.		
Stadium Rd. BD6	M15	66
Stadium Way LS11	Z13	73
Stafford Av. HX3	F21	94
Stafford Chase LS10	BB13	74
Stafford Par. HX3	F21	94
Stafford Pl. HX3	F21	94
Huddersfield Rd.		
Stafford Rd. HX3	F21	94
Stafford Sq. HX3	F21	94
Stafford St. BD4	O13	67
Stafford St. LS10	CC13	74
Stainbeck Av. LS7	Z 8	37
Stainbeck Cres. LS7	Z 8	37
Stainbeck Gdns. BD6	J15	65
Stainbeck Gdns. LS7	AA 7	37
Stainbeck Gro. LS7	Z 8	37
Stainbeck La. LS6	Z 7	37
Stainbeck La. LS7	BB 7	38
Stainbeck Rd. LS7	AA 7	37
Stainbeck Side LS7	Z 8	37
Stainbeck Sq. LS7	Z 8	37
Stainbeck St. LS7	Z 8	37
Stainbeck Ter. LS7	Z 8	37
Stainbeck Vw. LS7	Z 8	37
Stainbeck Wk. LS7	AA 8	37
Stainburn Av. LS17	CC 6	20
Stainburn Cres. N. LS17	BB 6	20
Stainburn Cres. S. LS17	BB 6	20
Stainburn Dr. LS17	BB 6	20
Stainburn Mt. LS17	CC 7	38
Stainburn Rd. LS17	BB 7	20
Stainburn Sq. LS9	BB11	56
Stainburn Ter. LS17	BB 7	38
Stainburn Vw. LS17	CC 6	20
Stainland Rd., Hal. HX4	F22	98
Stainmore Clo. LS14	GG 9	40
Stainmore Pl. LS14	GG 9	40
Stainton Clo. BD6	K15	65
Staircase La., Bram. LS16	V 1	2
Stairfoot Clo. LS16	Y 4	18
Stairfoot La. LS16	Z 4	19
Stairfoot Vw. LS16	Y 4	18
Stairfoot Wk. LS16	Y 4	18
Staithe Av. LS10	BB16	91
Staithe Clo. LS10	BB16	91
Staithe Gdns. LS10	BB16	91
Staithgate La. BD4	N14	67
Staithgate La. BD4	N15	67
Stallabrass St. BD8	M11	48
Hind St.		
Stamford Pl. LS10	BB10	56
Skinner La.		
Stamford St. BD4	O12	49
Stanacre Pl. BD3	N11	49
Stanage La. HX3	J15	65
Stanage Nook HX3	J15	65
Standale Av. LS28	S11	51
Standale Cres LS28	S11	51
Standale Ri. LS28	S11	51
Standard Pl. LS10	BB14	74
Norwich Av.		
Standard St. LS10	BB14	74
Norwich Av.		
Stanhall Av. LS28	S10	51
Stanhope Av., Troy LS18	V 6	17
Stanhope Dr., Hor. LS18	U 7	34
Stanks App. LS14	HH 9	41
Stanks Av. LS14	HH 9	41
Stanks Clo. LS14	JJ 9	41
Stanks Cross LS14	HH 9	41
Stanks Dr. LS14	JJ 9	41
Stanks Garth LS14	HH 9	41
Barwick Rd.		
Stanks Gdns. LS14	HH 8	41
Stanks Grn. LS14	JJ 9	41
Stanks Gro. LS14	HH 9	41
Stanks Av.		
Stanks La. N. LS14	HH 8	41
Stanks La. S. LS14	HH 9	41
Stanks Par. LS14	HH 9	41
Stanks Rd. LS14	HH 8	41
Stanks Ri. LS14	HH 8	41
Stanks Way LS14	HH 9	41
Stanley Av. LS9	CC10	56
Ashley Rd.		
Stanley Ct.	D19	93
Alabama St.		
Stanley Dr. LS14	DD 6	21
Stanley Pl. LS9	DD10	57
Compton Av.		
Stanley Rd. BD10	O 7	31
Bradford Rd.		
Stanley Rd. BD2	M 9	30
Stanley Rd. BD22	B 5	7
Stanley Rd. HX1	D20	93
Stanley Rd. LS9	CC10	56
Stanley St. BD10	O 7	31
Bradford Rd.		
Stanley St. BD16	H 5	10
Stanley St. BD18	M 8	30
Stanley St. HD6	L21	97
Stanley St. HX1	D19	93
Alabama St.		
Stanley St., Haworth	A 7	25
Stanmore Av. LS4	Y 9	36
Michaels La.		
Stanmore Gro. LS4	Y 9	36
Stanmore Hill LS4	Y 9	36
Stanmore Mt. LS4	Y 9	36
Stanmore Pl. BD7	L12	48
Stanmore Pl. LS4	Y 9	36
Michaels La.		
Stanmore Rd. LS4	Y 9	36
Stanmore St. LS4	Y 9	36
Stanmore Vw. LS4	Y 9	36
Michaels La.		
Stannary HX1	F19	95
Stannary La. HX1	E19	94
Stannary Pl. HX1	E19	94
Stannary St. HX1	E19	94
Stanner Hill Rd. BD7	K13	65
Stanningley Av. HX2	B16	78
Stanningley By-Pass, Pud. LS28	T11	52
Stanningley Dr. HX2	B16	78
Stanningley Field Clo. LS13	U10	52
Stanningley Rd. HX2	B16	78
Stanningley Rd. LS28	T10	52
Stanningley Rd., Stan. LS12	Y11	54
Stansfield Clo. HX1	E19	94
Hanson La.		
Stansfield Pl. BD10	O 6	13
Greenfield La.		
Stansfield Pl. LS12	Y11	54
Amberley Rd.		
Stansfield St. HX1	E19	94
Stansfield St. LS12	Y12	54
Staples La. BD21	B 7	25
Stapper Grn. BD15	E 8	27
Star St. BD5	M13	66
Star Ter. HD6	K23	100
State St. LS6	AA 9	37
Station Av. LS13	U10	52
Station Cotts. LS15	HH10	59
Station Cres. LS12	X11	54
Station La. BD11	R16	86
Station La. BD4	R16	86

Street	Grid	Page
Summerville Rd. LS28	S10	51
Sun Field LS28	S10	51
Sun Field Pl. LS28	S10	51
Sun Fold HX1	F20	94
Sun St. BD1	N11	49
Sun St. BD13	C 8	26
Halifax Rd.		
Sun St. BD21	C 4	8
Sun St. LS28	S10	51
Sun St., Haworth	ZZ 8	24
Sun St., Pud. LS28	T10	52
Sun Wood Av. HX3	H17	81
Sunbeam Av. LS11	AA19	73
Sunbeam Pl.		
Sunbeam Gro. LS11	AA13	73
Sunbeam Ter.		
Sunbeam Pl. LS11	AA13	73
Sunbridge Rd. BD1	M11	48
Sunderland Rd. BD15	M15	66
Sunderland Rd. BD21	B 4	7
Sunderland Rd. BD9	L10	48
Sunderland St. HX1	F19	94
Lord St.		
Sundown Av. BD7	K13	65
Sunfield Dr., Pud. LS28	T10	52
Sunfield Pl.		
Sunhill Dr. BD17	K 5	11
Sunhurst Dr.	ZZ 5	6
Sunningdale Av. LS17	Z 5	19
Sunningdale BD6	J11	47
Sunningdale Clo. LS17	AA 5	19
Sunningdale Cres. BD13	D 8	26
Sunningdale Dr. LS17	AA 5	19
Sunningdale Grn. LS17	AA 5	19
Sunningdale Way LS17	AA 5	19
Sunningdale Wk. LS17	AA 5	19
Sunny Bank Av., Hor. LS18	U 7	34
Sunny Bank BD12	J10	47
Sunny Bank BD18	L 7	30
Sunny Bank Cres., Greet. HX4	E23	98
Sunny Bank Dr., Greet. HX4	E23	98
Sunny Bank Dr., S.B. HX6	C21	93
Sunny Bank Grange HD6	L21	97
Sunny Bank Gro. LS7	CC 8	38
Sunny Bank La. BD3	Q10	50
Sunny Bank La., Greet. HX4	E23	98
Sunny Bank LS8	CC 8	38
Sunny Bank Rd. HX2	B16	78
Sunny Bank Rd., Greet. HX4	E23	98
Sunny Bank St. HX6	C21	93
Sunny Bank Ter. LS18	F18	81
All Souls Rd.		
Sunny Bank Vw. LS8	CC 8	38
Sunny Brow La. BD9	J10	47
Sunny Gro., Mor. LS27	Y15	72
Elland Rd.		
Sunny Hill Av. BD21	B 4	7
Sunny Hill Gro. BD21	B 4	7
Sunny Lea Ter. BD6	M15	66
Scott St.		
Sunny Mt. BD16	E 6	9
Sunny Rd., Hor. LS18	U 7	34
Sunny Side La. BD3	N10	49
Sunny View Ter. BD13	F15	63
Ladysmith Rd.		
Sunnybank Av. BD3	Q10	50
Sunnybank Av. BD5	M14	66
Sunnybank Gro. BD3	Q10	50
Sunnybank Rd. BD5	M14	66
Sunnybank Rd. HD6	L21	97
Sunnybrae Cres. BD16	J 6	9
Sunnydale Gro. BD21	D 4	8
Sunnydene LS14	FF10	58
Sunnymount Ter. WF17	T18	87
Leeds Rd.		
Sunnyridge Av. LS28	P11	50
Sunnyside HX3	M23	101
Sunnyside Rd. LS13	U10	52
Sunnyview Av. LS11	Z13	73
Sunnyview Gdns. LS11	Z13	73
Sunnyview Ter. LS11	Z13	73
Sunset Av. LS6	Z 7	37
Sunset Cres. HX3	G20	95
Sunset Dr. LS6	Z 7	37
Sunset Hill Top LS6	Z 7	37
Sunset Mt. LS6	Z 7	37
Sunset Rd. LS6	Z 7	37
Sunset Ri. LS6	Z 7	37
Sunset Vw. LS6	Z 7	37
Sunway HX3	G20	95
Surrey Gro. BD5	N13	67
Surrey Rd., Pud. LS28	S11	52
Sussex App. LS10	CC13	74
Sussex Av. LS10	CC13	74
Sussex Av., Troy LS18	V 5	17
Sussex Cres. LS9	CC12	56
Sussex St.		
Sussex Gdns. LS10	CC13	74
Sussex Grn. LS10	CC13	74
Sussex Pl. LS10	CC13	74
Sussex St. LS9	CC11	56
Sutcliffe Pl. BD6	M15	66
Sutcliffe St. HX2	D19	93
Sutcliffe Wood Rd. HX3	J19	96
Sutcliffes Ct. HX3	G20	95
Sutherland Av. LS8	DD 6	21
Sutherland Cres. LS8	DD 6	21
Sutherland Mt. LS9	DD10	57
Sutherland Rd. LS9	DD10	57
Sutherland St. LS12	Z12	55
Sutherland Ter. LS9	DD10	57
Sutton App. LS14	FF10	58
Sutton Av. BD2	N 8	31
Sutton Cres. BD4	P13	68
Sutton Cres. LS14	FF10	58
Sutton Dr. BD13	C 8	26
Sutton Gro. BD4	Q12	50
Sutton Gro., Mor. LS27	X17	89
Sutton Rd. BD4	Q12	50
Sutton St. LS12	Z12	55
Swain House Cres. BD2	O 8	31
Swain House Rd. BD2	N 8	31
Swain Mt. BD2	O 8	31
Swales Moor Rd. HX3	F16	80
Swallow Av. LS12	X12	54
Swallow Clo. LS17	CC 5	20
Swallow Cres. LS12	X12	54
Swallow Dr. LS17	CC 5	21
Swallow Mt. LS12	X12	54
Swan Bank La. HX3	F20	94
Swan Hill BD9	M 9	30
Swan La. LS16	Y 2	3
Swan St. BD5	N12	49
Swan St. LS1	BB11	56
Lands La.		
Swarcliffe App. LS14	HH 9	41
Swarcliffe Av. LS14	HH 9	41
Swarcliffe Bank LS14	HH 8	41
Swarcliffe Dr. E. LS14	HH 9	41
Stanks La. S.		
Swarcliffe Dr. LS14	HH 9	41
Swarcliffe Grn. LS14	HH 9	41
Swarcliffe Par. LS14	HH 9	41
Swarcliffe Rd. LS14	HH 8	41
Swarcliffe Towers LS14	HH 8	41
Swardale Grn. LS14	HH 9	41
Swardale Rd. LS14	HH 9	41
Swarland Gro. BD5	N13	67
Sweet St. LS11	AA12	55
Sweet St. W. LS11	AA12	55
Swift St. HX3	F21	94
Salterhebble Hill		
Swillington La., Swil. LS26	JJ14	77
Swincliffe Clo. BD19	R17	86
Swincliffe Cres. BD19	R17	86
Swinegate LS1	BB11	56
Swinnow Av. LS13	U10	52
Swinnow Clo. LS13	U10	52
Swinnow Cres., Stan. LS28	U10	52
Swinnow Dr., St. LS13	U10	52
Swinnow Garth LS13	U11	52
Swinnow Gdns. LS13	U10	52
Swinnow Grn., Pud. LS28	U11	52
Swinnow Gro. LS13	U10	52
Swinnow La. LS13	U10	52
Swinnow Pl., Swi. LS28	U10	52
Stanningley Rd.		
Swinnow Rd. LS13	U10	52
Swinnow Rd., Pud. LS28	T11	52
Swinnow St., Swi. LS28	U10	52
Stanningley Rd.		
Swinnow Ter., Stan. LS28	U10	52
Swinnow Vw. LS13	U10	52
Swinnow Wk. LS13	U10	52
Swinton Pl. BD7	L12	48
Swinton Ter. HX1	D20	93
Swires Rd. BD2	O10	49
Swires Rd. HX1	E20	94
Swires Ter. HX1	E20	94
Sycamore Av. BD16	G16	10
Sycamore Av. BD7	K12	47
Sycamore Av. LS15	GG11	58
Sycamore Av. LS8	CC 8	38
Sycamore Clo., Bram. LS16	O11	49
Sycamore Ct. LS8	EE 8	39
Sycamore Dr. BD16	G 4	10
Canal Rd.		
Sycamore Dr. HX3	L20	97
Sycamore Dr., Greet. HX4	F24	98
Sycamore Row LS13	U 9	34
Sycamore St. BD16	G 4	10
Foster St.		
Sycamore Way WF17	T18	87
Sycamore Wk., The, LS15	GG12	58
Sycamores, The, Bram. LS16	W 2	2
Sydenham Pl. BD3	O10	49
Sydenham Rd. LS11	Z12	55
Sydenham St. LS11	Z12	55
Sydney St. BD16	H 5	10
Sydney St. LS28	S10	51
Syke La. BD13	B21	92
Syke La. BD13	G15	64
Syke La. HX2	D14	62
Syke La., Brig. HX3	K18	82
Syke Rd. BD9	L 9	30
Sykes La. BD12	O17	84
Sykes La., S.B.	ZZ 5	6
Sykess Ter. HX3	E19	94
Sylvan Av. BD13	F15	63
Syringa Av. BD15	H 9	28
Tabbs Ct. BD19	N18	84
Tabbs La. BD19	N18	84
Talavera St. LS12	Z11	55
Talbot Av. LS4	Y 9	36
Talbot Av. LS8	CC 6	20
Talbot Cres. LS8	CC 6	20
Talbot Gdns. LS8	CC 6	20
Talbot Gro. LS8	CC 6	20
Talbot Mt. LS4	Y 9	36
St. Michaels La.		
Talbot Rd. LS8	CC 6	20
Talbot Ri. LS17	CC 6	20
Talbot St. BD7	L11	48
Talbot Ter. LS4	Y 9	36
St. Michaels La.		
Talbot Vw. LS4	Y 9	36
Tamar St. BD5	M13	66
Tan House La. BD15	E 8	27
Tan House La. HX3	H17	81
Tan La. BD4	O16	84
Tanfield Pl. LS2	AA10	55
Caledonian St.		
Tanfield Ter. LS2	AA10	55
Tanfield St.		
Tanhouse Hill HX3	J19	96
Tanhouse Hill, Hor. LS18	W 7	35
Tanhouse Pk. HX3	J19	96
Tanner St. BD19	O20	103
Tannery Sq. LS6	Z 7	37
Tannery St. LS6	Z 7	37
Green Rd.		
Tannett Grn. BD5	N14	67
Tanton Cres. BD14	J13	65
Tanton Wk. BD14	J13	65
Tarn La., Wike LS17	EE 4	21
Tarnside Dr. LS14	FF 9	40
Tasker Hill HX3	F19	94
Tatham Way LS8	EE 8	39
Tatlock St. LS12	Z12	55
Lord St.		
Taunton St. BD18	L 7	30
Tay Ct. BD2	P 9	32
Taylor La. HX1	F19	94
Taylor La. HX2	E13	63
Taylor Rd. BD6	M15	66
Pearson Rd.		
Taylor St. BD18	M 7	30
Phoenix St.		
Taylor St. HX1	E19	94
Taylor Ter. BD17	L 6	12
Green La.		
Taylors Yd. LS14	GG 9	40
Teal La. HX3	G17	81
Teal St., Roth. LS26	DD14	75
Queen St.		
Teasdale St. BD4	O13	67
Tees St. BD5	M13	66
Telephone Pl. LS7	BB10	56
Mushroom St.		
Telescombe Dr. BD4	P14	68
Telford Clo. LS10	BB14	74
Telford Ct. BD7	L12	48
Princeville St.		
Telford Gdns. LS10	BB14	74
Telford Pl. LS10	CC14	74
Woodhouse Hill Rd.		
Telford Rd. LS10	CC14	74
Telford St. LS10	CC14	74
Telford Ter. LS10	CC13	74
Telford Wk. LS10	CC14	74
Balm Rd.		
Temperance Field BD12	M17	83

Temperance Field BD19	N19	103	Thackley Old Rd. BD18	M 7	30	Thorne Clo. LS28	R11	51
Temperance St. LS5	X 9	36	Thackley Pk. BD10	O 6	13	Thorner La. LS14	JJ 7	41
Club Row			Thackley Rd. BD10	O 6	13	Thorner La., Thorner LS14	JJ 5	23
Tempest Cres. LS11	AA13	73	Thackley Vw. BD10	O 6	13	Thornes Pk. BD18	M 8	30
Tempest Rd. LS11	AA13	73	Thackray St., Mor. LS27	X17	89	Thornes Pk. HD6	L22	101
Templar La. LS15	HH 9	41	Thane Way LS15	JJ 9	41	Thornfield Av. BD6	M15	66
Templar La. LS2	BB11	56	*Mercia Way*			Thornfield Av. LS28	S10	51
Templar St. LS2	BB11	56	Thatchers Way BD19	R18	86	Thornfield Mt. WF17	U18	87
Templars Clo. HX4	E23	98	Theaker La. LS12	X11	54	Thornfield Pl. BD2	P 9	32
Templars Way BD6	K11	47	Theaker Vw. LS12	X11	54	Thornfield Rd. LS16	X 7	36
Temple Av. LS15	GG12	58	*Theaker La.*			Thornfield Ri., Greet.	E23	98
Temple Av., Roth. LS26	FF15	76	Theakston Mead BD14	J13	65	*Sunny Bank Rd.*		
Temple Clo. LS15	GG12	58	Thealby Clo. LS9	CC11	56	Thornfield Sq. BD2	P 9	32
Temple Cres. LS11	AA13	73	Thealby Lawn LS9	CC10	56	Thornfield St., Greet. HX4	E23	98
Cemetery Rd.			Thealby Pl. LS9	CC10	56	*Sunnybank Rd.*		
Temple Ct. LS15	FF11	58	Thearne Grn. BD14	J13	65	Thornhill Av. BD18	M 8	30
Temple Ct., Roth. LS26	FF15	76	Theodore St. LS11	AA14	73	Thornhill Av., Keighley	A 5	7
Temple Gate Av. LS15	GG12	58	Third Av. BD21	B 4	7	Thornhill Clo. LS28	R 8	33
Temple Gate Clo. LS15	GG11	58	*Lister St.*			Thornhill Cres. LS28	R 8	33
Temple Gate Cres. LS15	GG12	58	Third Av. BD3	P10	50	Thornhill Ct. BD5	W13	67
Temple Gate Dr. LS15	GG11	58	Third Av. HX3	E21	94	*Ripley St.*		
Temple Gate Gro. LS15	GG12	58	*Manor Dr.*			Thornhill Dr. BD18	M 8	30
Temple Gate LS15	GG11	58	Third Av. LS12	Z11	55	Thornhill Dr. LS28	R 7	33
Temple Gate Rd. LS15	GG12	58	Third Av., Roth. LS26	FF15	76	Thornhill Gro. BD18	M 8	30
Temple Gate Ri. LS15	GG11	58	Third St. BD12	N16	84	Thornhill Pl. BD3	Q11	50
Temple Gate Vw. LS15	GG12	58	Thirkleby Royd BD14	J13	65	Thornhill Pl. LS12	X12	54
Temple Gate Way LS15	GG12	58	Thirlmere Av. BD12	H23	99	Thornhill Rd. HD6	K23	100
Temple Gate Wk. LS15	GG11	58	Thirlmere Gdns. BD2	O10	49	Thornhill Rd. LS12	X12	54
Temple Grn. LS15	GG11	58	Thirlmere Gdns. LS11	Z15	73	Thornhill St. LS12	X12	54
Temple Grn., Wood. LS26	GG15	76	Thirlmere Gro. BD17	K 6	11	Thornhill St. LS28	R 8	33
Temple Av.			Thirsk Gro. BD14	J13	65	Thornhill Ter. BD3	P11	50
Temple Gro. LS15	GG11	58	Thirsk Row LS1	AA11	55	Thornhill Vw. LS12	X12	54
Temple La. LS15	GG11	58	*Wellington St.*			Thornhills Beck La. HD6	L21	97
Temple Lawn LS26	FF15	76	Thirteenth Av. LS12	Y12	54	Thornhills Bridge La.	L21	97
Temple Lea LS15	GG11	58	*Ninth Av.*			HD6		
Temple Park Clo. LS15	GG11	58	Thistle Way LS27	V16	88	Thornhills La. HD6	M21	97
Temple Park Gdns. LS15	GG11	58	Thomas Pl. BD18	M 7	30	Thornlea Clo. BD14	J12	47
Temple Park Grn. LS15	GG11	58	*High St.*			*Bradford Rd.*		
Temple Rhydding BD17	M 6	12	Thomas St. BD13	D10	44	Thornlea Clo. LS19	Q 4	14
Welwyn Dr.			*Longhouse La.*			Thornlea Down BD14	J12	47
Temple Rhydding Dr. BD17	M 6	12	Thomas St. HX1	F19	94	*Bradford Rd.*		
Temple Ri. LS15	GG12	58	Thomas St. LS6	AA 9	37	Thornlea Gro. BD14	J12	47
Temple St. BD9	L10	48	Thomas St. S. HX1	D20	93	*Bradford Rd.*		
Temple Stowe Cres.	HH10	59	Thomas St. W. HX1	E20	94	Thornlea Holme BD14	J12	47
LS15			Thomas St., Brig.	L22	101	*Bradford Rd.*		
Temple Stowe Dr. LS15	HH11	59	Thomas St., Elland	H24	99	Thornlea Mall BD14	J12	47
Temple Stowe Gdns.	GG11	58	HX5			*Bradford Rd.*		
LS15			Thomas St., Haworth	ZZ 7	24	Thornlea Thorpe BD14	J12	47
Temple Stowe Hill LS15	GG10	58	*Brow Rd.*			*Bradford Rd.*		
Temple View Pl. LS9	CC11	56	Thomas Yd. LS1	AA10	55	Thornlea Vills. BD14	J12	47
Temple View Rd. LS9	CC11	56	*Cankerwell La.*			*Bradford Rd.*		
Temple View Ter. LS9	CC11	56	Thompson Av. BD2	N 8	31	Thornlea Wk. BD14	J12	47
Temple Vw. LS9	CC12	56	Thompson Grn. BD17	L 6	12	*Bradford Rd.*		
Temple Wk. LS15	GG11	58	Thompson La. BD17	L 6	12	Thornleigh Mt. LS9	CC12	56
Templenewsam Rd. LS15	FF11	58	Thompson St. BD18	L 7	30	Thornleigh St. LS9	CC12	56
Templenewsam Vw. LS15	FF12	58	Thompson St. HX1	E19	94	Thornmead Rd. BD17	M 6	12
Ten Yards La. BD13	E10	45	Thoresby Gro. BD7	K13	65	Thornroyd Dr. BD4	Q14	68
Tenbury Fold BD4	Q13	68	Thoresby Pl. LS1	AA11	55	Thornsgill Av. BD4	P13	68
Tennis Av. BD4	P14	68	Thorn Av. BD9	J 9	29	Thornton Av. LS12	X11	54
Tennis Way BD17	L 6	12	Thorn Bank Av.	A 5	7	Thornton Clo. WF17	T17	87
Tennyson Clo. HX6	A21	92	Thorn Clo. BD18	N 7	31	Thornton Ct. BD8	K11	47
Tennyson Clo., Pud. LS28	T12	52	Thorn Clo. LS8	DD 9	39	*Lane Ends Clo.*		
Tennyson Pl. BD3	O11	49	Thorn Cres. LS9	DD 9	39	Thornton Gdns. LS12	X11	54
Tennyson Rd. BD6	L15	66	Thorn Cross LS8	DD 9	39	Thornton Gro. LS12	X11	54
Tennyson St. BD21	B 4	7	Thorn Dr. BD13	F15	63	Thornton La. BD5	M13	66
Tennyson St. HX3	E18	80	Thorn Dr. BD9	J 9	29	Thornton Moor La. BD13	B11	43
Tennyson St. LS28	S10	51	Thorn Dr. LS8	DD 9	39	Thornton Old Rd. BD8	J11	47
Tenter Hill	H12	46	Thorn Gro. BD9	J 9	29	Thornton Rd. BD1	N12	49
Green End			Thorn La. BD9	J 9	29	Thornton Rd. BD13	G14	64
Tenter La. LS1	BB11	56	Thorn La. LS8	CC 7	38	Thornton Rd. BD8	N12	49
Bridge End			Thorn Mt. LS8	EE 9	39	Thornton Rd., Brig.	K23	100
Tentercroft BD17	M 5	12	Thorn St. BD21	C 4	8	Thornton Rd., Denholme	D12	43
Tenterden Way LS15	JJ 9	41	*Park Wood St.*			Gate BD13		
Tenth Av. LS12	Z12	55	Thorn St. BD8	K10	47	Thornton Rd., Queens.	N12	49
Eighth Av.			Thorn St. WF17	T18	87	BD13		
Tern St. BD7	L13	66	*Middlegate*			Thornton Sq. BD5	M13	66
Ternhill Gro. BD5	N12	49	Thorn Ter. BD8	M10	48	*Marsh St.*		
Terrace St. HX6	B21	92	Thorn Ter. LS8	DD 9	39	Thornton Sq., Brig.	L22	101
West St.			Thorn Tree St. HX1	D20	93	*Bethel St.*		
Terrace, The, Pud. LS28	T13	70	Thorn Vw. HX3	F18	80	Thornton St. BD1	M11	48
Terrington Crest BD14	J13	65	Thorn Vw. LS8	DD 9	39	Thornton St. BD6	M14	66
Terry Hill Fold BD4	P13	68	Thorn Vw., Elland	H24	99	*Bank St.*		
Terry Rd. BD12	N16	84	Thorn Wk. LS8	EE 9	39	Thornton St. HX1	D20	93
Cleckheaton Rd.			Thornaby Dr. BD14	J13	65	*Fenton Rd.*		
Tetley Dr. BD11	R17	86	Thornacre Cres. BD18	N 7	31	Thornton Ter. HX1	D20	93
Tetley La. HX3	H17	81	Thornacre Rd. BD18	N 8	31	*Wainhouse Rd.*		
Town Gate			Thornbank Av. BD22	A 5	7	Thornton Vw. Rd. BD14	J13	65
Tetley Pl. BD2	N10	49	Thornbury Av. BD3	P11	50	Thorntons Arc. LS1	BB11	56
Tetley St. BD1	M11	48	Thornbury Cres. BD3	P11	50	*Briggate*		
Tewet La. BD16	H 4	10	Thornbury Dr. BD3	P11	50	Thornville Av. LS6	Z10	55
Tewit Clo. HX2	D15	62	Thornbury Gro. BD3	P11	50	Thornville Cres. LS6	Z 9	37
Tewit Grn. HX2	D15	62	Thornbury Rd. BD3	P11	50	*Brudenell Rd.*		
Tewit Hall Rd. BD3	P11	50	Thornbury St. BD3	P11	50	Thornville Ct. BD8	M10	48
Tewitt Hall Gdns. HX2	D16	79	Thorncliffe Rd.	A 4	7	Thornville Gro. LS6	Z10	55
Tewitt La. HX2	D15	62	Thorncliffe Rd. BD8	M10	48	Thornville Mt. LS6	Z10	55
Thackeray Rd. BD10	P 9	32	Thorncroft Rd. BD6	K14	65	*Harold Av.*		
Thackeray St. HX2	C19	93	Thorndale Ri. BD2	W11	49	Thornville Pl. LS6	Z10	55
Thackley Av. BD10	O 6	13	Thorndene Way BD4	R15	69	Thornville Rd. LS6	Z10	55

Street	Grid	Page
Thornville Row LS6	Z10	55
Thornville St.		
Thornville St. LS6	Z10	55
Thornville Vw. LS6	Z10	55
Thornville St.		
Thorp Garth BD10	O 7	31
Thorp St. HX1	E18	80
Thorpe Av. BD13	H12	46
Thorpe Av., Thorpe LS10	BB17	91
Thorpe Cres. LS10	BB17	91
Thorpe Gdns. LS10	BB17	91
Thorpe Gro. BD13	H12	46
Thorpe Gro. LS10	BB17	91
Thorpe Mt. LS10	AA17	90
Thorpe Pl. LS10	BB17	91
Thorpe Rd. BD13	H12	46
Thorpe Rd. LS10	BB17	91
Thorpe Rd. LS28	S11	51
Thorpe Sq. LS10	BB17	91
Thorpe St. LS10	BB17	91
Thorpe St. LS15	GG11	58
Thorpe Ter. LS10	BB17	91
Thorpe Vw. LS10	BB17	91
Thorverton Dr. BD4	Q15	68
Thorverton Gro. BD4	Q15	68
Threadneedle St. HX1	D20	93
Lombard St.		
Threshfield BD17	M 5	12
Threshfield Cres. BD11	R16	83
Thrift Way BD16	G 6	10
Throstle Av. LS10	AA17	90
Throstle Dr. LS10	AA17	90
Throstle Gro. LS10	BB17	91
Throstle Hill LS10	AA17	90
Throstle La. LS10	AA17	90
Throstle Mt. LS10	AA17	90
Throstle Mt., S.B. HX6	A20	92
Throstle Nest Vw., Hor. LS18	V 7	35
Throstle Par. LS10	AA17	90
Throstle Pl. LS10	AA17	90
Throstle Rd. LS10	BB17	91
Throstle Rd. LS10	CC16	91
Throstle Row LS10	AA17	90
Throstle Sq. LS10	BB17	91
Throstle St. LS10	AA17	90
Throstle Ter. LS10	BB17	91
Throstle Vw. LS10	BB17	91
Throstle Wk. LS10	AA17	90
Throston LS8	EE 9	39
Throxenby Way BD14	J13	65
Thrum Hall La. HX1	D19	93
Thryberg St. BD3	O11	49
Thurley Dr. BD4	O14	67
Thurley Rd. BD4	O14	67
Thurnscoe Rd. BD1	M11	48
Thursby St. BD3	O11	49
Thurston Gdns. BD15	H11	46
Thwaite La. LS10	DD13	75
Thwaites Brow Rd. BD21	D 4	8
Tichborne Rd. BD5	N13	67
Clough St.		
Tichborne Rd. W. BD5	N13	67
Humford St.		
Tickhill St. BD3	O12	49
Tilbury Av. LS11	Z13	73
Tilbury Rd.		
Tilbury Gro. LS11	Z13	73
Tilbury Rd.		
Tilbury Mt. LS1	Z13	73
Tilbury Par. LS11	Z13	73
Tilbury Pl. LS11	Z13	73
Tilbury Rd. LS11	Z13	73
Tilbury Ter. LS11	Z13	73
Tilbury Vw. LS11	Z13	73
Tile La. LS16	Z 5	19
Tile St. BD8	L10	48
Tile Ter. HD6	L22	101
Till Carr La. HX3	L19	97
Tilson Grn. BD13	H14	64
Tim La.	YY 6	6
Timber Pl. LS9	CC12	56
Timber St. HX6	D20	93
Timber St., Elland HX5	G24	99
Timble Dr. BD16	H 5	10
Timmey La., S.B. HX6	B20	92
Tinshill Av. LS16	W 5	17
Tinshill Clo. LS16	W 5	17
Tinshill Cres. LS16	W 5	17
Tinshill Dr. LS16	W 4	17
Tinshill Garth LS16	W 5	17
Tinshill Gro. LS16	W 5	17
Tinshill La. LS16	V 5	17
Tinshill Mt. LS16	W 5	17
Tinshill Rd. LS16	V 5	17
Tinshill Vw. LS16	W 5	17
Tinshill Wk. LS16	W 4	17
Tintern Av. BD8	J11	47
Tirley Sq. BD5	N13	67
Spring Mill St.		
Titus St. BD18	K 7	29
Tiverton Wk. BD4	Q14	68
Tivoli Pl. BD5	M13	66
Toby La. BD7	L12	48
Todd Ter. BD7	L13	66
Great Horton Rd.		
Todley Hall Rd.	YY 4	6
Todwell La. BD5	M13	66
Toft Pl. LS12	Y12	54
Toft St.		
Toft St. LS12	Y12	54
Tofts Av. BD12	M18	83
Tofts Gro. HD6	K23	100
Tofts Grove Gdns. Brig.	K23	100
Tofts House Clo. LS28	T11	52
Tofts Rd. LS28	S11	51
Toftshaw Fold BD4	P15	68
Toftshaw La. BD4	P15	68
Toftshaw New Rd. BD4	P15	68
Toller Dr. BD9	K 9	29
Toller Gro. BD9	K 9	29
Toller La. BD9	K 9	29
Toller Pk. BD9	K 9	29
Tolworth Fold BD15	H11	46
Tomlinsons Bldgs. BD10	O 6	13
Greenfield La.		
Tonbridge Clo. BD6	K15	65
Tonbridge St. LS1	AA10	55
Willow Ter. Rd.		
Tong App. LS12	V12	53
Tong Dr. LS12	V11	53
Tong Gate LS12	V11	53
Tong Grn. LS12	V11	53
Tong La. BD4	S15	69
Tong La. LS27	T14	70
Tong Rd. LS12	Z12	55
Tong Rd., Tong BD4	T14	70
Tong St. BD4	P14	68
Tong Way LS12	V11	53
Tong Wk. LS12	V11	53
Tongue La. LS6	Z 7	37
Toothill Bank HD6	L23	101
Toothill La. HD6	L24	101
Top Fold LS12	X12	54
Top Moor Side LS11	AA12	55
Topcliffe Av., Mor. LS27	Y17	89
Topcliffe Ct. LS27	Y17	89
Topcliffe La.		
Topcliffe Grn. LS27	Y17	89
Topcliffe La.		
Topcliffe La., Mor. LS27	Y17	89
Topcliffe Mead LS27	Y17	89
Topcliffe La.		
Topcliffe Ms. LS27	Y17	89
Topcliffe La.		
Tor Av. BD12	M18	83
Torbay Av. LS11	Z12	55
Torbay St.		
Torbay Gro. LS11	Z12	55
Torbay St.		
Torbay Pl. LS11	Z12	55
Torbay St.		
Torbay St. LS11	Z12	55
Torcote Cres. HD6	M24	101
Tordoff Av. BD7	K12	47
Tordoff Grn. BD6	L15	66
Tordoff Rd. BD12	M16	83
Cleckheaton Rd.		
Tordoff Ter. LS5	X 9	36
Toronto Pl. LS7	BB 8	38
Toronto St. LS1	AA11	55
Torre Clo. LS9	DD11	57
Torre Cres. LS9	DD10	57
Torre Dr. LS9	DD10	57
Torre Gdns. LS9	CC11	56
Torre Grn. LS9	CC11	56
Torre Gro. BD6	J14	65
Torre Gro. LS9	DD10	57
Torre Hill LS9	DD10	57
Torre La. LS9	DD10	57
Torre Mt. LS9	DD10	57
Torre Rd. BD6	J14	65
Torre Rd. LS9	CC11	56
Torre Sq. LS9	DD10	57
Torre Vw. LS9	DD10	57
Torre Wk. LS9	DD10	57
Tower Gdns. HX2	D21	93
Wakefield Gate		
Tower Gro. LS12	X11	54
Tower Hill HX2	B21	92
Tower La. LS12	W11	53
Tower Pl. LS12	W11	53
Tower Rd. BD18	K 7	29
Tower St. BD2	O10	49
Towers Sq. LS6	AA 7	37
Towers Way LS6	AA 7	37
Town Clo. LS18	U 6	16
Town St.		
Town Erfd BD7	L13	66
Town End Pl., Pud. LS28	T11	52
Town End Rd. BD14	H12	46
Town End, Gild. LS27	V15	71
Town Gate Av. HD6	M21	97
Town Gate BD10	O 7	31
Town Gate BD12	M18	83
Town Gate BD14	H12	46
Town Gate BD18	M 7	30
Town Gate BD19	N19	103
Town Gate HD6	M21	97
Town Gate HX3	H18	81
Town Gate LS28	R 7	33
Town Hall Sq. BD1	N12	49
Town Hall St. E. HX1	F19	94
Crossley St.		
Town Hall St., Elland	G24	99
Southgate		
Town Hall St., S.B. HX6	B21	92
Town Hill BD16	H 7	28
Town La. BD10	O 6	13
Town St. BD11	R16	86
Town St. LS10	AA16	90
Town St. LS11	Z14	73
Town St. LS12	X11	54
Town St. LS28	S 9	33
Town St. LS7	BB 7	38
Town St., Gild. LS27	V15	71
Town St., Hor. LS18	U 7	34
Town St., Raw. LS19	T 5	16
Town St., Rod. LS13	T 8	34
Town St., Stan. LS28	T10	52
Town Street Ms. LS7	BB 7	38
Townend Rd. LS12	X12	54
Greenside Av.		
Townfield BD15	F 8	27
Towngate HX3	J19	96
Towngate LS11	AA12	55
Towngate, Southowram HX3	H21	95
Townley Av. HX3	H21	95
Trafalgar Row HX1	E20	94
Trafalgar St. BD1	N11	49
Trafalgar St. HX1	E20	94
King Cross Rd.		
Trafalgar St. LS2	BB11	56
Trafalgar Ter. LS7	Y 8	36
Albert Gro.		
Trafford Av. LS9	DD10	57
Trafford Gro. LS9	DD 9	39
Trafford Ter. LS9	DD 9	39
Seaforth Av.		
Tranquility Av. LS15	HH10	59
Tranquility LS15	HH10	59
Tranquility Av.		
Tranquility Wk. LS15	HH10	59
Tranquility Av.		
Tranter Gro. BD4	Q12	50
Tranter Pl. LS15	FF11	58
Tredgold Av., Bram. LS16	W 2	2
Tredgold Clo. LS16	W 2	2
Tredgold Cres. LS16	W 2	2
Tree La. HX7	A16	78
Trees St. BD8	M10	48
Amber St.		
Trelawn Av. LS6	Y 8	36
Trelawn Cres. LS6	Y 8	36
Trelawn Pl. LS6	Y 8	36
Trelawn St. LS6	Y 8	36
Trelawn Ter. LS6	Y 8	36
Tremont Gdns. LS10	CC14	74
Tremont St. LS10	CC14	74
Woodhouse Hill Rd.		
Tremont Vw. LS10	CC14	74
Woodhouse Hill Rd.		
Trenam Park Dr. BD10	O 6	13
Trenance Dr. BD18	K 7	29
Trenholme Av. BD6	L16	83
Trenic Cres. LS6	Y 9	36
Trenic Dr. LS6	Y 9	36
Trent Rd. LS9	DD11	57
Trent St. LS11	AA12	55
Trentham Av. LS11	AA13	73
Stratford Ter.		
Trentham Gro. LS11	AA13	73
Stratford Ter.		
Trentham Pl. LS11	AA13	73
Stratford Ter.		
Trentham Row LS11	AA13	73
Stratford Ter.		
Trentham St. LS11	AA14	73
Trenton Dr. BD8	M10	48
Trescoe Av. LS13	W10	53

174

Name	Ref	Pg
Well St. LS28	S 9	33
Welland Ter. BD3	P11	50
Wellands La. BD19	O19	103
Wellcroft BD18	L 7	30
Wellcroft Rd. WF17	U18	87
Weller Av. LS9	CC10	56
Weller Clo. BD5	N13	67
Mumford St.		
Wellesley St. BD1	N11	49
Wellington St.		
Wellfield Pl. LS6	Y 9	36
North La.		
Wellholme HD6	L21	97
Wellington Bridge St. LS3	Z11	55
Wellington Cres. BD18	L 7	30
Wellington Garth LS13	V 9	35
Wellington Gdns. LS13	V 9	35
Wellington Gro. BD2	O10	49
Wellington Gro. LS13	V 9	35
Wellington Gro. LS28	S11	51
Wellington Mt. LS13	V 9	35
Wellington Pl. BD2	P 9	32
Wellington Rd. BD15	F 9	27
Wellington Rd. BD2	O10	49
Wellington Rd. LS12	Z12	55
Wellington Sq. BD21	C 4	8
Wellington St. BD1	N11	49
Wellington St. BD10	O 7	31
Bradford Rd.		
Wellington St. BD11	R16	86
Wellington St. BD13	G14	64
Brunswick St.		
Wellington St. BD16	G 5	10
Wellington St. BD18	M 7	30
Leeds Rd.		
Wellington St. BD4	P12	50
Wellington St. HX1	F20	94
Wellington St. LS1	Z11	55
Wellington St. W. HX1	E20	94
Wellington St., Allerton BD15	J10	47
Wellington St., Wilsden BD15	F 9	27
Wellington Ter. LS13	V 9	35
Wells Cft. LS6	Z 7	37
Wells St., Mor. LS27	Y15	72
William St.		
Wellstone Av. LS13	U11	52
Wellstone Dr. LS13	U10	52
Wellstone Garth LS13	U11	52
Wellstone Gdns. LS13	U11	52
Wellstone Grn. LS13	U10	52
Wellstone Rd. LS13	U11	52
Wellstone Ri. LS13	U11	52
Wellstone Way LS13	U11	52
Welton Clo. LS6	Z 9	37
Welton Mt. LS6	Z 9	37
Welton Pl. LS6	Z 9	37
Welton Rd. LS6	Z 9	37
Welwyn Av. BD18	N 7	31
Welwyn Dr. BD17	M 6	12
Welwyn Dr. BD18	N 7	31
Wembley Av. BD13	G12	46
Wenborough La. BD4	Q13	68
Wendron Way BD10	O 7	31
Wenlock St. BD3	O12	49
Wensley Av. BD18	L 7	30
Wensley Av. LS7	BB 7	38
Wensley Bank BD13	F12	45
Thornton Rd.		
Wensley Bank Ter. BD13	F12	45
Wensley Bank W. BD13	F12	45
Thornton Rd.		
Wensley Cres. LS7	BB 7	38
Wensley Dr. LS7	AA 7	37
Wensley Gdns. LS7	AA 7	37
Wensley Grn. LS7	AA 7	37
Wensley Gro. HD6	K23	100
Wensley Gro. LS7	AA 7	37
Wensley Rd. LS7	AA 7	37
Wensley Vw. LS7	BB 7	38
Wensleydale Rd. BD3	P11	50
Wensleydale Ri. BD19	N 5	13
Wentworth Av. LS17	AA 5	19
Wentworth Cres. LS17	BB 5	20
Wentworth Dr. HX2	D15	62
Wentworth Gro. HX2	D15	62
Wentworth Way LS17	BB 5	20
Wepener Mt. LS9	DD10	57
Wepener Pl. LS9	DD10	57
Wesley Av. BD12	M15	66
Wesley Av. LS11	Y11	54
Athlone St.		
Wesley Clo. LS11	Z13	73
Wesley Clo. LS11	Z13	73
Wesley Ct. HX3	F19	94
Crossley St.		
Wesley Ct. LS11	Z14	73
Wesley Dr. BD12	M15	66
Wesley Garth LS11	Z13	73
Wesley Grn. LS11	Z14	73
Wesley St.		
Wesley Gro. BD10	P 6	14
Wesley Pl. LS9	CC11	56
Wesley Rd. LS12	Y11	54
Wesley Rd. LS28	S10	51
Wesley Row, Pud. LS28	T11	52
Lidget Hill		
Wesley Sq. LS28	T11	52
Lowtown		
Wesley St. LS11	Z13	73
Wesley St. LS2	BB10	56
Wesley St. LS28	S 9	33
Wesley St., Mor. LS27	X17	89
Wesley St., Rod. LS28	T 9	34
Wesley Ter. LS13	V 9	35
Upper Town St.		
Wesley Ter., Pud. LS28	T11	52
Lidget Hill		
Wesley Ter., Rod. LS13	T 8	34
Wesley Vw., Rod. LS13	T 8	34
Wesleyan Ter. BD4	P13	68
West Av. BD15	G 9	28
West Av. BD17	M 5	12
West Av. HX3	E21	94
West Av., Brig. HX3	L19	97
West Av. LS8	EE 7	39
West Byland HX2	D15	62
West Cft. BD12	M18	83
West Church St. BD18	M 7	30
Church La.		
West Dene LS17	CC 4	20
West Dr.	ZZ10	42
West End App. LS27	W17	88
West End Clo., Hor. LS18	T 6	16
West End Dr., Hor. LS18	T 6	16
West End Gro., Hor. LS18	T 6	16
West End La., Hor. LS18	T 6	16
West End LS12	V13	71
Forge Row		
West End Rd. HX1	D20	93
Hopwood La.		
West End Rd. LS28	R 8	33
West End Ri., Hor. LS18	T 6	16
West End St. BD1	M11	48
West End Ter. BD18	L 7	30
Wycliffe Rd.		
West End Ter. BD2	O 8	31
West End Ter. LS6	Z 9	37
West End, Queens. BD13	F15	63
West End, Thornton BD13	F12	45
West Farm Av. LS10	AA16	90
West Gate BD17	M 5	12
West Gate BD2	P 9	32
West Grange Clo. LS10	BB14	74
West Grange Dr. LS10	BB14	74
West Grange Fold. LS10	BB14	74
West Grange Garth LS10	BB14	74
West Grange Gdns. LS10	BB14	74
West Grange Grn. LS10	BB14	74
West Grange Rd. LS10	BB15	74
West Grange Wk. LS10	BB14	74
West Grove St., Pud. LS28	T10	52
Richardshaw La.		
West Grove Ter. HX1	E19	94
West Hill Av. LS7	BB 7	38
West Hill St. HX1	E19	94
West Holme Rd. HX2	D19	93
West Holme St. BD1	M12	48
West Kirkstall HX2	C15	62
West La. BD13	F11	45
West La. BD19	R18	86
West La. HX3	G21	95
West La., Haworth	YY 7	24
West Lea Clo. LS19	Q 4	14
West Lea Cres. LS19	Q 4	14
West Lea Dr. LS6	AA 6	19
West Lea Garth LS6	AA 6	19
West Lea Gdns. LS17	AA 6	19
West Lea Gro. LS19	Q 4	14
West Lodge Gdns. LS7	BB 8	38
West Mount Pl. HX1	E19	94
Pellon La.		
West Mount St. LS11	AA13	73
South Ridge St.		
West Par. HX1	E20	94
West Par. LS16	X 7	36
West Par., S.B. HX6	C21	93
West Park Av. LS8	DD 5	21
West Park Chase LS8	DD 5	21
West Park Clo. LS8	DD 5	21
West Park Cres. LS8	DD 6	21
West Park Dr. E. LS8	DD 5	21
West Park Dr. LS16	X 7	36
West Park Dr. W. LS8	CC 5	20
West Park Gdns. LS8	DD 6	21
West Park Rd.		
West Park Gro. LS8	DD 5	21
West Park Pl. LS8	DD 6	21
West Park Rd. BD8	K11	47
West Park Rd. LS8	DD 6	21
West Park St. HD6	L22	101
Market St.		
West Park Ter. BD8	K11	47
West Pk. LS28	S11	51
West Rd. LS9	EE13	75
West Rd. N. LS9	EE13	75
West Royd Av. BD18	M 7	30
West Royd Av. BD2	O 9	31
West Royd Av. HX1	E20	94
Queens Rd.		
West Royd BD15	F 8	27
West Royd Clo. BD18	M 7	30
West Royd Cres. BD18	N 7	31
West Royd Dr. BD18	N 7	31
West Royd Mt. BD18	N 7	31
West Royd Rd. BD18	N 7	31
West Royd Ter. BD18	N 7	31
West Royd Wk. BD18	N 7	31
West Scausby Pk. HX2	D15	62
West Shaw La.	YY 9	24
West St. BD1	N12	49
West St. BD11	T16	87
West St. BD19	R18	86
West St. BD2	O 9	31
West St. HX1	E19	94
Oak La.		
West St. LS1	Z11	55
West St. LS28	T11	52
North St.		
West St., Brig. HX3	L21	97
West St., Mor. LS27	X17	89
West St., Northowram HX3	H17	81
West St., S.B. HX1	B21	92
West View Av. HX2	D19	93
West View Clo. BD18	N 7	31
West View Cres. HX2	D20	93
West View Dr. HX2	C19	93
West View Rd. HX3	E18	80
West View Ter. HX2	D19	93
West Vw. Av. BD18	N 7	31
West Vw. BD11	R17	86
West Vw. BD16	J 4	11
West Vw. BD19	N18	84
Well La.		
West Vw. BD4	O13	67
New Hey Rd.		
West Vw. HX3	E18	80
West Vw. St. LS11	AA13	73
West Wensley Bank BD13	F12	45
West Wood Ct. LS10	AA16	90
West Wood Rd. LS10	AA16	90
West Woodside LS12	X13	72
West Woodside LS27	X15	72
Westborough Dr. HX2	C19	93
Westbourne Av. LS11	AA13	73
Rowland Rd.		
Westbourne Cres. HX3	F21	94
Westbourne Mt. LS11	AA13	73
Rowland Rd.		
Westbourne Pl. LS11	AA13	73
Rowland Rd.		
Westbourne Pl. LS28	S10	51
Sun Field		
Westbourne St. LS11	AA13	73
Rowland Rd.		
Westbourne Ter. BD13	G14	64
Albert Rd.		
Westbourne Ter. HX3	F21	94
Westbrook Clo., Troy LS18	U 6	16
Westbrook La., Troy LS18	U 6	16
Westburn Av. BD21	B13	61
Westburn Av., Keighley	A 4	7
Westburn Cres.	A 4	7
Westburn Gro.	A 4	7
Westburn Way	A 4	7
Westbury Clo. BD4	P12	50
Westbury Gro. LS10	CC14	74
Westbury Pl. HX1	D20	93
Westbury Pl. LS10	CC14	74
Westbury Rd. BD6	J14	65
Westbury St. BD4	P12	50
Westbury St., Elland HX5	H23	99
Westbury Ter. HX1	D20	93
Westcliffe Av. BD18	L 5	12
Westcliffe Dr. HX2	C19	93
Westcliffe Rd. BD18	L 7	30
Westcombe Av. LS8	DD 6	21
Westcombe Ct. BD12	M17	83
Westcroft Av. HX3	H17	81
Westcroft Rd. BD7	L13	66

Street	Grid	Page
Whitebridge Av. LS9	FF11	58
Whitebridge Cres. LS9	FF10	58
Whitebridge Spur LS9	FF10	58
Whitebridge Vw. LS9	FF10	58
Whitechapel Clo. LS8	DD 8	39
Whitechapel Gro. BD19	O18	84
Whitechapel Rd. BD19	N19	103
Whitechapel Way LS8	EE 8	39
Whitechapel Yd. LS11	BB12	56
Meadow La.		
Whitecote Gdns. LS13	U 9	34
Whitecote Hill LS13	U 9	34
Whitecote La. LS13	U 8	34
Whitecote Mt. LS13	V 9	35
Newlay La.		
Whitecote Ri. LS13	U 9	34
Whitecote Sq. LS13	V 9	35
Whitecote St. LS13	V 9	35
Leeds & Bradford Rd.		
Whitegate Cft.	F21	94
Whitegate Rd.		
Whitegate Dr. HX3	F21	94
Whitegate HX3	F21	94
Whitegate Rd. HX3	F21	94
Whitegate Ter. HX3	F20	94
Whitegate Rd.		
Whitegate Top HX3	G21	95
Whitehall Av. BD12	L18	83
Whitehall Gro. BD11	S16	86
Whitehall Rd. BD11	T16	87
Whitehall Rd. BD12	P18	85
Whitehall Rd. BD19	P18	85
Whitehall Rd. E. BD11	R17	86
Whitehall Rd. HX3	L18	83
Whitehall Rd. LS1	AA11	55
Whitehall Rd. LS12	T16	87
Whitehall Rd. W. BD19	P18	85
Whitehall Rd., Lower Wyke BD12	L18	83
Whitehall St. HX3	J19	96
Whitehall Ter. BD19	P18	85
Whitehaven Clo. BD6	K15	65
Whitehead Dr. BD2	P10	50
Whitehead Pl. BD2	P10	50
Whitehead St. BD3	O12	49
Whiteheads Ter. HX1	D19	93
Hanson La.		
Whitehill Cres. HX2	D16	79
Whitehill Dr. HX2	D16	79
Whitehill Grn. HX2	D16	79
Whitehill Rd. HX2	D16	79
Whitehouse St. LS10	BB12	56
Whitelands Bldgs., Pud. LS28	T11	52
Whitelands Cres. BD17	M 5	12
Whitelands Rd.		
Whitelands LS19	R 5	15
Whitelands Rd. BD17	M 5	12
Whiteley Av. HX5	A21	92
Whiteley St. BD3	O11	49
Garnett St.		
Whiteley St. HX1	E20	94
Paradise St.		
Whitelock St. LS7	BB10	56
Sheepscar St. S.		
Whites Clo. BD9	J 9	29
Whites Ter. BD8	L10	48
Whites Vw. BD8	L11	48
Whiteways BD2	N 9	31
Whitfield Av. LS10	CC13	74
Whitfield Av.		
Whitfield Av. LS10	CC13	74
Whitfield Gdns. LS10	CC13	74
Whitfield Pl. BD8	L11	48
Whitfield Sq. LS10	CC13	74
Whitfield St. LS8	CC 9	38
Whitfield Way LS10	CC13	74
Whitkirk Clo. LS15	HH11	59
Whitkirk La. LS15	HH11	59
Whitley La. HX3	H20	95
Whitley Rd. BD21	B 4	7
Whitley St. BD16	G 5	10
Whitley St. BD3	O12	49
Garnett St.		
Whitley St. HX3	E17	80
Nursery La.		
Whittle Cres. BD14	H12	46
Whitty La. HX5	B20	92
Whitwell Av., Elland HX5	H23	99
Whitwell Dr., Elland HX5	H23	99
Whitwell Green La., Elland HX5	H23	99
Whitwell Gro., Elland HX5	H23	99
Whitwell St. BD4	O12	49
Whitwood La. BD19	M19	97
Wibsey Bank BD6	M14	66
Wibsey Park Av. BD6	K15	65
Wicken La. BD13	F11	45
Wickets Clo. BD6	M15	66
Wickham Av. BD6	M15	66
Wickham St. BD19	N19	103
Wickham St. LS11	AA13	73
Wide La.	YY 5	6
Wide La., Mor. LS27	Y17	89
Wigan St. BD1	M11	48
Wightman St. BD3	O10	49
Wigton La. LS17	CC 4	20
Wike La. LS17	EE 4	21
Wike Ridge La. LS17	DD 4	21
Wilcock Pl. BD18	M 7	30
High St.		
Wilcock St. BD18	M 7	30
Wrose Brow Rd.		
Wildred St. LS12	X13	72
Wildred St. LS15	GG11	58
Wildred Ter. LS12	X13	72
Wilfred Av. LS15	GG11	58
Wilfred St. BD11	R16	86
Allen Cft.		
Wilfred St. BD14	J13	65
Wilkinson Ter. BD7	K12	47
Willans Av., Roth. LS26	FF15	76
Willcock La. BD13	F13	63
William Av. LS15	FF11	58
William Henry St. BD18	K 7	29
Caroline St.		
William Ri. LS15	FF11	58
William St. BD13	D10	44
William St. BD18	K 7	29
William St. BD5	N12	49
William St. HD6	L22	101
William St. HX4	D20	93
William St., Chur. LS27	Y15	72
William St., Tong Street BD4	P14	68
William St., Tyersal BD4	P12	50
Fearnville Dr.		
William Vw. LS15	FF11	58
Williamson St. HX1	E19	94
Williamson St. LS11	Z12	55
Domestic St.		
Willis St. LS9	CC11	56
Willoughby Ter. LS11	Z12	55
Willow App. LS4	Z10	55
Willow Av. BD2	O 8	31
Willow Av. LS4	Z10	55
Willow Bank HX2	E20	94
Willow Clo. BD6	M15	66
Willow Clo. HX2	C20	93
Willow Clo. LS4	Z10	55
Willow Cres. BD2	O 8	31
Willow Cres. LS15	FF11	58
Willow Cres., S.B. HX6	C20	93
Willow Dene Av. HX2	C20	93
Willow Dr. BD6	M15	66
Willow Dr. HX2	C20	93
Willow Field Rd. HX2	C20	93
Willow Field Ter. HX2	D20	93
Willow Garth Av. LS14	GG 7	40
Willow Garth Clo. LS14	GG 7	40
Willow Garth LS4	Z10	55
Willow Gdns. BD2	O 8	31
Willow Gro.BD2	O 8	31
Willow Gro. BD21	B 5	7
Oak Gro.		
Willow Grove Rd. LS1	AA10	55
Tonbridge St.		
Willow Hall Dr. HX6	C20	93
Willow Hall La., S.B. HX6	C20	93
Willow Head Dr., S.B.	C20	93
Willow Park Dr. HX3	J16	82
Willow Rd. LS28	S10	51
Willow Rd. LS4	Z10	55
Willow Ri., S.B.	C20	93
Willow St. BD19	P18	85
Hunsworth La.		
Willow St. BD8	K11	47
Willow St. HX1	E19	94
Willow St., S.B. HX6	C21	93
Willow Terrace Rd. LS1	AA10	55
Willow Tree Clo. BD21	C 4	8
Willow Vills. BD2	O 8	31
Willow Well Rd. LS15	FF11	58
Willowfield Av. HX2	C20	93
Willowfield Clo. HX2	C20	93
Willowfield Clo., S.B.	C20	93
Willowfield Cres. BD2	O 8	31
Willowfield Cres. HX2	C20	93
Willowfield Dr. HX2	C20	93
Willowfield St. BD7	L11	48
Willowfield Vw. HX2	C20	93
Willows, The LS17	BB 6	20
Street La.		
Wilmer Dr. BD18	L 8	30
Wilmer Dr. BD9	L 9	30
Wilmer Rd. BD9	L 9	30
Wilmington Gro. LS7	BB 9	38
Wilmington St. LS7	BB10	56
Wilmington Ter. LS7	BB 9	38
Wilsden Old Rd. BD16	E 6	9
Wilsden Rd. BD15	G 9	28
Wilsden Rd. BD16	E 6	9
Wilson Ct. LS12	Z12	55
Wellington Rd.		
Wilson Fold BD12	M16	83
Wooler Rd.		
Wilson Rd. BD12	M17	83
Wilson Rd. BD16	G 5	10
Wilson Rd. HX1	D20	93
Wilson Sq. BD8	M10	48
Lumb La.		
Wilson St. BD12	M16	83
School St.		
Wilson St. BD8	M10	48
Lumb La.		
Wilsons Pl. LS11	AA12	55
Great Wilson St.		
Wilton Av. HD2	N24	102
Wilton Gro. LS6	Z 8	37
Wilton Pl. LS12	Y11	54
Parliament Rd.		
Wilton St. BD6	M12	48
Wilton St. HD6	K21	96
Wilton St. LS12	Y11	54
Parliament Rd.		
Wilton Ter. LS12	Y11	54
Wiltshire Mt. LS10	CC13	74
Wiltshire St.		
Wimborne Dr. BD15	J10	47
Winbrooke Ter. BD6	L14	66
Winburg Rd. BD7	L12	48
Winchester Mt. LS12	Y11	54
Winchester Rd. LS12	Y11	54
Winchester St. LS12	Y11	54
Winchester Vw. LS12	Y11	54
Windermere Rd. BD17	K 6	11
Windermere Rd. BD7	K13	65
Windermere Ter. BD7	K13	65
Windhill Old Rd. BD10	N 6	13
Winding Av.	F19	94
Winding Way LS17	AA 4	19
Windmill App. LS10	CC15	74
Windmill Clo. HX3	H18	81
Windmill Clo. LS10	CC15	74
Windmill Cres. HX3	H18	81
Windmill Dr. HX3	H18	81
Windmill Hill BD6	L14	66
Windmill Hill HX3	H18	81
Windmill Hill LS28	S12	51
Windmill La. BD6	M14	66
Windmill La. LS19	S 4	15
Windmill La., Mor. LS27	V16	88
Windmill Mt. LS10	BB15	74
Windmill Rd. LS10	BB15	74
Windsor Av. LS15	GG11	58
Windsor Cres.	YY 6	6
Windsor Ct. HX3	D18	79
Windsor Ct., Mor. LS27	X17	89
Windsor Grn.	YY 6	6
Windsor Gro. BD13	F12	45
Windsor Pl. LS11	GG11	58
Windsor Pl. HD2	N24	102
Windsor Pl. LS10	CC13	74
New Pepper Rd.		
Windsor Rd. BD18	L 7	30
Alexandra Rd.		
Windsor Rd. WF17	U18	87
Windsor St. BD4	O12	49
Windsor Ter. LS10	CC13	74
New Pepper Rd.		
Windsor Wk. HX3	L20	97
Windy Bank La. BD13	E16	80
Windy Gro. BD15	F 9	27
Windybank La. HX7	O20	103
Wine St. LS1	AA11	55
Infirmary St.		
Winfield Dr. BD11	Q16	85
Winfield Gro. LS2	AA10	55
Devon Rd.		
Winfield Pl. LS2	AA10	55
Devon Rd.		
Wingate Av.	A 4	7
Wingate Way	A 4	7
Wingfield Mt. BD3	O11	49

Name	Ref	Page
Wingfield St. BD3	O11	49
Winnie Ter. LS12	Z12	55
Winnipeg Pl. LS7	BB 8	38
Winrose App. LS10	CC15	74
Winrose Av. LS10	BB15	74
Winrose Clo. BD12	M17	83
Wycoller Rd.		
Winrose Cres. LS10	BB15	74
Winrose Dr. LS10	BB15	74
Winrose Garth LS10	CC15	74
Winrose Gro. LS10	CC15	74
Winrose Hill LS10	CC14	74
Winslow Rd. BD10	Q 9	32
Winstanley Ter. LS6	Z 9	37
Winston Gdns. LS6	Y 8	36
Winston Mt. LS6	Y 8	36
Winston Ter. BD7	L12	48
Winter Ct. BD15	H 9	28
Spring St.		
Winter St. HX1	D20	93
Fenton Rd.		
Winterbourne Av., Mor. LS27	X16	89
Winterburn La. HX2	B19	92
Winterburn Rd., S.B. HX6	A19	92
Winterton Dr. BD12	M16	83
Carr La.		
Winthorpe St. LS6	Z 8	37
Wintoun St. LS7	BB10	56
Wistons La., Elland HX5	H23	99
Witham Rd. BD18	K 7	29
Withens Rd. WF17	T18	87
Withins New Rd. HX7	A14	61
Wold Clo. BD13	F12	45
Wolley Av. LS12	V13	71
Wolley Ct. LS12	V13	71
Wolley Dr. LS12	V13	71
Wolley Gdns. LS12	V13	71
Wolley Dr.		
Wolscot St. LS11	AA12	55
Ladbroke St.		
Wolseley Av. LS4	Y10	54
Burley Rd.		
Wolseley Cres. LS4	Y10	54
Burley Rd.		
Wolseley Gro. LS4	Y10	54
Wolseley Mt. LS4	Y10	54
Wolseley Rd.		
Wolseley Rd. LS4	Y10	54
Wolseley St. BD4	J12	47
Wolseley St. LS4	Y10	54
Wolseley Ter. HX1	E19	94
Hanson La.		
Wolston Clo. BD4	Q14	68
Womersley Pl. LS28	S12	51
Carlisle Rd.		
Womersley St. HX1	D19	93
Hanson La.		
Wood Bottom La. HD6	J20	96
Wood Cft. HD6	A21	92
Wood Clo. BD17	L 6	12
Wood Croft Gro. HD6	K23	100
Wood End Ct. BD5	N14	67
Wood Gro. LS12	V11	53
Wood Hill Cres. LS16	V 5	17
Wood Hill Ct. LS16	V 5	17
Wood Hill Garth LS16	V 5	17
Wood Hill Gdns. LS16	V 5	17
Wood Hill Gro. LS16	V 5	17
Wood Hill Rd. LS16	V 5	17
Wood Hill Ri. LS16	V 5	17
Wood La. BD6	G 4	10
Wood La. BD2	N 9	31
Wood La. HX3	D18	79
Wood La. HX3	H19	95
Wood La. HX3	J20	96
Wood La. HX3	J21	96
Wood La. LS13	V 9	35
Wood La. LS28	R 7	33
Wood La. LS6	Y 8	36
Wood La. LS7	BB 7	38
Wood La., Hor. LS18	V 7	35
Wood La., Hough End LS12	V11	53
Wood La., New Farnley LS12	V14	71
Wood La., Roth. LS26	DD15	75
Wood La., S.B. HX6	A21	92
Wood Nook Clo. LS16	V 6	17
Wood Nook Dr. LS16	V 6	17
Wood Nook Garth LS16	V 5	17
Wood Nook La., S.B. HX6	C20	93
Wood Nook Rd. LS16	V 5	17
Wood Nook Ter. LS28	S10	51
Bradford Rd.		
Wood Pl. BD8	M11	48
Wood Pl. BD9	M 9	30
Wood Pl. LS1	AA13	73
Lodge La.		
Wood Rd. BD21	B 5	7
Wood Rd. BD5	N13	67
Wood Rd. BD9	M 9	30
Wood Row BD12	M16	83
School Rd.		
Wood Royd HX3	D18	79
Wood Side Vw. BD16	H 7	28
Wood Sq. HX3	E18	80
Mill La.		
Wood St. BD12	M16	83
Wood St. BD16	G 4	10
Wood St. BD17	M 6	12
Wood St. BD18	M 7	30
Phoenix St.		
Wood St. BD21	C 4	8
Park La.		
Wood St. BD8	M11	48
Wood St. BD9	J10	47
Wood St. HD6	L22	101
Wood St. HX3	F19	94
Wood St. LS27	W16	88
Wood St. N. HX3	E18	80
Mill La.		
Wood St., Elland HX5	H24	99
Wood St., Rod. LS13	T 8	34
Town St.		
Wood St., Troy LS18	V 6	17
Wood Top BD18	M 7	30
Leeds Rd.		
Wood Top, Brig.	K20	96
Wood View Ter. BD21	B 5	7
Haincliffe Rd.		
Wood View Ter. BD8	M 9	30
Wood Vw.	A 5	7
Wood Vw. BD13	C 9	26
Wood Vw. BD17	L 6	12
Green Rd.		
Wood Vw. BD8	M 9	30
Wood Vw., Chur. LS27	Y15	72
Wood Yd. BD13	G14	64
High St.		
Woodale Av. BD9	J 9	29
Woodbine Gro. BD10	O 7	31
Woodbine St. BD3	O11	49
Barkerend Rd.		
Woodbine St. HX1	E20	94
Hyde Park Rd.		
Woodbine St. LS28	S10	51
Bradford Rd.		
Woodbine Ter. BD10	O 7	31
Woodbine Ter. LS13	V 9	35
Upper Town St.		
Woodbine Ter. LS6	Z 8	37
Woodbourne Av. LS17	BB 6	20
Woodbourne LS8	EE 7	39
Woodbridge Clo. LS6	X 8	36
Woodbridge Cres. LS6	X 8	36
Woodbridge Fold LS6	X 8	36
Woodbridge Garth LS6	X 8	36
Woodbridge Gdns. LS6	X 8	36
Woodbridge Grn. LS6	X 8	36
Woodbridge Lawn LS6	X 8	36
Woodbridge Pl. LS6	X 8	36
Woodbridge Rd. LS6	X 8	36
Woodbridge Vale LS6	X 8	36
Woodbrook Av. HX2	C16	79
Woodbrook Clo. HX2	C16	79
Woodbrook Pl. HX2	C16	79
Woodbrook Rd. HX2	C16	79
Woodbury Rd. BD8	L10	48
Woodcot Av. BD17	M 5	12
Woodcross End LS27	X15	89
Woodcross Fold, Mor. LS27	X16	89
Woodcross Gdns., Mor. LS27	X16	89
Woodcross LS27	X16	89
Woodend Cres. BD18	M 7	30
Woodfield Av. HX5	E23	98
Woodfield Av. LS13	S 8	33
Woodfield Rd. BD13	D 7	26
Woodfield Ter., Pud. LS28	T12	52
Woodford Av. HX3	F21	94
Woodhall Av. BD3	Q11	50
Woodhall Av. LS5	W 8	35
Woodhall Cres. HX3	E21	94
Woodhall Ct. LS28	R 8	33
Woodhall Dr. LS5	W 8	35
Woodhall La. LS28	Q 9	32
Woodhall Park Av. LS28	R10	51
Woodhall Park Cres. E. LS28	R10	51
Woodhall Park Cres. W. LS28	R10	51
Woodhall Park Dr. LS28	R10	51
Woodhall Park Gdns. LS28	R10	51
Woodhall Park Gro. LS28	R10	51
Woodhall Park Mt. LS28	R10	51
Woodhall Pl. BD3	Q10	50
Woodhall Rd. LS28	Q11	50
Woodhall Rd. LS28	R 8	33
Woodhall Rd., Calverley BD3	R 8	33
Woodhall Rd., Thornbury BD3	Q11	50
Woodhall Ter. BD3	Q11	50
Woodhall Vw. BD3	Q10	50
Woodhead La. HD6	N22	102
Woodhead La., Gild. LS27	U15	70
Woodhead Rd. BD7	L12	48
Woodhouse Av. BD21	C 4	8
Woodhouse Cliff LS6	AA 9	37
Delph La.		
Woodhouse Clo. BD21	C 4	8
Woodhouse Dr.		
Woodhouse Dr. BD21	C 4	8
Woodhouse Grange BD21	C 4	8
Woodhouse Gro. BD15	H 9	28
Woodhouse Hill Av. LS10	CC14	74
Sandon Pl.		
Woodhouse Hill Cres. LS10	CC14	74
Woodhouse Hill Rd.		
Woodhouse Hill Gro. LS10	CC14	74
Sandon Pl.		
Woodhouse Hill Pl. LS10	CC14	74
Woodhouse Hill Rd. LS10	CC14	74
Woodhouse Hill St. LS10	CC14	74
Woodhouse Hill Rd.		
Woodhouse Hill Ter. LS10	CC14	74
Sandon Pl.		
Woodhouse Hill Vw. LS10	CC14	74
Woodhouse Hill Rd.		
Woodhouse La. HD6	L23	101
Woodhouse La. HX3	E21	94
Woodhouse La. LS2	BB11	56
Woodhouse La. LS6	AA 9	37
Woodhouse Rd. BD21	B 4	7
Woodhouse Sq. LS2	AA10	55
Woodhouse St. LS6	AA 9	37
Cross Chancellor St.		
Woodhouse Ter. BD6	M15	66
Pearson St.		
Woodhouse Way BD21	C 4	8
Woodhouse Dr.		
Woodhouse Wk. BD21	C 4	8
Woodkirk Gro. BD12	M18	83
Woodland Av., Swil. LS26	KK14	77
Woodland Cft., Hor. LS18	V 6	17
Woodland Clo. BD9	J 8	29
Woodland Clo. LS15	HH11	59
Woodland Cres. BD9	J 8	29
Woodland Dr. HX2	C20	93
Woodland Dr. LS26	JJ14	77
Woodland Dr. LS7	BB 7	38
Woodland Gdns., Thorner LS14	HH 4	23
Woodland Gro. BD9	J 8	29
Woodland Gro. LS7	BB 9	38
Woodland Gro., Swil. LS26	JJ14	77
Woodland Hill LS15	GG11	58
Woodland La. HX2	A17	78
Woodland La. LS7	BB 7	38
Woodland Mt. LS7	CC 9	38
Woodland Park Rd. LS6	Z 8	37
Woodland Pl. HD6	M22	101
Calder Rd.		
Woodland Rd. LS15	GG11	58
Woodland Ri. LS15	HH11	59
Woodland Ter. LS7	AA 7	37
Woodland Vw. LS7	BB 7	38
Woodlands Av. BD13	H14	64
Woodlands Av. BD19	R18	86
Woodlands Av. HX3	F18	80
Woodlands Av. LS28	S10	51
Woodlands Cres. BD19	R18	86
Woodlands Ct. LS16	X 6	18
Woodlands Dr. BD10	Q 6	14
Woodlands Dr. BD19	R18	86
Woodlands Dr. LS19	Q 6	14
Woodlands Dr. LS27	W16	88
Woodlands Dr., Raw. LS19	T 6	16
Woodlands Gro. BD13	H14	64
Woodlands Gro. BD16	H 7	28
Woodlands Gro. BD17	K 6	11
Woodlands Gro. HX3	F18	80
Woodlands Gro. LS28	S10	51
Woodlands Av.		

Woodlands Mt. HX3 — F18 80
Woodlands Park Gro. LS28 — S12 51
Woodlands Park Rd. LS28 — S12 51
Woodlands Rd. BD13 — H14 64
Woodlands Rd. BD16 — J 5 11
Woodlands Rd. BD19 — R18 86
Woodlands Rd. HX3 — F18 80
Woodlands Rd., Elland HX5 — G23 99
Woodlands Ri. — ZZ 8 24
Woodlands St. BD8 — M11 48
Woodlands Ter. BD8 — L10 48
Woodlands Ter. LS28 — S10 51
Woodlands Vw. HX3 — F18 80
Woodlea App. LS19 — Q 4 14
Woodlea Clo. LS19 — Q 4 14
Woodlea Dr. LS19 — Q 4 14
Woodlea Mt. LS11 — Z13 73
Woodlea Mt. LS19 — Q 4 14
Woodlea Rd.
Woodlea Pl. LS11 — Z13 73
Woodlea Rd. LS19 — Q 4 14
Woodlea St. LS11 — Z13 73
Woodlea Vw. LS19 — Q 4 14
Woodleigh Av. BD5 — N14 67
Woodler Ct. LS17 — DD 5 21
Woodlesford Cres. HX2 — B18 78
Woodliffe Cres. LS7 — AA 7 37
Woodman Av. HD2 — O24 102
Woodman Av. HX5 — G24 99
Woodman St. LS11 — AA12 55
Sweet St.
Woodman St. LS15 — GG11 58
Woodrow Dr. BD12 — N16 84
Woodroyd Av. BD5 — N14 67
Parkside Rd.
Woodroyd Dr. HX3 — D18 79
Woodroyd Rd. BD5 — N14 67
Woodroyd Ter. BD5 — N14 67
Woodryde Gdns., S.B. HX6 — A20 92
Woods Row LS28 — T10 52
Vernon Pl.
Woodside Av. BD16 — G 7 28
Woodside Av. BD18 — K 7 29
Woodside Av. LS4 — Y10 54
Woodside BD18 — M 7 30
Woodside Cres. BD16 — G 7 28
Woodside Cres. HX3 — E18 80
Woodside Ct. BD13 — C 8 26
Woodside Ct. LS5 — W 7 35
Tanhouse Hill
Woodside Dr. BD16 — G 7 28
Woodside Dr. LS27 — X15 72
Woodside Gdns. LS27 — X15 72
Woodside Gro. HX3 — F18 80
Bath Pl.
Woodside Hill Clo. LS18 — V 7 35
Woodside La. LS27 — X15 89
Woodside Mt. HX3 — E19 94
Woodside Rd.
Woodside Park Av. LS18 — V 7 35
Woodside Park Dr. LS18 — V 7 35
Woodside Pl. HX3 — E18 80
Woodside Pl. LS4 — Y10 54
Woodside Rd. BD12 — M17 83
Woodside Rd. HX3 — E18 80
Woodside Ter. HX3 — F18 80
Woodside Ter. LS4 — Y10 54
Woodside Ter., Greet. HX4 — F24 98
Woodside Vw. HX3 — E18 80
Woodside Vw. LS4 — Y10 54
Woodside Vw., Greet. HX4 — F24 98
Woodsley Rd. LS2 — Z10 55
Woodsley Rd. LS3 — Z10 55
Woodsley Ter. LS2 — AA10 55
Clarendon Rd.
Woodsly Rd. BD10 — O 8 31
Woodstock Clo. LS16 — Y 5 18
Woodstock Wk. BD5 — N12 49
Park Rd.
Woodthorne Cft. LS17 — DD 5 21
Woodvale Clo. BD4 — Q12 50
Woodvale Cres. BD16 — H 4 10
Woodvale Gro. BD7 — K12 47
Woodvale Way BD7 — K12 47
Woodview Av. BD17 — N 5 13
Woodview BD11 — S15 69
Woodview Dr. BD2 — P10 50
Woodview Dr. LS27 — T15 70
Woodview Gro. HD6 — K21 96
Woodview Gro. LS11 — AA14 73
Woodview HD2 — N24 102
Woodview Mt. LS11 — AA14 73

Woodview Pl. LS11 — Z15 73
Dewsbury Rd.
Woodview Rd. LS11 — AA14 73
Woodview Rd., Keighley — A 5 7
Woodview St. LS11 — AA14 73
Woodview Ter. LS11 — AA14 73
Woodville Av., Hor. LS18 — V 6 17
Woodville Clo. BD21 — C 4 8
Woodville Cres., Hor. LS18 — V 6 17
Woodville Ct. LD8 — DD 6 21
Park Vills.
Woodville Gro. LS10 — CC14 74
Woodhouse Hill Rd.
Woodville Gro., Hor. LS18 — V 6 17
Woodville Mt. LS10 — CC14 17
Woodhouse Hill Rd.
Woodville Pl. BD9 — K 9 29
Woodville Pl., Hor. LS18 — V 6 17
Woodville Rd. LS10 — CC14 74
Woodhouse Hill Rd.
Woodville St. BD18 — M 7 30
Leeds Rd.
Woodville St. HX3 — E18 80
Woodville St., Hor. LS18 — W 6 17
Woodville Ter. BD5 — M12 48
Woodville Ter., Hor. LS18 — V 6 17
Woodway BD16 — G 7 28
Woodway Dr., Hor. LS18 — V 7 35
Woodway, Hor. LS18 — V 7 35
Woodworth Gro. BD21 — B 5 7
Wooler Av. LS11 — AA14 73
Wooler Dr. LS11 — AA14 73
Wooler Gro. LS11 — AA14 73
Wooler Rd. BD12 — M16 83
Wooler Rd. LS11 — Z14 73
Wooler St. LS11 — Z14 73
Woolers Pl. W17 — T18 87
Upper Batley St.
Woolman St. LS9 — BB11 56
Woolpack St. BD21 — B 4 7
King St.
Woolrow La. HD6 — M20 97
Woolshops HX1 — F19 94
Woolwich St. LS11 — AA12 55
Meynell St.
Wooton St. BD5 — M13 66
Worcester Av. LS26 — CC17 91
Worcester Dr. LS26 — CC17 91
Worcester Pl. BD4 — O13 67
New Hey Rd.
Worden Gro. BD7 — K13 65
Workhouse La. HX2 — B19 92
Workhouse La., Greet. HX4 — F24 98
Wormald Lee BD4 — Q13 68
Worrall St., Mor. LS27 — W17 88
Worsnob St. BD12 — M16 83
Worsnop Bldgs. BD12 — M17 83
Starr Hill
Worsnop St. BD12 — M16 83
Common Rd.
Worth St. BD21 — C 4 8
Greengate
Worth Way BD21 — C 4 8
Worthing Head Clo. BD12 — M17 83
Worthing Head Rd. BD12 — M17 83
Worthing St. BD12 — M17 83
Worthington St. BD8 — M11 48
Wortley Gro. LS12 — Z12 55
Green La.
Wortley La. LS11 — Z12 55
Wortley Moor La. LS12 — X12 54
Wortley Moor Rd. LS12 — X11 54
Wortley Pk. LS12 — Y 2 3
Wortley Rd. LS12 — X11 54
Wortley St. BD16 — H 5 10
Wortley Tower LS12 — Z12 55
Wrangthorn Av. LS6 — Z 9 37
Wrangthorn Pl. LS6 — Z 9 37
Wrangthorne Ter. LS6 — Z 9 37
Brudenell Clo.
Wren Av. BD7 — K12 47
Wren St. — ZZ 7 24
Wrenbury Av. LS16 — V 4 17
Wrenbury Cres. LS16 — V 4 17
Wrenbury Gro. LS16 — W 4 17
Wright Av. — ZZ 5 6
Wright Ho. LS9 — BB11 56
Wrigley Av. BD4 — O14 67
Wrigley Hill HX2 — D16 79
Wroe Cres. BD12 — M17 83
Wroe Pl. BD12 — M17 83
Wroe Ter. BD12 — M17 83
Wrose Av. BD18 — M 8 30
Wrose Av. BD2 — O 8 31
Wrose Brow Rd. BD18 — M 7 30
Wrose Dr. BD18 — M 8 30

Wrose Gro. BD18 — M 8 30
Wrose Gro. BD2 — N 8 31
Wrose Hill Pl. BD18 — M 8 30
Bolton Hall Rd.
Wrose Hill Ter. BD18 — M 8 30
Wrose Mt. BD18 — N 8 31
Wrose Rd. BD18 — N 8 31
Wrose Vw. BD17 — M 5 12
Bank Wk.
Wrose Vw. BD18 — M 8 30
Wrosecliffe Gro. BD18 — N 7 31
Wycliffe Clo., Rod. LS13 — T 8 34
Wycliffe Ct. BD18 — L 7 30
Wycliffe Rd.
Wycliffe Dr. LS17 — BB 6 20
Wycliffe Gdns. BD18 — L 7 30
Wycliffe Pl. BD18 — L 7 30
Wycliffe Rd.
Wycliffe Rd. BD18 — L 7 30
Wycliffe Rd. LS13 — S 8 33
Wycliffe St. BD18 — L 7 30
Wycliffe Rd.
Wycombe Grn. BD4 — Q13 68
Wyke Cres. BD12 — M18 83
Wyke La. BD12 — M18 83
Wykebeck Av. LS9 — EE11 57
Wykebeck Cres. LS9 — EE11 57
Wykebeck Gdns. LS9 — EE11 57
Wykebeck Gro. LS9 — EE11 57
Wykebeck Mt. LS9 — EE11 57
Wykebeck Pl. LS9 — FF11 57
Wykebeck Rd. LS9 — EE11 57
Wykebeck Sq. LS9 — EE11 57
Wykebeck St. LS9 — EE11 57
Wykebeck Ter. LS9 — EE11 57
Wykebeck Valley Rd. LS9 — EE10 57
Wykebeck Vw. LS9 — EE11 57
Wykelea BD12 — M18 83
Wykelea Clo. BD17 — M17 83
Wyncliffe Gdns. LS17 — BB 6 20
Wyncroft Gro., Bram. LS16 — W 2 2
Wyndham Av. BD2 — N 9 31
Wynford Av. LS16 — X 6 18
Wynford Gro. LS16 — X 6 18
Wynford Mt. LS16 — X 6 18
Wynford Ri. LS16 — X 6 18
Wynford Ter. LS16 — X 6 18
Wynford Way BD12 — N15 67
Wynford Way BD6 — N15 67
Wynmoor Cres. LS16 — W 2 2
Wynmore Av., Bram. LS16 — W 2 2
Wynne St. BD1 — M11 48
White Abbey Rd.
Wynyard Dr., Mor. LS27 — W17 88
Wyther Av. LS5 — W 9 35
Wyther Gro. LS5 — W 9 35
Wyther La.
Wyther La. LS5 — W 9 35
Wyther Mt. LS5 — W 9 35
Wyther La.
Wyther Park Av. LS12 — W10 53
Wyther Park Clo. LS12 — W10 53
Wyther Park Cres. LS12 — W10 53
Wyther Park Grange LS12 — W10 53
Wyther Park Grn. LS12 — W10 53
Wyther Park Gro. LS12 — W10 53
Wyther Park Heights LS12 — W10 53
Wyther Park Hill LS12 — W10 53
Wyther Park Mt. LS12 — W10 53
Wyther Park Pl. LS12 — W10 53
Wyther Park Rd. LS12 — W10 53
Wyther Park Sq. LS12 — W10 53
Wyther Park St. LS12 — W10 53
Wyther Park Ter. LS12 — W10 53
Wyther Park Vw. LS12 — W10 53
Wyther Row LS5 — W 9 35
Wyther La.
Wyther St. LS5 — W 9 35
Wyther La.
Wyther Vw. LS5 — W 9 35
Wyther La.
Wyvern Clo. BD7 — K12 47
Necropolis Rd.
Wyvern Pl. HX2 — D19 93
Yarm St. LS11 — AA13 73
Yarmouth St. LS10 — BB12 56
Pearson St.
Yarn St. LS10 — CC12 56
Yarwood Gro. BD7 — K13 65
Windermere Rd.
Yate La. — ZZ10 42
Yeadon Dr. HX3 — H21 95
Yeadon Moor Rd., Yea. LS19 — T 4 16

Yeadon Moor Rd., Yea. LS19	U 3	1	York Cres. BD16 *York St.*	H 6	10	York Ter. HX3	E18	80
Yew Tree Av. BD8	J10	47	York La. LS9	BB11	56	Young St. BD8	K11	47
Yew Tree Cres. BD8	K10	47	York Pl. LS1	AA11	55	Zealand St. BD4	P13	68
Yew Tree Gro. BD8	K10	47	York Rd. LS14	GG 9	40	Zermatt St. LS7	BB 8	38
Yew Tree La. BD15	G11	46	York Rd., Scholes LS9	CC11	56	Zetland Pl. LS8	CC 9	38
Yew Trees Av. HX3	H17	81	York St. BD13	F14	63	Zion St. LS9	CC12	56
Yewdale Way BD10	P 8	32	York St. BD16	H 6	10	Zoar St., Mor. LS27	X17	89
Yewdall Gdns. LS13	S 8	33	York St. BD8	K11	47	Zulu Pl. LS9	BB11	56
Yewdall Rd. LS13	S 8	33	York St. HD6 *King Cross St.*	E20	94	*Argyle Rd.*		
Yewdall Rd., Rod. LS13	T 8	34				Zulu Ter. LS9 *Argyle Rd.*	BB11	56

NOTES

To help you record specific details, the following pages can be used to add your own notes.

NOTES

NOTES

NOTES